AF513143

Anthrogogy in Use

ANTHROGOGY IN USE

A Handbook for Language Educators

Edited by

Shree Deepa

Geetha Durairajan

Orient BlackSwan

ANTHROGOGY IN USE:
A HANDBOOK FOR LANGUAGE EDUCATORS

ORIENT BLACKSWAN PRIVATE LIMITED

Registered Office
3-6-752 Himayatnagar, Hyderabad 500 029, Telangana, India
Email: centraloffice@orientblackswan.com

Other Offices
Bengaluru, Chennai, Guwahati, Hyderabad, Kolkata,
Mumbai, New Delhi, Noida, Patna

First published 2026

ISBN 978-93-6973-596-9

042641

Typeset in Minion Pro 10.5/12.6 *by*
Shine Graphics, Delhi 110 094

Printed at
Manipal Technologies Limited., Manipal

Published by
Orient Blackswan Private Limited
3-6-752 Himayatnagar, Hyderabad 500 029, Telangana, India
Email: info@orientblackswan.com

We dedicate this book to Our Guiding Light His Holiness
Sri Sri Sri Tridandi Chinna Srimannarayana Ramanuja Jeeyar Swamiji,
Aaraavamudhan, and all our Acharyans and Gurus who inspired, taught,
and held us when we assumed that we thought, worded, and did.

Contents

Part III

A Compendium of Anthrogogic Tasks

Part IV

Ruminations on Anthrogogicity

Foreword

Public education, from its inception, has been based as much on values as on established technical principles and has thus remained a site for cultural and political debate. Over the last several decades, a range of thinkers have enriched the discourse around education: John Dewey, Paulo Freire, Henry Giroux, and Michael Apple, to name a few. Putative 'improvements' in education have come from scholars focusing on the conditions of human learning.

Alongside the edifice of institutionalised formal education, which has always been limited in its reach, the more informal arrangements under the broad label of adult education have provided the non-elite segments of society with avenues for learning opportunities. Malcolm Knowles' analysis of adult learning based on a distinction between pedagogy and andragogy was one useful contribution.

The establishment of the UK Open University in the 1960s was a major development in the realm of 'correspondence courses'. Its approach involved a massive commitment of resources to planning, curriculum design, pedagogic support, and quality assurance. Largely because of the discussion (more than mere publicity) around the Open University (OU) approach, it became the model for open universities in various countries.

The true significance of the OU approach lies in its conceptualisation of the learner or student. They were adults in their late-twenties or older who were going to 'university' after exiting from formal education after school. The OU treated them not as persons frozen in adolescence but as adults, citizens who had, in the 'lost' years, become workers, voters, spouses, parents, and members of social organisations. They were not registered at the OU to *prepare them for the future*, but were there as serious explorers of new experiences related to academic disciplines. The OU's concern was to give them the opportunity and the freedom to learn what appealed to them, as responsible adults.

This approach, recognising the agency of the adult learner, goes beyond the simplistic adult–child distinction made by Knowles. The scheme of anthrogogy elaborated in the present volume, as I see it, echoes the approach of the Open University.

The conceptual chapters and the additional examples of practical work with the anthrogogic approach will undoubtedly stimulate many readers to explore this new frontier.

Beyond that, I see in the volume a link to a key element in the yet-to-be written history of the early decades of CIE–CIEFL/EFLU. The Central Institute for Education (CIE) was set up initially alongside state English Language Teaching Institutes (ELTIs) and Regional Institutes of Education (RIEs) to support the reform of English teaching in the direction of skill development at the school level through re-orienting teachers—to promote skills supported by suitable new materials and evaluation schemes. The central target was the modification of the practices of teachers already in service. In the late 1960s, college teachers were brought into the ambit to orient them towards promoting language skills rather than to teach literature as found in textbooks.

The complexity of the mission to *change* the way teachers go about everyday teaching is worth reflecting on. Inputs are unquestionably important, but they need to engage with what the teacher already has as experience and expertise. Such in-service work engaging with teachers, which was once the centre of CIE's mission, is now a slim strand in the vast array of programmes offered at the English and Foreign Languages University (EFLU). Nevertheless, as the nature of the tertiary curriculum and the demography of the student population changes, the need for teachers to continually adapt remains. Support for this is presumably the role of the Academic Staff College. A parallel set of institutions exists at the school level, the State Councils of Educational Research and Training (SCERTs) and the District Institutions of Education and Training (DIETs). The target (clientele) here are adult teachers. The anthrogogy perspective presented in this volume is obviously relevant in these contexts.

I believe anthrogogy is much more than a 'more effective' approach. It is crucial. Teachers' sense of autonomy and self-efficacy needs to be preserved and enhanced. Insights that promote a deeper appreciation of how adults learn is the impact of this book that I most look forward to.

Jacob Tharu
Professor (retd.), Dept. of Evaluation
CIEFL/EFLU, Hyderabad

Foreword

The title of this book speaks volumes, for it is exactly what it claims to be: a handbook on anthrogogy. It will be useful, however, not just for teacher–educators but also for teachers and aspiring researchers in the field of English Language Education. The book is rooted firmly in the Indian soil, presented to the global English Language Education scenario. It encompasses the major areas of language and literature teaching, testing, and teacher education. The authors have presented their perceptions of the new domain, leaving scope for examining, analysing, and even critiquing their perspectives. There are a range of articles that deal with the applications of the principles of anthrogogic teaching practices and a few that focus on anthrogogic formative testing practices.

The contents page is an eye-opener for it indicates the research and scholarship available to the reader. After presenting the theoretical construct of anthrogogic teaching and testing in the first two chapters, preceded by a prolegomena, the rest of the book is an attempt at creative, innovative applications of the theoretical articulations, spanning a range of areas.

Generally, books on seminal topics present solid theory leaving the reader to explore possibilities for application. This book is reader friendly in the sense that it takes you by the hand. Twelve applications of the new theoretical perspective tried out in various contexts by research scholars are presented. There is also a whole section on anthrogogic tasks that can be tried out by any interested teacher or researcher. The reflective essays provide ample proof to any aspiring anthrogogic teacher that such practices actually work in classrooms. At the end of the book readers can happily tell themselves, 'Now I know what anthrogogy is, why it is necessary, how it can be applied, and what are its benefits'. A sense of satisfaction, fulfillment and achievement are the bonus points that the reader gets. And even if you are an ignoramus in this particular domain you are tempted to read the book.

The word 'prolegomena' is from a Greek word *prolegein* meaning 'to say beforehand'. The word 'prologue', its older cousin, is more common and refers to the introduction of a scholarly work. Both words are now used to refer to something that generally serves as an introduction. The prolegomena in this book, however, is not a formidable scholarly treatise, but is cleverly used to serve various purposes in the form of a dialogue which is extremely reader-friendly. The turns between Geetha Durairajan and Shree Deepa (the two editors) anticipate the readers' queries, doubts and anxieties—very much like a set of FAQs—but serve a valuable academic purpose. Their dialogue takes the readers by the hand and is like an appetizer or catalyst that motivates anyone interested to continue reading.

The first chapter by Shree Deepa is an excellent introduction to the topic. Practically a mini thesis, it is a brilliant and critical summary on the research literature in this domain, focusing also on the primary areas that have informed anthrogogy from the beginning till date. Questions that will occur to the reader—'what is pedagogy', 'what is andragogy', and last of all 'what is anthrogogy and how is it different'—are all answered explicitly and succinctly. The major argument made in the chapter is that the nature of learning in the case of adults with higher maturity and varied backgrounds needs to be celebrated, and that in these contexts classroom dynamics requires teachers to adopt the policy of 'we will agree to disagree' with students. Students are not captives or subordinates, but collaborators and contributors. The materials used in these teaching contexts should be a sourcebook and not a coursebook. The teacher has to adopt the role of a co-traveller. Indian teachers should avoid scaffolding which is teacher-centric and pedagogic. These initiatives must be student-centric. In brief, both teachers and students need to break free from the shackles of pedagogy, and enjoy and celebrate the responsibility of adulthood to be able to continue to grow, flourish and experience empowerment.

Geetha Durairajan's chapter on the principles of anthrogogic testing and assessment highlights the need for humane and joyful practices in testing. She argues for less stressful and tension-free tests and examinations; that it is important to ensure that tests should have washback as well as a wash-forward impact. A well-researched chapter, it presents a good critique of what is available and pinpoints the lacunae. She considers international tests as 'testing industries' and argues that the individual consequences of test-taking should supersede everything else. The mere handing over of a certificate to an adult is a demeaning act if that adult is not respected. It insults the abilities and decision-making power of adult students. Collaborative assessment, where teachers and students sit together, is what makes it genuinely anthrogogic. According to her, anthrogogic predictive validity becomes genuine only when the test can wash-forward into adult life beyond the classroom. The assignments given by teachers could be challenging and even exhausting, but should be exhilarating for the adult learner. If such assignments are not given, test takers are constrained to swim in fishbowls when they have the potential and ability to swim in the ocean. Thus, humane, test-taker friendly anthrogogic assessments contribute to empowering both the teacher and the learner.

In short, this book is a valuable asset for different categories of people. To the aspiring research scholar, here is a mine of information, critically presented. For the test designer, here is a guide on what should or should not be done. For the student, the reflective essays offer a bonanza of exciting experiences of anthrogogy. For the general public who have faced the agonies of repetitive lectures and memory-based testing, here is an eye opener. It may not be an exaggeration to say that this is a seminal book on anthrogogy in the adult classroom. It is a must read for one and all.

V. Saraswati
Professor of English (retd.)
University of Madras, Chennai

Acknowledgements

We confess that these ideas belong to all those good gurus and souls who watered and whisked our minds by being patient with us, teaching and inspiring us to push ourselves beyond boundaries.

Some others, by not believing in us and even throwing boulders and rocks at us, nevertheless became our muses. Our sincere thanks are offered to them as well, as they unleashed the best in us.

Our family members who put up with us, with all the scheduleless-ness and busy-nesses while contemplations, heated discussions, and exhilaration hit the roof, deserve a special mention for their selfless sacrifices.

To our extended academic family who understood our perspective by providing opportunities to present or workshop this perspective across the country and kept us on our toes, we reach out with grateful thanks.

A special and valued word of thanks to the many contributors who took this perspective seriously, believed in us, and, with their queries and applications, enabled the construct to mature. Without their dedicated work, writing and editing, this book would never have reached this form. Included here are the students who experienced anthrogogic courses and gave us valuable feedback.

The publisher and the array of dedicated team members who were available at all odd times and timelines were our strength throughout this process.

Prolegomena

Moving from Pedagogy to Anthrogogy

SHREE DEEPA AND GEETHA DURAIRAJAN

Geetha Durairajan (GD): How did our journey into the domain of anthrogogy begin? When did we begin getting dissatisfied with the idea of using the term 'pedagogy' with reference to adult education? I knew that I had no perturbation with the term when I wrote a book on assessment, intended for school-level teachers and titled it *Assessing Learners: A Pedagogic Resource* (Durairajan, 2015). However, although the term used was 'pedagogy', even in that book I did not talk down to our teachers and saw the book as enabling teacher development in a very adult—teachers as equal partners—professional manner. As Dr Prabhu stated in a personal conversation, (August 2017) after reading my book, 'It is obvious you know how to talk to teachers'.

Shree Deepa (SD): Both of us have worked for many years as educators and researchers: you at the university level, and I in schools and then at the university. We have experienced—even as students—boredom during classes where all we got were lectures, which we were forced to judiciously take down in the form of notes, to be reproduced in examinations. As a teacher–educator, you have attempted and successfully managed to move from this level of knowledge regurgitation to the analysis and application of theoretical concepts through your problem-solving, open-book examinations. As a teacher at the university level of both language ability and teacher-education courses, I too have tried the same for many years. My language proficiency and other examination papers at the undergraduate and postgraduate levels are very often attempted by students, who have not even attended a part of my course, out of nothing but sheer interest after hearing about the way my courses were taught and tested. They were willing to spend that kind of time to write the examination and ask for a 'grade' even if not submitted for certification, only because they wanted the exhilaration and stimulation of attempting such a paper.

With reference to teacher education, I have always felt that I do not need to be the warehouse of knowledge for students: at the postgraduate level, they can read, digest and internalise knowledge on their own. However, in many academic settings, we continue to use instructional models originally designed for children—methods that focus on rote learning, direct instruction, and rigid scaffolding—even though these approaches do not address or acknowledge the complexity of mature students. The students in our adult classrooms are not blank slates or *tabula rasas* waiting to be filled. They are individuals with rich life experiences, well-developed critical faculties and identities, and a deep sense of autonomy. Their academic journeys occur in vibrant, face-to-face communities where scholarship, debate, and personal engagement are central. And yet, too frequently, the methods we adopt remain rooted in either outdated or pedagogic paradigms. I have always believed in open-book/open-source examinations. Closed-book exams are like testing to find out whether students can swim inside a fishbowl when, in reality, we need to find out whether they can swim, if not in the ocean, at least in a lake. It is beyond my comprehension how a PhD student can even be given a closed-book exam as part of course work, when thesis writing is much more than mere access to an open library whether off or online. Co-creation of knowledge takes place between the supervisor and the doctoral student during the writing of a thesis. It is our discomfort with these existing paradigms that made us problematise this domain of the education of adults.

GD: Are you then saying that we need to impart knowledge only to children and once that is done, all education stops? Should we continue with education after they turn eighteen, and if yes, in what manner?

SD: Of course we continue. As human beings we believe in life-long learning, but here is where we have to make a distinction between the education of children and that of adults. In the twenty-first century, even with children, we talk about knowledge co-construction. With adults, it should not stop there but move into a collaborative co-creation of knowledge and collaborative assessment as well. Human society, from the perspective of physiology and psychology, has definitely made a distinction between children, adolescents, and adults with the awareness that the middle phase is where many changes take place. Physiologically, bones stop growing by the biological age of sixteen or eighteen years in most people. Cognitive maturity—after the stage of Piagetian abstract conceptualisation (Piaget, 1952)—also takes place by this time, or even earlier. However, given that human society perceives the need for education to continue, adolescents—and to some extent adults—ought to be educated but in a manner different from children. This distinction is not carried into the domain of education in a serious manner. The education of children is pedagogy; the education of adults must be primarily and qualitatively different. When we began problematising this domain a couple of years ago, I recall that you spoke about the differences between a banking system of education, and an education that is rooted in consciousness-raising.

GD: That is Freirian in origin (Freire, 1970/1993). The imparting of knowledge and expecting it to be regurgitated in memory-based, closed-book examinations where content is assessed, is worse than the Spolskian examination speech act (Spolsky, 1990). It is taking the banking system of education to its extreme conclusion where students are merely passive recipients of knowledge; teachers deposit knowledge the way we deposit money in the bank and we expect students to reproduce, or rather, regurgitate it. This type of education was critiqued by Freire more than fifty years ago, when neither the internet, search engines, or artificial intelligence existed and teachers could have been perceived as repositories of knowledge. Even then, he spoke about 'conscientization' which refers to critical consciousness. His focus was on adult literacy, but it has hence been applied to various levels of education. He may have used the term 'pedagogy' to problematise the education of the oppressed in the title of his book, but his focus was on adult learners, on literacy.

If the term anthrogogy had existed then, he would definitely have embraced it. The precursor to this supposition is his response to bell hooks when she asked him why he had not engaged with women in his philosophy. He succinctly replied that at that point in time, such a perspective was not that popular; if he had to rewrite the book he would have definitely incorporated it (hooks, 1994). Today such a conscientisation is not only crucial but essential. Teachers are no longer custodians of knowledge, only of experience. All the knowledge input that I have tried to share with my students during my years of teaching—by reading a large number of articles and books and picking out relevant arguments to get students to contemplate them critically—is now available at the click of a button and at the asking of a few questions or prompts to a Generative AI chat box. There was a time when I had found the need, as part of even a doctoral coursework programme, to read primary texts along with my students, or extracts from them when required; to comprehend, analyse, and critically evaluate the perspectives presented and arguments posited. One such example is Messick's articulation of validity which incorporated social consequences (Messick, 1990). Such a discussion may still be needed today, but the onus of such 'asking for help' has to come from the participant. Problem solving, critical thinking, dialoguing with the text: these are the necessary requirements of any course. This does not mean that we teachers are redundant and that AI can replace all of us. What questions to ask, what keywords to use, how to manage, traverse and exploit the large amounts of information that a search engine or an AI application may provide: these are the skills we need to enable and empower our students with.

SD: This is the perspective from which we decided to use the term 'anthrogogy' with reference to the teaching of adults, but not use the available notion of andragogy (Knowles, 1968, 1984). The term 'anthrogogy' is attributed in a large way to Trott (1991) and it is more inclusive. Andragogy carries with it a gender bias, for 'andra' means 'male' and, in the Knowlesian postulation, referred only to distance-education contexts and adult literacy. Our term, 'anthrogogy', is much more inclusive, is applicable to mainstream adult education, and incorporates in its purview, multilinguality, multiculturality, varied knowledge bases, caste, class, race, et cetera, where adults are respected for being themselves without any judgment or discrimination. This is a distinction that has not even been broached in higher institutes of education. Here, adults are taught in the same manner as children and pedagogic perspectives are continued, often leading to a Peter Pan syndrome (Kiley, 1983; Deepa, 2022a) where adults do not grow up and expect to be treated like children, to be told what to do. Teachers in the Indian context also provide lecture notes and expect those notes or information, possibly available in PowerPoint presentations form, to be reproduced in examinations. Adult students need some guidance, but not to access knowledge capital.

GD: What is the nature of this help and support that we are talking about? If, as teachers, we are expected to help adults with the kinds of questions they need to ask, with the key words they need to use in search engines, does this imply that we are the scaffolders for them, to use a Brunerian term? We are both aware that taking off from the notion of a zone of proximal development, (Vygotsky, 1978) Bruner applied it to language learning. He postulated that, along with a LAD (language acquisition device) there has to be a LASS (language acquisition support system) which is societal in nature, and that it is only with such scaffolding and help that language is acquired by children (Bruner, 1985). This notion of scaffolding (Wood, et al., 1976) has been picked up and used extensively in the arena of sociocultural theory over the past two decades or more, with the concepts of scaffolding, mediation, appropriation and regulation (Lantolf and Thorne, 2006) being applied to many domains of research where adults are the focus of study.

SD: The original postulation by Bruner was based on his observations of children trying to build pyramids with blocks and assistance provided by caregivers. The outcome and the nature of help that is to be provided in these contexts is pre-determined by the parent or caregiver who knows what the end product is, along with the processes, for the world view of the child is limited. This predetermined end product is also reflected in dynamic assessment (Poehner, 2008). In the context of anthrogogic education, therefore, we need to use a different analogy, that of road signs (Deepa & Durairajan, 2023). Scaffolds are primarily for buildings and are temporary structures to be removed when the construction is complete. Recall our thought experiment/speck: if an alien saw scaffolds around buildings, trees and humans, that alien could think that all three grow by themselves. But we know that buildings are made in a shape and size intended for them by other humans.

Growth is always other-oriented. Trees need nutritional help but grow on their own, breaking through their scaffolds or tree guards, or, in some cases, growing around them. Young children need gentle, parent/caregiver-regulated, pre-determined scaffolding to help them acquire language, basic skills, and world knowledge. However, for adult students who already possess a wealth of knowledge and experience, such constant pre-determined scaffolding can be limiting. Road signs, by contrast, offer guidance and information while leaving the final decisions up to the individual. They indicate possibilities, warn of obstacles, and invite personal judgment; they empower rather than constrain. In an anthrogogic set up, the goal is not to 'build up' the student from a state of dependency by imposing a fixed sequence of steps as is the case with a scaffold; instead, it is to provide informed, supportive cues that enable students to chart their own courses. An experienced driver on the road who is familiar with that route, may ignore all road signs, relying instead on personal experience and knowledge. Such a driver may also choose, when required, to make informed choices to overtake, cross double lines, or swerve off into a curb. Road signs are used when decisions have to be taken about when to navigate freely, when to turn or slow down, or take an alternative route if required based on road conditions or personal, informed judgment. When a novice or experienced driver is on an unfamiliar road, it could be road signs, or an app on the phone that will guide this person. The choice is left to the driver, in this case the student. If we continue to scaffold our students and treat them as those who need to be 'told what to do' we will only create 'Peter Pans' of them. They will be mentally stunted children who will remain in a state of perpetual reliance on external support rather than developing the independence essential for lifelong learning. When an educator recognises not only the cognitive capacities of a student but also honours the emotional, cultural, and experiential dimensions of that person, a learning environment can be truly liberatory. Such students will break free of the Peter Pan syndrome and become independent, self-directed thinkers who will co-create knowledge and not be passive absorbers and reproducers. Using pedagogic regurgitative methods will undermine their potential, resulting in frustration and disengagement where there should be creativity and intellectual vigour.

GD: Our conviction regarding the nature of scaffolding as pedagogic and the need for an alternative analogy, that of road signs, takes me into one other domain of anthrogogicity that we need to engage with: the role of tasks in anthrogogic education and whether we need something else, along with tasks, as an addition/alternative. Nearly forty years ago, task-based language teaching (TBLT) was introduced by Dr Prabhu (1987) in his Bangalore Project, which dealt with the education of children in Classes Four to Seven. TBLT and its offshoot TBLA (task-based language assessment) are used today to enable and evaluate not just the language proficiency of children, but also adults, and extends into teacher-education domains. Unfortunately, even with adults, many tasks have not been able to move away from the rigidity of the pre-task, task, post-task cycle. In the context of language ability, form-focused work also gets added to these tasks (Long, 2008; Ellis, 2016) thereby placing tasks with such a focus right in the middle of the pedagogic system.

SD: Tasks have their own place in the context of anthrogogic education. In many academic environments, closed-ended tasks that measure recall and reproduction of information, or move into the higher domains of the modified Bloom taxonomy focusing on applying, analysing, and even evaluating are used. While such tasks may work in certain contexts, they rarely capture the reflective, integrative, and creative aspects of learning that are critical for mature students. Tasks, like the analogy of the scaffold, have predetermined outcomes and fixed scoring criteria. This implies that they do not carry with them a wash-forward into real life where outcomes cannot be predicted and expecting the unexpected is the norm. In this context, thought seeds are a good innovation. They are designed as open-ended prompts that serve as catalysts for deep inquiry. They invite students to engage with abstract ideas, to connect theory with personal experience, and to articulate their insights without the pressure of having to provide a single 'correct' answer. In doing so, thought seeds transform the teaching–learning and assessment process from a static measure of performance into a dynamic, ongoing conversation with oneself and one's peers. Thought seeds enable and empower students to engage in a dynamic dialogue—a conversation that extends well beyond the confines of any type of teaching or testing task that is restrictive in its scope.

The origin of thought seeds can be traced to agriculture and organic farming, where seed balls covered in a muddy layer of soil are thrown onto a forest floor to germinate at will (Fukuoka, 1975; Bradley, 2010). In the context of anthrogogic education, thought seeds are problems, questions or issues raised and left in the mind of the adult student to ruminate on, germinate, flower, fruit, and even propagate if the conditions of enabling and empowerment are conducive to such growth.

GD: These thought seeds do not have any readymade or expected answers. They should be usable in any manner to push and aid the frontiers of the mind to make connections never made before. They are not a replacement for tasks, which have their own role to play. Like alternative assessments, which are not likely to replace all other forms of assessment, they are to be used by teachers and testers as and when required (Deepa, 2022b).

SD: The co-creation of knowledge, open-source examinations, road signs as an anthrogogic alternative to scaffolding, and thought seeds as an alternative to tasks are four major concepts that we have discussed. The concepts of road signs and thought seeds are not yet widely known. I would see these as a strength and valuable contribution of this book. Are there other strengths of our book that we need to highlight?

GD: With the awareness that anthrogogicity itself is a new concept, the illustrative tasks that form the third section of our book are one such contribution for it is proof that we are not talking from either an ivory tower, or out of thin air. The other contribution is actually student validation of our perspective, which is captured in the six reflective essays that form the fourth section of our book.

SD: There is one more important and crucial contribution that we need to highlight: this is the nature and power of the contributions of our twelve authors who have written the other chapters in this volume. The newness of the concept meant that conscientisation and critical discussions on the anthrogogic perspective were initially needed. These scholars, many of whom were our own doctoral students at one point in time, are now research guides in their own right. They were able to draw on their experiences and either pinpoint and write about what they were able to identify as their own anthrogogic enabling and empowering teaching/learning experiences, or carry out anthrogogic experiments in their own classrooms and document them. The end result is a different edited volume—not just invited chapters but a focused celebration of anthrogogic principles which has resulted in a rich tapestry with varied hues: chapters, tasks, and reflective essays.

GD: An overarching strong point of this book is its holistic approach. Rather than merely critiquing outdated models, it offers a robust alternative based on the full recognition of a student's potential. By challenging the heavy reliance on scaffolding and replacing it with the flexible imagery of road signs, and by introducing thought seeds as innovative catalysts for inquiry, this book seeks to provide a vision for the education of adults that is liberatory and empowering. It also pays careful attention to the diverse backgrounds and experiences that adult students bring to their academic lives, with the firm belief that true learning can only occur when these differences are not just embraced and integrated into the teaching process, but celebrated. It is not only language that is a form of life, as Wittgenstein put it (1953); education is also a form of lifelong learning. As students, participants, teachers, and doers we need to humanise ourselves through this process. The full range of human experience that values diversity and empowers students to become the architects of their own learning has to be celebrated. With this, anthrogogic education holds the promise of transforming not only individual lives but also the broader academic communities in which these students are embedded.

SD & GD: In a rapidly changing world, the education of adults must evolve. It must shed the constraints of models that treat students as passive recipients and embrace methods that nurture independence, creativity, and reflective inquiry. This transformation promised by anthrogogy is not an abstract ideal; it is a practical, actionable framework that can be implemented in classrooms, lecture halls, and academic institutions. It calls on educators, administrators, and policymakers to reimagine the purpose and practice of higher education in ways that are both inclusive and forward-looking.

As all of you—readers, researchers, and teachers—engage with this volume, we invite you to reflect on your own experiences with learning and teaching; to consider how existing models may have limited your potential and imagine how a shift toward anthrogogy might transform your educational landscape. Together, we can build a future in which the education of adults is not a relic of outdated practices but a vibrant, empowering process that transforms lives and enriches our society.

References

Bradley, K. (2010). Seed bomb. *Artlink*, *30*(2), 65–67. https://search.informit.org/doi/10.3316/informit.849802161912076

Bruner, Jerome. (1985). Vygotsky: A historical and conceptual perspective. In J. Wertsch (Ed.), *Culture, communication, and cognition: Vygotskian perspectives* (pp. 21–34). Cambridge University Press.

Deepa, S. (2022a). Pedagogic practices in higher education and the Peter Pan syndrome: An appraisal. *Fortell. 45*, 164–73. https://www.fortell.org/wp-content/uploads/2022/10/July-2022-164-173.pdf.

Deepa, S. (2022b). Thought seeds in anthrogogic learning contexts. *Journal of Indian Education*, *48*(2). 58–70. ISSN. 0972-5268.

Deepa S., & Durairajan, G. (2023). Scaffolds or road signs for anthrogogic language learners? A critical inquiry. In B. Nair, P. Ramalingam, & B. Nagalakshmi (Eds.), *Teaching of English: Theorizing from classroom.* (pp. 11–25). Tamil Puduvai.

Durairajan, G. (2015). *Assessing Learners: A Pedagogic Resource.* Cambridge University Press.

Ellis, R. (2016). Focus on form: A critical review. *Language teaching research, 20*(3), 405–28. https://doi.org/10.1177/1362168816628627.

Freire, P. (1993). *Pedagogy of the oppressed.* Penguin. (Original work published 1970).

Fukuoka, M. (1978). *The One-straw revolution* (L. Korn, Trans.). Rodale Press. (Original work published 1975).

hooks, b. (1994). *Teaching to transgress: Education as the practice of freedom.* Routledge.

Kiley, D. (1983). *The Peter Pan syndrome: Men who never grow up.* Dodd, Mead.

Knowles, M. S. (1968). Andragogy, not pedagogy. *Adult Leadership, 16*(10), 350–86.

Knowles, M. S. (1984). *The Adult Learner: A Neglected Species* (3rd ed.). Gulf Publishing.

Long, M. (2008). Focus on form in task-based language teaching. In R. Lambert, & E. Shohamy (Eds.), *Language policy and pedagogy: Essays in honor of A. Ronald Walton,* (pp. 179–92). John Benjamins Publishing Company.

Piaget, J. (1952). Logic and psychology. In H. E. Gruber, & J. J. Voneche (Eds.), *The essential Piaget* (pp. 445–77). Routledge and Kegan Paul.

Poehner, M. E. (2008). *Dynamic assessment: A Vygotskian approach to understanding and promoting second language development.* Springer.

Spolsky, B. (1990). Social aspects of individual assessment. In J. H. A. L. De Jong, & D. Stevenson (Eds.), *Individualizing the assessment of language abilities* (pp. 3–15). Multilingual Matters, Ltd.

Trott, D. C. (1991, October). *Anthrogogy* [Paper presentation] American Association for Adult and Continuing Education, Montreal, Quebec. https://eric.ed.gov/?id=ED342887.

Vygotsky, L. S. (1978). *Mind in society: The development of higher psychological processes.* Harvard University Press.

Wittgenstein, L. (1953). *Philosophical investigations* (G. E. M. Anscombe, Trans.). Basil Blackwell.

Wood, D., Bruner, J. S., & Ross, G. (1976). The role of tutoring in problem solving. *Journal of Child Psychology and Psychiatry, 17*(2), 89–100.

Part I

Theoretical Postulations

1

Principles of Anthrogogic Language Education

Shree Deepa

Anthrogogy versus Andragogy

There is a clear difference between teaching adults and children that is often consigned to oblivion by many researchers, academics and teachers across the globe. These differences—as envisaged or hastily and indifferently (mis)comprehended by many—are not ignorable, particularly when the terminal 'change' moves into the realm of principles that, when translated into classroom practices, bring about a sense of joint ownership of the classroom transaction processes between teachers and students. The term 'anthrogogy' is therefore proposed as a replacement for the term 'pedagogy' in higher education contexts. This term 'anthrogogy' can be traced from its ancestral term 'andragogy' but is a clear movement away from the latter and is much more inclusive. The term 'andragogy' was first coined in 1833 by a German teacher named Alexander Knapp (Knapp, 1833, as cited in Taylor & Kroth, 2009, p. 3) in an effort to expand Plato's theory of education. However, in recent times the term is most often associated with and attributed to Malcolm Knowles. He has inspired a lot of work at the higher education or tertiary level, and has spurred some serious debates on the principles that were derived from his postulations. The most important ones for this chapter are presented and discussed below.

The six principles of andragogy according to Knowles, et al. (2015, p. 17) are:

1. the learner's need to know,
2. self-concept of the learner,
3. prior experience of the learner,
4. readiness to learn,
5. orientation to learning, and
6. motivation to learn

These six principles are supposedly influenced by individual, situational and subject matter differences, which in turn will affect individual, societal and institutional growth. However, these andragogic thinkers have confessed that they have stayed only with the learning geographies of the United States and Europe, and have also acknowledged that 'these core principles are incomplete in terms of learning decisions' (p. 17).

This acknowledgment apart, there are three seminal problems with Knowles' six postulations. First, his theorisation is based on his work in counselling, which implies that the principles were based on work done with adults on a one-on-one basis and not based on the teaching of adults: as such, there is no educational perspective, but only a sociological orientation. Furthermore, there is nothing mentioned about classroom perspectives in this articulation but only theory accompanied by lists of 'oughts' and 'shoulds', therefore making it an extremely prescriptive perspective. Most importantly, his principles regarding education—in the few places where they are mentioned—have also been derived from work done with children by Bruner (Wood, et al., 1976) but applied to adults. The discrimination between child psychologists and adult psychologists is not maintained by Knowles in this regard. Finally, nothing is mentioned by him regarding teaching/teaching practices, nor about the educator's role; his focus is only on the learner's role.

Adult Learning Perspectives and Anthrogogy

The seminal contribution with reference to the term 'anthrogogy' can be traced to Trott (1991) who, in a conference, tried to resolve the confusion of the choice of the root word 'andra' that is of Greek origin, meaning 'man'; however, whether the reference was to the generic 'man' as representing human beings, or the specific gender 'male' is not very clear. In spite of this, the term attempted to answer the question 'Is there a generic set of principles that guide lifelong learning?'. He drew from Knowles' principles in the form of a table that included the following: (1) the anthrogogical concept of learning is identified as being lifelong; (2) the learner is conceived as being interdependent; (3) the learner's experiences are connected and stretched with new knowledge, experiences, and critical thinking; (4) motivation for learning is survival; and (5) the anthrogogical orientation to learning is holistic.

But, as with every new perspective, this postulation invoked a series of objections in the form of criticisms regarding the term anthrogogy as nothing but 'Gogymania' (Courtenay & Stevenson, 1983). This was an attempt to turn the pedagogy/andragogy debate away from further theorisation while ignoring the vehemence of the Ausubelian 'wishful thinking' (1962) argument, which referred to the processes of meaningful learning in adults in contrast with pedagogic perspectives. Trott had attempted to develop the term to represent anthrogogy with a humanistic system of a teaching model with seven dimensions: the student; learning groups; systems thinking; vision; direction and pathways; evaluation; and the teacher. However, there were no developments nor theorisations in this area beyond this attempt.

Prior to Trott's articulation of an anthrogogic perspective, the Ausubelian arguments in theorising language learning differences between children and adults contributed to the distinction, but he too, like Trott, does not take it further. He argues against the perspective that there are child superiority theses and hypotheses (1964) and states that whatever is seen as disadvantageous to adults' learning languages actually turn out to become overwhelmingly enjoyable advantages, and counterbalance the 'disadvantages' that are usually attributed to children. There are two major advantages in the context of adult language learning: one is the large repertoire of vocabulary in their 'native' languages that helps these adults comprehend abstract concepts with ease. The second is that adults can consciously make grammatical generalisations when they encounter a new language and apply them to 'suitable exemplars'. These positive and valuable distinctions notwithstanding, there are issues with Ausubel's theory: they are informed by child learning theories and articulations that focused only on expository teaching where the teacher lectures. For example, there is allusion to movement from old to new information and the need to link it with prior knowledge. The 'Advance Organisers' that adult learners are supposed to create are expected to be specified by the teacher who decides where the learner should go. This is like leading a cow by the horns!

The other thinker who refers to adult learning perspectives is Robert Gagne (1985) who does speak of teaching learning practices and refers to '9 stages/conditions of learning' but here again, like with Ausubel, the outcomes of these conditions are predetermined by the teacher. This implies that adults are treated like children with clear teacher-anticipated outcomes. He does indicate a learner and his/her role, but the learner's role is that of a sepoy following the instructions of a military officer. This ought not to be surprising, for his articulation of these principles evolved during the Second World War.

This whole debate on adult versus child learning theories has stayed only at the word/term level and has not been extended to either a full theorisation or applied to practices in the actual classroom. The resultant fizzling attempts led studies astray and shored up attempts into the foray of 'adult non formal/informal' education banks. This is even after a clear concomitance that exists between Freire (1970/1993) and Knowles (1975). In order to take the discussion further it is essential therefore to step into the discipline of psychology and attempt to construe the term anthrogogy from being treated as a mere 'word' and as an alternative to the word pedagogy into a perspectival branch of education. It is pertinent to arrive at the body of work in the discipline of psychology that treats adults and children separately and does not put the two groups under one umbrella perspective. Noticing, studying, and applying these differences lie at the crux of theoretical frameworks of teaching that 'inform' the field of education at large. It would be unfair to apply child-centric postulations derived from studies conducted either on animals—for example, the Pavlovian dog experiments—or children—for example, by Vygotsky, Bruner, Halliday—and then apply them forcibly and meaninglessly onto adult students, particularly at the tertiary or the university level.

A thorough analysis of various psychologists who worked with adults or the education of adults will undoubtedly have more to contribute than adapting the perspectives of those psychologists who have worked with children to the realm of the education of adults. A seminal contribution in the form of an attempt to bring in the impact of psychology on the nature of adult learning comes from Tennant (2006) where he categorises the approaches into three distinct and broad types. One is where psychology, sociology, and philosophy inputs are pragmatically valued for their relevance to adult education (Candy, 1991; Cross, 1981; Jarvis, 2004; Long, 1983; Merriam & Caffarella, 1999; Rogers, 2003 as cited in Tennant, 2006). Tennant further identifies the second approach that has, for him, a clearly articulated thesis that uses the literature to support the thesis being proposed (for example, Illeris, 2002 as cited in Tennant 2006; Knowles, 1978, 1984; Mezirow, 2000; Tough, 1979, 1982). Typically he observes that in the second type mentioned above, there is an attempt to apply a selected set of psychological, sociological, and philosophical concepts and principles to develop a programmatic stance that could occasionally become a prescriptive set of statements about adult teaching and learning. He further cautions that there could be a confusion as to whether the focus is on the psychological principles or on their application in adult learning contexts, and that this could lead to psychology being used in 'an uncritical way to support the normative rhetoric of adult education' (Tennant, 2006, p. 1). In the third approach, he summarises the need to adopt a critical analysis of research and theory that results from the above mentioned second approach so that teachers are encouraged to view their teaching practices with a critical lens. He further acknowledges that there could be drawings from a variety of disciplines that add to the approach apart from psychology. His conclusions suggest that there must be a psychological basis and the availability of critical postures to select applicable approaches that are firmly grounded in theory, so that adult educators develop 'a capacity for making informed choices which are defensible on rational, practical and political grounds' (p. 141). His confession of 'selected' psychological stances is laudable but needs to include a few more construals that work in South Asian contexts.

It is pertinent to therefore arrive at a set of principles and collate the ideas that have grown out of our experiences in adult classrooms. While valuing what Knowles, Ausubel, Gagne, Trott, Tennant, and others have contributed to this paradigm, we need to acknowledge that South Asian contexts and the contemporary global village syndrome connected by the web warrants a re-examination and a re-orientation of these stances. Studies in this domain, where present (Lavasani & Faryadres, 2011), are mediocre and nothing but an eyewash. Some studies (Omoregie, 2019) make flimsy connections and conclusions on how the educators of adults must work and strengthen their students' individuality, freedom and self-actualisation, and how seating arrangements are an essential aspect. Other attempts, such as the one by Rubayet and Imam (2021), focus on andragogy and its application in some Asian countries but not on mainstream higher-education classrooms.

Seminal and in-depth studies of anthrogogicity are, unfortunately, conspicuously absent in Indian education contexts and, even where available, are couched in an andragogic perspective. They are therefore sent to the periphery, clearly dismissed as not applicable to mainstream learning contexts such as the formal undergraduate, postgraduate, and research courses in higher-education learning spaces. These studies of anthrogogicity, in Indian contexts, are further ripped apart as they advocate for distance-education degree courses (NEP 2020) that are clearly dismissed as an inferior form of education for adults. Clearing the landscape of theorisations that suit the South Asian contexts in favour of India-specific studies is the need of the hour, with India rising as the new global superpower in more ways than one.

Educating Adults versus Adult Education

This leads us to a glade where we need to briefly clear up the terminological differences that exist between 'adult education' (AE) and 'educating adults' (EA). Clearing this confusion is pertinent because we need to leave the term 'andragogy' where it has flourished—namely, the AE contexts—and wish to bring in the term 'anthrogogy' and apply it to EA or the education of adults in mainstream education contexts such as a regular university or college classroom. If researchers and postulators of the andragogic perspective see it as valuable, they are welcome to shift to the more inclusive anthrogogic viewpoint.

The term 'andragogy' and AE, for us, alludes to adult literacy mostly, or in-service learning through workshops, modules, or training sessions. Further, for us, AE applies to areas such as human resources development (HRD), possibly as a part of the management discipline that targets adults at their post-employment stage. This clearly leads us to the necessity of operationally defining the term 'adult'. It is not easy to define this term without delving into the nuances of the impact of adulting that various perspectives have to offer and therefore help us define. There are umpteen ways of comprehending this term 'adult' and to approach it from different angles, contexts, and disciplinary lenses. In the discipline of allopathic medicine, a paediatrician treats the medical conditions of a person who is below fifteen years of biological age, and anyone above that biological age would be referred to a general medical practitioner who is not considered as a specialist who can treat paediatric conditions in India. However, someone who is biologically an adult but has cognitive impairments, though technically an adult, will not be seen as an adult for cognitive purposes and they will be scrutinised for an assessment of cognitive age using appropriate psychological tests and instruments.

In mainstream classrooms, the eligibility clauses of clearing previous levels of courses become the necessity for sitting in a particular classroom, no matter what the age of the adult is in a university or college context. There are instances where 'gifted' students have cleared courses that were actually meant for older adults. There are often cases where in the same classroom there could be a mix of different adult 'ages' depending on when they cleared the eligibility prerequisites. Similarly, even if someone is biologically and cognitively categorised as an adult, their emotional maturity may not match the unstated social expectations of an adult. There are instances in many hostels where 'adults' become so emotionally charged that it becomes impossible for them to sometimes decipher and deflect home-sickness, where they miss their home, and are perpetually faced with problems of adjusting to newer habitats.

To add to this conundrum, there is the legal discipline that defines an adult and it bases this on different biological ages in different countries. In India, for instance, a person is considered to be an adult eighteen years post their birth, and this person is bestowed with the opportunity to vote in an election in the country, apply for a driving licence, et cetera. From an emotional or intellectual perspective, youngsters and others are told to 'grow-up' or become 'mature' but this does not seem to have any connection with the biological age that a person carries on their body or their birth-certificate; it often has everything to do with how they are expected to follow certain norms of behaviour in particular contexts by society, family or friends.

It is therefore pertinent that we maintain the distinction between AE and EA and address the importance of defining and discussing the term 'adult' briefly using the literature available in this domain as a point of reference. Questions like, who is an adult and what are the markers (Lowe, 2013); is it subjective or objective (for example, Arnett, 1994, 1998, 2001, 2003; Nelson & Barry, 2005) are pertinent and need to be essentially clarified before we problematise and theorise the teaching or testing of adults in higher education spaces. Without such clarity in approach, perspective, and everyday transactions, it would not be an effective teaching/learning exercise in such academic spaces. The earlier mentioned studies further indicate that the subjective adult identity is rooted in what all adults are expected to do and most of them indicate the assumption of adjustments, self-regulation, social dynamics, initiative taking, et cetera by exploring their roles. Some studies deal with mentoring and engagement with community of different forms, and conclude that such engagements often lead to the conferment of developmental benefits (for example, Schulenberg, et al., 2004). It would make this task of defining the term adult easier if one were to simply ask the students to describe incidents where they actually felt like adults and how they have considered themselves as being mature as a reflective exercise. This would guide them to track their own milestones from their own life experiences with the traditional milestones being conspicuously absent, and provide us with the necessary clarity that needs to accompany such an important phase of life.

In this chapter, to retain an ease of understanding, the term 'adult' is defined as anyone who is legally an adult and therefore has the right to vote in their home country: in India, it is eighteen-plus years of biological age. The teaching of such adults in mainstream classrooms is considered as being within the purview of the term anthrogogy. This term is an all-inclusive one (all genders, languages, cultures, disciplines, capabilities, et cetera) when compared with andragogy that merely refers to informal or non-formal adult education, continuing education, or lifelong learning.

Andragogy, as Knowles (1950) has enumerated, carries a set of should-statements for adults. Adults should, according to him, acquire a mature understanding of themselves; develop an attitude of acceptance, love, and respect toward others; develop a dynamic attitude toward life; learn to react to the causes, not the symptoms, of behaviour; acquire the skills necessary to achieve the potentials of their personalities; understand the essential values in the capital of human experience; understand their society; and should be skillful in directing social change. Many discussions have taken place around these tenets.

First, as Merriam and Caffarella (1991) have pointed out, Knowles' conception of andragogy is an attempt to build a comprehensive theory (or model) of adult learning that is anchored in the characteristics of adult learners. Cross (1981) also uses such perceived characteristics in a more limited attempt to offer a framework to enable teachers to think about what and how adults learn. Next, Knowles seems to be informed by a wide range of thinkers that include Carl Rogers, Erik Erikson, Abraham Maslow, and also the behaviourist B. F. Skinner. Although he claims to be influenced by Carl Rogers, he endorses scientific curriculum making and behaviour modification, which are contrary to the Rogersian perspective. This implies that he uses ideas that are quite different and works with opposing traditions like the humanist and the behavioural. This is an indication that the model proposed by him is 'incomplete' even though perceived as pertinent as confessed by him (Knowles, et al., 2015, p. 17). Thirdly, according to Hartree (1984) it is not clear whether this is a theory or a set of assumptions about learning, or a theory/model of teaching that Knowles has attempted. It is possible that Knowles' definition of andragogy was seen as the art and science of helping adults learn, as against pedagogy which is the art and science of teaching children.

Hartree points out a few inconsistencies here. He goes on to ask: has Knowles provided us with a theory or a set of guidelines for practice? The assumptions, according to him, 'can be read as descriptions of the adult learner … or as prescriptive statements about what the adult learner should be like' (Hartree 1984, as cited in Merriam & Caffarella, 1991, p. 250). This links with a point made by Tennant (1988) that there seems to be a failure to set and interrogate these ideas within a coherent and consistent conceptual framework. Jarvis (1987) adds to this criticism when he states that throughout Knowles' writings there is a propensity to list characteristics of a phenomenon without interrogating the literature of the arena, namely andragogy, or looking through the lens of a coherent conceptual system. Undoubtedly Malcolm Knowles had a number of important insights, but since they were not tempered by thorough analysis, they were a hostage to fortune; they could be interpreted in a historical or a theoretical way. Nevertheless, the contributions of Knowles to anthrogogy cannot be ignored and need to be contended with as a foundation to build the theorisation of anthrogogy as a perspective. Knowlesian arguments are a mix of a list of principles and suggestions for practice. Moreover, all the work done was in the European or American context: we are placing it in the South Asian context. We also need to go beyond identifying gender as the only variable, as identified by Trott (1991), to change the term andragogy to anthrogogy. This alone is insufficient. In the South Asian context, it is necessary to bring into the fold perspectives on varied language use—namely multi or rather plurilingualism—multiculturalism and, in line with twenty-first century articulations, equity.

With these in mind, we propose a set of principles that can be used by the teacher in higher education classrooms where adult students populate the space to earn their degrees through certification processes. This will be done taking into account the dominant features of adulthood, particularly from South Asian contexts. These principles can and should inform all aspects of the classroom including teaching, testing, and material modification/creation, as well as research supervision.

Anthrogogic Teaching Principles

This postulation of the principles of anthrogogy is the outcome of many ideas and observations that grew out of classroom teaching and learning experiences at both the school (pedagogic) and college (anthrogogic) levels. These principles are a theoretically driven approach, gleaned from three decades of careful reflective practice which should lead to a perspectival change in existing methods. It is therefore pertinent to examine and discuss, as thoroughly as possible, each of the components of teaching/learning classroom practices. These include the nature of learning; nature of classroom talk; classroom dynamics; role of materials; student roles; teacher roles; syllabi; roles and responsibilities of teaching and learning; and along with it, wherever relevant, the underlying philosophy of learning and teaching and the underlying psychological principles that inform the teaching and learning that happens in the classroom.

Nature of Learning

Students at higher education institutes come to these places for various purposes that are very different from the children who are more often than not sent to learn by their parents. Adult students enrol at a higher education institute for purposes of certification and with the hope of finding employment later on the basis of the degree, diploma, or certificate they may receive. It is therefore essential and pertinent that the term 'learning' is problematised in order to understand and situate the term within this context of anthrogogy.

The term 'learning' according to Lachman (1997) is the process by which a relatively stable modification in stimulus–response relations is developed as a consequence of a functional environmental interaction via the senses. Should one desire to distinguish further learning from the effects of maturation, the two terms, 'maturation' and 'learning' may be appended rather than seen as a consequence of mere biological growth and development. In his elaborately studied definitions and in his recommendations, Lachman hints at differences between learning and the effects of maturation. He relegates the term 'maturation' to physiological growth, retaining the term 'learning' within the realms of cognitive psychology. This distinction is pertinent for us in the context of anthrogogy because the students in question are seen as adults with maturity. The relevant maturity in this context, is therefore, not just physiological but the mental maturity that adults come with, and this is undoubtedly at a higher level than that of children however vague the quantification processes may seem. It is this higher mental maturity of adults as compared to children, coupled with the learning that guides an anthrogogic teacher, which will determine the nature of learning in adults as being very different from the learning that occurs in children.

As such, the nature of learning that occurs with adults who have a higher mental and physical maturity and the various cultural, linguistic, class, caste and financial capabilities/backgrounds that the students come with must be acknowledged, accepted, and celebrated in the classroom as being a natural phenomenon. The nature of anthrogogic learning therefore should include a collaboration and a critical commutative collation of the matured or maturing diversities of each adult in the classroom. There cannot be a one-size-fits-all-for-all-time orientation regarding the nature of learning, but rather a mutual consultative, collaborative, negotiated evolutionary process instead of a fixed notional expectation from the teacher. For example, a course outline cannot be a non-tamperable (Prabhu, 2019b) teaching learning instrument that describes and expects a single process of learning as the norm. The learning processes must be tailor-made to meet the backgrounds, schemata, knowledge capital, and linguistic and cultural preferences of the adult students in question. The arbitrariness of the notional descriptions in the classroom transactions as envisaged and described in the course outline must be anticipated and allowed to go for a toss if it does not suit the particular class of students. It is not only the teacher's sense of plausibility (Prabhu, 1987, 2019c) but the adult student's/language-user's sense of plausibility that should be taken into account (Deepa & Ambati, 2026).

The nature of anthrogogic learning must therefore be determined by the realised actualities of the students and, as such, these forays into and attempts towards elasticity need to be valued as the only confirmed anticipated construct regarding anthrogogic learning. This implies that in an anthrogogic classroom the nature of learning must be dynamic, open, inclusive, dignified, consultative, collaborative, and evolving. One predominant reason for this is that motivation should actually never be perceived as a problem with adults. Adult students are fully aware of the underpinning reasons that sent them to these courses; they have enrolled of their free will knowing fully well that the outcome is certification in a course and therefore in the degree programme, with courses being the subcomponents of larger programmes such as a postgraduate degree. Another is that unnecessary artificial reliance on memory, particularly in the age of 'information overload' must be avoided: 'information overload is real. It is not a myth or a phantom' (Bawden & Robinson, 2020, p. 40). They caution us that this phenomenon needs to be taken more seriously than ever. The nature of learning must therefore mimic and be as close as possible to the professions that these students are being certified as capable or eligible for after the award of the degree.

Such learning must also align itself with advances in technology rather than witch hunt technological advances and its use in the classroom and peg a Hawthornian 'scarlet letter' on any student that wishes to approximate the authentic and newly natural context of the availability of information at a swipe on a mobile phone screen. The nature of learning in any anthrogogic classroom must be a sub-cosm of the world outside, but not an anti-cosm that is completely different from the contexts that lie outside the classroom. The pedagogic classroom is supposedly perceived as a microcosm of society at large, but ends up being the anti-cosm with no authentic societal ramifications of what is taught. The world outside includes social, personal, and professional contexts. As such, the nature of learning in an anthrogogic classroom needs to have macrocosmic implications and ramifications for students who are already responsible adults in a society with full voting rights. The nature of learning must involve real time problem-solving scenarios that are akin to the ones thrust by society onto adults routinely. Many anti-cosm courses that remain pedagogic in an adult classroom setup often dump content onto clueless students and outsource materials, equating the learning process to regurgitating the distributed content with obedience and precision, with no critical-thinking skills involved nor problem solving as the focus. Critical thinking/problem-solving skills are major departures from pedagogical contexts that involve children in terms of their complexities and response time. This will directly translate into the nature of classroom talk.

Nature of Classroom Talk

The nature of classroom talk should be in such a manner as though it is between two adults rather than between an adult and a child as is the case in a pedagogic classroom. There should not be any kind of talking down to the students but rather a sense of mutual dignity in the speech, or rather teacher talk, that is used. This classroom talk should be one that accepts, respects, and celebrates the diversities in the classroom rather than being lopsidedly judgemental. For example, classroom talk that bears racist or phobia-ridden undertones, or statements that undermine the life experiences of a particular individual or their (dis)abilities should never be a part of any classroom, more so in an anthrogogic classroom. Activation of the affective domain and implementation of higher order cognitive and affective domains (Anderson & Krathwohl, et al. 2001) characterise anthrogogic classrooms. The whole attempt must therefore be to build and use a constructive verbal disposition, and any feedback by the teacher ought to use constructive language choices of language potentiality (Deepa, 2022a), so that the teacher does not profess but rather enables and empowers the students to rediscover and reorient themselves towards the expectations of the teacher. Issues, if any, between the teacher and the students should be resolved through healthy, unbiased, and open discussions rather than being top-down and unidirectional. Students and teachers must display an equal partnership in the classroom while breaking the walls of silence from the students' side. Mutual respect and dignity must be the underpinning mood of any kind of talk, with the teacher probably being a few years older than the adult students.

Classroom Dynamics

In an anthrogogic classroom that is populated by adults (in the form of the teacher and students), the dynamics cannot be unidirectional either. Dignity, respect, and acceptance of all adults needs to be equally fostered. Processes will have to be consultative and collaborative in nature. For example, if there are certain disabilities displayed by the teacher in terms of a specific use of technological skills and if the students seem able, the teacher must be able to tap the potential of her students without shame (Deepa & Durairajan, 2023a). In a similar manner, if a student has some clarification regarding a teaching–learning point in the classroom, the student should be provided the same freedom of space and dignity to seek clarifications from the teacher/s or peers without fear of judgement from anyone. Ensuring a dignified, non-judgemental, safe environment for a civil discussion of beliefs that might seem contrary to one's own in a classroom that is populated by adults with an affective sensibility is the least expectation from someone who calls themselves an adult. Where there seem to be disagreements, it is expected to stay with a 'we will agree-to-disagree' as the worst case scenario.

The classroom dynamics must be such that it becomes the environment where there is a clear separation of the incident and the belief system from the person. If this is done, personal attacks will reduce and the Bloomian affective domain will blossom along with the cognitive and the psychomotor. For example, if an argumentative essay on *Money or Moral Values* is being explored in a language writing class and if one group chooses money over moral values, whatever one's individual opinion maybe, the classroom dynamic must provide space for all perspectives without judgement based on the choices the individual might prefer to make. Similarly, the power of 'I do not know' and 'What do you think about this?' must be explored, because in the real adult world these are oft-found stances and directions in any discussion. Such open-ended, non-judgemental, safe discussion spaces foster the development of interpretative spaces. Interpretative spaces are those spaces that exist between the discourses and the responses given to the discourses, where the identity, the schemata, and the cultural background of the individual acts as a catalyst in the construction of comprehension, and therefore the responses, to the discourse.

These spaces in anthrogogic classrooms need to be much larger than in pedagogic classrooms. The teaching of literature, poetry, prose, and drama allow for the maximum use of these spaces but this does not imply that it is not relevant in language classrooms. In the latter classrooms, for example, inferential questions that require opinionated and substantiated responses should supersede the accuracy type of questions, for these inferential questions require the activation and use of interpretative spaces.

Group dynamics should not be forcefully implemented among students. The students should be provided the freedom and space to choose to work alone, in pairs, or in convenient groups of their choice (Deepa and Durairajan, 2023b). This implies that there is mutual respect for the time spent by both the students and the teachers in anthrogogic classrooms.

Role of Students

Students in an anthrogogic classroom should not be perceived as captives or subordinates, but as individuals with a different set of experiences that function as assets in the teaching–learning processes. They are to be seen as the teacher's equal and a possible sequel in the near future. Every student is an independent, thinking individual who is also a part of the whole human race, with a huge knowledge capital that is both multilingual and pluricultural, making them clearly identifiable yet equally a part of the whole as a contributory person. Their human rights must rule supreme and preferences need to be respected and not judged. This implies that the independent decision-making powers of these students are to be respected. For this to become a reality, however, student training may be needed in some contexts because many adult classrooms in India are still pedagogic in their orientation and teachers treat adult learners like children. This might cause some initial confusion and the new-found responsibility might be difficult to negotiate. All adult students are expected and assumed to be naturally proactive. Here is where mainstream adult education must take a leaf out of online and open learning courses. In these contexts, the teacher briefs the students with the content and provides the context to the students to take charge of their own learning and proactively reach out to sources and resources while constantly keeping the teacher informed of their learning journey. Many self-learning courses such as the ones offered by the Regional English Language Office (RELO), the US government, and all MOOCs, online courses and distance-education courses offered in India, expect the students to negotiate the course materials provided to them and self-learn while taking responsibility for their own learning. The students in mainstream anthrogogic classrooms must also not just be expected to bring their multidisciplinary skills, and their diverse and multilevel knowledge systems gleaned from their unique world views, but use them skilfully to facilitate knowledge co-creation.

Role of Materials and Syllabi

The materials to be used in the anthrogogic classroom can never be the sole custody of the teacher in the form of a prescribed course book, but should function as a source book where the materials support the teacher and not function as a constraint to the learner/teacher. The students are to be seen as open, full-grown intellectuals and should be explicitly encouraged to copiously add on, modify, or bring alternative materials to the classroom as they deem fit. In anthrogogic classrooms, learning results from an 'interaction between input and investment, the amount of learning being proportionate to the amount of interaction' (Prabhu, 2019a, p. 83). The classroom materials are not to be seen as the Bible but as starting points of discussions, and should be amenable and amply tamperable with to suit the needs of the anthrogogic classroom (Prabhu, 2019b). Anything that sparks discussion can be defined as classroom materials (Tomlinson, 2023). These materials can even be multimodal in nature, such as recorded materials posted on YouTube or a meme posted on a social media site such as Facebook, or an audio from a podcast, et cetera. These materials should be such that they spark discussions on controversial issues in the classroom while also activating affective factors along with cognitive ones where mutual dignity is stressed and ensured.

Multilingual, multicultural, and multidisciplinary perspectives need to be encouraged in an anthrogogic classroom. The syllabus of any anthrogogic course should be a negotiated and spherical one rather than notional or structural. It is negotiated because the teacher and the students are considered as equal learning partners in the classroom, and knowledge- and skill-flow are multidirectional, contrary to the unidirectional flow (from the teacher to the students) in a structural or even communicative syllabus. Unlike older syllabi, both the teachers and the students are seen as knowledgeable and skilled adults in their own unique way in the classroom space. Both the anthrogogic syllabus and materials usually allow for such spaces in the classroom where multi-perspectival approaches are encouraged consciously while celebrating the diversity that the classroom represents. Materials are only complementary and supplementary in nature; further they are multimodal and open access, akin to the situation that the adult students will experience outside the classroom. The syllabus has to be a negotiated, spherical and emergent one, applicable to specific and general purpose programmes, tailor-made with a possibility of frequent change. Without such a syllabus, the materials used will remain a constraint and not support the teacher in an anthrogogic classroom.

Roles and Responsibilities of the Teacher and Underlying Philosophies

There is a lot of literature available on learner autonomy but very little on teacher autonomy. The focus moves to the end product of how students can be enabled to become autonomous learners (Choudhury, 2015) and discussions, if any, that deal with teacher ethics is all about what teachers should not do in classroom spaces, and how they must ensure administrative compliances (Deepa & Durairajan, 2022). It is well known, though, that teachers offer support only if requested by the students. In an anthrogogic setup the teacher must be a negotiator, a bridge between students and administration. She is a co-traveller with the students to see them off as successful degree-holders. The teacher brings her experiences to the table for discussion and functions as a beacon and suggests directions that the courses could take, but in consultation with the students. The philosophy she follows will be that of kintsugi of Japanese origin and guide the students to find their own ikigai. An understanding of the qualified monistic Indian philosophy or Vishishta Advaita of Swamy Ramanuja—where he says that different parts compose the whole and that every part being different is equally significant—will also ensure that all persons are treated with equanimity, equality, and equity. The ground rule in this philosophy, easily applicable to all anthrogogic classrooms, is one that says you do your own but at the same time, respect all. Furthermore although widely criticised for focusing too narrowly on individual transformation, the Mezirowian (1991) theory of transformative learning—which explains how adult learners make sense of their experiences—has been widely applied to various groups of adult learners. Within the domain of that contextual philosophy, the role of adult educators can be safely analysed and defined. It is situational, depending on their contextually adapted philosophies in the light of this transformational learning theory. Such a perspective pushes us further away from the Brunerian scaffolding technique (1985) which has to be seen as completely unsuitable to adult students. Although there may be other transformative learning cycles, the focus of the proposed Mezirowian model illustrates how a learner's transformation is impacted by a dynamic array of factors, including the educator's adapted philosophical perspectives, situational roles of educators, and the learners' needs, styles, experience, and motivation. The model supports a fresh look at prevalent humanistic and progressive philosophies, the role of adult educators as learning facilitators, and their relationship to transformative learning in the adult education field through the lens of a model of contextual philosophy (Wang & Sarbo, 2004). The anthrogogic approach and resultant classroom practices must be informed only by psychological studies that are conducted on adults, for example, Peter Pan syndrome (Deepa, 2022b; Kiley, 1983); Parkinson's law; and studies such as the ones carried out by Tennant (2006).

The Anthrogogic Classroom

The anthrogogic classroom must be viewed and accepted as an unwalled, building-free, and learning-prominent space that can always be expanded. Not confined to walls and benches, the world becomes the learning space. We need to remember that timetables are a necessity only for those physical classroom spaces that have to be shared by a group of teachers, and are not mandatory to enable teaching or learning. Even digital spaces such as a WhatsApp group doubles up as a classroom at the convenience of the teacher and her students. This also means that 'attendance' or marking of physical presence must not be forced by ruining their prime youth. Multimodal classrooms and a negotiated quantum of work/study can be encouraged rather than insisting on 'face staring' captivity in a confined cell behind locked doors usually termed as a classroom. The preferred methods of assessment are alternate, open source, project-based assignments and tests if any must be of the open source kind. Assignments must have negotiated and flexible timelines for submission. A comprehensive discussion of anthrogogic testing and assessment practices is delineated in Chapter 2 of this volume (Durairajan, 2026). Administrative compliance needs to be sent to the periphery and autonomy of teachers must be placed at the core. Wherever possible, collaborative scoring methods (Deepa & Durairajan, 2023b) need to be adopted.

Educating Adults in an Indian Classroom

There are a range of other issues that need to be taken into account in an anthrogogic classroom in the Indian context, regardless of whether the focus is on language empowerment for an adult language user or in courses where the focus is on student or teacher empowerment and professional development. The nature of learning and teaching can never follow the banking system of education and must always aim to raise awareness or conscientisation (Freire, 1970/1993). The focus can never be on the internalisation of a language system or the memorisation of content. Teaching adults is not like filling a pot, but like digging a well or finding an oasis together. Content cannot be disseminated but must always be co-constructed and ideas co-created. Most teachers are very wary of stating 'I do not know', or to ask, 'What do you think about this?'. These must become common statements in anthrogogic classrooms, for interpretative spaces are bigger than in pedagogic classrooms. This implies that the nature of tasks/questions in anthrogogic teaching must be problem-solving ones. We need to remember that adults do not need a scaffold but only a watering and nurturing of their roots. For this purpose, thought seeds will be much more fruitful than tasks (Deepa, 2022c). A practical application of the use of thought seeds in anthrogogic contexts, for the purposes of formative assessment to evaluate intercultural and interpersonal communication, can be found in two papers in this volume (Chekuri, 2026; Narke, 2026).

Student and teacher responsibilities in anthrogogic classrooms need to be equally shared and negotiated. The nature of teacher authority in a postgraduate diploma writing programme has been discussed by Chaudhuri and Pande (2026) while the nature of learner agency at the postgraduate and research level has been discussed by Chandrasekharan and Sultana (2026). It is possible, however, that when some adults—particularly in the Indian context—exhibit pedagogic tendencies, even in college-level classrooms, a certain amount of awareness-raising may be needed. But this does not imply that we as teachers can shun that responsibility. One of the essential, yet easy, ways to do this is to ensure that the nature of group/work is always voluntary. Some adults like to work in groups, others prefer to work alone. More often than not, this fact is not recognised by the teacher in adult classrooms and we go through a count from one to five or six and ask all the 'ones' to get into a group. This can become counter-productive in anthrogogic classrooms (Deepa & Durairajan, 2023b). Similarly, time allocation for tasks and assignment submissions must also always be negotiated through a consensus between teachers and students. An extension of academic time with justifications, however, should be made possible when required to enable students to submit assignments. We need to remember that adults have other responsibilities in their lives. If the responsibility of learning is with the adult student in an anthrogogic classroom, then, as adults they can exercise their power of choice and this must be recognised by teachers.

The choice exercised must include the nature of the helping hand that needs to be stretched out to the student: the request for help must come from the student. We need to remember that scaffolding, which is teacher-centric, is pedagogic. The nature of the helping hand stretched out to the adult student must be like road signs on highways. An experienced driver who knows the route will ignore them, while someone else may consult from time to time; a driver who is new to the route may even go to the extent of using Google Maps (Deepa & Durairajan, 2023a). Similarly, the initiative and request for assistance in any anthrogogic classroom must be student-centric.

Another crucial factor that must be taken into consideration is that the nature of road signs in India is multilingual. The bi/multilinguality of the highway road signs are only a reflection of the asset that multilinguality is to all Indians. This implies that the more enabled language, sometimes described as the first but not necessarily so, must be valued and celebrated. This language in the English classroom in India must be like a sampad, meaning as a 'resource', akin to natural resource and sometimes more than a resource or an asset; whenever needed teachers and students alike must be able to use it comfortably to provide dignity, equality and equity (Ghosh, 2026).

Such valuing of multilinguality alone is not sufficient. In an anthrogogic classroom, not just multilingual, but pluricultural and multidisciplinary platforms must be also celebrated and not just tolerated or recognised. This includes, not just language and culture, but all semiotics. Students may choose to answer assignments from different angles and perspectives, whether vertical, horizontal or spherical. Given the freedom, space, and choice, students may decide to write a poem, a play, or do a video as an assignment: the huge success of an anthrogogic classroom would be that assignments are submitted not in one singular mode but through written, spoken, or film mode.

The implications of these postulations is that, not just teachers, but also students need to be taught to break free from the shackles of the jails which are the pedagogic practices that have been ingrained in us. Teachers and students alike need to begin to explore anthrogogicity and learn to enjoy and celebrate the responsibility that adulthood brings with it. Teachers and students can then become joint learners in this domain of adults being educated with the hope that both will continue growing and flourishing.

References

Anderson, L. W., Krathwohl, D. R., Airasian, P. W., Cruikshank, K. A., Mayer, R. E., Pintrich, P. R., Raths, J., & Wittrock, M. C. (2001). *A taxonomy for learning, teaching, and assessing: A revision of Bloom's Taxonomy of Educational Objectives* (Complete edition). Longman.

Arnett, J. J. (1994). Are college students adults? Their conceptions of the transition to adulthood. *Journal of Adult Development, 1*, 154–168. https://doi.org/10.1007/BF02277582.

Arnett, J. J. (1997). Young people's conceptions of the transition to adulthood. *Youth & Society, 29*, 3–23. https://doi.org/10.1177/0044118X97029001001.

Arnett, J. J. (1998). Learning to stand alone: The contemporary American transition to adulthood in cultural and historical context. *Human Development, 41*, 295–315. https://doi.org/10.1159/000022591.

Arnett, J. J. (2000). Emerging adulthood: A theory of development from the late teens through the twenties. *American Psychologist, 55*, 469–480. https://doi.org/10.1037/0003-066X.55.5.469.

Arnett, J. J. (2001). Conceptions of the transition to adulthood: Perspectives from adolescence through midlife. *Journal of Adult Development, 8*(2), 133–143. https://doi.org/10.1023/A:1026450103225.

Arnett, J. J. (2003). Conceptions of the transition to adulthood among emerging adults in American ethnic groups. In J. J. Arnett & N. L. Galambos (Eds.), *New directions for child and adolescent development: Cultural conceptions of the transition to adulthood* (Vol. 100). (pp. 63–75). Jossey-Bass.

Ausubel, D. P. (1962). Can children learn anything that adults can-And more efficiently?. *The Elementary School Journal, 62*(5), 270–272.

Ausubel, D. P. (1964). Adults versus children in second-language learning: Psychological considerations. *The Modern Language Journal, 48*(7), 420–424.

Bawden, D., & Robinson, L. (2020, June 30). Information overload: An overview. In *Oxford Encyclopaedia of Political Decision Making.* Oxford University Press. https://doi.org/10.1093/acrefore/9780190228637.013.1360.

Bruner, J. (1985). Vygotsky: A historical and conceptual perspective. In J. Wertsch (Ed.), *Culture, communication and cognitions: Vygotskian perspectives* (pp. 21–34). Cambridge University Press.

Chandrasekharan, D., & S. Sultana, (2026). Anthrogogicity and learner agency in academic writing. In S. Deepa & G. Durairajan (Eds.), *Anthrogogy in use: A handbook for language educators* (pp. 122–135). Orient BlackSwan.

Chaudhuri, S., & Pande, M. H. (2026). Reimagining teacher authority in an anthrogogic framework: Reflections from a writing programme. In S. Deepa & G. Durairajan (Eds.), *Anthrogogy in use: A handbook for language educators* (pp. 97–121). Orient BlackSwan.

Chekuri, T. (2026). Incorporating thought seeds as an assessment tool in anthrogogic contexts. In S. Deepa & G. Durairajan (Eds.), *Anthrogogy in use: A handbook for language educators* (pp. 207–227). Orient BlackSwan.

Choudhury, M. T. (2015). *A study of teacher autonomy and its impact on classroom practices in secondary schools of Bangladesh* [Unpublished doctoral dissertation]. English and Foreign Languages University.

Courtenay, B., & Stevenson, R. (1983). Avoiding the threat of gogymania. *Lifelong Learning: The Adult Years, 6*(7), 10–11.

Cross, K. P. (1981). *Adults as learners.* Jossey-Bass.

Deepa, S. (2022a). Verbal disposition: The need for language potentiality in anthrogogic spaces. *Journal of English Language Teaching, 64*(6), 17–24. https://journals.eltai.in/index.php/jelt/article/view/JELT640603/388.

Deepa, S. (2022b). Pedagogic practices in higher education and Peter Pan syndrome: An appraisal. *Fortell, 45,* 164–173. https://www.fortell.org/wp-content/uploads/2022/10/July-2022-164-173.pdf.

Deepa, S. (2022c). Thought seeds in anthrogogic learning contexts. *Journal of Indian Education, 48,* pp. 58–70.

Deepa, S., & Ambati, A. (2026). Anthrogogic contexts and student sense of plausibility in language materials. In A. Sarkeshikian (Ed.), *Exploring the psychology of language materials development* (pp. 245–278). IGI Global Scientific Publishing. https://doi.org/10.4018/979-8-3373-2995-6.ch008.

Deepa, S., & Durairajan, G. (2022). Teacher autonomy: Ensuring equity and reinstating respect. *Journal of English Language Teaching, 64*(3), 17–23.

Deepa, S., & Durairajan, G. (2023a). Scaffolds or road signs for anthrogogic language learners? A critical inquiry. In B. Nair, P. Ramalingam, & B. Nagalakshmi (Eds.), *Teaching of English: Theorizing from classroom* (pp. 11–25). Tamil Puduvai.

Deepa, S., & Durairajan, G. (2023b). Learning through assessment in anthrogogic contexts: Wash-Forward. In A. L. Gokturk-Saglam, & E. Sevgi-Sole (Eds.), *Emerging practices for online language assessment, exams, evaluation, and feedback* (pp. 99–118). IGI Global.

Durairajan, G. (2026). Principles of anthrogogic testing and assessment: The need for humane joyful practices. In S. Deepa & G. Durairajan (Eds.), *Anthrogogy in use: A handbook for language educators* (pp. 27–55). Orient BlackSwan.

Freire, P. (1993). *Pedagogy of the oppressed.* Penguin. (Original work published 1970).

Gagne, R. (1985). *The conditions of learning and theory of instruction.* Holt, Rinehart & Winston.

Ghosh, D. (2026). Looking beyond the compulsion of 'need to be told': An attempt at anthrogocity in the undergraduate literature classroom. In S. Deepa & G. Durairajan (Eds.), *Anthrogogy in use: A handbook for language educators* (pp. 165–173). Orient BlackSwan.

Hartree, A. (1984). Malcolm Knowles' theory of andragogy: A critique. *International journal of lifelong education, 3*(3), 203–210.

Jarvis, P. (1987). Meaningful and meaningless experience: Towards an analysis of learning from life. *Adult education quarterly, 37*(3), 164–172.

Kiley. D. (1983). *The Peter Pan syndrome: Men who have never grown up.* Dodd, Mead.

Knowles, M. (1950). *Informal adult education.* Association Press.

Knowles, M., Holton III, E., & Swanson, R. (2015). *The Adult learner: The definitive classic in adult education and human resource development.* Routledge.

Lachman, S. J. (1997). Learning is a process: Toward an improved definition of learning. *The Journal of Psychology, 131*(5), 477–480. https://doi.org/10.1080/00223989709603535.

Larsen-Freeman, D. (2000). *Techniques and principles in language teaching.* Oxford University Press.

Lavasani, M. G., & Faryadres, F. (2011). Language learning strategies and suggested model in adults' processes of learning second language. *Procedia-Social and Behavioral Sciences, 15*, 191–197.

Lowe, S. R., Dillon, C. O., Rhodes, J. E., & Zwiebach, L. (2013). Defining adult experiences: Perspectives of a diverse sample of young adults. *Journal of Adolescent Research, 28*(1), 31–68.

Merriam, S. and Caffarella, R. (1991). *Learning in adulthood.* Jossey-Bass.

Mezirow, J. (1991). *Transformative dimension of adult learning.* Jossey-Bass.

Narke, P. (2026). Thought seeds as an instrument for assessing the intercultural competence of adult ESL learners. In S. Deepa & G. Durairajan (Eds.), *Anthrogogy in use: A handbook for language educators* (pp. 185–206). Orient BlackSwan.

Ministry of Human Resource Development (2020). *National education policy 2020.* https://www.education.gov.in/sites/upload_files/mhrd/files/NEP_Final_English_0.pdf

Nelson, L. J., & Barry, C. M. (2005). Distinguishing features of emerging adulthood: The role of self-classification as an adult. *Journal of Adolescent Research, 20*, 242–263. https://doi.org/10.1177/0743558404273074.

Omoregie, C. (2019). The theory and practice of andragogy. *Indian Journal of Adult Education, 80*(1), 27–31. ISSN: 2501-1111.

Prabhu, N. S. (1987). *Second language pedagogy.* Oxford University Press.

Prabhu, N. S. (2019a). Materials as support: Materials as constraint. In G. Durairajan (Ed.), *Perceptions of language pedagogy* (pp. 82–93). Orient BlackSwan.

Prabhu, N. S. (2019b). Rethinking language pedagogy: An interview. In G. Durairajan (Ed.), *Perceptions of language pedagogy* (pp. 314–330). Orient BlackSwan.

Prabhu, N. S. (2019c). Plausibility. In G. Durairajan (Ed.), *Perceptions of language pedagogy* (pp. 331–340). Orient BlackSwan.

Richards, J. C., & Rodgers, T. S. (2014). *Approaches and methods in language teaching*. Cambridge University Press.

Rubayet, T., & Imam, H. T. (2021). Adaptation of andragogy in the education system of Bangladesh: Emulating andragogical approaches of South East Asia. 212–33. *European Journal of Education Studies*, *8*(11). https://doi.org/10.46827/ejes.v8i11.3983

Schulenberg, J. E., Bryant, A. L., & O'Malley, P. M. (2004). Taking hold of some kind of life: How developmental tasks relate to trajectories of well-being during the transition to adulthood. *Development and Psychopathology, 16*, 1119–1140. https://doi.org/10.1017/S0954579404040167.

Smith, M. K. (2002). *Malcolm Knowles, informal adult education, self-direction and andragogy*. Infed.org. https://infed.org/mobi/malcolm-knowles-informal-adult-education-self-direction-and-andragogy/.

Taylor, B., & Kroth, M. (2009). Andragogy's transition into the future: Meta-analysis of andragogy and its search for a measurable instrument. *Journal of Adult Education*, *38*(1). http://files.eric.ed.gov/fulltext/EJ891073.pdf.

Tennant, M. (2006). *Psychology and adult learning: The role of theory in informing practice*. Routledge.

Thompson, M. A., & Deis, M. (2004). Andragogy for adult learners in higher education. In *Proceedings of the Academy of Accounting and Financial Studies*, *9*(1), 107–112.

Tomlinson, B. (2023). Humanising the course book: In B. Tomlinson (Ed.), *Developing materials for language teaching* (pp. 236–273). Bloomsbury Academic.

Wang, V. C., & Sarbo, L. (2004). Philosophy, role of adult educators, and learning: How contextually adapted philosophies and the situational role of adult educators affect learners' transformation and emancipation. *Journal of Transformative Education, 2*(3), 204–214.

Wood, D., Bruner, J. S., & Ross, G. (1976). The role of tutoring in problem solving. *Journal of Child Psychology and Psychiatry, 17*(2), 89–100.

2

Principles of Anthrogogic Testing and Assessment

The Need for Humane Joyful Practices

Geetha Durairajan

Introduction

This chapter makes a case for anthrogogic testing and assessment and enumerates the need for it, while drawing proof from existing practices that do not differentiate between pedagogic and anthrogogic testing and assessment. We will enumerate the principles of anthrogogic testing and assessment and their theoretical rationales along with operationalisations and realisations in the educational domain in the context of formative, and wherever possible, summative assessment practices.

The term 'anthrogogy' has been defined and delineated in an earlier chapter in this volume (Deepa, 2026). To reiterate that perspective, we are making a distinction between pedagogic—the assessment and evaluation of children—and anthrogogic testing and assessment practices as applied to mainstream higher education adult students. Anthrogogy as a term is preferred and has been systematically used in this chapter and book instead of the more common one, andragogy (Knowles, 1968, 1984), to remove the gender bias implied in the latter term and to make it more inclusive. Moreover, this book is located in the context of mainstream higher education and therefore the former term, anthrogogy, is preferred over the latter which has been in vogue only in the contexts of distance education and adult literacy programmes. As stated in Chapter 1, an adult is one who is over eighteen years of age and is old enough, in the Indian context, to vote and elect the prime minister of the country. In this chapter we will be focussing on anthrogogic assessment practices in higher institutes of mainstream education, preceded by a critical examination of some of the theorised constructs in the domain of testing and assessment and their manifested practices, to arrive at a clearer distinction between pedagogic and anthrogogic testing and assessment.

A test—in the context of this chapter, within the educational domain—is a procedure designed to elicit some kind of behaviour from which one can make inferences about certain characteristics of an individual (Carroll, 1968). Testing therefore implies using a calibrated instrument. No distinction is made in this chapter between examinations and tests within education; the latter is viewed as a smaller version of the former. Evaluation, in this context, is a broad umbrella term that implies that it can be done by the teacher in the classroom through the look of an eye, an assessment of body language, or the posture of a student in class (Bloom, et al., 1971). This chapter on anthrogogic testing and assessment, however, will not focus on evaluation, only on assessment and testing.

The term 'assessment' has been discussed in the context of formative and summative assessment (Hughes, 2003) and is also described as the informal assessment carried out by teachers (Bachman, 1990). In this chapter, it is construed as much more focused than evaluation; it has a value attached to it in the form of a grade or a mark, or some other performance indicator (Durairajan, 2015). There is an assessment procedure designed to elicit some form of behaviour, as with a test, but the 'instruments'—with reference to assessment—may be a task, a prompt, or specifications for a project. As such, these assessment instruments may not be calibrated and strict rules and procedures may not be followed. However, in the context of anthrogogy, assessments—rather than tests—ought to be the preferred mode of evaluation, for the inferences made will have more predictive validity. The focus of this chapter is on tests and examinations (where required), and more importantly, assignments—where the teacher has a part to play in the development, administration and evaluation—which includes the grading or marking of all formative, and wherever possible, summative assessments. The primary focus of this chapter, with reference to the principles of anthrogogic assessment and its operationalisations, is not on high-stakes or standardised tests. However, the construct of language proficiency itself, the primary arguments on test validation and the large body of research in the domain of language testing is located in this high-stakes domain; as such arguments will have to be drawn from there and applied to mainstream autonomous assessment contexts.

Existing Practices

It is pertinent and surprising to note that in the context of testing and assessment, 'age' is the first and foremost feature listed in physiological test taker characteristics (Bachman & Palmer, 1996, 2010; O'Sullivan, 2011), but surprisingly no binary distinction is made between children and adults, and no discussion can be found anywhere—either in practice or theory—about it to indicate such a distinction. There is no practical or theoretical research that distinguishes even between pedagogic and andragogic testing or assessment: the term 'anthrogogic' testing or assessment does not feature in the literature. Age seems to be an issue only with reference to the cognitive level appropriacy of the tasks, or as an eligibility criterion for taking a test, or as a mere demographic detail. In system-oriented tests that focus on the various competencies, however, it is possible that a younger child with a high level of language proficiency—even when the actual test is meant for adults—would be able to attempt that test paper and get a more than passable grade. This implies that the actual age of the test taker does not matter to the test developer, except as a nominal reference point or as a field to be filled in just like the 'Name' column. Other physiological test taker characteristics include gender and ethnicity along with short-term ailments, including even toothache, and extends to long-term ailments like dyslexia. Along with a listing of psychological characteristics like motivation and anxiety, experiential characteristics that could 'affect' test taking are listed, but these are limited to features like education, nature of communication in the target language, and the number of years of stay in the country of residence which may reduce anxiety (O'Sullivan, 2000, as cited in Weir, 2005, p. 51). The test takers whom the researchers are worried about are migrants or English language learners, not language users. Similarly, in recent times, the age, gender and locales—in terms of countries where standardised tests have been taken—have been researched, but only with reference to what is termed as a construct, 'shadow education', or test-preparedness—implying that it is an independent variable—to find out whether these factors have any effect on the supposed beneficial washback of such testing on teaching and learning. None of these characteristics are factored into the nature of the items in the test itself (O'Sullivan, et al., 2021).

Documented testing can be traced to the Han dynasty circa 206 BCE to 220 CE in China with reference to their Imperial examinations, to establish a system of testing with a centralised control to select, from a large number of candidates, the best who could work in government offices. This, described as the Chinese model, was later brought into the Indian and British civil services examinations (Spolsky, 1995, 2008, 2016). Such testing, though it was in the context of adults, could be described as merely andragogic in perspective, since it focused on the testing of male adults and did not have an all-inclusive perspective. Anthrogogic testing and assessment as a perspective that is all-inclusive, therefore, becomes a necessity with a sense of immediacy and urgency in today's modern scenario. Similarly, the growth from this initial testing through the three stages—that is the prescientific, the psychometric, and later the integrative sociometric, a move from essay type tests, to objective tests, to integrative communicative testing (Spolsky, 1995)—also dealt with adults, but all these tests focused mostly on language as a system of rules or as a communicative tool. They did not treat the test taker as a language user but treated them as deficient language learners, often also perceived as approximating to native speaker norms. None of them took into account the multilingual, pluricultural and multi-abilities of the test takers. At another level, none of these tests have attempted to assess the verbal disposition of the test takers who are language users (Deepa, 2022b). As such, these tests still remain either pedagogic or at the most andragogic, leaving a lacuna that this chapter attempts to fill through an open dialogue.

As a continuation of the three stages of proficiency testing and the break-up of proficiency into many parts—from the Unitary Competency Hypothesis (Oller, 1979) to the bi-partite BICS/CLP, and CALP/ALP (Cummins, 1980, 2000) and the four partite delineation (Canale and Swain, 1980)—powerful arguments have been made by Bachman (1990) and Bachman and Palmer (1996, 2010) to include Messick's notion of validity (1989) in such a way that their construct of language proficiency incorporates 'social consequences' and the impact of testing on test takers. Prior to this Messickian articulation, there was only an implicit awareness of the impact of social consequences, but it was never consciously and deliberately taken into account. Ethical considerations (Shohamy, 1997, 2001) and multilingualism (Shohamy, 2011) are two more aspects that have been added to this domain of social consequences. The import of this research work and the modification of the construct of language proficiency, along with its resultant operationalisations, cannot be undermined. However, the focus has stayed largely with construct validity—with some inputs from the fourth quadrant in

Messick's rectangle which focuses on the use of tests—which, along with relevance and utility, attempts to give great importance to the value implications of the test and its social consequences (Messick, 1989; this is elaborated briefly later in the chapter). The impact and use of tests and other assessment measures were brought to the forefront with the clear articulation that what is validated is not the instrument, but its suitability for that sample population and the strength of the score inference. The focus of such primary impact studies was, however, linked to fundamental issues regarding standards (whether they were the right ones for the purposes intended) and with reliable and valid measures. The worries displayed thereof were also about the nature of reporting and how they were linked to desirable outcomes, which in turn—it was posited—ought to lead to forms of appropriate and useful teaching (Davies, 2008).

The Messickian articulation—which is accepted and valued in the world of language testing—is that validity is always a matter of degree and that what gets validated is the nature of the inference made based on scores or other modes of assessment. The focus, however, has stayed with the adequacy and appropriateness of actions (1989) that are based on score inferences. It is further postulated that these inferences are perceived to have 'social consequences', but no mention has been made of the affect or the effect of test taking on the test-taking individual, as though the test does not have any consequences for them along with the society that they are a part of. Further, an awareness of the legality of these 'consequences'—influenced by what popular media describes as 'certificate chasing lawyers'—led to the postulation not only of the 'language use' of the test-taker argument (Bachman & Palmer, 1996) but also to the need to couch all work done with language proficiency in legal terms, with a clear outlining of claims, warrants, evidence and rebuttals leading to an assessment-use argument (Kane, 2006; Bachman & Palmer, 2010). The purpose of these realisations was to largely provide evidence that test takers—and when relevant, other stakeholders—have been treated in a fair and reliable manner.

A large volume of such work in the literature is, however, in the domain of standardised testing; not with reference to the certification of tests and assessments that lead to the award of a degree, and definitely not in the context of formative assessments. Some of the evidence collected and presented, however, does attempt to ensure that what has been taught in the context of formal teaching and learning, has been tested. This is reflected in the assessment and evaluation projects taken up at the university level (Bachman & Palmer, 1996). Research in the domain of consequential validity is also reflected in the work done with entrance and selection examinations, where ensuring fair gatekeeping is attempted through beneficial washback (Chang, 2002); but it has become a conundrum with no reference or attention paid to the consequences on the test taker who is the primary user of the test.

Testing in the context of international level selection tests and examinations has become an industry and a business. The major test purpose with all international examinations is for selection, or elimination in some cases. It is an allied certification which is not a part of any educational programme. The test results are used for admission purposes by those in the educational domain for purely gatekeeping purposes, termed as 'users' (Alderson, 1991). These 'users', surprisingly, are not the students or examinees who take the test, but those who use the test results to decide on cut-off scores to permit or prevent entry into a range of institutions for further studies or employment. The nature of the test—or its administration and evaluation—and its affect and effect on the individual is never the primary concern of the educationists, or school/college/university-level administrators, employers, and decision makers. This is notwithstanding the fact that Bachman and Palmer's (1996) 'language use' tasks are supposedly situated in the actual language-use context that they call, 'real life domains' (p. 44). These perspectives seem to remain at the level of postulation and have not seen their way into the actual test items that are constructed or administered, thus enabling the flourishment of the testing industries.

These testing industries are often controlled by examination syndicates and services which encompass or oversee the range of international tests that certify individuals as eligible to pursue some course of study or employment. These include tests of language and also a measuring of content knowledge and application. In these tests, accountability and parity take precedence after ensuring, through major research exercises, that the inferences made are valid ones as far as the construct is concerned. In line with the validity-is-a-matter-of-degree Messickian argument, research in this area is always ongoing with a range of domains that include test design; nature and adaptation of tasks; administration; scoring and interpretation of results; and dynamic assessment (Tiekstra, et al., 2016), ending with overall evaluation that focuses on the joint impact on the stakeholders and the community (Kunnan, 2019).

In international certification tests and examinations, the need for parity across the board gets prominence and to ensure that this is applied worldwide—whether pencil-paper or computer-based—the tests are administered at the same time. To ensure that no one individual gets undue advantage, even personal needs such as toilet breaks (termed as 'comfort breaks' sometimes) are monitored. Such care may be perceived as essential for purposes of accountability, but these tests and examinations land up converting all the 'subjects' who take the test into an object and all of them are either subjected to (or as adults), subject themselves to testing (Foucault, 1978/1991). With this perspective, it is immaterial whether the test taker is a child or an adult, for administrative systems remain the same. The representation of the construct is hopefully age- and cognitive-level appropriate. Steps are usually in place to ensure that there is no Messickean construct under-representation, and one assumes that construct-irrelevant variance (1989) from the standardised test perspective is minimal. Social consequences in any case, however, do not go beyond an awareness of gatekeeping—who is kept out and who is given admission. These include ensuring that only relevant target-language skills are tested, that gender/ethnic sensitive topics are avoided, and that there are no unfamiliar item types or that test scores are not misused.

With reference to language testing at the international level, in order to ensure that there is positive washback, there is a full-fledged curriculum, syllabus and materials production industry in place. The test creators also become materials producers: communicative and academic language coursebooks of all kinds are written and published, claiming to equip the test taker to achieve the desired band or grade in this or the other test. Sample test tasks are available for free on the internet, often accompanied by notes to the teacher. This makes it a business enterprise. The concern of the test developer and examination syndicate is not about the mental strain or tension of the test taker, or the money that has to be dished out by the test taker for the coursebooks, online courses, and the actual examination/test. The coursebooks divide the skills to be developed into tiny bits and attempt to teach them separately. Thus there are units in these textbooks on cohesive markers, and even some aspects of grammar and vocabulary, that get taught under the nearly fifty-year-old premise that second language learners of English need the weak form of communicative language teaching which includes a focus on not only communicative functions but also on the forms of language (Widdowson, 1978). Such 'preparatory' materials and online practice tests attempt to ensure that test difficulty—which is one of the two aspects of construct-irrelevant variance, (Messick, 1989)—will not be a problem for the test taker. All such course books have tasks covering the various skills, similar to what is in the actual examination, but also carry sample papers. This implies that the test developer can vouchsafe that this variance will not interfere with, or rather pollute, the inference made using the score obtained by the candidate. The tensions of test preparation and test taking, however, are rarely taken into consideration.

Another facet of such an attempt to ensure that construct-irrelevant variance does not affect or pollute the test score and inference, is through the arena of accommodations. It was initially restricted to facilities for those with disabilities and later extended to those who do not speak English as a first language—the so-called English language learner group (Abedi, 2010, 2014). Instructions were to be provided in the 'migrant's' first language to ensure that they could work to their full cognitive capacity. The history of educational and assessment reform in the USA has unfortunately been the outcome of legal cases and of certificate-chasing lawyers and clans who convince huge groups of people to fight for their 'rights'. The work in this domain of accommodations is also one such outcome. Couched in the language of social consequences, the focus seems to have shifted from the effect of scores and inferences on the actual individuals who are test takers—and therefore primary 'users' of the tests and their results—to test-administration conditions. It is still prodded by the social consequences of the use of test results and its impact on the individual, but only as either 'gate keeping or door opening' (Bachman & Purpura, 2008) after the results have been announced. In the context of critical-language testing, an attempt to ensure social justice has led to schools in the USA being asked to practice multilingual testing. But this is to either avoid or overcome violations of language rights which, if left unchecked, will lead to legal battles (Shohamy, 2022).

The literature stops there abruptly with no credible references made to the test taker as the primary test user, which is a huge lapse in the domain of testing and assessment. The test taker remains an object that is assigned either a nominal value (a CGPA or a grade) or ordinal values (like ranking or percentiles). This is silently projected as though the test takers carry a label (in the form of a grade, or score or a CGPA, et cetera) with them and offer themselves for further scrutiny or stay with that certification stamp that marks them forever as either proficient, with low level ability, or as wanting in some respect.

In this chapter, we therefore postulate that there is an urgent and a massive need to include the notion of 'individual consequences' along with social consequences. The primary test 'user' is the test taker before anyone can use it for whatever purpose. Under this postulation the test taker's characteristic of 'age' becomes very important because pedagogic tests (testing and assessing children) and anthrogogic tests (testing and assessment of adults) should make a clear distinction between these two types of users. The pedagogic test user has different individual consequences when compared to anthrogogic ones. The adult test user might use the results of the test to either get her/himself a chance at employment, to decide if s/he wants to pursue higher studies, or take a repeat test to improve the score. These primary users of the tests are not lifeless objects, particularly adults who are full-fledged sentient beings leading full lives. These tests have a major role to play in both short- as well as long-term goals, and impact their plans in life which might impact their families too in many ways. For example if an Indian adult (say a doctor) qualifies in the IELTS test and is planning to use the score to try her luck at a job or aim for further studies in a country like the UK, the individual consequences for her would be to decide on the impact of shifting to a new country. If she is a married woman with children, the test results would impact her family and children. She might have to decide whether she would take her children along with her or leave them back in India. Different consequences are possible for her if she does not qualify—over and above the cost factor, the affective factors, more preparation time, et cetera—all of which will be outcomes. As such, the inclusion of individual consequences is tantamount and this is closely dictated by the fully rounded adult and her family who are impacted by the test use, in whatever fashion. Sometimes a situation may arise where an individual may qualify as per organisational requirements in a test such as the IELTS or TOEFL but because of the family or children taking prominence, the well 'qualified' test result that could have otherwise been 'useful' could be tossed out of the window unapologetically for the sake of familial bonding. In such a context, the culture and value systems that the individual holds will decide on the actual use of the test! The individual consequences of test taking and the results, should therefore supersede any other kind of consequences, social or otherwise, for predictive and consequential validity stems from this root notion.

Anthrogogic Perspectives on Consequential Validity

Messick (1987) critiqued the traditional ways of cutting validity and introduced a unified framework where he argued that construct validity subsumes content- and criterion-related validity. He also introduced the argument that tests are not conducted in a vacuum and that the social consequences of testing must be taken into account, bringing in consequential validity into the purview. He also postulated that facets of validity must include both test interpretation and test use, and that both the evidential and consequential basis of such interpretation and use must be considered. This postulation gave rise to what is well known as the Messick quadrant:

Table 2.1: *Facets of Validity*

	Test Interpretation	***Test Use***
Evidential basis	Construct Validity	Construct Validity + Relevance/ Utility
Consequential basis	Value Implications	Social Consequences

Table 1 (Messick, 1987, p. 17)

For Messick, tests are interpreted based on the validity of the construct, while the evidential basis for test use must provide information regarding the relevance of the test to the specific applied purpose in the applied setting. The consequential basis of the interpretation of tests should carry an awareness of value implications, where the term 'value' refers to the meaning of the score assigned to an individual. Messick (1987, p. 18) cites Cronbach (1971) to state that a test can be used to either describe a person or to make decisions about a person. However, the use of the term 'to describe, or to make decisions' implies that someone else is expected to describe or make decisions, and most often it alludes to the gatekeeping process. 'To interpret a test is to use it' is acknowledged, by Messick (1987, p. 17), but the question that needs to be asked is: by whom? The test taker is never recognised as a test user in this postulation. The consequential basis of test use, the fourth quadrant in Messick's rectangle, incorporates the 'appraisal of potential and actual social consequences of the applied testing' (p. 17) but whose appraisal is not stated. The implication—based on the reference to the Cronbachian reference to descriptions of or decisions about a person—is that someone else—the test user, who is in a position of power—is the appraiser.

This is one of the probable reasons why there is very little research in the domain of the fourth quadrant, the consequential basis of test use, of the Messickian rectangle. The focus of most research in this domain is restricted to washback studies in the past, and social justice in more recent times, primarily because of the way the test taker is viewed by the testing industry; not as an individual, but as someone who can be described by someone else. The perspective is pedagogic in its orientation. Test takers, although they are mostly adults—as is the case with international tests of proficiency whether for higher studies or employment—are not seen as mature, responsible adults. Decisions about what and how to test are made by test developers and test users. The test taker is never accounted for as a test user and this is the basic difference between pedagogic and anthrogogic testing and assessment.

In anthrogogic testing and assessment, the test taker must be given prominence and be at the centre of all decision making. This non-recognition of the test taker as a test user leads to the second issue that needs to be problematised in anthrogogic assessment: consequential validity focuses only on social and not individual consequences, primarily because the affect and effect of the test/examination on test takers is not accounted for. This implies that the individual's psychomotor, cognitive, and affective factors must be accounted for in all anthrogogic testing and assessment. When this happens, it will then be no longer sufficient to claim consequential validity by linking it with mere beneficial washback into teaching and learning, or expand into accommodations to ensure social justice. These are carried out at the level of social consequences because washback is for a whole class that is taught and accommodations are for groups of test takers, not individuals. At any given point in time, for a standardised/international test, it is possible that accommodations are made available for one particular test taker, but that individual functions only as a token of one type of student; whether an English language learner or a student with disabilities. In India, such accommodations are not yet part of mainstream education; the exception is in the form of scribes for those who are visually impaired.

The arguments being made in this chapter are not couched within the domain of standardised or international tests. However, parallels are being drawn from that domain to make a case for incorporating individual consequences in anthrogogic testing domains in India. Such a parallel is different from the theorisations in the literature that primarily come from these standardised/international tests. In that context, the postulations and operationalisations are violently thrust into the domain of classroom teaching and testing contexts in mainstream higher education/adult classrooms, which focus on the certification of degrees after successfully clearing the courses that make up a programme for which the degree is awarded. Furthermore, the literature consistently avoids considering the test taker as the primary test user, for such decisions in pedagogic contexts are made by parents or caretakers; but adults decide for themselves how to use the test. The adult students in mainstream higher education classrooms, namely anthrogogic students, come with a full plan of what to do for a living and make informed choices. They are thereby bound by their individual choices and are aware of the consequences that might impact their choice. It is not by fluke or random magic that adults sit down to be assessed, to mechanically handover a grade or a score or a certificate paper (or soft copy) to someone outside of themselves to treat them like objects of either praise or ridicule in the form of either denying them entry or opening doors for them. This is to demean and insult the abilities and decision-making power that rests with adult students.

Adults who take a test or an assignment, who are willing to be assessed, subject themselves to such an assessment either to move into a higher course of learning, to seek employment, or to better their employment opportunities. There are two kinds of assessments here: one is the standardised testing or 'industrial grading' as it is in the discipline of chemistry where a watered-down strength of chemicals used in industries are indicated as opposed to a purer version of chemicals termed as 'therapeutic grading', which is akin to the university certification processes followed in a country like India where there are formative and summative assessments to mark the completion of a programme such as an undergraduate degree. It is pertinent to note that not all graduates from a country like India subject themselves to these international standardised tests, probably because Indians are happier working inside and for their country rather than being de-homed. The testing industries leech themselves into mainstream higher education classrooms, convincing educational organisations to shell out large sums of money. These industries enter through the back door and try to meddle with not only the certification processes, but also the teaching–learning processes in the form of additional English classes—termed 'optional'—that focus only on preparation for these standardised tests. Such preparation, rather than leading to beneficial washback, only results in mere industrial rather than therapeutic grading which—by contrast—will empower the individual. In India, there are 'competitive examinations' such as bank or public service examinations at various levels that function as employment placement tests which fulfil the purpose of gatekeeping.

This chapter does not focus on such examinations but focuses on assessments, both formative and summative, that lead to the acquisition of a degree after the fulfilment of a certain number of successful credit hours in regular mainstream classrooms that house adult students. Many summative examinations/assessments in Indian contexts happen in an autonomous setup, where the teacher/s are the instructors, test constructors, and evaluators, although there are a few exceptions where this pattern is not followed. In such contexts where autonomy is not available at the summative level, there are, however, clear systems in place to include autonomy in formative assessments. In either case, this chapter focuses only on the autonomous setup and does not consider the other tests that build businesses out of examinations that lead to a laundering method of washbacks with a laundromat's 'precision' of test 'clearance'.

Anthrogogic Assessment Postulations

A primary argument made in this chapter is that instead of a mere washback to teaching and learning, assessments should wash-forward (Allan, 2020; Deepa & Durairajan, 2023b) into life where tests do not get taken or written, but projects and assignments will definitely need to be taken on or carried out. In this anthrogogic assessment context, the purview and extent of wash-forward should also reach far beyond a professional wash-forward for the teacher into other courses (Deepa & Durairajan, 2023b). It is the responsibility of the evaluator/assessor to ensure that students/test takers also benefit from the assessment in such a way that their test taking experience—which should contain problem-solving tasks and not be tests of memory or system based regurgitations—can wash-forward into adult life beyond the classroom. This is genuine anthrogogic predictive validity.

The relevance and utility of the test/examination/assignment (Messick, 1989) cannot refer only to the score given and to the inference that is made. The test taker must also be seen as the primary test user, not only those who are in a position of power to use the scores. The assignments and projects must therefore, to be useful to the test taker, be similar (in a holistic manner) to the kinds of demands the adult student will face in real life, with the taken-for-granted assumption that non-familiar tasks will not feature in any test, examination, or assignment.

Test interpretation implies test use by the test taker, and this value consequence must be factored into the design of the test/assignment. If social consequences refers to the appraisal of both potential and actual social consequences of the test, then the consequences for the individual's 'self appraisal' must also be taken into account. The test taker cannot be reduced to the Foucaultian subject who is merely made into an object of testing and then subjected to taking the test or examination (Foucault, 1978/1991). In anthrogogic assessment contexts, the test taker is not a child whose parents/caregivers force that child into a test taking position. The test taker is an adult who is the decision maker. The assessment/examination, when not part of ongoing formative assessment, is usually taken to either move on to higher studies or to exit education and look for employment. Either way, that assessment must enable the test taker to get into higher studies and grow there, or get, keep, and grow in the job.

This implies that the assessment/test should not be a mere checking of the language system or expect a regurgitation of content. Test takers should be able to use the test-taking exercise itself, the score—which will hopefully be a grade and not a mark—and the inference made by the evaluator to get a sense of themselves. The grade must be complemented by a set of 'can-do' descriptors, without which any credible 'use' of the grade earned or assigned is not valid for either higher studies or employment in the real sense of the word. Even a CGPA system is a clever conversion between numbers (marks), grades (letters), and/or a smaller number where it is a mere game of camouflage between letters and numbers that are not different from a random allotment. In order for them to be useful, they must be collaboratively arrived at by the teacher and the student concerned where possible (Deepa & Durairajan, 2023c), and supplemented by a set of can-do descriptors for the test taker to use, enumerating what s/he can do if they have been allotted a particular grade or score. Wherever possible, in formative assessment contexts, for example, these grades or scores can be arrived at in collaboration with the test takers themselves.

Such collaborative scoring—where the student and the teacher sit together and the score or the grade is arrived at consensually—is 'assessment for learning' in the genuine sense, where the student and the teacher take the assessment as an opportunity to learn about their teaching–learning processes and further convert this collaboration to feed forward. This collaborative scoring process is an anthrogogic move where the assignment of the scores or grades is not random or one-sided, but a conscious attempt and process that respects the adultness of the student and explains to them the connection between the criteria for assessment and the submission done by the student. This process opens up a dialogue to resolve differences between how the teacher perceives the assignment/test response and how the student actually intended it to be perceived.

Very often the space for such dialogues is not even available with the assumption that 'the teacher is always right' and 'the student remains a learner and not a user of language'. It is pertinent to revisit this concept in the light of arguments where Bachman and others have used the term 'user' to indicate the test taker and not as a language learner (Bachman & Palmer, 2010). Yet, no attempts have been made either in theory or in practice to treat these adult students as users of the language, particularly when such grading or scoring happens, opening doorways of 'teacher-centred' scoring/grading systems that become subjective even in objective types of items such as Multiple Choice Questions or MCQs (Deepa, 2022a).

Such collaboration also needs to be backed up by test taker trust and not a suspicion of test taker motives and moves. Formative and summative tests within the educational domain in India, and standardised and international tests elsewhere, operate with an interpretation that is full of suspicion of the test taker (Ricouer, 1983). All technical devices and affordances are denied to this test taker for it is assumed that test takers will misuse the technology—be it a cell phone, access to the internet, or to AI tools—and that the score obtained and its inference will not be a true reflection of ability. But such suspicious interpretation will not contribute to genuine anthrogogic predictive validity, for in real time all these facilities—perceived as affordances (Hutchby, 2001; Levy, 2009)—will always be available. The trust that is referred to here is not just about the issues of 'cheating' but about treating the test taker as a well-rounded individual who can make her/his own choices, with her/his own perspectives and outlook on life, cultures, languages, and as a whole person that comes through the responses that are submitted for the testing or assessment processes. It is also about aligning the responses with the teachers' expectations and being given a chance and a choice to defend their perspectives alongside the teachers'. In the absence of such a purview, the whole process of testing/assessment would degenerate to that of the teacher's word against the word of the student where there is an inbuilt and unstated supremacy attached to the teacher's perspective: if the student's response aligns with hers, s/he is seen as being 'correct' and otherwise 'wrong'. It also seems criminal to softly and stealthily bully the adult student into 'submission' with any grading done based only on the perspective of the teacher evaluator/assessor/scorer. This is why collaborative scoring is crucial in anthrogogic assessment (Deepa & Durairajan, 2023c). Imposed, teacher-centered scoring negates the adulthood and thinking capacities of the students who might come with multiple realities, abilities, and resources that they would otherwise have access to consult or an opportunity to discuss/defend their views, which could then be closely connected to predictive validity and thereby begin to function as predictive-validity evidence.

Further, if the predictive evidence for certification is to be linked to the criterion for certification (Messick, 1987), then such predictive evidence, in the form of assignments, and its consequences for the individual test takers' self-appraisal must also be taken into account. Every test/assessment must answer the question about what the test taker sees in that instrument and what decisions it affects, in terms of the self and also with respect to affective factors. This is one of the primary reasons behind the attempt to move from using tasks in the form of assignments, to thought seeds by two researchers in the undergraduate classroom (Chekuri, 2026; Narke, 2026). The former was able to assess interpersonal communication in the context of summative assessment by using a thought seed-based term paper, while the latter assessed intercultural competence through two assignments.

Value implications in both educational and psychological measurements derive not only from the construct labels but from ideologies that give theories their perspective and purpose. Individual perceptions are valued as essential to learning (Kelly, 1980 as cited in Messick, 1987, p. 104) but this assertion has not gone beyond a theoretical stance. The social consequences of test interpretation and use are expected to include both intended and unintended consequences, including side effects, which have been incorporated by the appraisal of the functional worth of testing/assessment that encompasses individual, institutional, societal, and systemic aspects (Messick, 1987). However, the extent of individual consequences have stopped with the inclusion of accommodations, which is like buttering-up the minority so that their voices can be silenced. By bringing in accommodations into the arena of testing (Abedi, 2010, 2014) attempts have been made to minimise or account for these side effects which are perceived as contributing to construct-irrelevant variance (Messick, 1989). Beginning with students with learning disabilities, it moved to including English Language Learners (Stansfield, 2011).

Today, accommodations are being made in the domains of policy, design and test development, with proactive rather than retrospective measures, including an awareness of the affordances and constraints of technology. The attempt has been made to incorporate equity, access, and inclusion in testing accommodations, but in all these contexts, the focus is on the design and use of accommodated tests for language learners, *not language users* with specific needs (Taylor & Banerjee, 2023a, emphasis mine). Accommodations also highlight the importance of establishing a transparent and close relationship between the language teaching–learning situation and the language assessment context (Taylor & Banerjee, 2023b); this is where social consequences are frozen. The nature of the tests/assignments need to carry with them predictability and echoes of what the test taker will use those capabilities for in real life, after the scores or grades in the form of results have been declared. In anthrogogic contexts, particularly in a country like India, this test taker is always a language user with multilinguality as a point of reference (Agnihotri 2007a, 2007b), and in actuality adult students come into the classroom with multiple perspectives and with a strong sense of multiple realities and truths rather than the teacher-driven or teacher-oriented ones alone. Such an inclusion of multilinguality is the stance behind the two studies presented in this volume on the teaching and formative assessment of literature in the undergraduate classroom (Baruah, 2026; Ghosh, 2026). In a pedagogic context, children are in their formative years of such a construction of their own realities and truths while grappling with the changes in their bodies, for example, during adolescence. As adults these students are expected to have figured out major issues related to their goals and directions in life that might impact their own lives, family, and society at large. Accommodations that allow for the inclusion of discussion of the test/assessment in this light is of paramount importance and a necessity in an anthrogogic classroom, particularly when such scores/grades affect their livelihoods and directions in life that seem to be in the hands of the scorer/grader or the teacher evaluator. Such collaborative assessments will ensure that the role of the test taker as the primary test user is justified and that genuine autonomy is ensured in the assessment process for both the teacher and the student.

Further, rather than merely ensuring that certain accommodations are in place for certain groups of test takers, anthrogogic assessments should attempt to ensure that the test/examination/assignment has value, relevance, and utility for the test taker as a user, by functioning as a last class: where the test taker (also the student) is pushed into turning a corner not ventured into before, where the task demands are a wee bit more challenging than what had been taught that far. One of the ways in which this can be done is by asking the students to make links across topics and to bring in fresh perspectives. It will enable the teacher to go far beyond the additive pattern of conventional tests and assignments which have a series of either standardised or limited-in-scope tasks for each predefined sub-topic in the syllabus. Such a corner-turning will empower both the teacher and the student. Teachers will also grow professionally for they will want to invest their best efforts into designing these assignments. This is a luxury rarely experienced by teachers. Initially, it is possible that the teacher might struggle to create such assignment prompts, but that is what genuine teacher growth is all about. Teachers will use their own sense of plausibility, without certainty (Prabhu, 1987, 2019b), but maybe to identify what works and what doesn't. Such assignment prompts will empower students and, through self-reflection, teachers will learn to create, use and modify—with assurance and confidence—empowering assignments. With such assignments, the students as test takers will experience and enjoy their end-of-term examinations/assignments as akin to a last class (Tharu, personal communication, August 5, 2021). The assignments will be perceived as difficult and challenging, but will contribute not just to a learning through assessment but also a wash-forward into real life (Deepa & Durairajan, 2023b).

Such a challenge is very different from the postulation of test difficulty which contributes only to construct-irrelevant variance. The purpose of such an exam-as-last class is not to make it difficult and undoable. The aim of the assignment writer is to ensure that task engagement for the test taker is doable, but a tad difficult. To paraphrase the experience of one such test taker, it was an exhausting but exhilarating experience. Its purpose is to ensure predictive validity and wash-forward into real life along with ensuring authenticity. In such contexts, individual differences in capability also have to be accounted for, but instead of merely ensuring group accommodations, help in terms of a discussion or extra time to complete an assignment, or even a student capability oriented assignment that could be more or less difficult, must be provided but on a one-on-one, case-to-case basis. Technological tools like Grammarly, spell checks, and all types of Artificial Intelligence will not just be permitted, but encouraged, because in real time when such assignments need to be completed, or projects taken on, enabling and empowering assistance will always be available both in the form of technological or academic tools, or in the form of peers or colleagues.

Pedagogic scaffolding (Bruner, 1985) includes enabling/aid by a more abled peer. That being the case, in anthrogogic contexts teamwork and collaboration is not just to be expected or only welcomed, but encouraged and valued. However, the nature of such help or assistance provided should be like the signs on highways and roads and not like pedagogic scaffolding. Any experienced driver who knows the route will not bother to even look at road signs; at the same time, a new-to-that-route or novice driver is likely to need/use such information. Similarly, an experienced driver knows when to move to the side of the road by crossing the yellow line, or when to overtake, ignoring the road-dividing line (Deepa & Durairajan, 2023a). The accommodations permitted in the literature do not carry with them the possibility of test-taker–chosen assistance. Any assistance needed by the student as a test taker ought to be provided and not be limited to the kind of 'accommodations' that are permitted in the literature. This will enable a genuine wash-forward (Deepa & Durairajan, 2023b). But such a demand for a wash-forward also implies that a different level of authenticity should be aimed at, and not just reflect—as posited by Bachman and Palmer in their two seminal works in bits and pieces—as sub-abilities of target language use (1996, 2010). Authenticity will then get linked to predictive validity and wash-forward, and will carry positive individual consequences for such openness of opportunities wherever possible, even in summative contexts.

Examinations and tests, in summative contexts where they have to be administered, should not be closed-book, memory-based ones which will only result in empty examination speech acts (Spolsky, 1990). If sit-down examinations are unavoidable, they must not be merely open-book (Durairajan, 2013) but open-source examinations (Deepa & Durairajan, 2022). The zone of negotiated responsibility (Chalhoub-Deville, 2009) of the anthrogogic test/assignment developer has to reach far beyond the impact and social consequences of the test/assignment on teaching and learning in the classroom. The nature of such responsibility cannot stop with the awareness of the distal versus proximal use of the test. Examination and assessment spaces themselves need to become domains of shared responsibility between test developers and test takers, and not only the users of test scores perceived as teachers at all levels who are expected to interpret these scores and make decisions of selection and placement, or workplace officials who make decisions regarding careers and promotion (Kunnan, 2019). This implies that the test scores/grades play a pivotal role in the life of the primary test taker, that is, the student.

Test scores are used for selection, placement, certification and, in the context of formative assessments, to help learners and teachers modify their own practices. But test/examination takers who are the primary users in the anthrogogic context, and more importantly, assignment writers as users, should also be able to use the test-taking experience to know what they can and cannot do and how far they can stretch themselves. This is not a mere stretching of physical muscles or mental memory. From a psychomotor perspective, particularly with reference to India and possibly other similar countries, examinations are handwritten, but today, in the twenty-first century, students do not spend time taking notes. A three hour, sit-down examination is a toil of terror and severe muscle pain, for that test taker is expected to 'scratch' on the answer sheets using pens when otherwise they would have typed all of it on a computer, smartphone, or even 'voice-typed', as they do outside the examination hall all the time. In all possibilities these students/test takers would not have 'practised' the physical or the psychomotor skill of writing for ages in their real lives, but it is thrust upon them in the examination hall. Forcing such an unpractised psychomotor skill in a high-stakes examination time and place, and scoring based on this 'ability', is not biasing for the best (Swain, 1985) but biasing for the worst, pushing it into the Messickian construct-irrelevant variance domain. Today in the twenty-first century, in India, computers are being given out by governments to children who come from economically backward families. Most adults use computers or laptops to write their assignments or work on their projects. From a cognitive perspective, most formative and all summative assessments in India require nothing other than a memorised regurgitation of facts and possibly some interpretation of them, which is tantamount to timed one-shot writing (Wiegle, 2002). From an affective perspective, these tests and examinations only increase tension, stress, and fear in the primary test user, that is, the student/test taker. None of these are factors that any adult language-user needs to cope with in daily life. There may be times when timelines have to be met, but that is usually within the context of teamwork and collaboration. All anthrogogic real-time writing or speaking, which includes listening and speaking, are done in the context of Cronbachian typical performance and never under maximum performance conditions (1970). Tension and stress do not come from outside of the individuals and assistance is available whenever needed. In the literature, although there is a faint recognition that tests can be perceived as tools of power by test takers and zones of negotiated responsibility are being identified to mitigate this power, not much is being done with adult test takers in a serious manner. The zone must expand to become a domain of negotiated responsibility, not just between the test user (read in the literature as the industry and not the test taker as discussed above) and the test developer, but between the primary test user—who is also the test taker—and the developer, and the eventual user who uses the inference based on the assessment score to take a decision on further studies or employment for the test taker. In anthrogogic contexts, the test takers are the major decision makers.

This implies that all decisions regarding test design, time allocation, weightage for different sections in the examination paper (if a sit-down one) break up of marks (if allotted), and scoring criteria for free response tasks, must be collaborative and a part of this negotiated domain of responsibility. Such collaborative assessment in anthrogogic contexts can essentially draw from the Prabhuvian 'productive self-evaluation' (2019a) where test takers or assignment writers, in collaboration with the teacher who is also the evaluator, can assess and score/grade themselves. In research studies on peer/self-evaluation, researchers confess that the rubrics are decided on by the teacher and this is then used for self, peer, and teacher evaluation (Wang, 2017). In anthrogogic contexts, the rubrics must also be collaboratively worked out by both students and teachers. These scoring criteria or rubrics in anthrogogic contexts for free-response tasks must also go beyond being merely task-specific criteria, but such long-sighted vision is absent in many studies in this area (for example see Mukhopadhyay, 2015), where it is retained at the pedagogic level, for this is also teacher pre-determined and features only as a pedagogic scaffold (Deepa & Durairajan, 2023a) during the planning stage of writing. It is not just the criteria for evaluation but also the nature of the assignments, focus, weightage for various sections in the assignment/test paper, that must be collaboratively decided upon (Deepa & Durairajan, 2023c) by the language users who are the adult students in the classroom and the teacher who is the test developer.

Tests, examinations, and assessments of adults impact those who take it, not just in terms of the score they get, the certification obtained, or the employment achieved. Every such test or assessment must carry with it an awareness, by the test creators and administrators, of what it does to the individual during those hours or days of evaluation, how it impacts gatekeeping, and their image of themselves as individuals, not just as subjects or objects of testing and assessment. The individual consequences from intrapersonal affective factors must also be accounted for. Enough has been written about students with examination fear in pedagogic contexts, of children being petrified and miserable and concocting fevers and stomach upsets on 'test' days. But it is even more important in the context of anthrogogy, where these adults need to be tested, examined and evaluated in a manner similar to the way in which they will use the skills and knowledge gained—and on which they are being evaluated—in the real world and in their future lives. One of the major justifications for the shift from the psychometric to integrative sociometric testing was that these tests and examinations would reflect and capture the ways in which language would be used communicatively in the real world, implying that these tests were authentic realisations, in an examination setting. Such tests and examinations ought to be tests of typical and not maximum performance (Cronbach, 1970). But this has never been the case. Any test or examination implies not only that a test taker prepares for it, but also goes into it knowing that the best performance needs to be aimed at. Bias for the best is an argument made theoretically in language testing (Swain, 1985) but no test taker can put in a typical performance during a test or examination and expect to get a high score or grade. The test taker is always expected to set aside other considerations, ignore stress or tension, not take real life affordances into account, and work at maximum ability during the actual 'testing time'. The mind is expected to work at peak capacity like a well-oiled, serviced machine. This is not how the mind is used day-in and day-out to tackle everyday communication or work. If tests, examinations and assessments do not reflect real world use, then we are only claiming to test our students to swim in an ocean, but actually confining them to small goldfish bowls (Deepa & Durairajan, 2022), where even if not as severe as the panopticonical gaze, (Foucault, 1978/1991) the fish—or rather the test takers—are always observable. They are forced to go round and round that small bowl, hoping that somehow such practice and experience will give them the knowledge and expertise to move from the fish bowl to an aquarium, to a small lake, and eventually to the vast ocean. If students of content subjects and language users need to learn to swim in an ocean, but we continue to test them in fish bowls with the limited understanding that a few spoonfuls of water carefully taken from various parts of the ocean to ensure adequate sampling is sufficient, such a test/assessment will not have any beneficial wash-forward (Deepa & Durairajan, 2023b).

It will also not be an authentic test/examination/assignment where authenticity carries with it predictive validity. This is particularly crucial in the context of anthrogogic testing where the degree or postgraduate degree examination might be the last one that they take. In the context of language proficiency, authenticity can no longer be justified as existing when it is broken up into target-language domains and where the individual parts are tested separately and sometimes in some amalgamated form. Authenticity was initially defined as the link between the characteristics of the test task and the target-language use task (Bachman & Palmer, 1996), and replaced by a range of qualities like consistency, meaningfulness, generalisability, relevance, et cetera, associated with specific claims and warrants (Bachman & Palmer, 2010). The break-up of language ability into many parts is like stating that 1 +1 +1... to the power of a hundred, when totalled, will provide a perfect hundred. It will, in mathematics, but not with constructs, however well-honed and fine-tuned and calibrated. Practice jumps and leaps may enable individual skills, but that will not give the gymnast a perfect ten in any competition. The whole is always greater than the sum of its parts. Even fifty years ago, Carroll (1968) was able to state that the 'integrated' domain, the testing of the skills in his table, was more than just the sum of the three systems and added the secondary tables to indicate this. The whole, in the context of anthrogogic testing, must reflect reality to ensure predictive validity and take care of consequences, not just of inferences but the manner of test preparation and test taking for the individual. Thus far, social consequences—except for the token movement with accommodations which has also not considered the individual as a separate being with tensions and fears that 'I may cease to be'—have not taken into account the affect and effect of testing and assessment on every test taker.

To cite two examples from outside language education, examinations in medicine, law, and accountancy are still memory-based and expect the candidate to remember all kinds of information. In reality, once that person has become a doctor, lawyer, or chartered accountant, in most cases the internet, or books on these areas, or cross checks with a specialist or domain expert are always available. Even today, the offices of lawyers and accountants are lined with shelves of material which carry this information. When in doubt they always look up the information needed. No lawyer or accountant needs to justify to the client why a law book or set of acts are consulted. Similarly, no doctor needs to justify the checking-up of symptoms or the referral to another expert for diagnosis except in emergency situations that demand an immediate, reflexive-action type of involvement with the patients in a casualty room or the call for a code-blue!

A similar perspective is required in the context of language testing. Proficiency tests are closed-book ones. Open book 'allows' for the use of a dictionary or a couple of printed papers or books. Today, with Artificial Intelligence and applications such as Grammarly, and a thesaurus and a dictionary available at the click of a button, no student needs to know grammar rules or pragmatic/paradigmatic alternatives for a lexical term. Report writing is done in a jiffy with the use of internet tools or simple, freely downloadable applications that sit on smartphones. Our examinations therefore need to reflect and echo all these facilities that are available at our digital fingertips. Once upon a time, knowledge of either a language system or bodies of various disciplines had to be supposedly carried at our fingertips so that we could spout them to pass examinations. Today, all of that is available with the click of a mouse or a trackpad, or the swiping of a few keys on a phone.

Anthrogogic (teaching and) testing and assessment must certainly prepare language users for life. If we take education seriously and assume that it should prepare the individual to face the travails of life, then every one of our examinations, the formative and particularly the summative ones, in anthrogogic contexts should not be a testing, trying time which is the cause of tears and fears, but as stated earlier, like a last class where some kind of learning takes place even as the examination paper is being answered. Existing tests and examinations, particularly in the Indian context of not just language education but all other disciplines and bodies of knowledge, follow the regurgitation principle: memorise, reproduce, apply knowledge in some cases, but get rewarded for proving that you have the ability to fulfil, very successfully, an empty examination speech act. Examination tasks and questions or problems should enable the student to turn a corner never turned before. Examinations today are often exhausting, but at the same time, unnerving and frightening, never exhilarating. More often than not, they are exhausting either because in a short span of time a large number of multiple choice items have to be answered (all examples of examination speech acts), or essay questions attempted at great speed, that too in the form of timed one-shot writing (Wiegle, 2002). Examinations need to be exhilarating, challenging experiences the way problems in life are.

More importantly, tests and examinations ought to be joyful experiences, filled with learning experiences. To enable this, it is important to make all anthrogogic testing and assessment genuinely collaborative, challenging yet as tension-free as possible. Anthrogogic testing and assessment practices need to follow one major edict: no decision is to be made by the teacher/tester without dialogue and discussion with the students who should be co-creators of the testing paper/assessment task/project (Deepa & Durairajan, 2023c). Ownership of what has to be done and responsibility for that act are anthrogogic qualities. Anthrogogic assessment must be done in a humane and realistic manner, where no adult who takes a test, examination, or writes an assignment feels that they are doing it out of compulsion or pressure. At the same time, such humane anthrogogic testing must lead to both teacher and test-taker empowerment.

References

Abedi, J. (2010). Research and recommendations for formative assessment with English language learners. In H. L. Andrade and G. J. Cizek. (Eds.), *Handbook of formative assessment* (pp. 181–197). Routledge.

Abedi, J. (2014). Accommodations in the assessment of English language learners. In A. J. Kunnan (Ed.), *The companion to language assessment: Volume III: Evaluation, methodology, and interdisciplinary themes* (pp. 1115–1129). Wiley Blackwell.

Agnihotri, R. K. (2007a). Identity and multilinguality: The case of India. In A. B. M. Tsui & J. W. Tollefson (Eds.), *Language policy, culture, and identity in Asian contexts* (pp. 185–204). Lawrence Erlbaum Associates, Inc.

Agnihotri, R. K. (2007b). Towards a pedagogical paradigm rooted in multilinguality. *International Multilingual Research Journal, 1*(2), 1–10 .

Alderson, C. (1991). Bands and scores. In C. J. Alderson, and B. North (Eds.), *Language testing in the 1990s: The communicative legacy* (pp. 71–86). Macmillan.

Bachman, L., & Palmer, A. (1996). *Language testing in practice.* Oxford University Press.

Bachman, L., & Palmer, A. (2010). *Language assessment in practice.* Oxford University Press.

Bachman, L., & Purpura, J. (2008). Language assessments: Gate-keepers or door-openers?. In B. Spolsky, and F. M. Hult (Eds.), *The handbook of educational linguistics* (pp. 456–468). Blackwell Publishing.

Baruah, N. (2026). Unveiling anthrogogic practices: Teaching novels to English literature students. In S. Deepa & G. Durairajan (Eds.), *Anthrogogy in use: A handbook for language educators* (pp. 174–184). Orient BlackSwan.

Bloom, B. S., Hastings, J. T., & Maduas, G. F. (Eds.). (1971). *Handbook on formative and summative evaluation of student learning.* McGraw-Hill Book Company.

Bruner, J. (1985). Vygotsky: A historical and conceptual perspective. I. J. Wertsch (Ed.), *Culture, communication and cognitions: Vygotskian perspectives* (pp. 21–34). Cambridge University Press.

Carroll, J. B. (1968). The psychology of language testing. In A. Davies (Ed.), *Language testing symposium: A psycholinguistic approach* (pp. 46–69). Oxford University Press.

Cronbach, L. (1970). *Essentials of psychological testing* (3rd ed.). Harper International Edition.

Chekuri, T. (2026). Incorporating thought seeds as an assessment tool in anthrogogic contexts. In S. Deepa & G. Durairajan (Eds.), *Anthrogogy in use: A handbook for language educators* (pp. 207–227). Orient BlackSwan.

Canale, M. & Swain, M. (1980). Theoretical bases of communicative approaches to second language teaching and testing. *Applied Linguistics, 1*(1), 1–47. https://doi.org/10.1093/applin/I.1.1

Cummins, J. (1980). The cross lingual dimensions of language proficiency: Implications for bilingual education and the optimal age issue. *TESOL Quarterly, 14*(2) 175–87.

Cummins, J. (2000). *Language power and pedagogy: Bilingual children in the crossfire.* Multilingual Matters.

Davies, A. (2008). Accountability and standards. In B. Spolsky, & F. M. Hult (Eds.), *Handbook of educational linguistics* (pp. 483–494). Blackwell Publishing.

Deepa, S. (2022a). Options in multiple choice questions: Oh Really! Yours sincerely adult learners! *Language and Language Teaching*, 11(2:22), 81–86. https://llt.org.in/wp-content/uploads/2023/01/LLT-issue22-Options-in-Multiple-Choice-Questions.pdf

Deepa, S. (2022b). Verbal disposition: The need for language potentiality in anthrogogic spaces. *Journal of English Language Teaching, 64*(6), 17–24.

Deepa, S. (2026). Principles of anthrogogic language education. In S. Deepa & G. Durairajan (Eds.), *Anthrogogy in use: A handbook for language educators* (pp. 3–26). Orient BlackSwan.

Deepa, S., & Durairajan, G. (2022, Oct. 26–28). *Breaking the goldfish syndrome: The need for open-source summative language use examinations in anthrogogic contexts* [Paper presentation]. 8th International Conference of Asian Association of Language Assessment, Chennai, Tamil Nadu, India.

Deepa S., & Durairajan, G. (2023a). Scaffolds or road signs for anthrogogic language learners? A critical inquiry. In B. Nair, P. Ramalingam, & B. Nagalakshmi (Eds.), *Teaching of English: Theorizing from classroom* (pp. 11–25). Tamil Puduvai.

Deepa, S., & Durairajan, G. (2023b). Learning through assessment in anthrogogic contexts: Wash-forward. In A. L. Gokturk-Saglam, & E. Sevgi-Sole (Eds.), *Emerging practices for online language assessment, exams, evaluation, and feedback* (pp. 99–118). IGI Global.

Deepa, S and Durairajan, G. (2023c, Jun. 21–23). *Learning to assess language potentiality through student feedback: A case study* [Paper presentation]. MATSDA-Bilingual International School Conference–Materials for Testing, Rufina, FI, Italy.

Durairajan, G. 2013. Open-book examinations: The need of the hour in teacher education. In P. Powell-Davies (Ed.), *Assessing and evaluating English language teacher education, teaching and learning* (pp. 35–44). British Council.

Foucault, M. (1991). *Discipline and Punish: The Birth of the Prison.* Vintage Books (original work published 1978).

Ghosh, D. (2026). Looking beyond the compulsion of 'need to be told': An attempt at anthrogogicity in the undergraduate literature classroom. In S. Deepa & G. Durairajan (Eds.), *Anthrogogy in use: A handbook for language educators* (pp. 165–173). Orient BlackSwan.

Hutchby, I. (2001). Technologies, texts and affordances. *Sociology, 35*(2), 441–456. https://doi.org/10.1177/S0038038501000219

Kane, M.T. (2006). Validation. In R.L. Brennan (Ed.), *Educational measurement* (4th edition, pp. 17–64). American Council on Education/ Praeger.

Knowles, M. S. (1968). Andragogy, not pedagogy. *Adult Leadership, 16*(10), 350–386.

Knowles, M. S. (1984). *Andragogy in action: Applying modern principles of adult education.* Jossey-Bass.

Kunnan, A. J. (2019). An agenda for language assessment development, research and pedagogy. *The Journal of Asia TEFL, 16*(1), 327–333. http://dx.doi.org/10.18823/asiatefl.2019.16.1.21.327.

Levy, M. (2009). Technologies in use for second language learning. *The Modern Language Journal, 93*, 769–782. https://doi.org/10.1111/j.1540-4781.2009.00972.

Messick, S. (1987). *Validity: Research report.* Educational Testing Service.

Messick, S. (1989). Validity. In R. L. Linn (Ed.), *Educational measurement: Third edition* (pp. 13–03). American Council on Education. Macmillan Publishing Company.

Mukhopadhyay, L. (2015). Using evaluation criteria to plan writing performance: A study of pre-service teachers of English. In G. Pickering, & P. Gunashekar (Eds.), *Innovation in English language teacher education. Selected papers from the fourth International Teacher Educator Conference Hyderabad, India* (pp. 116–124). British Council.

Narke, P. (2026). Thought seeds as an instrument for assessing the intercultural competence of adult ESL learners. In S. Deepa & G. Durairajan (Eds.), *Anthrogogy in use: A handbook for language educators* (pp. 185–206). Orient BlackSwan.

Oller Jr., J. W. (1979). *Language tests at school: A pragmatic approach.* Longman.

O'Sullivan, B., & Green, A. (2011). Test-taker characteristics. In L. Taylor (Ed.), *Examining speaking: Research and practice in examining second language speaking* (pp. 36–64). Cambridge University Press.

O'Sullivan, B., Dunn, K., & Berry, V. (2021) Test preparation: an international comparison of test takers' preferences. *Assessment in education: Principles, policy & practice, 28*(1), 13–36. https://doi.org/10.1080/0969594X.2019.1637820.

Ricoeur, P. (1983). On Interpretation. In A. Montefiori (Ed.), *Philosophy in France today* (pp. 175–197). Cambridge University Press.

Shohamy, E, 1997. Testing methods, testing consequences: Are they ethical? Are they fair? *Language Testing, 14* (3), 340–349.

Shohamy, E. (2001). *The power of tests: A critical perspective of the uses of language tests.* Longman.

Shohamy, E. (2011). Assessing multilingual competencies: Adopting construct valid assessment policies. *Modern Language Journal, 95*(3), 418–429.

Shohamy, E. (2022). Critical language testing, multilingualism and social justice. *TESOL Quarterly, 56*(4). https://doi.org/10.1002/tesq.3185.

Spolsky, B. (1990). Social aspects of individual assessment. In J. H. A. L. De Jong, & D. Stevenson (Eds.), *Individualizing the assessment of language abilities* (pp. 3–15). Multilingual Matters, Ltd.

Spolsky, B. (1995). *Measured words: The development of objective language testing.* Oxford University Press.

Spolsky, B. (2008). Language assessment in historical and future perspective. In N. H. Hornberger (Ed.), *Encyclopedia of language and education* (pp. 2570–2579). Springer. https://doi.org/10.1007/978-0-387-30424-3_192.

Spolsky, B. (2016). History of language testing. In E. Shohamy, I. Or, & S. May (Eds.), *Language testing and assessment* (pp. 1–11). Springer. https://doi.org/10.1007/978-3-319-02326-7_32-1.

Stansfield, C. W. (2011). Oral translation as a test accommodation for ELLs. *Language Testing, 28*(3), 401–416.

Swain, M. (1985). Large scale communicative testing: A case study. In Y. P. Lee, A. C. Y. Y. Fok, R. Lord, & G. Low (Eds.), *New directions in language testing: Papers presented at the International Symposium on Language Testing, Hong Kong* (pp. 35–46). Pergamon Press.

Tiekstra, M., Minnaert, A., & Hessels, M. G. (2016). A review scrutinising the consequential validity of dynamic assessment. *Educational Psychology, 36*(1), 112–137. https://doi.org/10.1080/01443410.2014.915930.

Wang, W. (2017). Using rubrics in student self-assessment: student perceptions in the English as a foreign language writing context. *Assessment & Evaluation in Higher Education, 42*(8), 1280–1292.

Weir, C. (2005). *Language testing and validation: An evidence based approach.* Palgrave: Macmillan.

Wiegle, S. (2002). *Assessing writing.* Cambridge University Press.

Widdowson, H. G. (1978). *Teaching language as communication.* Oxford University Press.

Part II
Anthrogogic Applications

The distinction between pedagogy and anthrogogy was not an easy one to establish. The two of us, Geetha and Shree, had been practicing what we now term as 'anthrogogy' for a long time, but did not have the conceptual clarity earlier in our academic lives. It evolved through ruminations, discussions and a deep-seated conviction, as stated in our prolegomena. This being the case, striving to get a group of researchers to either take our theorisations into the classroom, reflect on their own experiences, or experiment with these new modes of enabling and empowerment was not an easy task, to say the least. We reached out to a large number of scholars; some were unable join this endeavour, others fell by the wayside for a range of reasons. The twelve chapters in this section of the book are more than just a set of researched and contributed articles. They are the culmination of many conversations and discussions on various threads of the concept of anthrogogy. The authors have not just contributed to our volume; their chapters are living, written proof that we are not building or postulating a castle in rarefied or non-existent air. Their conviction and belief in this perspective is celebrated in their chapters. Each of the authors have delved into their own teaching/learning/classroom experiences, and reflected on and critiqued themselves to present these gems.

The chapters cover three major domains: teacher education, critical language awareness, literature teaching and language empowerment. Sweta Mukherjee, locating her reflections in the domain of pre-service teacher education in Chapter 3, questions the nature of existing relationships between mentors and mentees and makes the case for a collaborative relationship between the two. The reciprocity of mutual growth is highlighted: stringent and sharp self-reflectivity are the distinctive features of her evolving process.

The focus of Chapter 4 is on in-service teachers to ascertain the integration of ICT tools in ESL classrooms. Shadab Khan's study proved that while teachers in pedagogic contexts are comfortable with teacher-centred tools, those teaching in anthrogogic contexts would prefer to be familisarised with student-centred tools.

Monishita Hajra Pande and Sayan Chaudhuri, like Sweta, have also used self-reflection as a tool. Through a self-reflexive mapping and analysis of experience in Chapter 5, they have shown how teacher authority—when working with postgraduate students as agentive adults—can be negotiated and repositioned by critically analysing four different episodes from a critical writing course.

Chapter 6 by Deepesh Chandrasekharan and Sajida Sultana is also a study on academic writing at the doctoral level. Their focus is on learner agency. They reached out to a range of research students who felt that most research supervision is supervisor led. Their recommendation is that adult supervisees should be able to push the envelope of academic writing to ensure collaboration and freedom.

Another self-reflective study, rooted at the undergraduate level, is by Shravasti Chakravarty with the focus on her own teaching in two countries: India and Uzbekistan. In Chapter 7, she examines six vignettes with stringent criticism, separates her pedagogic teacher moves from anthrogogic ones, and suggests ways in which students can be taught to take charge of their own learning.

Chapters 8 and 9 are also located at the undergraduate level in India, but the focus shifts to the teaching of literature. In Chapter 8 Diganta Ghosh explores, using self-reflectivity, how it is possible to push his students to go beyond the need to be told, to tap their own interpretative spaces and experience shared learning. Narji Baruah, in Chapter 9, carefully documents how she was able to bridge the gap between students and 'unfamiliar' Jane Austen novels by drawing parallels to similar novels in Assamese and Bengali literature.

Pankaj Narke and Tabitha Chekuri, in Chapters 10 and 11, move into a different space. They have both focused on the use of thought seeds rather than tasks at the undergraduate level. Pankaj's focus is on how he used thought seeds in his own classroom to assess intercultural competence in a more insightful manner through assignments, by enabling students to think critically and identify biases within themselves. Tabitha's focus is on interpersonal communication in the context of summative assessment. She used thought seeds as the basis for a term paper and documented student reflections to prove that her altered assessment structure converted a normal examination speech act into one reflecting the complexities of real world communication.

Chapter 12, by A. Amaratheja, is written from the perspective of an observer who was able to critically document the ways in which questioning can be taught anthrogogically in an undergraduate classroom using the Samvaad technique, to enable students to move from merely mastering the syntax of the interrogative to exploring authentic language use.

In Chapter 13, Sruti Narra critically examines some tasks used in undergraduate classrooms, identifies their pedagogic orientation, and—using teacher and student responses—suggests ways in which the tasks can be made anthrogogic.

Chapter 14 by Meghna Anand and Nidhi D. M. is a unique contribution to this book for it captures the perspective of two students who experienced two content courses that were taught anthrogogically. Reflecting on their own experiences, they recommend a paradigm shift in adult education, with an emphasis on student-centred strategies that value student autonomy, critical thinking, and creativity.

3

Mentor–Mentee in a Collaborative Anthrogogic Relationship to Develop a Supportive Professional Community

Sweta Mukherjee

Introduction

In the literature on teacher education, mentoring refers to the process where someone who is usually the more knowledgeable other (MKO) (Vygotsky, 1934) facilitates and assists another individual's development (Kamarudin, et al., 2020). In this chapter, I will make an attempt to challenge this idea and claim that mentoring within an anthrogogical framework is a collaborative learning exercise where both the learner/s and the mentor understand and explore different aspects of learning together. By creating a mentor–mentee relationship, in a pre-service teacher education programme, both the mentor/s and the mentee can exchange knowledge and experiences, offer guidance and feedback, and ultimately contribute to each other's overall development. This mutually collaborative relationship allows both the mentor and mentee to share their expertise and wisdom, help each other navigate challenges, make informed decisions, and develop necessary skills for their professional journey.

One of the most significant stages in the process of becoming a teacher occurs perhaps during the transition from a student to a student-teacher, and eventually to a novice teacher (Peterson & Williams, 1998). It is during this period that a new teacher can be supported by a mentor. Mentoring has always been an accepted form of training new teachers as they take their first steps towards their teaching career. However, the present study argues that mentoring needs to become an anthrogogic (Trott, 1991; Deepa, 2022a) tool or a way of teaching and learning within the framework of anthrogogicity in any teacher-education programme that is designed for pre-service teachers. As posited in this chapter, the relationship of a mentor and a mentee needs to shift from a hierarchical to a more equal space where each contributes to the other's growth. Only when mentoring is seen as a collaborative journey can it be anthrogogically effective.

In this chapter an attempt will be made to explore teacher-education programmes within the framework of anthrogogicity. The chapter also builds a case for mentoring as one of the most effective anthrogogic tools to teach pre-service teachers. Pre-service teacher-education programmes are an essential part of adult teaching–learning programmes, and hence there is a need to explore an approach that specifically caters to adult professionals. The chapter posits that mentoring is one of the most effective ways for trainee teachers to develop their personal philosophy of teaching, examine their beliefs, and develop teaching strategies. One-on-one discussions with the mentor/s not only helps trainee teachers learn skills but also helps them in building a deep insight into their own belief systems and experiences. This in turn helps them develop skills and strategies that will be relevant for teaching their learners.

Scope of the Chapter

This chapter discusses core aspects related to mentoring. The mentor–mentee relationship is a critical component of teacher education and plays a key role in the development of a supportive professional community. Mentors are usually understood to be guides who support the development of knowledge and hone the skills of new teachers to help them achieve their professional goals. The present chapter seeks to incorporate an additional dimension to mentoring, claiming that mentoring as an anthrogogic tool enables teachers to become co-creators of their own knowledge base/skills and further enables them to design and achieve their own goals. It seeks to establish that mentoring is the most effective anthrogogic practice as it works on the fundamental principles of personalised learning, where learners take control of their own learning situations. Through the study, an attempt will be made to differentiate between mentoring and coaching as applicable to teacher education, define mentoring using principles of anthrogogicity, and argue that mentoring is indeed a practice towards personalising learning and developing lifelong learners. The main aim of the chapter is to provide a new understanding of mentoring as one of the most effective ways of teaching adults and developing a professional community of practice for prospective teachers.

Theoretical Background

In this section of the chapter, the core theories that have helped in the formulation of the arguments will be discussed. This section will also help us understand the ways in which the key terms 'mentoring' and 'anthrogogy' are used in the chapter. It will also discuss the different theoretical arguments and literature related to anthrogogicity and the role of mentoring in pre-service teacher education programmes.

Anthrogogy

We already know that every individual learns differently; as such, it is only natural to assume that strategies for adult learning are different from the strategies that are used to teach young learners. The term 'pedagogy', as we know, refers to teaching children, however the principles of pedagogy cannot be directly translated into adult learning as approaches to adult learning are completely different (see Deepa, 2022a, 2026 for a detailed discussion). Adult learning is characterised by certain specific features including the experiences that adult learners have, their readiness to learn, their orientation to learning, and their motivation to learn (Knowles, 1984). This was termed as andragogy. However, this term has always been contested owing to certain sexist connotations, and that most andragogical principles seem to be taken directly from pedagogical practices (Deepa, 2022b), thus providing a very limited understanding of adult learning which may not capture the nuances of such adult learning. Andragogy also seems to acquire meaning only when compared to pedagogy and, therefore, essentially becomes a subset of pedagogy.

Hence, for this chapter we will use the term anthrogogy (Trott, 1991). As a term, anthrogogy is both gender neutral and humane (Deepa, 2022a, 2026). It also views adult learners as those who come with very unique experiences, biases, and prejudices. As educators we cannot disregard these when we teach adult learners. In fact, it is these experiences that help them learn and also make them understand that they might need to unlearn their biases and prejudices. As mentioned, a few of the principles of anthrogogy might be drawn from andragogy, but anthrogogy is regarded more as a generic set of principles that tend to guide lifelong learning (Trott, 1991). Using the term anthrogogy would also help us get out of the dichotomy of andragogy/pedagogy and will ensure that we adapt a more holistic and inclusive approach to adult learning. It is in the light of this theoretical framework that I would be discussing the concept of mentoring, specifically as it applies to pre-service teacher-education programmes.

Mentoring

As the National Education Policy (NEP) 2020 of India very clearly states, higher education plays a significant role in promoting human as well as societal well-being, and eventually creating individuals who would help develop India. This is truly a lofty aim for any teacher to achieve. To be able to achieve this, a teacher first needs to form their own philosophy of teaching. They need to equip themselves with skills that will help them teach their learners to grow into complete and socially responsible individuals, to gain an understanding of their own selves, realise their biases, and be ready to unlearn and relearn. This is only possible when the process of learning how to teach is a personalised process, and the trainee teacher is constantly involved in a one-on-one relationship with their mentor.

Mentoring is an activity where an educator or a mentor is engaged professionally to develop their mentee (Winston & Dahlber, 2019). The word mentor comes from the character of Mentor in Homer's *Odyssey*, who teaches and advises Telemachus. Thus, the term has often been used to refer to someone who guides and educates, helping an individual grow. It may prove to be a transformative experience for both the mentor and mentee as they delve deep into each other's belief systems, learn, and grow together.

Research in mentoring reveals that there are two primary functions of a mentor: a) providing psychosocial support, and b) providing instrumental support and helping the mentee improve their skills (Kram, 1983). However, over the last twenty years mentoring has undergone quite a few changes and is now understood more as a reciprocal and dynamic relationship. Some of the major aspects of mentoring relationships include commitment to the relationship, sharing responsibility with the mentor, and most importantly, clearly communicating expectations and needs (Hartwig, 1999).

Mentoring has always been a very prominent aspect of training novice teachers (Schwille, 2008). Educative mentoring (Feiman-Nemser, 2001, as cited by Schwille, 2008), refers to mentoring pre-service or novice teachers, as the mentor does not have a supervisory approach but rather considers the learner to be an active participant in the learning process.

It creates learning opportunities for pre-service or novice teachers to gain a better understanding of teaching, learning, and learning how to teach (Schwille, 2008). Mentoring is sometimes a complex and dynamic process and hence it may be difficult to arrive at a single definition of it. However, for the purpose of this chapter, I have considered mentoring as a term where the mentor is not merely an academic guide but is also involved in transforming the mentee's belief systems and helping them develop their own teaching philosophy, eventually becoming independent lifelong learners.

Mentoring as an Anthrogogical Tool

As has been previously posited, anthrogogy is a holistic approach to adult learning, and mentoring perhaps is one of the most important tools that can be used within this framework to train pre-service teachers to become lifelong learners. As summarised by Arnesson (2017), scholars such as Hultman and Sobel (2013), Lauvås and Handal (2015), and Lindgren and Morberg (2012) conceptualise mentoring as a democratic process that fosters reflection, dialogue, and deeper knowledge sharing.

It is precisely because of this equal platform that mentoring provides, that it becomes a very significant tool in teacher-education programmes. Pre-service teachers are adult learners; they sometimes may include individuals who have professional expertise in fields other than teaching, for they may be individuals who have decided to make a career shift to teaching. Therefore, it becomes important that they are treated as adults and their experiences are considered in the learning process.

Mentoring provides a space for them to use their experiences for professional development. It helps them develop their own goals, and the mentor then only supports them to achieve their goals. Being an adult learner as a trainee teacher can be a very challenging experience. This challenge is because most of these adult learners come with domain expertise, but may need support in transforming from being an expert to an educator. This is where the mentor's role becomes very important as they provide the emotional and psychological support needed for this transformation. This chapter posits that, within the framework of anthrogogy mentoring is viewed as a participatory learning process where the mentor and mentee are a part of the learning community, and they learn when they interact with each other (Arnesson & Albinsson, 2017). Here, learning becomes an active process where both the mentor and the mentee share an equal relationship. This humanising and personalising of learning, where a mentor and their mentee form a deep, personal relationship, can form the basis of an effective transformation process.

The Context

The ideas for this chapter are rooted in my own experiences and interactions with a group of twenty-four mentees whom I have worked very closely with for a duration of nine months. I was teaching a postgraduate diploma in an international education programme offered by a university in the United Kingdom in collaboration with a research centre in Bangalore, India. A unique aspect of this programme was the emphasis on mentorship or mentoring as a primary tool in the teaching process. As a result, I was able to exclusively mentor my group throughout the duration of the programme.

My mentees belonged to the age group of 25–45, and had varied professional and academic experiences and interests in fields ranging from engineering, special education, commerce and management, to literature and language, et cetera. All my mentees were from India, except one person who was from the United Kingdom. One of my mentees had a doctoral degree in special education; all other mentees had no earlier experience in education. All my mentees were making a shift from different careers in the corporate sector to teaching. They had enrolled in this teacher-education programme to acquire a formal degree that would help them teach in any international curriculum across the globe.

Methodology

The findings reported and analysed in this chapter are a result of my interactions with my twenty-four mentees over a period of nine months. I met my mentees every week individually for around thirty minutes. The objective of these meetings was to discuss their progress in the course, clarify their doubts if they had any, and also discuss the importance of these sessions in their learning experiences. The major data for this study is from these conversations, and notes taken by me and my mentees. Post their graduation from the programme, I also had a few conversations with them and had recorded their responses on a Google form that was sent to them. This participation was entirely voluntary, and interestingly enough all my mentees responded to the questionnaire. What follows is an in-depth discussion and analysis of these responses and conversations. In order to understand the role that I as a mentor have played in their learning, to explore their beliefs about teaching and learning, to learn about mentoring as a process and its efficacy, it is important to explore these responses in detail and analyse the narratives of my mentees.

A Thematic Analysis of Mentee Responses

In this section, I have made an attempt to thematically categorise the different conversations and responses from my mentees and explore the emerging meaning of mentoring as an effective tool in adult learning; specifically, in the context of pre-service teacher education programmes. To ensure complete confidentiality, the mentee responses have been coded as M1 to M24.

Meaning of Mentoring

Let me begin by stating that before they enrolled in this programme, my mentees were not familiar with the process of mentorship. In order to understand how my mentees understood mentoring, I had asked them to explain what they knew about the role of a mentor or mentoring. According to them, a mentor is a person who supervises. They believed that most mentors limited their discussions to the present academic concerns of their mentees and regarded the process as a more formal interaction with a more knowledgeable other (MKO) in a formal and constrained environment. However, this belief changed as they had continuous interactions with me as their mentor, through one-on-one sessions.

As one mentee responded (M1), 'I initially was apprehensive of meeting my mentor as I felt she would only question me on the progress of my work. However, my meetings have really helped me discover the concepts that I was confused about, it has also started to make me rethink my lesson plan design …'

At the end of the course when M1 was asked once again to explain what mentoring meant to them, they responded,

> I think for me my mentoring sessions were not just limited to academic discussions, in the middle of the programme I was struggling to meet deadlines and almost felt like giving up … although my mentor never interfered with my personal life, her constant encouragement and persistence with me did help me confront the challenges and complete

> the programme. Therefore, for me, being a mentor is also like being an emotional anchor … that is what she was to me …

Let us now look at another response from a mentee. According to M9,

> I came into the programme thinking this is a traditional chalk-talk teaching programme, I had no idea about who a mentor is… so when I was assigned ____ Maam, I wasn't sure what to expect … At the beginning of the programme I used to miss my appointments and thinking I do not really need these one-on-one sessions, however, Maam made sure she was always present and was patient with me … eventually I realized I needed guidance and support, she gave constructive feedback, and to a large extent understood the context that I was working in … what also helped is she always informed me of the meeting agenda in advance, that helped me be prepared and less anxious about my meetings … I feel as a mentor one needs to understand each student as an individual and allow them to learn at their own pace.

When one analyses these and similar responses, we see that most adult-learners did come with some preconceived notions about mentoring. They seemed to be mostly apprehensive of meeting their mentors because they felt that the mentor was playing a very supervisory role. As adults, being supervised all the time or being questioned can be a very intimidating experience and can even hamper the learning process. However, what stands out is their change in attitude once they started interacting with their mentor. They seemed to have been able to arrive at a much more enhanced understanding of the role of a mentor and had begun to see the mentor as an emotional guide, a trusted friend who lets the learners learn at their own pace. This lays a more equal ground for the mentee to form a strong relationship of mutual respect with the mentor.

The Role of a Mentor in Professional Development

To establish mentoring as an anthrogogic tool in pre-service teacher education programmes, it is important to understand how my mentees viewed the role of the mentor in their own professional development. When my mentees were asked how their mentor has helped them in their professional development, the following were their responses:

> *M3*: 'I used to have weekly meetings with my mentor, I have always made notes in these meetings. These meetings help me get a clear picture of

my idea, her inputs help me think critically and guide me in the right direction. While starting my research proposal, I wasn't able to think deeply about all the aspects of the topic. But discussions with my mentor helped me to identify and analyze sociological issues which could have arisen. Like ethical issues and emotional concerns that could be faced in the future if continued.'

M14: 'I believe I have always reflected on my practice, however, I also think that discussions with my mentor have brought in intentionality and direction to my reflection.'

M18: 'As I made new meaning and gained insights my mentors were helping me to direct my own learning. This constant interaction with my mentor was prompting me to take action on my fast-emerging newfound metacognitive connections about learning, so that I could broaden and organize my thinking.'

M2: 'In the mentoring sessions I was not asked to learn in any particular way but rather was given the space needed to understand my own self better. Through dialogues and reflections, I feel that my mentor had enabled me to choose my own method of learning and this has made me aware of an emerging sense of ownership and autonomy; I now know that I create my own contexts for learning and believe that I am responsible to lead my learning.'

M24: 'My mentor meetings were very interesting, because our discussions were not just limited to official meeting hours. Most of the time I could text my mentor and she would reply to my queries. As I was already doing an internship this arrangement helped me a lot. Also, my mentor knew that I was not so great with deadlines, her gentle but firm reminders have helped me immensely in completing my work on time.'

What is interesting in all these is the ability of these adult learners to see their own growth. We need to note that in none of these responses do we find any overt attempt by the mentor to create a difference. However, it is just the way that the mentoring took place that led to learners' understanding themselves better. Dialogue with the mentor emerges as a powerful means of building a relationship of mutual trust and respect. It is important to remember that all these mentees were adult learners, hence respecting and valuing their time, giving importance to their individual preferences and experiences, and helping them to lead their own learning were strong reasons for the success of the process. Almost all the mentees unanimously agree that the mentoring process has been vital to their professional development.

Characteristics of an Effective Mentor

The efficacy of the mentoring process seemed to depend on the relationship between the mentor and their mentees. In their responses to the question, 'What do you think are some of the most important characteristics to be an effective mentor', there were varied responses.

> *M1*: 'I think for me it's the time that my mentor gives me. I am a working professional, getting back to being a student was hard. I am thankful my mentor treated me as an equal and gave me the time to figure things out . . .'
>
> *M22:* 'I feel that a good mentor needs to set the expectations clearly, at first I was not sure what exactly my mentor expected from me and this created a lot of anxiety, however, I did communicate this to her and then I think we both worked on setting the expectations! That worked I guess!'
>
> *M3:* 'Well, I think patience, empathy, and kindness, also a bit of firmness! These are very necessary for effective mentoring.'
>
> *M17*: 'I am not sure I can point out specific characteristics, but yes in my case, I am a very self-dependent learner, so I take time to open up with anyone . . . my mentor was not very probing. . . . She let me be but also would be approachable when I needed, I liked that she respected my space.'
>
> *M21*: 'I got back to studies after a 16-year-long gap, so you know . . . I was anxious and confused in the first few modules . . . I also did not take feedback very positively as I was not used to being critiqued for my work. One thing that worked is communication with my mentor. I was very straightforward with her and told her exactly how I felt . . . she was a bit taken aback I think but eventually we could develop a more common understanding of how we needed to communicate with each other . . .'

These are some enlightening responses. What is interesting is that each individual had their own definitions of what a good mentor needs to do or be. From analysing these narratives, we can say that one of the most important characteristics of an effective mentor is understanding differences in learner backgrounds. As is evident from the responses, my learners came from diverse backgrounds; some had come back to being students after long gaps and hence made the difficult journey of unlearning what they knew about traditional classrooms; some thought of themselves as self-dependent learners, while others wanted constant reassurance and feedback. Their learning preferences impacted their expectations of the course; one of my learners, for instance, was extremely feedback driven. Although she had completed her Master's in English, she was not confident of her writing abilities and needed constant guidance.

Having a profile of the learners and then making individual adjustments to fit their needs seemed to have worked in this case. For instance, for one particular mentee I had to allot more than thirty minutes for mentoring. In this learner's case, mentoring was not just about sharing her academic concerns, but also involved talking to her about challenges in communication and writing. From the responses mentioned above, it is also clear that mentees expect to be respected and treated as equals by their mentors. Being a good listener, letting your learners be, and also being firm whenever needed: these are some of the characteristics that stand out. One important aspect of mentoring is also setting the expectations clearly. This is true for both the parties involved. This helps in ensuring that all channels of communication are open and there is always the flexibility to discuss and develop new strategies to work together. Collaboration is an extremely important aspect of mentoring.

The Overall impact of Mentoring

In this section of the chapter, I have collated responses where my mentees have discussed how mentoring has impacted them. This was important for me to further build a case for mentoring as not just a requirement in teacher education programmes, but a necessary anthrogogic intervention.

When asked 'Is there anything that you feel has changed in you due to the mentoring process? You can write how it has impacted you overall, and also do you think it was an effective part of this programme', my mentees responded as follows:

> *M4*: 'Before I entered this programme, I thought I will be taught using traditional classroom methods, to be honest, initially I was not happy with having to meet my mentor weekly, because it felt more like a

compulsion.... But as I proceeded with the programme, I realized that these discussions did help me shape up my assignments ... now that I have graduated from the course, and am teaching in a school, I reflect back on these conversations and I feel that I did learn a lot of things from these, I feel that these have helped me develop a better understanding of my own teaching.'

M8: 'I think mentoring was the key aspect of my learning in the programme, I did find classes useful but the individual attention and the discussions I could have with my mentor have helped me unlearn, and relearn, this could not have been possible in a traditional classroom.'

M13: 'Unlike most of my classmates, I was a homemaker until very recently. I also was not very fluent in English and this has always held me back. I also did not initially feel comfortable talking in the class in front of all my classmates ... that's why for me mentoring sessions were extremely useful ... these sessions helped me clear my doubts without feeling embarrassed, also there were times when I was going through some challenges, my mentor did give me the time to talk my anxiety and fear out ... I think without mentoring I would not have been able to have the confidence to get through this programme ...'

M15: 'I think mentoring was the best part of the programme, also I could talk to other mentors as well and my mentor did not really have a problem with that ... so that was cool ... mentoring ensured that I had individual attention also I could learn the way I want ... I think discussions with my mentor/s helped me build a philosophy of my own ... my mentor did respect my view and that definitely helped me further question my own prejudices and also what I learned front the course.'

M23: 'My discussion with my mentor helped me get an understanding of myself as a learner and also as an aspiring teacher ... I did go through a lot of emotions during my discussions with my mentors ... I have learned how to take critical feedback without being upset about it ... I also learned how to give feedback ... when I reflect on my learning journey ... I think these mentoring sessions were instrumental in my learning journey ... they still continue to be ... I think it was important for me that my mentor respected my views and worked with me ...'

M19: 'I think the best part of this programme is my time with my mentor ... I felt this was a very personalized process, I also felt respected and important in this journey ... it may not be easy to accept all the discussions that I had with my mentor because we did have differences

> of opinion in some cases, but there was also a mutual respect so we could overcome these differences and continue to work. I think as a student I liked being valued and respected and the fact that my choices were given importance.'

What emerges once again as the most important aspect is respect. When adult learners feel respected, they become more flexible to adapt to different perspectives. Respecting the views that mentees already held and then creating a platform to co-learn seemed to be an important aspect of the process. This is evident in the responses of M13, M15, M23, and M19.

As these learners had the ability to choose their learning processes, time, and pace of learning, they felt valued in the journey. As a mentor, I was not merely a supervisory authority but rather a co-participant in the journey. Each of the sessions made me re-look at my own teaching practices. Here, I would like to share one particular incidence where my mentee (M15) was required to design a lesson to teach the concept of perimeter. As she discussed her lesson with me, I was intrigued by the idea of using a game such as Minecraft to teach the concept of perimeter. Sessions with her were enriching for me as well. Similarly, my mentee who had a doctorate in special education made a presentation on how our brain understands concepts. While discussing her presentation, I also learned how concept formation happens in the brain. Hence each of these mentoring sessions were spaces for mutual learning.

A major aspect of any learning process is feedback. It is critical that learners understand and implement feedback in their learning, as is evident in M23's response, 'I have learned how to take critical feedback without being upset about it . . . I also learned how to give feedback . . .'. Constructive feedback helped my mentees understand their concepts, as is evident from the response by M9, 'eventually I realized I needed guidance and support, she gave constructive feedback, and to a large extent understood the context that I was working in . . . what also helped is she always informed me of the meeting agenda in advance, that helped me be prepared and less anxious about my meetings . . .'.

For adult learners, sometimes accepting critical feedback is challenging as it shatters their prejudices and existing ideas about their own selves and their work. As M21 states, 'I got back to studies after a 16-year-long gap, so you know . . . I was anxious and confused in the first few modules . . . I also did not take feedback very positively as I was not used to being critiqued for my work …'. It was difficult for some of my mentees to accept feedback. However, in such cases, regular communication with the mentees helped me to gauge their challenges in accepting feedback. I realised that my learners were sensitive to criticism and also did not know how to act on feedback. I, therefore, changed my strategy from pointing out their mistakes to asking probing questions that would help them discover what was wrong and then further come up with solutions. This strategy empowered my mentees and made them feel that they were not being treated as children but as adults who can take charge of their own learning.

Conclusions and Thoughts as a Mentor

Mentoring is not only a transformative journey for the mentee but also for the mentor. It is therefore only appropriate that I, as a mentor, conclude this chapter with some insights into my own journey as a mentor.

My Journey

I feel that as a mentor having respect for the mentee is non-negotiable. All my mentees are individuals and they need to be respected for their decision to begin a new career at different stages in their life. I also learnt that communication is extremely important and, more than what is communicated, how it is communicated can make a huge impact on the kind of responses received from the mentees. As a mentor I learned to be constantly mindful of my mentee's emotions. I realised that my role moved beyond academic advising to being an emotional anchor, helping my mentees lead their learning, and also to have clear and transparent discussions with them regarding their work. I treated my mentees as equals and valued their participation in their own learning. Unlike a pedagogical process where there is an innate hierarchy in the terms used for the role of a teacher and learner, I felt that the process of mentoring was a co-learning process where I, along with my mentees, learned and discovered many things about ourselves. In that sense, it was a transformative journey for me as well. This is exactly why I feel that mentoring should be a major aspect of all teacher-education programmes.

Although mentoring has been used in teacher-education programmes, it has mostly been used within the framework of pedagogy, that is, the role of a mentor is mostly seen as a supervisor in a hierarchical teaching–learning context. But if we are to look at mentoring from an anthrogogic perspective, we will be able to create more inclusive and humane learning mechanisms for teachers. As pre-service teacher-training programmes mostly cater to novice teachers, mentoring as an anthrogogical tool becomes even more relevant. It allows pre-service teachers to understand themselves, equips them to take charge of their own learning, develop their own beliefs about teaching and learning, and eventually become effective teachers.

Individual Professional Growth: A Brief Self-Reflection

As a teacher–educator, I strongly believe that this chapter on mentoring needs to leave some food for thought for the reader, hence I have attempted to conclude this chapter with a self-reflective note on my encounters with different aspects of mentoring and how that has impacted my own understanding of mentoring.

My first academic mentor was my research guide, Dr K. Padmini Shankar, with whom I had been working since my Masters' programme. Academically, she gave me the opportunity to discover my research interests and strengths. She also gave me complete academic freedom. What was most unique about this relationship was our mutual ability to explore a relatively new research area together. I distinctly remember Dr Padmini telling me to go ahead and work on my research area and that we would both learn about that area together. For the next four years, we both learned to be co-travellers in my research journey.

During my research, I was in the United States for a period of nine months on an international scholarship. Here, I had a very different experience with my mentor. Initially my mentor was very authoritative; she was extremely critical of my work in India. Her sharp criticism often involved telling me what is wrong with my work. However, her feedback never included what I could do better. As a young researcher this made me resent the criticism, and I think I became more stubborn as I resisted her feedback. The relationship ended on a bitter note as she made me feel very inadequate about myself. This bitterness and fear stayed with me for a long time, till one day, as a young professional teaching at a university, I started reflecting on my time with her. I realised that as a twenty-five year old, I was not prepared to accept blatant criticism because of my preconceived notions of who a mentor should be. I looked at a mentor more as a guide who would 'tell' me things and I would follow them. Hence, I was not able to use the feedback constructively at that time. I used to dread the meetings that I would have with her as this would mean me feeling more unsure about myself and my work. This relationship has taught me an important lesson: that as teachers or mentors, we often tend to focus on feedback, not really understanding how it feeds forward. Feedback needs to be critical. It has to critique the work but, at the same time, it is important as a mentor to value the emotional temperature of the mentee. Mentors need to focus not just on the academic maturity of their mentees but also their emotional maturity to take critical feedback.

My most recent brush with toxic mentoring was in a professional situation, where my immediate reporting authority—who was also supposed to be the team mentor—created a toxic work atmosphere. Not only was this person sharply critical of everyone's work, she would make it a point to demoralise the whole team. Unclear instructions, unrealistic expectations, micromanaging every aspect of work, incomprehensible reactions to tasks assigned, and most importantly, being suspicious of her own team, were some of the traits she displayed. The situation was challenging for everyone as it made working with her very difficult. She would pit one team member against the other, use personal information publicly to humiliate and harass her team, demand work with no prior clarity in instruction, blame and shame the team for failures that the team was unaware of, hide relevant information, lie about student feedback, and ensure that the team never succeeded. Such an atmosphere made it extremely difficult to work. All attempts of raising this issue and providing feedback fell on deaf ears, and eventually I quit that workplace. This incident left an indelible mark on me. I went through a period of extreme stress and it took me some time to recover. In retrospect, this taught me what a mentor should not be. Mentoring is not just about knowing or studying who a mentor is. Mentoring is about practicing what one preaches. More importantly, in adult learning situations a mentor is a co-participant in the journey. They need to probe you, they need to be the voice of your conscience, and also to be the silent force that pushes you to do better.

Dr Geetha Durairajan, a teacher who has known me as a student from my Master's days, continues to mentor me even now. She and I have evolved in our relationship over many years. As a mentor, she has treated me as an equal and is available for a conversation whenever I have needed to sound my ideas out. One of the most unique aspects of this relationship is her ability to understand my professional demands and challenges. There are times when I have not been able to meet deadlines, or have not even been able to respond to her messages immediately. However, instead of getting angry or upset over this, she has been persistent in approaching me and ensuring that I am okay. Over a period of time, this has instilled in me a trust that she would understand my situation and would still push me to give my best to complete the tasks. I have been able to work on my academic commitments because of this. As a mentor, she never gave up on me and that has made me not give up on myself, despite having many other professional commitments. This level of understanding and trust has been built over a long period of time and continues to strengthen.

The discussions above were important to understand my personal beliefs about mentoring. I do not see mentoring as a supervisory role. As I have shown, from an anthrogogic perspective mentoring needs to be viewed as a more equal partnership between two individuals sharing an academic space. This partnership then lays the foundations for growth of both the individuals. In the course of writing this chapter, Dr Durairajan and I have also deliberated on how we need to challenge the term 'mentor', which implicitly brings in a supervisory perspective. We now intend to find a term that redefines mentoring as we understand it.

References

Arnesson, K. & Albinsson. G. (2017). Mentorship–a pedagogical method for integration of theory and practice in higher education. *Nordic Journal of Studies in Education Policy*, *3*(3), 202–17.

Deepa, S. (2022a). Thought seeds in anthrogogic learning contexts. *Journal of Indian Education*, *48*(2), 58–70.

Deepa, S. (2022b). Pedagogic practices in higher education and Peter Pan syndrome: An appraisal. *Fortell*, *45*, 164–73.

Deepa, S. (2026). Principles of anthrogogic language education. In S. Deepa & G. Durairajan (Eds.), *Anthrogogy in use: A handbook for language educators* (pp. 3–26). Orient BlackSwan.

Hartwig, E. O. (1999). Mentoring. *Oceanography*, *12*(2), 4–6.

Kamarudin, M., Kamarudin, A., Darmi, R., & Saad, N. (2020). A review of coaching and mentoring theories and models. *International Journal of Academic Research in Progressive Education and Development*, *9*, 289–98.

Knowles, M. S. (1984). Andragogy in action: Applying modern principles of adult education. Jossey-Bass.

Kram, K. (1983). Phases of the mentor relationship. *Academy of Management Journal, 26*(4), 608–25.

Ministry of Human Resource Development (2020). *National education policy 2020.* https://www.education.gov.in/sites/upload_files/mhrd/files/NEP_Final_English_0.pdf.

Peterson, B. E. & Williams, S. R. (1998). Mentoring beginning teachers. *The Mathematics Teacher, 91*(8), 730–34.

Schwille, S. A. (2008). The professional practice of mentoring. *American Journal of Education, 115*(1), 139–67.

Trott, D. C. (1991). *Anthrogogy* [Paper presentation]. Meeting of the American Association for Adult and Continuing Education, Montreal, Quebec.

Vygotsky, L. S. (1934). *Thought and language.* MIT Press.

Winston, A. B & Dahlber, M. L. (Ed.). (2019). The science of effective mentorship in STEMM. *A Consensus Study Report of Science, Engineering, Medicine.* The National Academic Press. https://doi.org/10.17226/25568.

4
Decoding the Digital Classroom
A Study on In-Service Teachers' Experiences with ICT Tools

Shadab Khan

> If I stay in education, it will be because of the kids. If I leave education, it will be because of the adults.
>
> —*Anonymous (via X, formerly Twitter)*

Introduction

The integration of Information and Communication Technology (ICT) in English as a Second Language (ESL) classrooms has become increasingly prominent in recent years, offering numerous benefits such as enhanced student engagement, personalised learning experiences, and improved access to resources (Ghavifekr & Rosdy, 2015). Despite these advantages, the perception and adoption of ICT tools by experienced in-service teachers, particularly those with over a decade of teaching experience, remain under-explored in educational research. This gap is significant as these educators bring a wealth of practical knowledge and teaching expertise, yet their unique challenges and needs in adapting to digital tools are often overlooked.

Recent studies highlight that while younger in-service teachers are generally more adept at integrating ICT due to their familiarity with digital technologies, experienced teachers may encounter different barriers. These barriers include resistance to change, lack of adequate training, and insufficient support structures within educational institutions (Siddiq, et al., 2017). Understanding these challenges is critical, as digital literacy involves not only the ability to use technology, but also the critical evaluation of digital content and the effective integration of digital tools into pedagogical practices (van Laar, et al., 2020).

Moreover, the COVID-19 pandemic has further emphasised the critical role of ICT in education, pushing many educators to rapidly adapt to remote teaching environments (Bond, 2021). This sudden shift has spotlighted the varying levels of preparedness among teachers and the urgent need for comprehensive training programmes that cater specifically to the needs of experienced educators. Studies have shown that the successful integration of ICT in education depends significantly on the attitudes and perceptions of teachers towards these tools. Teachers with positive attitudes towards ICT are more likely to implement these technologies effectively in their classrooms, leading to improved educational outcomes (Tondeur, et al., 2017).

In this context, the present study aims to explore the experiences and perceptions of experienced in-service teachers regarding the use of ICT tools in both pedagogic and anthrogogic ESL classrooms. By concentrating on educators with substantial teaching experience, this research aims to uncover the specific challenges these teachers face, the impact of ICT on various age-groups of learners in ESL teaching and learning, and the adequacy of current training and support structures. Understanding these factors is crucial for developing targeted interventions that support the professional development of experienced teachers and enhance their ability to leverage ICT for effective ESL instruction.

Additionally, the study examines the differential impact of ICT tools on students across various age groups, specifically in pedagogic (children and adolescents) and anthrogogic (adult learners) contexts. As elaborated by Deepa (2026), the term 'anthrogogy' in this volume refers to inclusive, experience-based learning practices for adult learners in mainstream higher education, distinct from both pedagogy and andragogy. Pedagogic settings often benefit from interactive and multimedia-rich ICT tools that can enhance engagement and motivation among younger learners (Shadiev, et al., 2018). In contrast, adult learners in anthrogogic settings may derive greater benefits from ICT tools that offer flexibility and opportunities for self-directed learning. For instance, in their insightful study 'Learning Through Assessment in Anthrogogic Contexts: Wash-Forward', Deepa and Durairajan (2023) explore how assessment practices can profoundly influence future learning experiences for adult learners. They argue that traditional assessment methods, which prioritise rote memorisation and immediate performance, are inadequate for adult education, an observation that aligns with Durairajan's 2026 formulation of anthrogogic assessment, which foregrounds individual consequences and advocates assessment designed to 'wash-forward' into future practice. They advocate for assessment approaches that encourage critical thinking, practical application, and incorporate peer and self-evaluation. These methods not only foster deeper understanding and reflection, but also promote continued growth and the application of knowledge, essential for adult learners.

Furthermore, Deepa and Durairajan emphasise the concept of 'wash-forward', (2023) a dynamic and forward-looking approach to assessment that actively contributes to the ongoing educational journey of adult learners. Their study highlights the importance of project-based assessments, self-assessments, and peer evaluations in fostering a deeper understanding and long-term retention of knowledge among adult learners. This approach aligns well with the requirements of adult learners, who seek ICT tools that accommodate their need for flexible and autonomous learning environments.

This distinction between pedagogic and anthrogogic learners is crucial as it underscores the need for differentiated ICT strategies that cater to the unique learning styles and needs of diverse age groups. By addressing these needs, educational institutions can better support both teachers and students in maximising the potential of ICT in ESL education. Effective ICT integration requires a comprehensive understanding of the diverse challenges faced by experienced educators and a commitment to providing tailored support and training to facilitate the adoption of digital tools in varied educational contexts.

The Study

Research Design

This study employed a qualitative research design, utilising semi-structured interviews to gather in-depth insights into the experiences and perceptions of in-service ESL teachers regarding the integration of ICT tools in their classrooms. This research aims to explore the nuances of ICT integration and identify key themes that contribute to the ongoing discourse in this area, providing a foundation for further investigations and practical applications in the field.

Research Questions

1. How do in-service ESL teachers perceive and experience the integration of Information and Communication Technology

(ICT) tools in both pedagogic and anthrogogic learning environments?
2. What are the key challenges and support needs for experienced ESL teachers in successfully integrating ICT tools to enhance language learning outcomes for both pedagogic and anthrogogic learners?
3. What are the implications of in-service ESL teachers' perceptions and experiences for the effective use of ICT tools in promoting learner engagement and improving educational outcomes across different age groups?

Participants

The participants in this study comprised six in-service ESL teachers. Among them, four were teaching at the university level and two were teaching at public schools. Each teacher had over ten years of teaching experience. This selection criterion ensured that the teachers had substantial exposure to both traditional and technology-enhanced teaching methods. Consequently, this provided a rich basis for exploring the evolution of their experiences and perceptions regarding ICT integration.

Table 4.1: *Participants' Details*

Teacher	*Years of Teaching Experience*	*Type of Institute*	*ICT Experience*
Teacher 1	Over 30 years	Central University	Yes
Teacher 2	18 years	Central University	Yes
Teacher 3	14 years	Central University	Yes
Teacher 4	22 years	Central University	Yes
Teacher 5	26 years	Government Public school	Yes
Teacher 6	Over 10 years	Government Public school	Yes

Data Collection

Data was collected through semi-structured interviews, which allowed for both structured questioning and the flexibility to probe deeper into specific areas of interest as they emerged during the conversations. This method was chosen to capture the complexity and depth of the teachers' experiences while providing the opportunity for them to express their views in their own words.

Interview Process

The interviews were conducted individually with each participant, ensuring a comfortable and confidential environment to encourage open and honest dialogue. Each interview lasted approximately sixty minutes and was guided by an interview protocol that included a series of open-ended questions designed to elicit detailed responses about the teachers' experiences, challenges, and perceptions related to ICT integration.

Data Analysis

Experiences and Perceptions Over the Past Decade

All the teachers in both pedagogic and anthrogogic settings initially faced significant resistance and challenges while integrating ICT tools into their teaching practices. One teacher described the initial phase as 'very frustrating', highlighting the mental strain involved in learning to handle various commands and tools. Another teacher shared, 'The initial learning is very challenging . . . learning to handle those different commands is mentally very tiring'. However, over time, teachers gradually adapted to the new ICT tools and recognised their potential to enhance teaching efficiency and effectiveness.

Impact on Teaching Practices and Student Learning Experiences

In implementing ICT tools in ESL classrooms, it is crucial to distinguish between pedagogic and anthrogogic environments, as the use and effectiveness of these tools vary significantly. Based on interviews with in-service ESL teachers, this analysis reflects the diverse perspectives and experiences of these educators.

The two teachers teaching in pedagogic settings noted that teaching for them remains predominantly teacher-centered. They emphasised that simpler, less complex tools are often more effective. One teacher mentioned, 'In a classroom with younger learners, we tend to use basic tools like PowerPoint and educational apps that align with the structured learning environments these students need.' They highlighted that multimodal learning, involving multiple methods of content delivery, is often less effective for younger learners. According to these teachers, when ICT is used to promote multimodal learning in these scenarios, it sometimes fails to facilitate actual language learning and can reduce lessons to mere gimmicks without substantial educational value.

In contrast, the four teachers teaching in anthrogogic classrooms pointed out that these environments require a more learner-centered approach. Adult learners benefit significantly from collaborative environments where they can share experiences and provide feedback to one another. One teacher shared, 'In my experience with adult learners, tools like Google Docs and online forums are incredibly effective. They foster an interactive and engaging learning atmosphere.' These teachers emphasised the importance of gradually introducing adult learners to technology, ensuring they have the necessary support to utilise these tools effectively.

Multimodal learning, when implemented in anthrogogic scenarios, was found by these teachers to significantly enhance engagement and interest. They observed that using ICT in this context increases attention and facilitates a deeper understanding of the material. One teacher remarked, 'Adult learners bring diverse experiences to the classroom, and they benefit from a variety of content delivery methods that cater to different learning styles.'

All six teachers believed that regular training and staying updated with the latest ICT tools were crucial for integrating these technologies effectively. Furthermore, they emphasised the importance of 'anthropological' awareness—understanding the cultural and social contexts of learners, particularly adult learners. This involves selecting and implementing ICT tools in ways that are sensitive to these contexts, considering factors such as the accessibility of technology and the digital literacy of learners.

Overall, the effective integration of ICT tools in ESL classrooms requires a nuanced approach that considers the distinct needs of pedagogic and anthrogogic learners. By recognising these differences, teachers can better tailor their methods and tools to enhance learning outcomes for both groups.

Challenges in Integrating ICT Tools

The teachers highlighted several challenges related to ICT integration. They expressed concerns about the lack of adequate training and support for utilising ICT tools, often having to figure things out on their own or seek help from colleagues. For instance, a teacher teaching in the pedagogic setting mentioned that they've 'never received formal instruction on using digital grading systems', highlighting a lack of basic structured training. This exacerbated the learning curve for many teachers, ultimately limiting their ability to seamlessly integrate ICT into their lessons. Another teacher teaching in the anthrogogic setting stated the challenge, saying, 'it takes a lot of mental strain and struggle to learn this new technology', further emphasising the difficulties faced without proper guidance.

All six teachers expressed concerns about inequitable access to ICT tools among students. For instance, some students lacked laptops or smartphones, hindering their participation in classroom activities. One teacher highlighted the challenge of integrating ICT tools when students without devices appeared 'laid back' or 'inaccessible': phrases used to describe how these students became withdrawn or disengaged, not due to disinterest, but because they lacked the means to participate fully. This underscored the difficulty of fostering inclusion in a classroom where resource disparities persist. Additionally, teachers noted their own struggles in accessing premium ICT tools, citing prohibitive costs as a barrier to adopting more effective technologies.

Teachers often face challenges in locating and utilising high-quality tutorials and materials for ICT tools. A common issue is the inconsistency between tutorials and the actual tools, particularly when comparing different operating systems like Windows and Mac. Instructions often differ significantly between Windows and Mac, and even between mobile devices and PCs, making it difficult for teachers to follow along accurately. Additionally, the alignment and interface of websites or tools frequently change over time. For instance, a teacher teaching in the anthrogogic setting noted that the recording button on Google Meet tends to 'play hide and seek', moving to different locations with each update. Similarly, the three lines (hamburger menu ☰), which might initially be at the top left, can suddenly shift to a completely different position in a single update. These constant changes exacerbate the difficulties teachers face, making the struggle to effectively integrate ICT tools into their lessons even more challenging.

Teachers also raised concerns about time management and monitoring student engagement while using ICT tools. Managing class time effectively and ensuring all students are engaged can be challenging with digital tools. One teacher teaching in the pedagogic setting noted the difficulty in monitoring group activities and ensuring active participation, stating, 'it's very difficult for us to monitor when it comes to group activities.'

A significant challenge identified in the interviews is the perception of ICT tools among colleagues and administrators. Many senior teachers and administrators resist ICT integration, viewing it as unnecessary or a distraction from traditional teaching methods. One participant teaching in the anthrogogic setting noted, 'Senior professors, with extensive experience or administrative roles, often perceive ICT tools negatively', which creates barriers to the adoption and effective implementation of these technologies. For example, when fellow teachers propose new courses that incorporate ICT, administrators often do not approve these initiatives. The teacher further said, 'Even when ICT courses are introduced, the curriculum is kept largely theoretical rather than practical', reflecting scepticism about the tangible benefits of ICT. Additionally, a teacher teaching in the anthrogogic setting mentioned, 'There is a prevailing negative attitude towards non-traditional assessment methods. Many administrators and senior teachers prefer traditional pen-and-paper exams and resist digital modes of assessment, believing them to be less rigorous or reliable.' These attitudes highlight the need for targeted professional development and systemic support to shift perceptions and foster a more positive view of ICT integration in education.

Teachers also struggled with finding high-quality online resources, expressing frustration with 'a lot of ads or fake apps or the paid apps'. They emphasised the importance of ensuring that ICT tools enhance rather than overshadow the actual language learning process. One teacher teaching in the anthrogogic setting cautioned that technology can sometimes be perceived as just something trendy or impressive rather than a genuine educational tool, highlighting the risk of it becoming a gimmick instead of truly benefiting education.

Infrastructure issues were another challenge. Teachers often dealt with unreliable internet connections and inadequate technological resources in their schools. These issues disrupted lessons and made it difficult to rely on ICT tools consistently.

Evolution and Adequacy of ICT Training

The six teachers reported insufficient formal training in using ICT tools, often relying on self-learning or informal peer support. One teacher teaching in the pedagogic setting shared, 'I've never gone and learned how to use MS Word or anything else . . . learning takes a lot of mental strain and struggle.' This lack of structured training often resulted in frustration and limited the effective use of ICT tools. Training sessions, when available, were frequently rushed and predominantly theoretical. Teachers emphasised that most training did not translate into practical classroom applications. As one teacher teaching in the anthrogogic setting noted, 'Training often feels rushed, and most of the time, it's just theory and not in practice', highlighting the disconnect between training content and real-world teaching needs. The teacher said, 'This gap has often left teachers feeling unprepared and unsupported in integrating technology effectively into our classrooms.'

Necessary Support for Successful ICT Integration

The six teachers interviewed were passionate about integrating ICT tools into their teaching practices but emphasised the need for more appropriate training. They highlighted the importance of hands-on training and practical experience rather than just theory, delivered in a supportive environment with access to technical assistance and guidance from experts. The teachers passionately advocated for dedicated technical support staff. One teacher teaching in the anthrogogic setting said, 'We all know there's an issue. We're constantly grabbing our laptops and running around trying to find someone to help. What we need is a system like the central training hubs they usually have in universities and colleges, with readily available support staff.'

One teacher teaching in the pedagogic setting believed that ongoing professional development (PD) programmes are crucial to help teachers keep up with the rapid pace of technological advancements. They suggested that these programmes should be made compulsory, especially for new recruits, and should be arranged at regular intervals of at least six months. They said, 'Continuous support is necessary to learn new tools and troubleshoot problems.' A significant concern is the outdated and non-adult-friendly manuals for ICT tools. A teacher teaching in the anthrogogic setting suggested that manuals should be made more accessible and user-friendly, tailored to the needs of adult teachers. They recommended creating anthrogogic manuals that incorporate user-friendly language and visual aids, making them easier to understand and useful for all ages.

Two teachers, from both pedagogic and anthrogogic settings, stressed the need for appropriate training to identify student-friendly and teacher-friendly tools based on their needs and the student's needs. One teacher said, 'Continuous professional development should focus on giving hands-on training to teachers, and administrators should be open to different modes of testing and evaluation, including supporting ICT in examinations. For example, supporting open-source examinations and providing training for teachers to design such exams can help integrate ICT into assessment processes and eliminate the fear of technology among educators.' Peer support and collaborative learning were also emphasised, with teachers advocating for more opportunities to share experiences, learn from each other, and co-create resources and teaching materials through student–teacher collaboration, peer-to-peer support, workshops, and online communities. The teachers highlighted the importance of fostering a collaborative learning environment, where they can share their experiences, challenges, and solutions.

One teacher teaching in the anthrogogic setting highlighted the need for a balanced approach to using ICT in the classroom. While ICT tools can be effective for certain tasks, they emphasised that technology should not replace traditional teaching methods but rather complement them. This approach promotes active learning, collaboration, and critical thinking. Integrating ICT tools effectively requires a multifaceted approach that includes proper training, support, and collaboration, fostering a culture of shared learning and continuous professional development for successful ICT integration in the classroom.

Training Methods for Different Age Groups

All six in-service teachers expressed the view that teaching methods, particularly when incorporating ICT, must be tailored to the specific age groups of learners. They consistently highlighted the distinct cognitive levels, interests, and learning needs of young learners versus adults, emphasising the need for different pedagogic and anthrogogic approaches.

One teacher, who had experience teaching both primary and high school students, observed that while animated cartoons worked well to bring textbook stories to life for primary students, these same tools were not as effective for high-school learners. These tools' animated and visually appealing nature engaged and motivated younger learners, capturing their attention. However, for older students, these methods did not align with their learning needs and interests. Instead, high-school students benefited more from tools that promoted brainstorming, idea-sharing, and interactive discussions, which resonated with their cognitive development and preference for collaborative learning.

The two teachers working at the school level (pedagogic context) emphasised that educational games and multimedia resources were highly effective in maintaining engagement and motivation among younger learners. These tools supported skill development in a manner suited to the developmental stage of children. However, the four teachers working at the university level (anthrogogic context) found these same tools less effective for adult learners. Even when developing similar skills, adults engaged with and processed information differently, often requiring ICT tools that were more practical and aligned with real-world applications to maintain their engagement.

The interviews also revealed distinct challenges faced by the teachers themselves, particularly older teachers. One educator in the anthrogogic setting highlighted that adult in-service teachers often face unique challenges that are seldom addressed in training programs. They may have less patience for long, theoretical sessions and prefer practical, immediately applicable training. The teacher pointed out that 'adult teachers tend to seek hands-on solutions that directly address their professional challenges.'

Overall, while ICT tools offer significant potential for enhancing learning, their effectiveness heavily depends on age-appropriateness. Tailoring these tools to meet the specific needs of different age groups can significantly improve learning outcomes. Therefore, teacher training must include strategies for implementing ICT tools in ways that are most effective for the targeted age group, recognising the unique characteristics and needs of both young and adult learners, as well as the practical challenges educators themselves face.

Discussion

The integration of ICT tools in ESL classrooms has significantly transformed teaching practices, offering valuable insights into in-service teachers' experiences and perceptions. This discussion highlights the profound impact of ICT, explores the challenges faced, and examines its varied effects in both pedagogic and anthrogogic contexts.

Research Question 1

How do in-service ESL teachers perceive and experience the integration of Information and Communication Technology (ICT) tools in both pedagogic and anthrogogic learning environments?

Evolving Teacher Experiences and Perceptions

The initial phase of ICT integration was marked by significant resistance and frustration among teachers, reflecting a broader trend in the adoption of new technologies in education. Studies by Tondeur, et al. (2017) and Howard, et al. (2021) corroborate this initial resistance, emphasising the mental strain and learning curve associated with mastering new digital tools. However, over time, teachers' perceptions evolved as they adapted to the technology and began to recognise its potential to enhance teaching efficiency and effectiveness. This shift aligns with the findings of Mueller, et al. (2008), who noted that sustained exposure and gradual familiarisation with ICT tools can lead to more positive attitudes and increased usage in educational settings.

Research Question 2

What are the key challenges and support needs for experienced ESL teachers in successfully integrating ICT tools to enhance language learning outcomes for both pedagogic and anthrogogic learners?

Challenges in ICT Integration

Despite the potential benefits, the integration of ICT tools in ESL classrooms is fraught with challenges. Inadequate training and support emerge as significant barriers, echoing the findings of Ghavifekr and Rosdy (2015), who highlight the need for comprehensive and continuous professional development. The study's participants reported relying heavily on self-learning and peer support, which is insufficient for mastering complex digital tools. This inadequacy is compounded by the lack of high-quality, accessible training resources, a problem also noted by Rienties, et al. (2013).

Accessibility issues further complicate ICT integration, particularly in resource-constrained environments. The digital divide, as discussed by Warschauer and Matuchniak (2010), remains a critical issue with disparities in student access to devices and reliable internet connections creating inequities in educational experiences. This study's findings underscore the need for policy interventions and institutional support to address these disparities and ensure equitable access to digital learning tools.

The Evolution and Adequacy of ICT Training

The study highlights a significant gap in the adequacy of ICT training for teachers. The training sessions available are often theoretical and rushed, failing to equip educators with the practical skills needed for effective technology integration. This aligns with the findings of Darling-Hammond, et al. (2017), who advocate for experiential learning and ongoing professional support in teacher education. Effective ICT training should be hands-on and context-specific, providing teachers with the skills and confidence to integrate digital tools into their pedagogical practices seamlessly.

Support Systems for Effective ICT Integration

The call for more appropriate training, dedicated technical support staff, and ongoing professional development programmes reflects a widespread recognition of the need for systemic changes in ICT integration support. This aligns with the broader pedagogical shift towards collaborative professional development models, as discussed by Avalos (2011). Teachers emphasised the importance of fostering a collaborative learning environment where they can share experiences, challenges and solutions. This echoes Deepa's description of the anthrogogic classroom (Deepa 2026) as a negotiated, dignity-centred space in which adult learners and teachers exercise agency and co-construct knowledge. This peer support and collaborative learning approach is crucial for building a community of practice that can collectively navigate the complexities of digital pedagogies.

Research Question 3

What are the implications of in-service ESL teachers' perceptions and experiences for the effective use of ICT tools in promoting learner engagement and improving educational outcomes across different age groups?

Impact of ICT on Pedagogic and Anthrogogic Practices

The differential impact of ICT tools in pedagogic and anthrogogic settings is a critical finding of this study. The study indicates that, in pedagogic contexts, simpler, teacher-centered tools such as basic educational apps and PowerPoint underscore the importance of age-appropriate technological interventions. These tools, which often support structured, direct instruction, align well with the needs of younger learners by providing clear and focused content delivery. This observation is supported by Taufik, et al. (2023), who argue that younger learners benefit more from such straightforward and less complex digital tools, as more intricate multimodal approaches may overwhelm them and detract from core learning objectives.

Conversely, in anthrogogic settings, the study highlights the efficacy of collaborative and interactive tools like Google Docs and online forums, which align with the learner-centered approach favoured in adult education. Philipsen, et al. (2019) similarly emphasise the importance of leveraging adult learners' experiential backgrounds and promoting interactive learning environments to enhance engagement and learning outcomes. These findings suggest that the successful integration of ICT in ESL classrooms requires a nuanced approach, tailored to the distinct cognitive and developmental needs of different learner groups.

Tailored Training for Different Age Groups

The study underscores the importance of tailored training approaches for educators working with different age groups. The distinct cognitive levels, interests, and learning needs of young learners versus adults necessitate differentiated pedagogic and anthrogogic strategies. This differentiation is supported by recent research, such as Hamidi and Chavoshi (2018), who emphasise the need for age-appropriate digital interventions and training programmes. Effective ICT integration in ESL classrooms requires training that is specifically designed to meet the unique needs of both young and adult learners, ensuring that digital tools are implemented in ways that are developmentally appropriate and pedagogically sound.

Conclusion

This study provides a comprehensive examination of the integration of ICT tools in ESL classrooms, highlighting the diverse experiences and perceptions of experienced in-service teachers. The findings illuminate the transformative potential of ICT in enhancing teaching practices and student learning experiences while also underscoring the challenges and barriers that persist.

The evolution of teacher experiences from initial resistance to eventual adaptation and recognition of ICT's benefits mirrors broader trends observed in educational technology adoption. Teachers' initial frustrations and the mental strain associated with learning new tools gradually gave way to more positive attitudes as they became familiar with these technologies. This shift emphasises the importance of sustained exposure and gradual familiarisation with ICT tools.

The study's findings underscore the necessity of differentiating between pedagogic and anthrogogic contexts when implementing ICT in ESL classrooms. In pedagogic settings, simpler, teacher-centered tools proved more effective, aligning with younger learners' cognitive and developmental needs. In contrast, anthrogogic environments benefited significantly from collaborative, learner-centered tools, which fostered interactive and engaging learning experiences for adult learners. This distinction highlights the importance of tailoring ICT interventions to the specific needs of different learner groups.

Despite the potential benefits of ICT, the integration process is fraught with challenges. Inadequate training and support, accessibility issues, and infrastructural constraints emerged as significant barriers. The lack of formal, hands-on training and the reliance on self-learning and peer support limited teachers' ability to effectively utilise ICT tools. Additionally, the digital divide and disparities in access to devices and reliable internet connections exacerbated inequalities in educational experiences.

The study also highlighted the need for systemic changes in ICT integration support. Teachers emphasised the importance of dedicated technical support staff, ongoing professional development programs, and collaborative learning environments. These support systems are essential for fostering a community of practice capable of collaboratively navigating the complexities of digital teaching and learning.

Limitations and Scope for Future Research

While this study provides valuable insights into the experiences and perceptions of in-service ESL teachers regarding ICT integration, several limitations must be acknowledged. First, the study's sample size was limited to a specific geographic region and educational context, which may limit the generalisability of the findings. Future research should aim to include a more diverse and representative sample to capture a broader range of experiences and perspectives.

Second, the study relied on self-reported data which may be subject to biases such as social desirability and recall bias. Future research should consider using a mixed-methods approach, incorporating observational data and quantitative measures to triangulate findings and enhance the robustness of the results.

Third, the study focused primarily on the perspectives of teachers with limited input from students. Understanding students' experiences and perceptions of ICT integration is crucial for developing a holistic understanding of its impact. Future research should include student voices to provide a more comprehensive view of ICT's role in ESL education.

Additionally, future research should explore the long-term effects of ICT integration on teaching practices and student learning outcomes. Longitudinal studies can provide valuable insights into how the sustained use of ICT tools influences educational processes and achievements over time.

Finally, there is a need for research on the development and evaluation of tailored professional development programmes for ICT integration. Such programmes should focus on providing hands-on, context-specific training that addresses the unique needs of both pedagogic and anthrogogic learners. Evaluating the effectiveness of these programmes can inform best practices, and guide policy and practice in ICT integration in ESL education.

References

Avalos, B. (2011). Teacher professional development in teaching and teacher education over ten years. *Teaching and Teacher Education*, *27*(1), 10–20. https://doi.org/10.1016/j.tate.2010.08.007.

Bond, M. (2021). Schools and emergency remote education during the COVID-19 pandemic: A living rapid systematic review. *Asian Journal of Distance Education*, *15*(2), 191–247. https://doi.org/10.5281/zenodo.4425683.

Darling-Hammond, L., Hyler, M. E., & Gardner, M. (2017). Effective teacher professional development. *Learning Policy Institute*. Retrieved October 14, 2024, from https://learningpolicyinstitute.org/product/effective-teacher-professional-development-report.

Deepa, S., & Durairajan, G. (2023). Learning through assessment in anthrogogic contexts: Wash-forward. In Gokturk-Saglam, A, L., & Sevgi-Sole, E. (Eds), *Emerging practices for online language assessment, exams, evaluation, and feedback* (pp. 99–118). IGI Global. https://doi.org/10.4018/978-1-6684-6227-0.ch006.

Ghavifekr, S., & Rosdy, W. A. W. (2015). Teaching and learning with technology: Effectiveness of ICT integration in schools. *International Journal of Research in Education and Science, 1*(2), 175–191. https://doi.org/10.21890/ijres.23596.

Hamidi, H., & Chavoshi, A. (2018). Analysis of the essential factors for the adoption of mobile learning in higher education: A case study of students of the University of Technology. *Telematics and Informatics, 35*(4), 1053–1070. https://doi.org/10.1016/j.tele.2017.09.016.

Howard, S. K., Tondeur, J., Ma, J., & Yang, J. (2021). What to teach? Strategies for developing digital competency in preservice teacher training. *Computers & Education, 165*, 104149. https://doi.org/10.1016/j.compedu.2021.104149.

Mueller, J., Wood, E., Willoughby, T., Ross, C., & Specht, J. (2008). Identifying discriminating variables between teachers who fully integrate computers and teachers with limited integration. *Computers & education, 51*(4), 1523–1537. https://doi.org/10.1016/j.compedu.2008.02.003.

Philipsen, B., Tondeur, J., Pareja Roblin, N., Vanslambrouck, S., & Zhu, C. (2019). Improving teacher professional development for online and blended learning: A systematic meta-aggregative review. *Educational Technology Research and Development, 67*(5), 1145–1174. https://doi.org/10.1007/s11423-019-09645-8.

Rienties, B., Brouwer, N., & Lygo-Baker, S. (2013). The effects of online professional development on higher education teachers' beliefs and intentions towards learning facilitation and technology. *Teaching and Teacher Education, 29*, 122–131. https://doi.org/10.1016/j.tate.2012.09.002.

Shadiev, R., Hwang, W. Y., & Liu, T. Y. (2018). Investigating the effectiveness of a learning activity supported by a mobile multimedia learning system to enhance autonomous EFL learning in authentic contexts. *Educational Technology Research and Development, 66*, 893–912. https://doi.org/10.1007/s11423-018-9590-1.

Siddiq, F., Gochyyev, P., & Wilson, M. (2017). Learning in Digital Networks–ICT literacy: A novel assessment of students' 21st century skills. *Computers & Education, 109*, 11–37. https://doi.org/10.1016/j.compedu.2017.01.014.

Taufik, M. F., Sakina, R., & Pratama, S. H. H. (2023). The use of ICT by EFL Teachers in young learner classroom during Covid-19 pandemic at a state school in Garut. *JEPAL (Journal of English Pedagogy and Applied Linguistics), 3*(2), 111–120. https://doi.org/10.32627/jepal.v3i2.627.

Tondeur, J., Van Braak, J., Ertmer, P. A., & Ottenbreit-Leftwich, A. (2017). Understanding the relationship between teachers' pedagogical beliefs and technology use in education: A systematic review of qualitative evidence. *Educational Technology Research and Development, 65*, 555–575. https://doi.org/10.1007/s11423-016-9481-2.

van Laar, E., van Deursen, A. J., van Dijk, J. A., & de Haan, J. (2020). Determinants of 21st-century skills and 21st-century digital skills for workers: A systematic literature review. *Sage Open, 10*(1). https://doi.org/10.1177/2158244019900176.

Warschauer, M., & Matuchniak, T. (2010). New technology and digital worlds: Analyzing evidence of equity in access, use, and outcomes. *Review of Research in Education, 34*(1), 179–225. https://doi.org/10.3102/0091732X09349791.

5

Reimagining Teacher Authority in an Anthrogogic Framework

Reflections from a Writing Programme

Sayan Chaudhuri and Monishita Hajra Pande

Introduction

Teaching is inevitably a constant negotiation with notions of authority. As Sriprakash's work on teacher reform programmes points out, teachers may find it difficult to initiate themselves into non-hierarchical embodiments of teaching (being democratic, accessible, friendly) since they are socialised within fundamentally hierarchical assumptions about who a teacher needs to be (Sriprakash, 2011). While teachers may ethically agree with the values of classroom democracy, practical concerns come in the way. There is often a gap between the theoretical agreement with values of democracy and the practical negotiation of a classroom, or between the teachers' theoretically-espoused and practically-embodied beliefs about teaching. This gap hinges on a rather tricky question: how does a teacher control the classroom, garner respect from the student, and be respected in society, if they *cede* authority? Further, as Sarangapani has shown, a teacher's self-identification is often framed in terms of particular relational hierarchies—the teacher is an adult guiding a younger person, or the teacher is a patron initiating a protege, or the teacher is doubling up as a parent to discipline the child (Sarangapani, 2003). These hierarchies are further, albeit in complicated ways, bound up in sociocultural assumptions about the teacher as a 'guru' or as a socially sanctioned disciplinarian. While these assumptions may be increasingly challenged in progressive education discourse, they continue to be internalised as dispositions, tendencies, and behavioural attributes of teachers. And while these frameworks of self-identification are prominent in narratives of school teaching, it is worth asking to what extent this is applicable in higher education spaces, where the teacher is ostensibly teaching 'adult' learners.

Unfortunately, the teacher–student relationality in Indian higher education settings is hardly problematised. At undergraduate and postgraduate levels, there doesn't seem to be any institutional framing of the student as an agentive adult. The student is still considered as one who needs to be subjected to a combination of top-down guidance, disciplining, and surveillance. There are two aspects to this problem: institutional and pedagogic. First, the institutional structures of the university are enmeshed in top-down bureaucratic structures, which largely restrict the autonomy of both the teacher and the student, and prevent the active questioning of the normative ritualisation of hierarchical classroom roles, norms, and practices. These institutional structures are also enmeshed in paternalistic and meritocratic discourses of caste, class, and gender, which further withdraw or oppose the agency of students from marginalised communities. This, in turn, informs the dominant pedagogic culture within higher education settings. The normative pedagogic assumption is that students must be prescribed and imparted standardised information (across institutional settings) which they learn to (re-)produce in standardised assignments and exams. Further, such assumptions are often shaped by the kinds of classrooms teachers have themselves inhabited as learners—the imagination of what it means to be a teacher, or how a teacher behaves and positions themselves, are also affectively and behaviourally inherited. At the same time, there are inevitable negotiations that teachers and students undertake, to creatively rework and personalise the teaching–learning process. Teachers are mediating between their own inherited beliefs, institutional rituals and agendas, and political and pedagogic desires. Further, there are different kinds of institutes within the higher education landscape, affording varying degrees of teacher autonomy. If we take a cynical view, we might be stuck with the understanding that there are systemic hurdles that are impossible to bypass—the teacher is doomed to be a 'meek dictator' working at the behest of larger forces. But that also begs the question: how do we imagine alternatives? In other words, what can the teacher do to inhabit alternate frames of embodiment and relationality?

There could be two starting points to think through this question. First, we might wish to problematise dominant notions of 'pedagogy' itself. Not only is it mediated by a hierarchising and infantilising institutional logic, but it also leads to a conceptual impasse. A 'pedagogic' relation or practice would dominantly assume a child learner and a top-down transmission of knowledge. To use this word uncritically, then, might result in a grave contradiction. A second important starting point could be to map the kinds of authority the teacher is already negotiating with—an authority that is both socially sanctioned yet in some ways institutionally disempowered; an authority that is mediating between a complex self-embodiment and ritualistic, reified practices. Such a mapping might open up insights into how the teacher can consciously negotiate and reposition themselves at both a personal and institutional level. This chapter will explore modalities through which such an exercise—both the mapping and the repositioning of the teacher—can be undertaken.

This chapter will take as its central focus the authors' experience of teaching adult learners at a multi-disciplinary liberal arts fellowship and, through a self-reflexive mapping and analysis of experience, will provide certain conceptual tools to work through the problem of how one can negotiate and reposition notions of teacher authority. The chapter will be divided into three subsequent sections. The first will lay out the field of study, as it were, which is the Critical Writing programme at the Young India Fellowship programme. It will describe the details of the programme, what it entailed and aimed to do, and then go on to introduce the writing courses that the authors were teaching. The second section will present four anecdotes, where each author will anecdotally reflect on two significant experiences from their courses respectively, to open up both approaches as well as tensions towards challenging hierarchical teacher–student relations, and reposition the teacher as inhabiting a counter-hegemonic, self-critical vantage-point. The third section will attempt a critical discussion of the anecdotes, where their teaching and political implications will be drawn out. It will be shown how there are particular modes of enquiry and modalities that are immanent in the critical pedagogic projects of both the authors. These modes of enquiry and practices, we believe, can lend themselves to a generative 'anthrogogic' reimagining of the teacher's positionality and role in the classroom as well as a restructuring of the teacher–student relation towards more liberatory outcomes.

The method being used in this chapter is a self-reflective mapping of teacher experience. We find such an approach particularly pertinent for the kind of (self-)enquiry we are developing, which is not merely about providing a set of principles or theoretical positions on how we understand the negotiation of teacher authority but a path towards reconstructing teacher embodiment and positionality. The reflective mapping and discussion will be organised around two hermeneutic frames, or what we will call 'modes of enquiry': first, the deconstruction of the teacher–student relational dynamic and second, the co-creation of knowledge. We consider both of these frames or modes to be crucial in developing an anthrogogic orientation (see Deepa, 2026 for a detailed discussion). Further, they entail a set of modalities, or critical practices, that could facilitate a transformative enquiry towards developing an anthrogogic orientation. These include practices such as co-teaching with students, dialogic feedback, modelling self-critique, and role-playing, among others. An anthrogogic orientation, we think, cannot be conceptualised as a set of prescriptive practices—instead, we imagine it to be a processual, reflective, and self-critical inquiry towards re-orienting dominant teacher–student relations.

The choice of using self-reflective anecdotes as the primary mode of inquiry is inspired by the narrative inquiry method that studies the experience of practitioners as stories, which is a way of thinking about experience and generating knowledge. Narrative enquiry is a methodology that views experience as a phenomenon under study (Connelly & Clandinin, 2006).

There is one caveat though. One may ask how the experiences of two teachers in an elite, private, liberal arts programme can be useful or instructive for teachers across institutes, especially when the degree of autonomy afforded by institutes differs widely. While we acknowledge our relative privilege in having the autonomy to shape our own curriculum and experiment with teaching methods—an opportunity not available to many higher education teachers—our interest is in putting forward a certain self-reflexive approach to analysing both teacher embodiment as well as the complexity of the teaching experience. Even if our experiential context may not be relatable to all, we hope our method of inquiry—and its associated, and hopefully not overstated, transformative promise—will find critical resonance across many different spaces.

Setting the Context

The Critical Writing course (CW) located within the curriculum of the Young India Fellowship (YIF)—a year-long, residential postgraduate diploma programme—is a unique space for experimentation with adult teaching–learning processes. The YIF draws its participants from a wide age group (21–29 years) and is a relatively more diverse community within the Ashoka University ecosystem. Students come from a wide variety of disciplines, ranging from the humanities to the sciences, from the performing arts to professional courses The CW courses are offered in smaller groups with a small class size of twenty to thirty Fellows in each group and each CW instructor has the freedom to execute the course through various themes in the social sciences and humanities, such as sociology, anthropology, literature, education, et cetera. It involves a considerable amount of innovation with genres of writing across multiple disciplines and aims at developing a metacognitive awareness of one's own reading and writing practices. Teaching writing to a group that is not only diverse in disciplinary training but also in terms of work experience makes the YIF classroom unpredictable and demanding, and a site ripe for rich conversations on the anthrogogic reimagining of the teacher–student relationship. The CW curriculum views writing as 'central to processes of knowledge acquisition, production, and consumption' and over the last eleven years, 'the programme has developed a pedagogy geared towards building critical reading, writing and thinking skills that help Fellows [participants who are enrolled in the YIF are called Fellows] engage with the world of ideas and enable them to develop and express their own ideas in a well-reasoned, lucid, and engaging manner' (Ashoka University). The fact that the participants are not primarily referred to as students or learners, but as Fellows, highlights how this academic space aims to distinguish itself.

The CW course aims to put the experiences of the Fellows to a critical examination in a collaborative class environment where critical dialogues become a way to negotiate multiple meanings and perspectives on issues ranging across a diverse spectrum—social, political, linguistic, psychological, and so on. There is an emphasis on peer learning—peers are supposed to mould, influence, lead class discussions and are also expected to contribute to critical conversations around curricular goals and materials used for the course. A process-based approach to writing is adopted which involves multiple rounds of peer review, instructor feedback, and whole-class workshops to arrive at a *final draft* for each writing assignment.[1] Also, for syllabus design, the process-based

---

[1] Process approach, unlike the product approach, does not focus on form. Instead, the emphasis is on this process by which a text is produced. Schmitt (2002) highlights that in the process approach, the act of composing is seen as recursive, explanatory, and generative. There are different stages in a process approach; however, these stages are not always linear. A typical model of process writing consists of five stages: prewriting, composing/drafting, responding/feedback, revising/editing, and evaluation.

approach is explored within a framework consisting of core curricular goals that are common for the CW course across groups. The CW course also attempts to borrow from post-process approaches by prioritising content and meaning over form and rhetorics. Therefore, each instructor designs a writing course with common curricular goals but unique content drawing from their expertise in various disciplines within the social sciences and humanities. Some of the CW courses offered by different instructors include *Anthropological Unsettlements*; *Education, Literacy and Justice*; *History and Politics of Representation of Madness in Literature and Art*; *Politics of Language and Multilingualism; Writing the City*; and *Internet Culture and Memes.*

The CW classroom is a potential space where discussions in other courses of the YIF may come together and provide the Fellows with an opportunity to make connections across the curriculum. Reflections on reading and writing practices, and classroom tasks that raise the metacognitive awareness of the Fellows, are intended to assist their learning trajectories across courses. Writing is explored within a multimodal framework where Fellows are encouraged to critique literacy practices, question hierarchies in knowledge production and dissemination, and reflect on their own choices as critical thinkers and writers within a sociocultural framework of writing. In this chapter, we will draw from the CW course that we taught over two semesters from August 2020 to April 2021 through the following themes: *Politics of Language and Multilingualism* and *Education, Literacy and Justice.* These themes have a lot of overlapping concerns, yet there are certain differences in their orientations.

The CW course on *Politics of Language and Multilingualism* focused on sub-themes such as language politics, debates around language policies and linguistic diversity. It hoped to enable participants to critically examine their role as a bi/multilingual thinker, reader and writer. The course outline stated that 'this course aims to introduce you to a range of debates around language policy, implementation, linguistic diversity and multilingualism to develop a nuanced understanding of the complex relationship between language, access to education and participation.' This theme naturally lends itself to discussions around writing and reading and how language use takes place within a complex web of sociopolitical and cultural contexts. It encouraged fellows to reflect on their biases towards languages/language users and critically examine their own educational experiences to find alternative ways to address problems within the education system stemming from linguistic considerations. The course content was used to discuss the writing genres common across all CW courses: critical summary, opinion editorials, literature review, and synthesis paper.

The CW course titled *Education, Literacy, and Justice* was framed as an introduction to critical pedagogy and critical literacy, broadly oriented towards critically mapping the relations between pedagogic praxis and socio-economic justice. The course aimed to connect macro contexts of education planning, political economy, and cultural ideology with micro structures of classroom experience, curriculum negotiation, and teaching methods. In this course, students wrote a response summary, a literacy narrative, and a research-based paper, reflecting on areas of education they wanted to probe and intervene within. The themes covered in the course included the politics of curriculum, liberatory discourses of pedagogy, ethnographies in education, alternative evaluation strategies, and social movements in education, among others. The course was oriented towards making students reflect on their educational experience, not merely to analyse the various aspects of that experience but also to orient them towards the question and agenda of reconstructive praxis. Towards that end, classroom discussions were often on what could change, and how different participants in education would need to be mobilised towards effecting changes at both a macro and micro level.

Reflections

In this section, we will present four anecdotes, titled A1, A2, A3, and A4, where both of us have reflected on aspects of our teaching experience. Each of us has written two anecdotes—A1 and A2 by Sayan, A3 and A4 by Monishita—where we have discussed constructed moments as well as 'critical incidents'[2] from our courses. While the anecdotes refer to

[2] Richards and Farrell (2010) define a critical incident as an 'unplanned and unanticipated event that occurs during a lesson and that serves to trigger insights about some aspect of teaching and learning' (p. 13). Critical incidents allow teachers to document and analyse teaching incidents in order to reflect on the long-term implications, learn from them, and improve practice. This process of documentation and reflection provides opportunity for teachers 'to learn more about their teaching, their learners and themselves' (p. 114).

specific moments or situations, we specifically chose them since they are indicative of the larger ethos of our classrooms. They sharply point out practices, orientations, and choices that are fundamental to our teaching praxis, and that we are making across classes and batches. They have been written in the first person, and in an introspective register, to provide a sense of the curiosities and confusions that marked the experience of these moments/situations.

Anecdote 1 (A1)

Unpacking Classroom Experience: Empowering Students to Critique Pedagogic Processes

One of the abiding themes in classroom discussions was to think through how everyone was thinking and feeling about our course. In the first class, I introduced the term 'hidden curriculum', and gave a few examples of how often there is a contradiction/gap between the officially-stated values of a course and what actually transpires. I deliberately used the example of how teachers might profess to believe in ideas of deliberative democracy, but the classroom practices might reproduce and sanction unequal power dynamics. Then I asked the students to keep enquiring into the hidden curriculum of our course—its contradictions, complications, and contestations. But I also felt that merely introducing these critical terms or inviting students to participate in a critical conversation on classroom practices might not be enough to shake up the normative classroom embodiments most of us have been conditioned into.

In a class where I wanted to discuss certain ideas of ethnographic research in education, I decided that we could turn a bit 'meta'. Different groups of students had to study different aspects of the classroom—how I presented my lecture, how students were behaving and responding—and then also interview me (the teacher) and a smaller group of students on their experience of the class. The subsequent discussion was an interesting one: students began to open up about why some felt distracted or passive, or why they felt certain readings did not work, not in a complaining tone as much as a reflective one. I presented some of my own reflections as a teacher: how I plan for class, how I choose my readings, how I negotiate my own sense of disappointment when students don't read for class.

In subsequent classes, there were many more conversations like these. We would identify a problem affecting either some or most members of the class—whether it is student absenteeism, or students feeling a sense of exclusion from peer groups, or how I sometimes felt thwarted as a teacher when students didn't care enough for the content—and then discuss it more analytically. I did feel vulnerable often. I wasn't always sure what this would lead towards, or how it would help simply overcome the problem we were discussing. But I would always say that I couldn't solve these problems on my own, and it would be unfair to expect the teacher to have such dynamic capacities. But it did seem to produce an awareness that we are in this together and that we must accept each other for who we are—not for who we ideally should be—and that to work towards transforming teacher–student relations, we need to do slow, reflective work. It did help that my course was on critical pedagogy, but I do think this can be done in all classrooms.

Anecdote 2 (A2)

Feedback as Dialogue: Thinking Through the Politics of Feedback

In a one-on-one session with a student, I noticed that a section of their argument was incoherently phrased. I asked the student, 'What did you try to say here, could you explain?' The student provided a little more clarity about what their intention was. The student re-read the section themselves and found it a bit awkwardly phrased and felt a bit embarrassed. I reassured them that it was no big deal and that we will work through the problem. But now I asked a different question: 'How could we phrase this section?'. I summarised their ideas; I suggested a tentative sentence template. They picked up on it and began developing the sentence. Both of us knew that we were on the right track, but it would take some work to develop the alternative phrasing. The student said that they would work on it. I continued the feedback process in a similar mode. There were moments when I sensed they were unsure or sceptical, and I asked them if they agreed with my feedback or if my language was not specific enough. There were other moments when I told them what the ideas in their paper reminded me of, and these brief tangents and associations generated some fun, and often insightful, conversation. At the end of the session, I asked them what they thought of the overall feedback, what stood out for them, and what they would want to add to it. They didn't emphasise what I thought stood out for me, and I found that difference in perspective interesting. Right before they left, I asked them if they had any other questions, and they asked me something entirely disconnected from our conversation: 'Have you read this book? I was thinking of you when I read it, you should have a look'. We concluded the session with a sense of both overlaps and differences in our thinking—the student had a set of starting points for reworking their paper and I hoped they also got the sense that it was their journey, that they didn't have to do this to please or impress me.

Anecdote 3 (A3)

Where Is My Voice?: Reclaiming the Classroom Space Through Co-teaching

One of the sub-themes of the course was language policies and politics. To explore this sub-theme, I designed a few tasks around an Economic and Political Weekly article titled *Constituent Assembly Debates on Language* authored by Professor Rama Kant Agnihotri. During class discussions, I noticed that not all voices in the classroom were represented in the interactions. Since I had administered a questionnaire at the beginning of the course to create a detailed participant profile, I knew that if the voices of the Fellows from minority-language–speaking communities went unheard, it would be an incomplete construction of knowledge in the classroom. A Fellow from the Maithili community, another from Urdu, one from Dogri and a Meitei speaker from Manipur—their opinions, understanding of the issues raised in the article, and lived experiences were central to the exploration of the theme. However, I noticed that these fellows preferred to stay quiet and not voice their opinions. I wondered if it was their choice to stay out of the conversation in overt ways or did they experience hesitation to speak against the dominant voices? That's when I decided to reach out to them during our teacher–Fellow conferencing session and understand their thoughts on the article and what kept them out of the class discussions. I was reassured that their engagement was deeper than what any class discussion could unravel. Their lived experiences gave them agency and confidence to deconstruct the arguments of the author and the contradictions and struggles of the Constituent Assembly debates played out in their lives in innumerable ways. They deployed several critical reading strategies such as text evaluation, asking questions around the text, relating personal experiences to the text, comparing arguments of the author with other authors, et cetera. They were articulate, passionate and connected with the text. However, all of them suffered from self-doubt and felt their experiences and opinions were not valuable enough to be shared with the class. I also understood that for years these students had remained silent in their classrooms probably due to the dominant classroom practices that often alienate voices that come from marginalised or minoritised communities, and yet such classrooms debate issues in caste, identity, and politics. I convinced them to become part of a team-teaching endeavour where they would be co-instructors preparing with me for class, and we planned to rehearse some of the conversations that we wanted to unfold in the classroom. After this initiation, I noticed that these participants opened up on their own in subsequent class discussions and I could safely go into the background and let them claim their space in the classroom discourse. Later, these participants recalled this moment of team teaching with the instructor as a breakthrough moment in their writing journey. They connected it with their exploration of academic voice in constructing their texts.

Anecdote 4 (A4)

Role-playing: Teachers become Students

Sayan and I wanted to explore team-teaching to learn from each other and put into conversation our varied styles of teaching. Towards the end of the semester, in December 2020, we planned a session to explore the technique of role-playing as a teaching tool in a writing classroom. The theme for discussion was peer feedback and its complex implementation in the educational context. Peer feedback was interrogated through a role play in which Sayan and I demonstrated the complexity of peer interactions where gender, personalities, varying socio-economic backgrounds of the participants, and systemic norms/structures have a subtle influence on the process of providing feedback. Sayan played the role of a 'socially superior' peer who seems to be well-read, self-aware, and dominating, and I took up a more submissive role of a self-doubting individual who is in awe of a more enabled peer. We exaggerated some of the aspects of feedback to highlight certain issues such as hierarchies in knowledge production (written versus oral texts), theory versus practice, power relations generated due to gender, class, et cetera. After we enacted the role play, we opened it up for critique and discussion. Fellows shared their insights and observations that allowed us to problematise the concept of peer feedback and arrive at some conceptions of the term in the context of a writing classroom. The Fellows identified with the characters we played; some even shared their own experiences of feeling alienated/overwhelmed while participating in peer feedback. It led to a critical conversation on institutional norms, knowledge structures, and politics of feedback. The theorisation was grounded in experiences and reflections that embraced the emotions and feelings of the participants. For me, it was a moving experience to see how the Fellows connected and empathised with the vulnerabilities of our characters. It was a difficult choice to let go of my authority as a teacher (completely) and play a character that exhibited her insecurities and powerlessness, but it was rewarding in terms of the teaching and learning process.

Discussion

The four anecdotes presented above (A1–A4) highlight practices and modes of reflective teaching that open up the possibility for an anthrogogic reimagining of the classroom. Broadly, they challenge the dominant teacher–student relational dynamic rooted in hegemonic social hierarchies and reimagine the classroom space as a site for the co-creation of knowledge. We will discuss these two themes by analysing the anecdotes through the modes of enquiry and modalities that they incorporate, to arrive at an evolving template for incorporating an anthrogogic orientation in language teaching. We define modes of inquiry as the interpretive processes that we cultivate and model to negotiate interaction and meaning-making in the classroom, such as critical reflection, demonstrating institutional norms and practices, reflective conversations, and so on. The modalities refer to the specific practices and techniques that we used to generate particular modes of enquiry—these include role-playing, dialogic feedback, co-teaching, choosing strategic content, and so on.

Deconstructing the Teacher–Student Relational Dynamic

All the four anecdotes promote the anthrogogic principle of challenging teacher–student power relations by striving towards creating a democratic space for classroom discourse. Politically, our approach borrows heavily from critical pedagogy frameworks, emphasising the need to critique the mode of teaching itself and pushing for a self-critique oriented towards institutional change (Freire, 2018; Giroux, 1988; Kincheloe, 2008). Institutional structures and practices codify the teacher–student relationship in ways such that deconstructing their relational dynamics is often difficult. It requires conscious effort on the part of the teacher to get out of their comfort zone and explore alternate practices that need constant nurturing and experimenting with ideas.

These anecdotes use reflection as their dominant mode of inquiry. Reflection that questions fundamental, taken-for-granted assumptions is critical and is both an individual as well as a collaborative process. Fook (2010) states that critical reflection allows one to question one's own socially dominant assumptions which can be restrictive, and makes way for more empowering ideas and practices, thereby triggering social change at an individual level. Fook and Askeland (2007) suggest that critical reflection needs to connect individual identity and social context. Cressey, Boud, and Docherty (2006) further argue that it can be highly productive and can help individuals to evolve as agents bringing change in their contexts. The dialogic nature of reflection allows an individual to unearth deeper assumptions, beliefs, experiences and perspectives which can all contribute to a better understanding of the teaching and learning situation.

The dominant modalities through which the deconstruction of teacher-student relationship is explored in the above anecdotes include setting up meta conversations, dialogic feedback, co-teaching with students and role-playing. Let's discuss each of these modalities in the context of deconstructing teacher–student relational dynamics.

Setting up Meta Conversations

A1 involves setting up meta conversations which requires the teacher to explicitly make their teaching practices the site of critique and inquiry to understand concepts and ideas. A meta conversation draws attention to the constructedness of a conversation, or in other words, the style and form of the conversation. By going meta, the focus is on *how* particular conversations are forged and cleaved, how the material and social conditions shape the conversation, and how the conversation has effects on its participants. A1 encourages students to observe and critique the classroom itself. The classroom becomes an object of study thereby exposing hidden power relations between the teacher and the students, and between students themselves. The use of a concept such as the 'hidden curriculum' helps build the meta conversation—the teacher is inviting the student to reorient their gaze towards the framing of classroom practices, value systems, and norms. The ethnographic impulse is strong in this reorientation—the teacher is inviting the student to be a participant-observer in a sense, to experience the classroom but also analyse it, critique it. Further, there is attention drawn to the relational aspects of the classroom experience, particularly the teacher–student relation. Rather than thinking of the teacher and the students as stable, reductive, binarised or demarcated identities, they are understood in mediation with a host of other factors—the material environment, subjective histories, social and cultural contexts, and so on. In A1, the classroom is framed as a critical text that can be deconstructed, disassembled. The classroom is read in terms of both processes which take place within it, as well as the structural and institutional conditions which produce the classroom. This exercise is helpful in questioning and reconstructing teacher–student relationship patterns and exploring alternative classroom conversations.

Dialogic Feedback

A2 demonstrates ways in which the teacher–student relationship can be shaped to share feedback in an equitable dialogic space. Students are often exposed to feedback cultures, where they may expect teachers to guide/direct/instruct them from an authoritative vantage-point. There is an element of performance in feedback too: students may intentionally or unconsciously play a more passive role in the transaction of feedback, where they obediently, uncritically accept the teacher's feedback. They may not wish to displease the teacher by challenging them, or fear consequences for disagreement, or not have the requisite vocabulary or insight to know how to demonstrate what they disagree with. The teacher, in this scenario, can play a more pre-emptive role. The teacher, in a sense, has to intuit, anticipate, suggest, or create a space for the student to critically participate in the conversation. Rather than determinately or prescriptively providing feedback, the teacher consciously invites the student into a dialogue where both are building a reflective and critical assessment of the content, writing choices, and framing of the paper. In dialogic feedback, there is an attempt to cultivate the agency of the student, partially by providing them particular tools/schemas for self-assessment and partially by reorienting the agency of the teacher. The teacher is suggestive, asking the student to think through the feedback rather than passively implement it. The student arrives at alternate framings, through the process of the conversation, rather than being handed a predetermined template.

What does the teacher gain from this exercise? Providing feedback is a process through which teachers can reflect on their own assumptions, speech styles, listening capacities, communication practices. In dialogic feedback, teachers are also receiving feedback as they ask the student to think through and respond to their feedback. Further, the teacher is also at times pursuing a more open-ended conversation, not strictly limited to the formal bounds of the paper—there are digressions and even personal anecdotes that reflect or build on tangents in the paper. This can reorient the teacher–student relation in other ways too. The student can feel more comfortable discussing their intentions and aspirations beyond the purview of merely writing an assignment. What a student is supposed to take away from the feedback conversation is more open-ended as a result; it is not determinately scripted or controlled by the teacher.

Co-teaching with Students

A3 highlights the problem of representation of student voices in classroom discourse. It argues that the voice of every participant needs to be valued and is often necessary for a holistic construction of knowledge. It inquires as to which voices get heard in the classroom and why. What is the politics of classroom discourse and how can it be made more accessible? This internal dilemma of the teacher pushed her to think of alternate ways to include students in the class discussion. Co-teaching with students was tried out as a classroom practice to address this problem of unequal representation of student voices. In adult classrooms, the teacher may feel the need to maintain their aura as an expert in domain knowledge, which undoubtedly they are. However, creating spaces where the students take control of the content and discourse can be highly rewarding. It diffuses the teacher–student hierarchy when students take up the teacher's role and experience the struggles that a teacher faces on a regular basis—planning, organising and facilitating classroom procedures. Co-teaching also allows the teacher to actively involve students in the decision-making process that shapes class discussions. Sharing authority during a classroom interaction and at the planning level also stems from the acceptance that the teacher herself may not have lived experiences of the theoretical conceptions under introspection, and therefore considers it enriching for other participants to bring those insights to question dominant narratives in the classroom.

Co-teaching with students as a strategy helps to bring their experiences, opinions and ideas about the text under discussion to mainstream classroom discourse. Planning and shared decision-making with students allows them to access the classroom space in a more equitable manner, especially students who come from marginalised/ minority backgrounds who find it even more challenging to claim their space in any classroom discourse. Co-teaching breaks the hierarchy between teacher and student and promotes democratic classroom processes. This strategy has two benefits: first, it allows otherwise shy students to claim their space in class discussions and secondly, it allows the expert teacher to shape students' perspectives about issues and make them more multiperspectival and nuanced. She does so by tapping into their experiences and helping them theorise effectively to make sense of their experiences, and analyse them in a more complex manner than look at them in simplistic and reductionist ways. The content, perspectives, and insights that they bring in, the teacher herself may not have access to. She may lack some of those lived experiences that are needed to explain conceptual frames that need sharing of experiences and subject positions that are complex. However, her role as a mediator and facilitator takes a more powerful form through co-teaching.

Role-Playing

A4 demonstrates the use of role-playing as a tool to deconstruct the relational dynamics between student and student, teacher and teacher, and even teacher and student. A role-play makes explicit the performative and behavioural aspects of a particular practice—in this case, the act of providing and exchanging feedback. Further, the sociological construction of a moment—how characters are inhabiting or performing particular 'roles' and 'identities', how they may have inherited or are reproducing particular tropes of behaviour—is made more explicit. In the role-play that we did, the power dynamic between the two characters is made palpable, not just through what they say but the gestural embodiment and non-verbal interaction of the characters. The role-play also allowed the teacher to unsettle their own vantage-point and inhabit (even if partially) the embodiment of a student. To witness the teacher as a (more vulnerable) student already inverts and complicates the default image of a teacher and allows an entry-point into questioning the power dynamics in the classroom. The questioning and subsequent analysis, however, is not a reductive one—it doesn't simply amount to saying that one character is bad, and another is good, that one is a hero and another a villain—but a layered one, where both 'authoritative' and 'passive' students/teachers are analysed in relation to their social, cultural, and psychological contexts. Further, even though the teacher may be playing the role of a student, they are inviting the students to scrutinise them too. The authoritative student has a parallel with the authoritative teacher; the teacher is asking students to critique their embodied behaviour too.

It was not an easy exercise since it involved exposing ourselves as more vulnerable, as being implicated within institutional hierarchies and power relations, but the outcomes were generative and worth the effort in planning, executing and, performing the act. Many of the students reported how they related to one or both the characters and empathised with them thereby critically reflecting on their own peer interactions. They also later reported how the role-play allowed them to theorise from practice and reflect on their prior beliefs and assumptions about peer feedback, and how they began to change their practices and develop a more analytic approach towards both imparting and receiving feedback. Seeing the teachers in students' shoes, they were able to view the classroom as a different space—a site for developing critical insights into existing structures with empathy and understanding the complex interplay of multiple factors.

Co-creation of Knowledge

Co-creation of knowledge is at the heart of the process of writing. Through writing, participants control and negotiate knowledge production and thus fully participate in situated learning (Lave and Wenger, 1991). If they fail, it may lead to a sense of isolation and, therefore, as not belonging to the social practice—this could mean the immediate class, programme or the university. Thus, we look at critical writing as a social practice that encourages participants to explore what they know, co-create knowledge in a collaborative space, and also explore who they are in a community through text production.

Through writing, knowledge is created, negotiated, debated, and new directions and insights emerge. Moreover, the text becomes a medium for sharing new insights and a means to communicate with the outside world. In the process of writing, a number of choices have to be made and these choices are crucial for knowledge production. What to include and what to leave out? What is the focus and what serves as background?

Who to cite and whom to ignore (Kamler & Thomson, 2014)? Which vocabulary and style is fit for the content, message and reader? These choices are influenced by a complex web of factors since academic genres are situated in sociocultural conditions that are historically shaped (Wegener, 2017).

A text has the power to transform its readers and trigger social change—it is a living being and not a static entity (Canagarajah 2005). Therefore, a writing classroom involves epistemological questions of knowledge and knowledge production as well as ontological questions of how we perceive reality and understand ourselves. Through the different teaching strategies employed during the course, we were constantly involved in the creative co-creation of writing practices thereby providing a space for self-growth, reflection, and self-expression.

The term co-creation, when applied to educational settings, includes ideas of teacher–student dialogue, collaborative learning, sharing a common commitment to knowledge production, and having meta-communication (Bateson 1972) to create new learning experiences and innovations in teaching. Shaw (2002) in her complexity theory sheds light on the nature of user-driven design that can be applied to teacher–student dialogue that facilitates the co-creation of knowledge. Shaw (2002) explains that honest, open, and meaningful communication is essential for generative dialogue. This type of communication captures the interest of participants and reflects a willingness to explore and improvise. The teacher listens to what students say and allows associations to emerge: 'I am describing the process of weaving in our actions one with one another to co-create the future' (Shaw, 2002, p. 70). Thus, teacher–student dialogues not only lead to understanding each other's preconceptions but also lead to the co-creation of new ideas. The teacher in the form of a facilitator encourages meaningful dialogues in the classroom that allow different views, conflicts, and voices to co-exist with awareness and critical negotiation. For co-creation of knowledge to occur in the classroom, the teachers and the students need to be open to a learning experience that questions the conventional sense of authority in the classroom. Teachers need to let go of fixed agendas and lesson plans and instead lead conversations that help students articulate issues and themes as they emerge, and participate genuinely in the expression of ideas thereby co-creating knowledge.

This theme of co-creation of knowledge emerges powerfully in the reflective anecdotes. By knowledge, we mean both the discursive and interpretive understanding of the readings/materials used in the course or what would be conventionally classified as critical domain knowledge, but we are also referring to a more expanded understanding of the social, emotional, and material conditions within which the domain knowledge is produced and constructed. In other words, the discovery and unpacking of the knowledge of writing practices, the social and emotional dynamics of classroom experience, and institutional politics, become as important as the specific domain knowledge—the student and the teacher are participating in a joint exercise to uncover both the form and content of their educational experience. This entails comprehending and developing conceptual vocabularies to facilitate such an exercise. It is, of course, interesting to note that the same concept (for example, the use of 'hidden curriculum' in A1 or 'minority language community' in A3) often helps enquire into both a critical awareness of the domain (in this case, education and sociolinguistics) as well as classroom dynamics. This, in a way, is an enactment of a critical teaching praxis—it helps generate awareness of the conditions of knowledge production, to build an agentive capacity for transforming and expanding knowledge. The teacher–student relation is inevitably interrogated in such an exercise. The teacher—by foregrounding their intermediary and self-interrogative, rather than determinate and authoritative, self-status in generating knowledge—invites the students into a collective enquiry for the transformation of knowledge production. The students, meanwhile, are encouraged to inhabit a participatory, agentive, and generative mode of learning and thinking. The ethic of collective transformation—in terms of the meaningful implementation of content-learning, the growing awareness of the socio-emotional dynamics shaping human interactions in the classroom, and the expansion of knowledge from discursive to affective, sociocultural and behavioural domains—provides the justification for why everyone is engaging in this collective exercise, why everyone is 'in it together', so to speak.

The modalities used to carry out such an exercise include the strategic choosing of content (in the form of readings, videos, presentations), the use of reflective tasks and assignments to interactively frame the content as well as facilitate directions of enquiry, and the conscious modelling of critical, introspective self-reflection by the teacher. We will briefly comment on each modality, in terms of the techniques and practices used as well as the mode of enquiry it generated. We will also point out certain limitations and tensions marking each of these modalities.

Choosing Content

In A1 and A3, the choice of content is deliberate. To facilitate a methodological understanding of how an ethnographic study happens as well as establish the context of teacher reform, Sayan chose a particular reading. The reading immediately helped develop a particular vocabulary: for example, the idea of how teachers are 'repositioning' themselves vis-á-vis child-centred frames of teaching, or how the role of the teacher has been dominantly framed through the imaginary of the adult–child relation. Similarly, Monishita chose a reading to foreground the idea of power dynamics within and between 'language communities' that play out in policy-making processes. The concept of the language community is powerful, since it helped frame a discussion on both experiential processes (the experience of speaking particular languages in particular sociocultural contexts) as well as structural norms mediating such processes (the institutional definitions and delimitations of language communities). The content chosen in both A1 and A3, attempted to facilitate an application of the concept while encouraging analytic abstraction. The student as well as the teacher were encouraged to make sense of their experience through the reading, but also think of how their individual experience is organised and mediated through structural forces. This back-and-forth between experiential and structural enquiry—or more specifically, to think of the mediations between experience and social structures—was particularly productive for interrogating teacher–student relationality.

However, it cannot be assumed that the content will necessarily anticipate the desired form of enquiry—that requires a particular mediation through assignments and tasks, which we will describe in the next section. Further, the content chosen in A1 and A3 are perhaps more suited to such an interrogative exercise since they have been chosen from the domain of education and sociolinguistics—domains that easily lend themselves to experiential reflection. It may be more challenging to think of how domains such as theoretical syntax or computational linguistics can facilitate similar forms of enquiry.

Designing Tasks and Assignments

In A4, the role-play was centrally used to facilitate a sensory as well as discursive interpretation of both the mechanics and politics of feedback. The role-play, however, was consciously contextualised within the discussion of both theoretical and experiential content. In preparation for this class, Monishita and Sayan designed three exercises. First, an experience-sharing exercise where everyone was encouraged to share an anecdote about how they have experienced evaluation in a formal or non-formal setting. This was followed by brief presentations by Monishita and Sayan to provide the conceptual and technical vocabulary to think through evaluative procedures and cultures (for example, norm-based versus criterion-based evaluation, power dynamics in feedback, and so on). Then the role-play was enacted, where students would think and reflect using some of these conceptual categories, along with categories or parameters they found relevant or pertinent. Finally, students were encouraged to reconstruct and personally contextualise the broad interpretation of the role-play by writing about what they would prioritise in their own feedback of other's writing. Feedbacking was presented as an essential mode of generating knowledge about what they were learning, especially since students were expected to provide feedback on each other's main assignments and also informally help each other out in (re)drafting assignments for the course. The choice of the task here was to help build critical agency in learning to effectively feedback, and to learn to critique how teachers provided informal and formal feedback. This, in turn, became a self-interrogative exercise for the teachers. They were encouraged to unpack their own assumptions, approaches, and motives in providing feedback (or for that matter, grading assignments).

Further, this task consciously chose a 'representative' example based on an enquiry into how students may have previously experienced feedback or how they assume dominant feedback cultures to be. While the task did entail a degree of binarisation of the roles of those providing and receiving feedback, it did imply the kinds of implicit or explicit power hierarchies usually undergirding the relation between a socially and institutionally sanctioned authoritative subject and a socially and institutionally neglected/disfavoured subject. This principle was used across tasks and assignments. The choice of a representative example, or a situation/context that both the teacher and students could relate to or have a lived experiential access to, was supposed to facilitate the enquiry of the mediation between experiential contextualisation and abstraction, theoretical understanding and practical implementation.

However, this exercise can also lead to a rather complicated negotiation of power and authority for the teacher. By willingly choosing to deconstruct their ideology and practice, they have to contend with their own blind spots, insufficiencies, and inconsistencies. This can be seen as a transformative process for the teacher as well as for the teaching–learning process, but can also be destabilising and painfully vulnerable. The teacher has to also put in a greater degree of labour to fine-tune and connect different tasks within a single class as well as across classes. There is a risk of glorifying this excess labour keeping in mind the material precarities and justifiable limitations of cognitive–emotional capacities amongst teachers. Not all teachers across institutional settings can afford to partake in, or are supported in, the exercise of this labour. Further, it is important to keep in mind that students may occasionally approach an assignment insincerely, half-heartedly, or even cynically, despite the transformative promise of it. This is not a fault of the task itself, but how students may be dominantly conditioned and oriented owing to a series of institutional experiences—an assignment is meant to be 'hacked', or 'winged' at the last minute, not meaningfully engaged with. In the YIF, for example, students had to navigate a high assignment load across courses. This would sometimes exhaust them and diminish their engagement, even in an immersive course like Critical Writing, despite their positive intentions and willingness to engage. While exercises (such as the role-play) can generate an honest conversation on how students may wish to avoid or overcome a functional, cynical, or de-motivated attitude towards assignments, the problem may not be overcome without larger shifts in institutional culture and educational conditioning.

Modelling Self-Critique

In A1 and A4, the teacher was presented as a subject to be examined and interrogated. In A2, the teacher displaced themselves from the position of an authoritative subject imparting knowledge, to a more tentative, reflective, and to some extent, uncertain subject, curiously figuring out what knowledge to impart. In A3, the teacher was repositioning themselves as a co-curator of the classroom, inviting students to collaborate and re-orient the content of teaching as well as the controlling role of the teacher in determining content. In each of these scenarios, the modelling of self-critique became a necessary conduit to re-orienting the role of the teacher. We call this a modelling to draw attention to its intentional constructedness. The self-critique is not being presented spontaneously, randomly, abruptly; instead, it is a particular template of conversation that the teacher reinforces and demonstrates. The ethic of doing such an exercise is also reinforced—that it is important to narrativise self-critique towards transformative ends.

The teacher is consciously and explicitly articulating their own limitations and contradictions in a non-defensive yet analytic language. This is not about the teacher trying to be humble or ironic or self-deprecatory or caring in a predetermined way, but the teacher cultivating a disposition where they contemplatively arrive at what they want or need to be. Further, this modelling provides students both an ethic as well as a framework to think through their own experiences, positionality, and relations with others within the educational setting. Students are encouraged to frame their experiences in an analytic language, to move beyond a mere admission or rant or confession towards a complex critique of one's choice, disposition, behaviour, and identity.

This modelling, as A4 points out, entails a certain negotiation with one's own vulnerability. While the expression of vulnerability can provide a powerful conduit to rethink power relations and open the teacher to critique, it can also feel like a dissonant task for the teacher since the institutional identity of the teacher derives its authority and legitimacy from its hierarchical demarcation from the identity of the student. Further, in choosing to share classroom space with a colleague and inviting students to examine our relational dynamics (albeit within a role-play), we are also opening the risk of immediate comparison. The teacher is meant to be taken seriously, respected, and deferred to. To humanise the teacher, to expose them as flawed and limited and vulnerable, to consciously open them up for comparison with other teachers, might make them more accessible to the student but also breaks their institutional and intellectual aura and can also lead to the anxiety that students may not take them as seriously anymore. In the context of the YIF, this was an anxiety that we had to sometimes grapple with—the fact that students could demand a lot more of our time and make more claims on us because now the teacher is akin to a 'friend'. We hesitate from taking a simple position on this situation. While it is liberatory to develop emotionally honest relationships between teachers and students, it is also fraught with tensions that cannot be easily resolved. Often it takes a particular kind of personality, with critical emotional support from other quarters in life (family, friendships, having like-minded colleagues) to be able to sustainably carry out such vulnerable self-critique. However, the promise of such an exercise must be acknowledged—it can be deeply transformative for both teachers and students.

Conclusion

In this chapter, we have attempted to demonstrate an approach towards analytically working through and reimagining the teacher's positionality as well as the teacher–student relationship in a higher educational space. Although our context and nature of the course content highly facilitated such an introspection and experimentation, we hope that our approach can lend itself to different contexts and make the conscious repositioning of teacher authority possible, especially if the teacher is open to critical reflection and embraces fresh perspectives on their own teaching practices. We have highlighted modalities that could be used and adapted to mobilise such an approach. This, as we have shown, requires a self-critical yet delicate negotiation with notions of authority embedded within dominant 'pedagogic' practices. This, in turn, opens the possibility of an anthrogogic orientation—an orientation aimed at deconstructing and reworking dominant pedagogic relations and processes—that can facilitate a generative and self-reflexive praxis for both teachers and students.

References

Agnihotri, R. K. (2015). Constituent Assembly debates on language. *Economic & Political Weekly, 50*(8), 47–56.

Ashoka University. (2024). *Critical writing—Inquiry and expression.* Ashoka University: Young India Fellowship. https://www.ashoka.edu.in/yif-critical-writing/.

Bateson, G. (1972). *Steps to an ecology of mind.* Chandler Publications.

Canagarajah, S. (2005). Understanding critical writing. In H. Luria, D. M. Seymour, & T. Smoke (Eds.), *Language and linguistics in context* (pp. 307–314). Routledge.

Connelly, F. M., & Clandinin, D. J. (2006). Narrative inquiry. In J. L. Green, G. Camilli, & P. B. Elmore (Eds.), *Handbook of complementary methods in education research* (pp. 477–487). Lawrence Erlbaum Associates Publishers.

Cressey, D, Boud, P., & Docherty, P. (2006). *Productive reflection at work.* Routledge.

Deepa, S. (2026). Principles of anthrogogic language education. In S. Deepa & G. Durairajan (Eds.), *Anthrogogy in use: A handbook for language educators* (pp. 3–26). Orient BlackSwan.

Dewey, J. (1916). *Democracy and education: An introduction to the philosophy of education*. Macmillan.

Freire, Paulo. (2018). *Pedagogy of the oppressed* (Myra Bergman Ramos, Trans). Bloomsbury Academic.

Fook, J. (2010). Beyond reflective practice: Reworking the 'critical' in critical reflection. In Helen Bradbury, Nick Froast, Sue Kilminster and Miriam Zukas, *Beyond reflective practice*. Routledge.

Fook, J., & Askeland, G. (2007). Challenges of critical reflection: 'Nothing ventured, nothing gained'. *Social Work Education*, *26*(5), 520–533.

Giroux, Henry. (1988). *Teachers as intellectuals: Towards a critical pedagogy of learning*. Bergin and Garvey.

Kamler, B., & Thomson, P. (2014). *Helping doctoral students write: Pedagogies for supervision*. Routledge.

Kincheloe, Joe L. (2008). *Critical pedagogy*. Peter Lang.

Lave, J., & Wenger, E. (1991). *Situated learning: Legitimate peripheral participation: Learning in doing: social, cognitive, and computational perspectives*. Cambridge University Press.

Richards, J. C., & Farrell, T. S. C. (2010). *Professional development for language teachers*. Cambridge University Press.

Sarangapani, P. (2003). *Constructing school knowledge: An ethnography of learning in an Indian village*. SAGE Publications.

Schmitt, N. (Ed.). (2002). *An Introduction to Applied Linguistics*. Arnold & Oxford University Press.

Shaw, P. (2002). *Changing conversations in organisations: A complexity approach to change*. Routledge.

Sriprakash, A. (2011). Being a teacher in contexts of change: Education reform and the repositioning of teachers' work in India. *Contemporary Education Dialogue*, *8*(1), 5–31.

Thomson, P., & Kamler, B. (2010). It's been said before and we'll say it again-research is writing. In P. Thomson, & M. Walker (Eds.), *The Routledge doctoral student's companion: Getting to grips with research in education and social sciences* (pp. 149–160). Routledge.

Wegener, C. (2017). Co-creating the joy of writing: Creative analytical writing practices. In Tatiana Chemi and Lone Krogh (Eds.), *Co-creation in higher education* (pp. 117–130). Sense Publishers.

6

Anthrogogicity and Learner Agency in Academic Writing

Deepesh Chandrasekharan and Sajida Sultana

Rethinking Higher Education Practices

A quick survey of existing academic institutions of higher education in India indicates that academia and its institutional structures are steeped in colonial practices and regulations. The democratic ideals that are politically sought after outside academia seem to be largely absent inside it, and its rigid structures are extremely difficult to dismantle. For this chapter, we have classified all Indian higher-education institutions (HEIs) broadly into three categories in order to present the nature of the university and the space for academic freedom allowed at various HEIs. This classification is based on the autonomy they have from outside institutions or regulatory bodies. While a few central universities and institutes of national importance, such as the Indian Institutes of Technology (IITs) and Indian Institutes of Management (all primarily funded and run by the Union Government of India), used to enjoy reasonable autonomy with some of them having had proud histories of innovation and readiness to adapt to bottom-up change without losing sight of academic rigour, even these institutions have lately faced an onslaught of top-down regulations preventing them from acting democratically. These make up the first category. The second category is a set of elite, private or semi-government institutions that run predominantly on student tuition fees and are relatively free from outside interference and regulations except for the bare minimum. These well-funded HEIs are, however, primarily driven by rankings and ratings that are often determined by regulatory bodies which then leaves little scope for free academic work and minimal supervisory practices. The third set of institutions are resource-crunched private institutions that charge relatively low fees, pay very low salaries to faculty and staff, and are the least open to democratic practices in both academic administration as well as the teaching–learning process.

How academic writing is undertaken is different in each of these three types of institutions. Many studies (Cumming, 2006; Graff & Birkenstein, 2007) have identified the role of the English language in a university setting and the importance of including academic writing as a course for college/university level students. The necessity of a course in academic writing emerges from the gaps in the needs of the students who are part of the academic community and the requirements that the institution has from these students. In NEP 2020 (section 15.9.), we see that institutions are encouraged to offer credit-based courses in improving the writing skills of researchers: 'All fresh Ph.D. entrants, irrespective of discipline, will be required to take credit-based courses in teaching/education/pedagogy/writing related to their chosen PhD subject during their doctoral training period' (p. 43). This reflects that there are now institutional requirements to ensure that when a student graduates they need to show 'high' reading and writing skills in order to reflect the 'high standards' of the university, thereby leading to a 'template driven' approach to language teaching. It can be argued that British colonialism, with its long hold over academic institutions, is responsible for creating the current situation regarding academic writing in HEIs.

Colonial Hangover in Academic Writing Practices and Regulations

Scholars have referred to modern academic writing practices—in their tendency to 'maintain sterility'—as failing to capture the essence of aspects of identity: 'Where do the non-words get translated into words in our writing process?' ask Guttorm, et. al (2021, p. 114). In this section, we try to understand the ways in which academic writing practices continue to maintain colonial practices with a control-oriented flavour, and, in the process, restrict students/writers from going beyond the scope of well-defined boundaries.

Academic writing is a term we use broadly to encompass all writing that students and faculty in tertiary-level academic institutions use to describe and report their learning and research activities. This typically includes term papers, dissertations, theses, journal articles, and chapters in books. While there prevails an unwritten philosophy of 'publish or perish' in academia, and faculty and students are rewarded for publications in reputed journals, how the process takes place works differently in different institutions.

There is an overarching tendency to follow a routine procedure, which seems like a to-do checklist both for the process of research as well as in reporting the findings in a paper or article. With the assistance of technology in writing, we see that for any writing—whether collaborative or individual in nature—there is a list of items given to the author(s) that are considered necessary to be complied with for academic writing. These include writing the introduction, literature review, methodology, results and discussion sections of the article; including properly formatted citations and references; and similar items.

What we find from such instances is that there are fixed templates for writing which are built over the years through various forces—top-down institutional policies in HEIs that regulate how theses, dissertations, project reports, and similar academic documents have to be written; style manuals of journals and other such powerful spaces which house a lot of academic writing; and even individual teachers who are themselves trained by teachers who adhere to these institutional and journal style guidelines and requirements, and are unwilling to leave any scope for creativity in these aspects.

As part of academic career growth, researchers and faculty engage in intellectual discourse by publishing in various journals. These publishing houses invite papers on specific themes where we see that the content must conform to certain rules, such as the use of the 'correct' font size and using bold/italics to distinguish between various texts presented. Appropriate capitalisation and proper use of 'foreign' vocabulary are given as much (if not more) importance as the original ideas of the researcher/author. These ideas remind us of what several scholars have decried as prescriptivism (Pullum, 2004) and verbal hygiene practices (Cameron, 1995).

This situation is further complicated by the colonial tendency of language gatekeeping prevalent among the authorities in Indian academia where the slightest use of Indian languages or Indianisms is frowned upon, to the extent that a sense of shame is cultivated amongst Indian postgraduate students and research scholars in the use of Indian languages or language expressions in their academic writing, even if there is a somewhat greater tolerance for such use in any literary work.

Regulatory bodies like the University Grants Commission (UGC), accrediting agencies such as the National Assessment and Accreditation Council (NAAC) and the National Board of Accreditation (NBA), as well as ranking methodologies adopted by popular ranking bodies such as the National Institutional Ranking Framework (NIRF) for example, all perpetuate a standard model of research and writing that is widely acceptable and ruffles no feathers. To be divergent or creative in this field is close to impossible.

Scholars (Ajil & Blount-Hill, 2020, for example) are beginning to focus on decolonising the process of thought that goes into the process of academic writing as well:

> As the academic universe becomes increasingly diverse, we are witnessing the emergence of critical perspectives from the inside that challenge largely Eurocentric and hegemonic dynamics in the system of knowledge production. Decolonial perspectives have recently entered academic debates, calling for epistemological decolonization, including critical engagement with the heritage of White Anglo-European hegemonic thinking ... An important aspect of decolonization focuses on the inclusion of voices from the periphery and the Global South, and the decentralization and "indigenization" of knowledge production, merging with calls for "minority perspectives". (pp. 84–85)

In our experience and in discussions with various faculty across institutions, we have found that universities and colleges are very conservative when it comes to modifying the application of a template for academic writing artifacts such as theses. There is, however, an increasing groundswell for the inclusion of decolonial perspectives as well as indigenous processes in the act of writing in academic contexts. Added to this is the idea that at the tertiary level of education, the students are adults and can (and should) no longer be treated as children who have to be moulded into doing things in particular ways.

The Pedagogic Nature of Academic Writing, Teaching, and Guidance

HEIs not only use rigid rules and regulations for all longer pieces of writing for evaluation, such as dissertations and theses, the teachers tend to use practices that can be termed as pedagogic in nature to enforce writing practices among adults. We agree with Deepa's argument (2026, 2022a, 2022b) that the term 'pedagogy' fails to capture the essential difference in the teaching/enabling that happens/should happen in HEIs (that teach adults) from the teaching of children that happens in schools. Adults, by way of their own experiences in life, bring a lot of world- and word-knowledge (especially so in plurilingual India) and are also more pragmatic and goal-oriented than children, thus making them more responsive to problem-solving and self-directed tasks. Like her, we prefer to use the term 'anthrogogy' (and not pedagogy) to refer to the enabling of learning that happens (or should happen) at HEIs.

The term 'pedagogy' is so deeply ingrained in the system that it often goes unnoticed. For example, it is likely that you, as readers, missed reading the term 'pedagogy' as problematic in the line 'will be required to take credit-based courses in teaching/education/pedagogy/writing related to their chosen PhD subject' quoted above from the NEP 2020. Several private or semi-government universities follow a process of revising their syllabus to incorporate new courses or review existing courses, and this is a good practice. During this process, the faculty members are required to submit proposed revisions to the courses via an institutional format or template. Along with sections titled 'Unit Description' and so on, is a section that is usually called 'Pedagogy' to refer to the teaching methodology or approach employed by the teacher. Such nomenclature is problematic as the terms we choose to use influence how we conceptualise teaching and, as a result, the nature of teaching that takes place. Through our chapter, we propose that the term to be used in institutional documents be 'teaching style', for example, instead of pedagogy in order to consider the fact that the learners are adults who bring a significant level of agency to the learning environment.

To look at the aspect of learner agency in greater detail, we reached out to respondents who are (or recently were) research students. Agency seemed to be missing for the adult research scholars even in aspects such as the selection of a research supervisor in several of the institutions where our respondents are/were doing their research.[1]

[1] Respondents ranged from those who completed their PhD recently to those who are nearing completion. Most of them belonged to the English and Foreign Languages University, Hyderabad where both the chapter-authors completed their PhDs from. The other respondents were/are from different Indian universities including a few central universities, a state private university, and private colleges affiliated to state universities, including a few aided ones. All the respondents agreed to have their information shared but most of them requested anonymity. Hence, while maintaining anonymity, we have avoided dehumanising them by labelling their responses with numbers or alphanumeric codes, and have chosen to paraphrase them or merely quote them anonymously.

Going back to the three categories of institutions referred to earlier, it was clear that the more autonomous an institution is from government or regulatory control, the more likely that the learners in the institutions felt a sense of agency. We therefore suggest that institutions must aim to build a culture that encourages such agency.

As for the question whether they would call their research supervisor-led or researcher-led, many respondents actually felt that the research was supervisor-led. If we consider the fact that this is the reality in an anthrogogic context, this should not be the norm. Additionally, many respondents admitted that their research supervisor actually asked them to include the latter's names in published papers as co-authors. Irrespective of whether this was a valid request or not, the fact that the supervisor felt the need to ask the 'supervisee' to add their names as co-authors comes across as a sign of pedagogic transaction in an anthrogogic context. To be fair to a few of the supervisors, who were also our respondents, that any research paper published during the research process includes the research supervisor as co-author was an institutional requirement (including in some of the authors' present or earlier affiliating institutions). Some of the other supervisors chose the co-author status since, 'we worked together on every aspect of the paper. Moreover, we had a lot of discussions throughout the production process'.

As for the question of the approach used by their supervisor, many respondents seemed to be reconciled to the way in which the supervisor guided or helped them in their research, but some of them expressed disappointment. One of them said, 'There are times when you just don't understand what your supervisor tells you. No matter how crystal clear it may seem. All this can be avoided if the supervisor is less intimidating and let's (sic) the scholar communicate without any hesitations'. In contrast, there are respondents who report that their supervisors are responsive, empathetic, and encouraging. Some respondents, for example, said that their supervisor '(M)aintained open lines of communication'; were 'approachable, and responsive … encouraged discussions, asked probing questions, and listened to ideas and concerns'; 'worked collaboratively to define research goals, establish milestones, and develop a timeline'; 'encouraged autonomy and was mindful of work-life balance and well-being'; was 'respectful towards his PhD students', et cetera. Such responses are clear indications that where it does not exist, there is a dire need for the anthrogogic (and not the pedagogic) spirit in PhD guidance. It is amply clear to us that an agency-enabling environment is not only a prerequisite for anthrogogic contexts, but it also nurtures better possibilities for academic excellence and better research outcomes.

We have had close friends who got their supervisor changed or even gave up their PhD owing to the rigidity of the supervisor who followed the usual top-down approach with little scope to take into account the learner's agency. Respondents who had changed their supervisor cited problems such as, 'Lack of expertise in the area', '*usage of insensitive language in classes*', and 'lack of guidance and feedback on drafts and write-ups' (emphasis ours). One of the supervisors who had 'taken up' a researcher from a colleague, while enumerating reasons for the change, said, 'One of the scholars (not willing to mention names) came to me with a very bad experience with (his/her) previous supervisor. The scholar was not offered decent treatment, and academic/research-based discussions were not entertained by the previous supervisor'. An anthrogogic approach, in our view, would not have led to such unfortunate instances.

In a project that is high-stakes—as it is make-or-break in many ways—it is imperative that the researcher-learner feels involved and responsible enough throughout the process. At the least, as a researcher suggested, 'A blend of both research supervisor-led approach and research student focused approach would be effective'. In discussions following the initial responses, we noticed that a democratic/humane approach displayed by the supervisor could have helped sort things out better. Supervisors in most HEIs typically tend to be invested with immense power and tend to (mis)use this disproportionate power to control most aspects of research without being sensitive to the researcher's abilities, needs, and personal choices. There are ample instances of PhD students being asked (against their wish) to teach, evaluate students and invigilate tests and exams, all normal academic duties of the supervisor. There is ample anecdotal evidence available of other oppressive practices of research supervisors in HEIs. Research scholars are forced to ghostwrite for others who are not capable enough to write (or contribute to) papers but must publish articles before submitting their PhDs. Research scholars have complained of even having to do household chores for their research supervisors, and having to host lavish treats and parties for academic benefits. All this stems from the fact that the research scholar lacks agency. We argue that this situation can be avoided by using an anthrogogic approach.

As far as academic writing is concerned, even the empathetic teacher-supervisor may tend to err on the side of caution when it comes to following academic conventions/rules/styles. One of us (Deepesh), for example, faced a few difficulties while drafting their PhD thesis because the supervisor—who could otherwise be described as an empath—insisted on avoiding the first-person pronoun in the thesis chapters, arguing that the PhD thesis is expected to be a somewhat impersonal, objective text. [2] The supervisor's anxieties also stemmed from the fact that the thesis is primarily evaluated by an external examiner who may not subscribe to the objectives of using the first-person pronoun for the purpose of 'taking ownership and responsibility' for the writing. The ensuing struggle between the researcher and the supervisor luckily ended with the latter suggesting that a footnote be included at the first instance of use of the pronoun, clarifying the purpose and intention clearly. As was expected, the PhD examiner (thesis evaluator) took this up at the viva-voce, and the examinee and the supervisor were able to defend the use of the first-person pronoun in the text. Our argument is that even in contexts where the supervisor is 'benevolent' or 'empathetic', there is a need for a dialectical process—taking into account the adult learner's views or voice—before reaching a conclusion on what expressions and tone to use in academic writing. In the said thesis, the author's intention of using the first-person pronoun comes across in its use throughout most chapters of the thesis, and through the use of the footnote at the beginning.

The Way Forward

Since all writing, including academic writing, carries the voice of the author, it must be seen as a way to build a learner's identity, as a writer, an academic, and a scholar. It may be argued that developing an identity is an internal activity, but we also need to understand that when students in college or university write, their writerly identity, their world, their ideas, their experiences are (and must be) visible in their work. To help learners achieve greater agency, a probable way forward would be to build an egalitarian teacher–learner relationship.

---

[2] The research supervisor, Professor Geetha Durairajan, has evolved from that position, as is obvious from the fact that she is one of the editors of this book on anthrogogicity.

The concept of learner agency has been defined in multiple contexts. In a broad sense, Ahearn (2010) defines agency as 'the socio-culturally mediated capacity to act' (p. 28) where there is an influence of cultural, linguistic, and social aspects of human actions, beliefs, and intentions. Writing about language learner agency Mercer (2012) states, 'Viewing agency holistically also implies considering it as temporally situated connecting together the dynamics of a person's ongoing life history including their past and present experiences as well as their future goals, expectations and imaginations' (p. 57).

One of the ways in which we can promote learner agency in anthrogogic contexts and ensure the decolonising of academic writing, we argue, is to provide tasks that focus on making students reflect on the role of English and their other languages in their lives, and how the present course that they are enrolled in requires them to learn something new that they have/have not experienced earlier. Such tasks can be given after a brief discussion of the course overview so that the students know what exactly they need to reflect on. Keeping in mind this significance of learner agency in the context of multilingual India, we draw attention to the following responses of a few of our students:

> *Response 1*: 'I started my education at a government school with the medium of instruction as my mother tongue, Malayalam. Till my higher secondary school, I used to write my answers in Malayalam. I still remember how we started learning English pronunciation in the third standard. We used to write the Malayalam words instead of understanding this language.' (PhD Scholar)
>
> *Response 2*: 'My first exposure to English was when I enrolled in an English-Medium School in Guwahati. English was used as the medium of instruction. However, as a 5-year-old child, I was not at ease with the language. I could read the language effortlessly, but it took some effort to phrase a sentence in English that I could easily phrase in Assamese. It wasn't until sixth grade that I began to feel comfortable with the language.' (PhD Scholar)
>
> *Response 3*: 'My first experience to come in contact with English language was at primary school in the class 5th when one subject was basic English and I first learned to write and pronounce English alphabets for about a month. The medium of instruction my village school was completely Marathi, hence we were learning English seeking full support of Marathi.' (MA Student)

These responses give the teacher/instructor a brief idea of the past experiences and challenges that the learners have had in learning the English language. They also help the teacher/instructor become aware of the struggles her learners have faced while writing in the past, including dealing with English in an already richly-multilingual context. A teacher/instructor may use these samples of writing to steer her teaching style to address the university's language requirements. Instead of using the typical mindset of the West, where migrant languages are commonly perceived as roadblocks in learning English, learners can be asked to celebrate the rich repertoire of languages and linguistic expressions they have, and to delve into this repository suitably, even in academic writing. For example, knowing that the learners have spent their schooling in the first language, the teacher/instructor could encourage them to use high-quality texts from their first language to gain more clarity on the concepts discussed in their programme of study (MA or PhD). Once the learner understands the concepts, the responsibility of a language teacher/instructor would be to see that the learner has expressed her ideas clearly in the assignment. This places equal responsibility on the learner as well as the teacher/instructor in the learning process, thereby enabling learner agency.

> *Response 1*: 'I completed my schooling with good marks, and for my Bachelor's degree, I moved to another city which is Trivandrum. From my college days, only I started writing in English for every subject . . . the Covid thing happened, and I spent two years in my home town, and during that time, the use of English was minimal.' (PhD Scholar)

> *Response 2*: 'When I was young, I was not very fond of English songs or movies but now I enjoy listening to an English song or watching an English movie without a subtitle. I have always attended English-medium schools and colleges. Even in the workplace, English is used as an official language. And I am very much comfortable using it as my primary language. At home or with friends although I would like to communicate in Assamese or Hindi, inadvertently I end up speaking one or two sentences in English.' (PhD Scholar)

Considering that the learners are adults with fluency in more than one language, the memories that a learner brings to class about their first experience with the English language would help a teacher/instructor understand the relationship that the adult learner has been maintaining between/among the home/first language(s) and the English language.

In some cases, university students come back to pursue education after a break from their academics. In such scenarios, a reflection on their English language learning makes the learners pay greater attention to their actual linguistic achievements. The teacher/instructor needs to then think of providing ways to help students speak their ideas, and this may, in a way, also relate to an individual's personality. Building on ideas presented by Larsen-Freeman (2019), in the case of adult learners we suggest that, to sustain learner agency, the teacher/instructor needs to be open to the idea of transformation in teaching practices for adult learners so as to allow learners to create their own style of writing in the areas of academic tasks. The way we understand it, language is not a closed system and teachers/instructors need to provide space to adult learners to be agents in the creation and presentation of ideas.

While teaching adult learners, if the teacher gets a thorough understanding of the sociocultural background of the learner through a learner-description of their journey of learning English at school/college/home and how they use it, it will go a long way in building possibilities for giving learners more agency in their learning or research process. The responses from students reveal quite a lot of information for a teacher to organise her sessions, and more importantly, understand the factors that resulted in the way a student performs or why they are facing issues in language or in conveying their ideas.

The imbalances in the power held by certain groups of adult learners also result in the denial of access to these resources for learners from marginalised backgrounds. As a teacher of adult learners, the teacher needs to keep in mind the agency that each learner brings to the learning process, and each learner's agency needs to be recognised. Even as we emphasise the agency of the learner and the creative freedom with which they need to be able to express their agency in their writing, the learners must be oriented towards taking responsibility for any consequence that the employment of creative freedom may have. This, in our opinion, is as important as the emphasis on learner agency. While the onus of allowing for and giving space to learner agency may lie with the teacher, the adult learner has the responsibility of taking charge of their authorial identity.

All in all, the supervisor or teacher needs to apply the principles of anthrogogy to avoid any problems that their supervisee-researchers may face during the research process. Following Deepa's enumeration of the principles of anthrogogy (Deepa, 2026) based on Knowles, et al.

(2015), we recommend that teachers in anthrogogic contexts follow these broad guidelines:

1. The nature of learning is based on knowledge co-creation with large interpretative spaces.
2. The learner plays the role of an independent, thinking individual as the teacher's equal.
3. The nature of teaching is based on problem-solving and co-creating knowledge.
4. The role of the teacher is to co-travel and not impose.
5. The nature of the syllabus is 'negotiated, spherical and emergent'.
6. Teaching materials are negotiated with the learners.
7. Teachers and learners share the responsibility to create an ambience for learning.
8. The world is the learning space (and not merely the classroom), and attendance and timetables are not seen as restrictions but merely as guidance-points or conveniences.
9. Classroom talk is mutually respectful, full of open-minded discussions and enabling.
10. Individual learners decide the group dynamics, with the choice of individual-, pair- or group work based on personal choice.
11. Assessment is open-source, project-based, autonomous, and flexible.

Teachers in anthrogogic contexts need to be empathetic to the world of adult learners and negotiate the learning process based on the individual language requirements of the learners, by following democratic practices. Following anthrogogic principles and aspects of decoloniality, we recommend that PhD supervisors shun any know-it-all attitude portraying themselves as custodians of knowledge and power, and embrace a more inclusive role of a guide and mentor, someone who may merely have a better grasp of the workings of the academic world. In this context, the supervisor and the adult supervisee can build a partnership of equals and, as collaborators, they can negotiate the ideas that need to be sharpened and researched in a better way, including the language employed for writing the PhD thesis. Through this chapter, we reiterate that each adult supervisee can push the envelope of academic writing, even if it is one divergence at a time, by applying their own rationale in negotiation with the supervisor in a spirit of collaboration and academic freedom. It is only then that we can imagine the richly creative use of language to capture much-needed and well-researched ideas that are unencumbered by rigid, arbitrary, and arguably pedantic rules of spelling, punctuation, convention, and grammar.

As for our recommendations for HEIs, the greater the autonomy in the teaching–learning and research processes, the greater the scope for academic success and creative solutions to existing problems. This, we argue, is the true objective of research in these institutions.

References

Ahearn, L. (2001). Language and agency. *Annual Review of Anthropology, 30*(1), 109–137. https://doi.org/10.1146/annurev.anthro.30.1.109.

Ajil, A., & Blount-Hill, Kwan-Lamar. (2020). "Writing the other as other": Exploring the othered lens in academia using collaborative autoethnography. *Decolonization of Criminology and Justice, 2*(1), 83–108. https://doi.org/10.24135/dcj.v2i1.19.

Cameron, D. (1995). *Verbal hygiene.* Psychology Press.

Cumming, A. (2006). *Goals for academic writing-ESL students and their instructors.* John Benjamins Publishing Company.

Deepa, S. (2022a). Pedagogic scaffolding and anthrogogic learning contexts: Issues in metaphor mismatch. *Journal of English Language Teachers' Interaction Forum, XIII*(2), 3–7.

Deepa, S. (2022b). Options in multiple choice questions: Oh Really! Yours sincerely Adult learners! *Language and Language Teaching, 11*(2:22), 81–86. https://llt.org.in/wp-content/uploads/2023/01/LLT-issue22-Options-in-Multiple-Choice-Questions.pdf.

Deepa, S. (2026). Principles of anthrogogic language education. In S. Deepa & G. Durairajan (Eds.), *Anthrogogy in use: A handbook for language educators* (pp. 3–26). Orient BlackSwan.

Ministry of Human Resource Development. (2020). *National Education Policy 2020.* https://www.education.gov.in/sites/upload_files/mhrd/files/NEP_Final_English_0.pdf.

Graff, G. and Birkenstein, C. (2007). *They say/I say: The moves that matter in academic writing.* W.W. Norton & Company.

Guttorm, H., Kantonen, L., Kramvig, B., & Pyhälä, A. (2021). Decolonized research-storying: bringing indigenous ontologies and care into the practices of research writing. In P. K. Virtanen, P. Keskitalo, & T. Olsen (Eds.), *Indigenous research methodologies in Sámi and global contexts* (pp. 113–143). Brill.

Knowles, M., Holton III, E., & Swanson, R. (2015). *The Adult learner: The definitive classic in adult education and human resource development.* Routledge.

Larsen-Freeman, D. (2019). On language learner agency: A complex dynamic systems theory perspective. *The Modern Language Journal, 103*, 61–79. https://doi.org/10.1111/modl.12536.

Pullum, G. K. (2006, Dec. 13). Ideology, power, and linguistic theory [Unpublished conference paper]. https://www.lel.ed.ac.uk/~gpullum/MLA2004.pdf.

7

Identifying Anthrogogic Practices through Classroom Vignettes

Shravasti Chakravarty

Introduction

Adult learners, by dint of their age and years of experience, tend to perceive what is taught differently from young learners. Similarly, different adult learners perceive the same problem in a variety of ways that is unique to every individual. Further, they are focused on their goals and are practical in their approach to life; they carry this into their classrooms. Therefore, the adult learning situation should not be pedagogic or scaffolding in nature, and freedom of thinking should be encouraged in the various facets of the teaching–learning process. This argument first took hold in the works of Knowles (1968) who opined that 'the biggest obstacle to the achievement of the full potential of adult education has been that it has been tied to and ... has been hamstrung by the concepts and the methods of the traditional education of children' (cited in Deepa, 2022d, p. 1). Moreover, with the ease of availability of information and resources, the teacher in an adult classroom is simply a facilitator, a 'guide on the side' rather than the 'sage on the stage' (King, 1993). Therefore, for an adult learning scenario, it was necessary to establish the difference. The term 'andragogy', as found in the literature, was examined and found to be limiting in its nature especially in terms of representation of gender. Consequently, attuning to the argumentation put forward by Deepa (2022a, 2022b, as cited in Chakravarty, 2023b), the different terms used in the article to refer to the concept being discussed are 'anthrogogy', 'anthrogogic', and 'anthrogogicity'.

Understanding Anthrogogicity

The concept of anthrogogicity shares its core values with the tenets of universal human values that have been emphasised in India's National Education Policy (NEP) 2020. The thinking adult carries the onus of sustainable development practices that are built along the lines of equity for both the human and the natural world. Further, in such a class, mutual respect is aspired to be maintained between the teacher and the adult learner. Some of the well-established principles of andragogy are:

- the learners' need to know
- self-concept of the learner
- prior experience
- readiness to learn
- orientation to learning
- motivation to learn (Knowles, et al., 2015)

In this chapter, the term has been used according to the definition given by Deepa (2022d, 2026), which is a working definition. It entails understanding gender, multilingualism, multiculturalism, encompassing disciplines, and the repertoire of adult learners' pre-existing information. It is concerned with informal education, non-formal education, and also educating adults within the folds of regular teaching.

Trott (1991) talks about anthrogogy from a humanistic approach, and his classification comprises seven dimensions that include: the student, learning groups, systems thinking, vision, direction and pathways, evaluation, and the teacher. Therefore, in the present study, the tenets of anthrogogicity have been analysed within the scope of the classroom from the perspective of the teachers, with emphasis on the nature of teaching and roles of the teacher. These are labelled as anthrogogic and pedagogic moves made by the teacher during the sessions. Each session has been identified as a vignette.

Defining the Anthrogogic Teacher

An anthrogogic practice-centred teacher works as an excavator/unraveller of learners' pre-existing information. This means that instead of being the supplier of information, the teacher treats the adult learners as adults, and gets them actively involved in the teaching–learning process. In an anthrogogic teacher-led class, the learners spearhead classroom processes. Detractors of the ideology might opine that this gives teachers the freedom to go off track; nevertheless, it calls for added preparedness on the part of the teacher. On the one hand, the teacher needs to be able to relinquish her position as the only source of information and refrain from making unwanted intrusions into the knowledge acquisition process of the adult learner, and on the other hand, she also needs to don the hat of the guide without turning into the provider of the solution; a fine balance needs to be maintained. Therefore, it is important for an anthrogogic teacher to discern the differences between her anthrogogic and pedagogic moves. These will be discussed later in the chapter.

It is important to note that although in my teaching I was inherently incorporating aspects of anthrogogic practices, these were done without awareness of the principles. It is only in retrospect that I was able to review my practices from the lens of anthrogogicity.

While a vast amount of research has been conducted in the areas of learner autonomy (Smith, 2008, Smith, et al., 2015), and teacher autonomy (NFER, 2020), very little has been done from the lens of anthrogogicity. LeClaire and Binks (2022) maintain that as a fallout of the pandemic it is more important than ever to make learners responsible and involved in their learning process. Consequently, this chapter aims to identify the role of the teacher in an anthrogogic scenario.

Considering the lacuna identified in the literature as presented earlier in the chapter, the research question that drives this study is: What is the nature of teaching and the kind of teaching roles adopted by the teacher in an anthrogogic classroom?

Methodology

Participants

In this chapter I have analysed the adult teaching–learning scenario that I experienced as a teacher in India and Uzbekistan. Both countries define legal adulthood as the age of eighteen years. An adult is a part of mainstream education practices starting from the college-level onwards. Instruction is provided within a formal higher education context (tertiary level). Consequently, I have limited the data collection site for this chapter to my experience of teaching at three private universities.[1]

Further, an adult learner is one who,

- is autonomous and self-directed
- has vast amount of life experiences and knowledge

[1] The identities of the institutions and respondents have been deliberately kept anonymous for the purposes of confidentiality. Necessary permissions have been obtained from the concerned persons.

- is pragmatic and goal-oriented and
- responds better to problem-solving and task-oriented learning (Knowles, 2015)

My experience in teaching English ranges from Bachelor of Arts (BA Honours and general)- and Master of Arts (MA)-level courses in English literature to teaching the language as an elective and compulsory subject to students in the streams of Engineering (BTech), Pharmacy (BSc), Law, Media and Communication (BA), as well as the sub-category of teaching communication skills to undergraduate and graduate students of Business Administration programmes (BBA and MBA). I have also taught English as a Foreign and a Second language (EFL/ESL). Although the focus and content of the courses differed, the common element in these experiences was the tertiary-level adult learners. Detailed information about the students for each vignette are mentioned in the ensuing sections. The words 'student' and 'learner' have been used interchangeably across the chapter.

Data Collection and Tools

Data collection was undertaken using video recordings of the sessions, introspective analysis reports of the teacher, teacher's observations of the sessions, experiences of learners using self-reflective reports, and feedback from the students, along with semi-structured interviews that were useful for triangulating the data.

Retrospective analysis of specific sessions that I have taught in the last four years of my teaching journey forms the principal tool for this study. Research shows that when teaching experiences are put through this lens of retrospection, it often highlights missed perspectives (McMurtry, 2023). In most cases, I have highlighted teaching incidents that occurred on a single day. Each session was preceded and followed by related sessions based on the same topic. The data presented here comprises the teacher-researcher's (T) observations and feedback from learners/students as and where available (S).

As discussed earlier, information has been taken from eight instances of teaching (vignettes from the classroom) identified hereafter with the letter, 'V', equally divided into literature (V3, V4, V5, and V8) and language (V1, V2, V6, and V7) segments. Vignettes 1 and 2 are from classrooms in Uzbekistan and the remaining are from the teaching–learning scenarios experienced by the teacher-researcher in India.[2]

The term 'vignette' was originally defined by Finch (1987) as a short hypothetical story. Jeffries and Maeder (2004–2005) have further streamlined the definition of this qualitative data-gathering tool to 'incomplete short stories that are written to reflect, in a less complex way, real-life situations in order to encourage discussions and potential solutions to problems where multiple solutions are possible' (p. 18). The context of the stories can be obtained directly from the learners' experiences, records maintained by other researchers, or from other studies conducted in the area (Bradbury-Jones, et al., 2014). In this study, the term has been used to identify a specific incident or a short series of interconnected incidents that form a small part of the larger classroom process—akin to a highlight from a longer session. Vignettes collected from both the teacher-researcher's and the learners' experiences lend themselves to the analysis of anthrogogic practices.

For every session, the detailed lesson plan was first written down in a paragraph. Next, the various steps were identified with respect to the roles of the teacher-researcher and learners. After that, the information was tabulated for ease of arriving at themes and categories that eventually gave rise to the different kinds of anthrogogic and pedagogic moves as presented in the results and discussion section. In the following section, the eight episodes have been described in detail.

Vignette 1: Project based on 'Developing Interview Skills'

A project was conducted with bridge-course (International Foundation Studies Programme) students at the university level in an English as a Foreign Language (EFL) scenario. Most students had an International English Language Testing System (IELTS) band of around 5.5. Instructions were given on asking questions. Students were also taught basic structures to reduce grammatical inaccuracies. This was done by introducing the difference between 'wh' and 'yes/no' answer type questions.

---

[2] The context of a few of the vignettes described here have been used in another article where the data, unlike this one, has been examined from the learner's perspective. The analysis there focuses only on learner responses and feedback.

Next, a multi-stage assignment, to be completed in three steps, was designed. Stage one comprised two parts of data collection. The first part involved an excursion to places of historical interest within the city of Tashkent. This ensured that learners found foreigners with whom the need to communicate in English would arise. The places of tourist interest selected for data collection were narrowed down after conducting a student poll, thereby, taking into consideration the students' preferences. This choice resonates with the concept of learner autonomy highlighted earlier (Smith, 2008, 2015). The places visited include Amir Timur Square, Broadway Street, Chorsu Bazaar, and Mason's mosque complex. We used the metro service and walked to commute from one place to the next. Learners encountered travellers from Korea, Japan, China, Turkey, India, Pakistan, Russia, Estonia, Bangladesh, Portugal, and Brazil. This variety was possible because of an ongoing world Kurash Tournament that led to a momentary influx of foreigners to the country.

The learners divided themselves into groups or pairs depending on their preferences (Deepa & Durairajan, 2023). Working alone, although another option, was not actively encouraged considering the quantum of work that needed to be submitted. The excursion started at 2 pm and continued till 8 pm. It ended with sharing food at a nearby mall: Samarkand Darvoza.

During the data collection, the students found that some foreigners were not comfortable speaking in English, therefore, they started conversing in Russian, Turkish, and Spanish depending on the preference of the tourists being interviewed.

The second part of the data collection required learners to interview their elderly family members to identify the changes that had been observed over the past three decades of the country's independence from the Russian confederate. Stage two of the assignment required learners to create a video, documenting the process of data collection.[3] Using Facebook to showcase the work was inspired by the findings of the study conducted by Özmen & Atıcı (2014a, 2014b, as cited in Chakravarty, 2023a). Students also presented the information gathered through PowerPoint presentations (PPTs). The conversations that took place with the tourists were enacted in the classroom using role plays.

---

[3] A video sample of Stage 2 of the project can be accessed on the following link: https://www.facebook.com/shravasti/videos/1463015487432363.

In the third stage, learners submitted a self-reflective write-up describing their experiences during the data collection process.

Vignette 2: Storytelling through PowerPoint Presentations

BTech and BSc Computer Science students are expected to master the skills of making presentations as part of their communication skills syllabus. While some students falter at the sentence construction level, the speaking capability of the majority could be placed more or less around the level of the IELTS band 6.5, as identified from their test scores that they submitted during the time of admission to the programme.

A trend observed among these students was the memorisation of stock phrases related to their subject area: Information Technology. Their register of these ideas is well developed. However, they normally face difficulties when trying to express themselves in other areas. This often poses a challenge since students are expected to think on their feet at the time of group discussions during the campus recruitment process. Further, many students usually work either full-time or part-time during which they are required to make presentations in English, which is a foreign language for them. A lot of time is often spent on preparation as it involves memorising entire speeches in English to ensure a faultless performance during the actual task.

Therefore, to enable them to improve their efficiency and skills, one component of their formative assessment as part of the course was to deliver a presentation. However, rather than allowing them to stick to their regular course-related topics—which the majority recycled across the semesters of their degree programme—in this session they were asked to present something 'that caught their eye beyond studies'. They were further instructed to 'tell their story' using the presentations (Zak, 2014). This resulted in a variety of activities, such as making origami after receiving proper instructions; talking about their dream business ideas like opening a cosmetic surgery beauty parlour, a coffee shop, online garment manufacturing business; talking about their love for the book and movie *The Queen's Gambit*, and so on. The enthusiasm of the learners in trying to describe the things that appealed to them enabled them to become self-sufficient and gave direction to their learning process. Simultaneously, it ensured their real-life application when these budding entrepreneurs made business pitches to prospective investors.

Vignette 3: Reading Poetry with a Twist

As part of the BA English Honours syllabus, I taught students the poem 'Elegy written in a country churchyard' by Thomas Gray. However, they were not very enthusiastic about it. Within a span of two years they had to study it thrice—as part of their Class 12 syllabus; once again as part of the Compulsory English course in the first semester of their BA; and the third time as part of the second year '18th Century Poetry' syllabus which I was teaching. Therefore, having to study it all over again was excruciating for them.

However, at that time I did not have the administrative liberty to engineer any change especially since it was in the middle of the semester. Consequently, I modified the approach to teaching the poem. I flipped the teaching–learning process and in the first session assigned to the lesson, students came prepared to make presentations explaining it. Components at this stage included the basics of any literature class and involved providing information about the poet, describing his oeuvre, identifying other major contemporaneous poets, and noteworthy poems centred around the same theme and time. In addition, students by themselves wanted to share their thoughts and personal experiences related to the theme. The class thus turned into a cornucopia of students' poems, essays, monologues, letters to family members since phone connectivity was sporadic in the mountains, and lyrics sung accompanied by the guitar. Studies conducted (Kobayashi, 2023; Ribosa and Duran, 2022) indicate the efficacy of using such learner-created materials for effective learning. During the session itself, some students went to the blackboard and drew images related to the theme to set the tone of the class. One such example was the drawing of the Grim Reaper standing near a grave on a crescent moon night. The image was depicted on one side of the board and on the other side was the rest of the graveyard with eerie bats and a dead tree with branches in silhouette. This matched the mood of the poem. Beneath the picture were quotations such as 'memento mori', 'the breezy call of incense', 'no more shall rouse them from their long sleep', and 'long lingering look behind'. The output thus generated in this session was used as formative assessment tasks. Hence, students exhibited the ability to take charge of their own teaching–learning process and ensured anthrogogic practices.

Appendix 1 is an excerpt of students' writing based on the theme of the poem in the syllabus.

Vignette 4: Using Brainstorming as a Pre-Reading Task

Some of the BTech students I taught were required to study elective English courses. Often overloaded with their subject-specific courses, they did not prioritise studying English. Thus, towards the beginning of the semester itself, I found out the hard way that it was impossible to make the class interactive. Trying to navigate this situation, I introduced the oft-used technique of incorporating a pre-reading task: brainstorming ideas. The idea for this had its roots in a previous study (Chakravarty, 2018) that highlighted the effectiveness of using brainstorming to arrive at robust and creative discussion points when used as a pre-task before participating in group discussions. During the present session I wrote the title of the text in the centre of the blackboard and invited each student to write one idea/word that they thought could be linked to the text. Sometimes students would play a prank and put up something completely off-track. Instead of reprimanding the action, I asked them to explain the connection for the benefit of the whole class. I made a conscious effort to not reprimand them and instead say 'Let's wait and watch if you are on the right track'. Students would maintain a record of these connections either by jotting them in their notebooks, or digitally by clicking photos. Over the following few sessions, as they made their presentations, I would ask them to revisit the brainstorming. Often, what initially started off as a completely off-the-track idea turned into an interesting link with others' ideas and the given text. Such connections were arrived at through a whole-class activity. Once the method proved successful, the anthrogogic approach adopted by the learners was further highlighted. In the concluding session for the topic, I displayed the photograph of their brainstorming session and walked them through the development of their ideas and the connections established with the text therein.

Vignette 5: Role-playing for Increased Learner Engagement

Using role-play has often proved effective in making the class communicative (Larsen-Freeman, 2007; Ishak and Aziz, 2022). The course was designed for BTech students and included teaching English short stories in translation from different languages. Studying elective English was not prioritised by these students. Moreover, this class was scheduled at 9 am. This proved to be a further challenge for the students to participate actively, especially on cold winter mornings. As a result,

the need of the hour was to make students more interested and invested in their learning process.

Therefore, I adopted a novel strategy. The class was divided into groups; students were free to decide on their team members. I also divided the short story under purview—'How Much Land Does a Man Need?' by Leo Tolstoy—into smaller units. Lots were drawn and each group was handed one part of the story. Students turned the events depicted in the story into a short script in which they had the flexibility of adding their own dialogues, while ensuring that the important components of the storyline were adhered to. Flexibility was also given in terms of the tone of the role play. Thus, one group turned their story segment into a series of monologues for each of the characters present. Another group turned their part into a humorous segment. To add a rustic flavour to the Russian short story, some Indian language dialogues were also incorporated by a third group. In this way, the six groups of the class took turns and presented the entire story in an entertaining yet engaging format for the whole class. Once the presentation was completed, students were asked to reflect on it and identify the various themes that the author was talking about. The progression of the characters in the story was also easy to follow as a positive outcome of the dramatisation. Through this approach, an otherwise dull class was transformed into an anthrogogic experience.

Vignette 6: Learning the Ropes of Negotiation

In the communication skills course designed for students of business management, most students come with work experience. This means their concept of 'prior experience' (Knowles, et al., 2015) is very rich. Therefore, the sessions turned learner-driven by recollecting their experiences. One such incident occurred when introducing the skills of negotiation. Apart from recounting scenarios that they encountered in their workplaces, they gave more relatable experiences of instances when they made use of their negotiation skills. Some responses include, 'negotiating for the extra piece of *gulab jamun* in the mess' (S4); 'negotiating with the teacher for extra time to complete assignments' (S38); and 'when we tried to negotiate an early return from the adventure trip to the jungle' (S52). This last encounter between the class representative and the faculty in charge was further enacted by the students as a role-play.

In the former experiences, the students were usually successful in their negotiation skills. However, the third was an example of a failure to negotiate their way out of the situation. That became the central point of teaching for the class wherein students analysed and identified the positives and negatives of the negotiation process. Further, they provided scope for improvement to the role-players. The *a priori* concepts of ethos, pathos, and logos to enhance the argumentation used were further demonstrated during the debriefing stage. Thus, the session was largely learner driven, with the teacher as a 'guide on the side' (King, 1993). It concluded with the learners incorporating the feedback in the negotiation role-play task that was used as the production activity. Appendix 2 is a sample of brainstorming for a task on negotiation.

Vignette 7: Giving Peer Feedback in Group Discussion Tasks

Business schools in India usually follow a trimester system. Business communication students of MBA programmes in these institutes generally have placement opportunities arising at the end of the first semester itself, therefore leaving very limited time to hone their skills. A task that these students need to participate in is group discussions. This is used as a parameter for eliminating students to select the crème de la crème of the class. However, this task type did not feature in the syllabus since different student bodies and the alumni association have traditionally taken charge of this group discussion preparation process. Nevertheless, the students here showed proactiveness and requested a session on group discussions to be included in the syllabus. This is a clear example of adult learners taking charge of their learning needs, which in turn is an example of anthrogogic practices.

The two components of this business communication course are 'effective communication' and 'understanding critical feedback'. To make the learners more self-reliant, I combined the two. The first was explained through a practice round of group discussions, and the second was embedded into the discussions under the guise of peer feedback, since this process has been found to be effective across professional courses (Lerchenfeldt, et al., 2023). The first step of the class was to explain the tenets of group discussions and the concept of providing constructive criticism. This explanation was carried out using PPTs. It was followed by a round of group discussions. The audience—that is, the other students of the class—acted as the eyes and ears who identified one discussant and gave constructive feedback to enhance their group discussion performance. This gave them the opportunity to practice giving feedback while at the same time ensuring that they imbued the principles of

active critical listening. Thus, the feedback given incorporated manner of speaking, body language, points raised, and overall group dynamics. The method in which the feedback was delivered was also categorised as taking on the appearance of the 'cheese sandwich' and 'gluten-free' methods (Flatt, 2011) using 'I', including positive praise, focusing on the action/behaviour of the discussant, and providing actionable feedback. The idea that all criticism should come from a place of empathy was also highlighted since it is deemed necessary for becoming effective and emotionally intelligent managers. The anthrogogic attitude of the learners was further evidenced by the fact that before the commencement of the following session, the class representative came over to negotiate the format, the number of discussants, and the duration of the task making it a better practice segment before the actual discussion in front of the recruiters. A sample of the first step in the peer feedback is presented in Appendix 3.

Vignette 8: Master's Class with a Difference

The MA in English course that I taught was unique in its structure: irrespective of the Bachelor's programme that students had successfully completed, they were allowed entry into it. Therefore, some students in the class were exposed to English-medium education for the first time during my sessions. Such students found it difficult to interact during class discussions. A possible reason for that was their inability to do critical thinking and express themselves in the new language. Numerous studies over the years (Hayes, 1990; Tung and Chang, 2009; Cananau, 2021; Zhang, 2022) have shown the efficacy of using the literature class for developing critical thinking skills and vice versa across age groups. Therefore, I incorporated it as part of the syllabus. To ensure adequate classroom participation and reduce the overall teacher-talk time, I implemented a variety of critical thinking approaches. Two are highlighted here:

a. **Using mind maps**: I introduced the story of the novel being studied in the class by providing a very basic outline in which I highlighted the names of the various characters and their intertwining relationships. This was put up in the form of a flowchart/mind map on the blackboard. Students then had to identify specific characters and critically analyse them. This informal presentation was done orally. However, should a learner so decide, he/she had the liberty to use a PowerPoint presentation. Once the presentation was completed, others in the class asked questions using the Socratic method to flesh out details about the character. Sometimes, they also added information which might have been ignored by the presenter. I intervened only at the insistence of the students. In the initial stages of using the method, students were permitted to use their mother tongue to speak as required. This was translated into English by another student for the benefit of the foreigners in the class who were unable to understand the local language. Appendix 4 is an example of this for the session on *Nagamandala* by Girish Karnad.

b. **Themes in the text**: When discussing the themes found in the text, another approach augmented classroom participation. I wrote down all the themes associated with a given text on the board or on a PPT. Then, I invited the students to discuss and identify them as portrayed in the novel. Using this method ensured that the sessions were learner driven, and discussion based. As a result of using this technique, by the end of the semester—once all the texts of the syllabus were completed—students were able to identify the intertextuality of the themes across the syllabus. Further, they drew comparisons between the various characters across the texts. They took this mode of analysis a step further and gave free reign to their creative imaginations by placing characters from one novel in a situation found in another novel, and trying to analyse how they would behave within the new context. This took the sessions above and beyond the requirement of the course objectives. To identify better with the characters, the graduate students also shared personal narratives that were similar to those described in the novels. This led to complete engagement with the texts. *The White Tiger* (Arvind Adiga), *Shadowlines* (Amitav Ghosh), *Nagamandala* (Girish Karnad), 'My Grandmother's House' (Kamala Das), and *The Sari Shop* (Rupa Bajwa) were some of the texts used in this course. Foreign students from Nigeria who were enrolled in the course enriched the sessions by sharing texts from their linguistic and cultural backgrounds (Chinua Achebe's writings) thereby, enlivening the spirit of a truly multicultural classroom. The flexibility that was offered to the students ensured that the erstwhile silent ones felt more confident to speak up since they were able to take charge of their own learning process. Following are in-verbatim excerpts shared by students over WhatsApp in the form of personal correspondence:

> You would try to make us speak in class and even if the points we speak out wasn't very relevant you would tell that in a positive manner so that we still have the confidence to talk next time. In fact, many of my friends started speaking in other classes too because of the way you pushed them. (S2)
>
> You would make us think by asking questions and discuss it. (S5)
>
> You have always encouraged criticism. Your methods are very clear and concise. (S7)
>
> You have amazing way of breaking things down so that they are easily understandable for us and helped us to think and bring our own stories to the class. (S8)

So far, the various vignettes from which data for the present study were collected have been described. In the following section, these will be analysed to identify the patterns that lend themselves to anthrogogic and pedagogic practices as observed across the teaching-learning scenarios.

Results and Discussion

The aim of the study was to identify the principles of anthrogogic practices that already exist among most teachers inherently, without conscious awareness. These have been referred to as the anthrogogic moves made by the teacher in the class and are in opposition to teacher-centric pedagogic moves. As stated previously, the patterns that emerged from the vignettes shared have been categorised broadly under teacher roles, and the kind of teaching that happens. These have been further subdivided into the anthrogogic and pedagogic moves that were being made by the learners and teachers and are presented below.

Anthrogogic Moves

Content

Learners across the sessions showed some autonomy when it came to the content they brought to the class. This included the language used for collecting their data and the tone they adopted when presenting the short story as a skit. They were also instrumental in requesting permission to present their own writings as part of the syllabus to be covered (see Appendix 1). This included their life experiences in the form of personal narratives. Learners further exhibited their anthrogogic attitude towards the mechanics of the task when they negotiated the format for group discussion in order to sync them with industry requirements. Some quotes from the teacher-researcher's observations are as follows:

- Students decided on the language in which the question was asked, depending on the convenience of the foreigners being interviewed. (V1)
- The tone (happy/sad/serious/angry/enthusiastic) of the presentation was at the learner's discretion. (V5)
- They had the liberty to structure their presentations as they saw fit. No specific format was provided. (V1)
- Students decided not to study the poem in the regular manner since it was a repetition. (V3)
- Students arrived at the idea to present their writings. (V3)
- Students created the teaching materials. (V3)
- They wrote their own dialogues to portray the information in the text. (V5)
- Students brought in their life experiences. (V3)
- Students volunteered to enact the negotiation scene for the benefit of the class. (V6)
- Students decided the format for the group discussion in sync with their needs that were different from what I had practiced initially. (V7)
- They shared personal narratives in sync with the situations encountered by the various characters: personal experiences, heard narratives from grandparents. (V1)
- No spoon-feeding information to the learners with respect to the kind of questions to be asked. (V1)

Creative Thinking

Another anthrogogic move identified in the teacher's attitude was with respect to giving reign to creative thinking among these adult learners. There was rarely any spoon-feeding of information. None of the responses were designated incorrect; they were perceived as only points to be clarified further. This encouraged the learners to put on their creative thinking hats and suggest out-of-the-box solutions to the problems encountered during the sessions. Students were also instrumental in the decision-making process and decided to provide a moral of the story as they deemed fit, irrespective of its presence in the original text. Learners adding ideas to the pre-existing information showed an increased level of confidence. Practical issues were problem-solved (see Appendix 2), and learners asked for help which resulted in the modification of the sessions (V7). Samples from the researcher's observations are as follows:

- Allowing them to take decisions by themselves with respect to the order of the questions asked. (V1)
- These were not countered by the teacher: there were no wrong answers. (V3)
- I did not reprimand them for putting up bizarre words. (V4, V8)
- Students had the liberty to choose their topic. (V1, V3)
- I did not comment on the content of the presentations although they were not in sync with my personal belief systems. (V2)
- Students of their own accord presented the moral of the story (Group 6). (V5)

Critical Thinking

Thinking critically and asking questions was another aspect in which the anthrogogic moves by the teacher were evident in giving free rein to the learners. This supported the notion of 'interpretative spaces'(Deepa 2026) that adult learners have access to (Ghosh, 2026). Instead of providing direct answers to queries, I threw the question back at them and asked, 'What do you think?' (V4, V8). This would open the floor for other learners to respond. This was accompanied by using the Socratic method of asking questions to take the sessions forward. They eventually became confident to think critically about the texts and connect the characters across the syllabus. This was especially observed in the literature classes. When using the mind-map technique, instead of providing the information, as the teacher I would encourage the learners to guess the connections. This further enabled them to become confident (Baruah, 2026) (see Appendix 4). Some observations made by the teacher-researcher during the sessions are:

- Highlighting creativity, students superimposed characters from one book into a situation presented in another. (V8)
- Other students also tried to make the connections. (V3, V8)
- Students tried to guess and expand on the themes. (V8)
- Students arrived at their own interpretations of the texts introduced by their classmates. (V3)
- Depending on the segments of the story, students analysed the characters. (V3, V4, V8)
- Learners identified the intertextuality of the themes and highlighted similarities and differences among characters across the texts. (V4, V5, V8)

Classroom Dynamics

It was easy to observe pre-existing unconscious anthrogogic moves when it came to the classroom dynamics among learners. To maintain autonomy, they decided whether to work in groups, pairs or individually (V1, V3). The group members were also left to their discretion. The number of participants they would be comfortable working with was also largely their decision. Identifying the places to visit for data collection for maximum impact was also left to the learners, further enabling them to become responsible for their decisions. This preference for autonomy resonates with the findings among other anthrogogic students as well (Deepa and Durairajan, 2023). The oft-used statement by the teacher was 'You tell me where we are likely to find the maximum number of people' (V1). In line with the principles of anthrogogicity, the decision to create ambient learning conditions also rested with the learners. Therefore, they decided when to organise the excursion for data collection, the time designated for it, the locations to be visited, and so on. Further, those who were unhappy with the quality of data revisited the places to redo the work. They took the collective decision to ask for a session on group discussions (V7) to prepare better for their summer internship programmes. In some classes, to aid the linguistically challenged students, the more able peer took it upon themselves to explain the concept in the mother tongue for better understanding (V1, V4, V8). Some snippets of learner behaviours include:

- Students could choose their pairs and groups. (V1, V5, V7)
- It became a whole class activity. (V3, V4, V8)
- Students took the decision to wait for a few others before starting the trip. (V1)

- Those who were unable to make it to the excursion on the given day, took the liberty to go for data collection at their convenience. (V1)
- I did not show them the connections immediately but waited for them to arrive at their own conclusions. (V8)
- They planned and directed their segment of the lesson. (V5)

Pedagogic Moves

Although the sessions from which data was collected exhibited numerous instances of anthrogogic moves by the teacher, there were some moves that are synonymous with pedagogic practices in which the teacher is at the helm of the classroom processes. These are referred to as the pedagogic moves and presented below.

First Encounters

One predominant stage of the sessions wherein the role of the teacher was pedagogic was the first session for each class. In most of the episodes described above, this was the first time students encountered such autonomy. Therefore, they required time to get acclimatised to the new teaching–learning process. Consequently, some initial handholding was necessary. Nevertheless, for a particular group, repeated exposure to the same modality reduced the pedagogic moves required during the initial session since orientation would no longer be necessary. Some observations made across the episodes are presented here:

- Initial instruction in asking questions was provided by using videos, reading materials, as inputs and writing and speaking in class as the by-products of the sessions. (V1)
- We practised some sample questions in class to give the less proficient students an idea since this was the first time they were undertaking such a task. (V1)
- Introduced the pre-reading task of brainstorming as a modality of teaching. (V4)
- All sixty students in the class perforce walked up to the board and wrote their ideas. (V4)
- I delegated chapters to a specific range of roll-numbers and called them at random to present that part of the story for the benefit of the class. (V5, V8)

- I displayed the photograph from the first session. I walked them through some of the ideas that were discussed. (V4, V5, V8)
- Introduced the basics of group discussions. (V7)
- I drew a skeleton mind-map of the story with a basic outline and naming the characters. (V8)
- I introduced critical articles to the class based on the characters. (V8)
- Chose role-play as a modality to make the class interactive. (V5)

Syllabus Decisions

In some sessions, students wanted to change the content of the syllabus. However, the kind of change that would be permissible was a decision taken by the teacher. It was negotiated and primarily teacher-driven. Therefore, in V3 we saw that while the poem in the syllabus was not studied like the others, learners created their own materials based on the themes derived from it. Students wanted a session on group discussion, therefore I incorporated a brief lecture that was predominantly teacher-speak (V7). Further, I prohibited the students from recycling their presentation topics which was the norm for them until then (V2). Some other decisions that were pedagogic in nature are:

- The order in which the tasks needed to be completed was provided. This was the task for evaluation. (V1)
- I could not allow the students to skip the poem altogether as was their initial suggestion since it was a part of the syllabus. (V3)

Time Management

The time allocated for a specific task or assignment was fixed by the teacher in consultation with administrative requirements. In some cases, I had to manage the time for specific presentation tasks and get them to stop midway (V2). This was necessary to ensure that everyone in the class got the same opportunity to showcase their skills. Some other instances are included in the following observations:

- The total time within which the work was to be completed was provided by me in sync with administrative needs. (V1, V2, V8)
- I was the manager ensuring that everyone completed the work at a given site within the time specified so that we could proceed to the next spot without difficulty. (V1)
- I was timing the presentations. (V1, V2, V7)

- I gave fifteen minutes in every session for them to practice their segments in the class since it was not possible for them to interact outside class. (V1, V5).

Assessment

One important area where the pedagogic moves were the maximum was the evaluation and assessment of learners. For all the sessions from which data was collected, the final evaluation was predetermined by administrative requirements. This was mostly in the form of internal assignments and end-term exams. The detailed criteria for evaluation implemented for the various writing tasks was not shared with the learners since it was not the norm in the institutions where data was collected. However, the criteria for speaking tasks were shared to aid peer-evaluation practices. This was necessary since it was the first time learners were undertaking peer evaluation and, therefore, a scaffolding was required. Nevertheless, the learners were unable to evaluate their own performances based on those criteria. This shows that self-evaluation and self-awareness require repeated practice. Some observations made by the teacher-researcher are presented here:

- Teacher responded to the learners' queries so that the work continued. (V1, V3)
- The evaluation criteria was set by me. (V1, V2, V3, V5, V7)
- The materials created by the learners became a part of the student portfolio for formative assessment. (V3)
- I provided the parameters for them to evaluate others/themselves. (V7)

Giving Directions

Another significant area wherein pedagogic moves by the teacher were predominant was giving direction to the session. Once students completed their presentations either in the literature or the language sessions, there appeared to be a brief limbo. To ensure the flow of the sessions, the teacher stepped in by using Socratic questions and encouraging learners to initiate critical thinking whenever a lacuna was felt. Following are certain directions that were shared with the learners:

- I added the component of critically analysing the student's creations in class like a regular text. (V3)

- At the end of the presentation of the material by each participant, I was directing their attention to the various themes that the texts exhibited. This was done by asking Socratic questions based on the text. (V4, V8)
- I showed them the different methods of providing feedback. (V7)

Linking Ideas

In the literature sessions specifically, towards the end of a chapter the need was felt to make the learners discern the connection between and among the texts. This process of meaning making is an essential part of any literature course, especially at the Master's level. Therefore, the pedagogic move to initiate this habit was necessary. However, later in the semester students didn't need any handholding by the teacher to link ideas intertextually. So, a clear shift from pedagogic moves could be identified in the teacher's role. Given below are some sample observations on the pedagogic move of linking ideas.

- I was continuously linking their writings with the poem in the syllabus. (V3)
- I also asked them questions to enable them to link the situations with other texts that formed a part of the syllabus. (V4, V8)
- I directed their attention to the themes. (V4, V8)
- I directed their attention towards the language function of negotiation. (V6)
- I added extra information as pertinent. (V1, V3, V4, V5, V6, V7, V8)
- I pitched in as required with extra information or more detailed insight into the characters. (V4, V5, V8).
- I delegated chapters to a specific range of roll-numbers and called them at random to present that part of the story for the benefit of the class. (V5, V8)

In this section, we have looked at the various anthrogogic and pedagogic teacher moves that were found across the eight episodes. Components that required a certain amount of creativity or the ability to work with others seemed to emerge from the learners themselves. Both are indicative of autonomy at their end. However, certain administrative factors, like time management and giving direction to the sessions, required intervention from the teacher. Assessment was another area that required more involvement from the teacher. This can be attributed to the need to conform to a norm for effective administration leading to the larger process of academic advancement.

Conclusion: Changing the Moves

As indicated by the data, learners brought their concerns to my notice and we changed the trajectory of the session. Materials created by learners were used (V3, V4) and learners were encouraged to bring their sociocultural experiences to enrich the sessions further (V8). Continuing with the concept of anthrogogicity being embedded in giving autonomy to the learners (Smith, 2008; Smith, et al., 2015), I tried to keep that spirit alive in my sessions. In the sessions that were chiefly learner-directed, I relegated myself to the sidelines and let them take the lead, intervening only when necessary. Quite often this was to take permission or to seek a point of clarification. Also, when providing the clarifications, instead of telling them what to do, I tried to provide examples and asked them to find the connection to arrive at their own unique solutions. Such an activity requires time, patience, and bravery on the part of the teacher. In the initial days, it had the propensity to turn into a hit-and-miss segment of the session.

As teachers following anthrogogic practices, it is imperative that we push aside our biases. One such incident when I had to make a conscious effort was experienced in V2. The learner made a presentation on the need for plastic surgery to enhance the beauty of women. The concept goes absolutely against my personal views; however, in the spirit of equal give-and-take and to avoid cultural appropriation, I held back my views and was a silent spectator when the presentation was underway. Since my opinion was not solicited, the feedback that I provided was limited to the presentation style and steered clear of the content.

Once again, adhering to the concept by King (1993), V5 turned me into the 'guide on the side'. After forming the groups, my contribution was limited to providing vocabulary support when required. As discussed earlier, in the other episodes as well (V6, V7, V8) similar instances were observed.

Further analysis of the vignettes suggests that with a little planning and the willingness to take risks, anthrogogic practices can be easily incorporated into our ESL/EFL classrooms. Some components of the classroom processes—such as the role of the teacher and the material to be used—lend themselves to this practice with ease. However, it requires a certain amount of trial and error, and also a change in the mindset of the learners themselves. Just as the teacher has to learn to give away control, the learner should also be oriented towards taking charge of their learning (Chakravarty, 2023b, 2026). They need to grow out of their Peter Pan syndrome (Rubayet et al., 2021; Deepa, 2022c). The notion that the teacher is the only source of information must change.

To make the learners more anthrogogic, one approach that will prove useful is to make them self-reflective and introspect on their learning behaviour. This will increase their level of confidence and also bring their learning needs to light. However, this process is time-consuming and requires appropriate practice. Nevertheless, it will benefit adult learners by treating them as such, unlike pedagogy which is geared towards teaching children.

References

Adult. (2003, Jan. 9). In *Wikipedia*. https://en.wikipedia.org/wiki/Adult#:~:text=In%20contrast%20to%20a%20%22minor,%2C%20country%2C%20and%20psychological%20development.

Baruah, N. (2026). Unveiling anthrogogic practices: Teaching novels to English literature students. In S. Deepa & G. Durairajan (Eds.), *Anthrogogy in use: A handbook for language educators* (pp. 174–184). Orient BlackSwan.

Bradbury-Jones, C., Taylor, J., & Herber, O. R. (2014). Vignette development and administration: A framework for protecting research participants. *International Journal of* Social Research Methodology, *17*(4), 427–440. https://doi.org/10.1080/13645579.2012.750833.

Cananau, I. (2021). Critical thinking and English literature in higher education: The theoretical models and the Swedish syllabi. *Nordic Journal of English Studies, 20*(2), 99–128.

Chakravarty, S. (2018). Exploring the understanding and use of the metacognitive strategy of brainstorming in group discussions (Revised). *International Journal of Language, Literature, Culture and Education.* https://www.academia.edu/69458817/Exploring_the_Understanding_and_Use_of_the_Metacognitive_Strategy_of_Brainstorming_in_Group_Discussions.

Chakravarty, S. (2023a). New online delivery methods beyond the era of the pandemic: varied blended models to meet the COVID-19 challenges. In U. G. Singh, C. S. Nair, & S. Gonçalves (Eds.), *Digital Teaching, Learning and Assessment* (pp. 221–239). Elsevier. https://doi.org/10.1016/B978-0-323-95500-3.00014-6.

Chakravarty, S. (2023b). Overcoming Peter Pan syndrome using anthrogogic practices in the EFL/ESL classroom. In D. K. Giri (Ed.), *Compendium of scholarly essays: Conference proceedings of 10th ELT Symposium.* (pp. 90–97). ETC, UTAS-Shinas.

Chakravarty, S. (2026). Learners' roles and responses: Existential humanities and the English classroom in India. In K. M. Kudale, R. J. Valiyamattam, R. Kotte, & G. V. Nayak (Eds.), *Teaching and learning English language and literature in India* (pp. 149–161). Springer. https://doi.org/10.1007/978-981-95-5883-4_12.

Deepa, S. (2022a). Pedagogic scaffolding and anthrogogic learning contexts: Issues in metaphor mismatch. *Journal of English Language Teachers' Interaction Forum, XIII*(2), 3–7.

Deepa, S. (2022b). Options in multiple choice questions: Oh Really! Yours sincerely Adult learners!. *Language and Language Teaching: A Peer Reviewed Journal, 11*(2:22), 81–86.

Deepa, S. (2022c). Pedagogic practices in higher education and Peter Pan syndrome: An appraisal. *Fortell, 45*, 164–173. https://www.fortell.org/wp-content/uploads/2022/10/July-2022-164-173.pdf.

Deepa, S. (2022d). Thought seeds in anthrogogic learning contexts. *Journal of Indian Education, 48*(2), 58–70.

Deepa, S. (2026). Principles of anthrogogic language education. In S. Deepa & G. Durairajan (Eds.), *Anthrogogy in use: A handbook for language educators* (pp. 3–26). Orient BlackSwan.

Deepa, S., & Durairajan, G. (2023). Learning through assessment in anthrogogic contexts: Wash-forward. In A. L. Gokturk-Saglam, & E. Sevgi-Sole (Eds.), *Emerging practices for online language assessment, exams, evaluation, and feedback.* IGI Global. https://doi.org/10.4018/978-1-6684-6227-0.ch006.

Durairajan, G. (2015). *Assessing learners: A pedagogic resource.* Cambridge University Press.

Finch, J. (1987). The vignette technique in survey research. *Sociology, 21*(1), 105–114. https://doi.org/10.1177/0038038587021001008.

Flatt, M. (2011, Dec. 21). *How to give feedback that works.* Inc. https://www.inc.com/michael-flatt/how-to-give-feedback-that-works.html.

Ghosh, D. (2026). Looking beyond the compulsion of 'need to be told': An attempt at anthrogogicity in the undergraduate literature classroom. In S. Deepa & G. Durairajan (Eds.), *Anthrogogy in use: A handbook for language educators* (pp. 165–173). Orient BlackSwan.

Hayes, W. H. (1990). Critical Thinking through Literature: A Dialogue Teaching Model [Master's thesis]. *Critical and Creative Thinking*

Capstones Collection. 140. https://scholarworks.umb.edu/cct_capstone/140

IELTS Speaking Band Descriptors (public version). https://assets.cambridgeenglish.org/webinars/ielts-speaking-band-descriptors.pdf.

Ishak, S. A., & Aziz, A. A. (2022). Role play to improve ESL learners' communication Skills: A Systematic Review. *International Journal of Academic Research in Business and Social Sciences, 12*(10), 884–892. http://dx.doi.org/10.6007/IJARBSS/v12-i10/14851.

Jeffries, C., & Maeder, D. W. (2004–2005). Using vignettes to build and assess teacher understanding of instructional strategies. *The Professional Educator, 27*(1-2), 17–28. http://files.eric.ed.gov/fulltext/EJ728478.pdf.

King, A. (1993). From sage on the stage to guide on the side. *College Teaching, 41*(1), 30–35.

Knowles, M. (1968). Andragogy, not pedagogy. *Adult Leadership, 16*(10), 350–386.

Knowles, M. (1984). *Andragogy in action: Applying modern principles of adult education*. Jossey-Bass.

Knowles, M., Holton III, E., & Swanson, R. (2015). *The Adult learner: The definitive classic in adult education and human resource development*. Routledge.

Kobayashi, K. (2023). Learning by creating teaching materials: Conceptual problems and potential solutions. *Frontiers in Psychology, 14*, 1095285. https://doi.org/10.3389/fpsyg.2023.1095285.

Larsen-Freeman, D. (2007). *Techniques and principles in language teaching*. Oxford University Press.

LeClair, R. J., & Binks, A. P. (2022). Unbound education: Curriculum no longer confined by time and space. In U. G. Singh, C. S. Nair, Craig Blewett, & Timothy Shea (Eds.), *Academic voices* (pp. 461–64). Chandos Publishing. https://doi.org/10.1016/B978-0-323-91185-6.00011-2.

Lerchenfeldt, S., Kamel-ElSayed, S., Patino, G., Loftus, S., & Thomas, D. M. (2023). A qualitative analysis on the effectiveness of peer feedback in team-based learning. *Medical Science Educator, 33*, 893–902. https://doi.org/10.1007/s40670-023-01813-z.

McMurtry, T. (2023). "Changing the course of the stream": A retrospective analysis of artful language learning opportunities. *Journal of Adolescent and Adult Literacy, 67*(2), 74–84. https://doi.org/10.1002/jaal.1301.

Ministry of Human Resource Development (2020). *National education policy 2020*. https://www.education.gov.in/sites/upload_files/mhrd/files/NEP_Final_English_0.pdf.

Özmen, B., & Atıcı, B. (2014a). The effects of social networking sites in distance learning on learners' academic achievements. *European Journal of Open, Distance and E-Learning, 17*(2), 61–75. https://doi.org/10.2478/eurodl-2014-0019.

Özmen, B., & Atıcı, B. (2014b). Learners' views regarding the use of social networking sites in distance learning. *The International Review of Research in Open and Distributed Learning, 15*(4), 21–42. https://www.irrodl.org/index.php/irrodl/article/view/1790/3048.

Ribosa, J., & Duran, D. (2022). Do students learn what they teach when generating teaching materials for others? A meta-analysis through the lens of learning by teaching. *Educational Research Review, 37*, 100475. https://doi.org/10.1016/j.edurev.2022.100475.

Rubayet, T., & Imam, H. T. (2021). Adaptation of andragogy in the education system of Bangladesh: Emulating andragogical approaches of South-East Asia. *European Journal of Education Studies, 8*(11), 212–233. http://dx.doi.org/10.46827/ejes.v8i11.3983.

Smith, R. (2008) Learner autonomy. *ELT Journal, 62*(4), 395–397. https://doi.org/10.1093/elt/ccn038.

Smith, R., Kuchah, H., & Lamb, M (2018). Learner autonomy in developing countries. In Chik, A., Aoki, N., & Smith, R. (Eds.), *Autonomy in Language Learning and Teaching* (pp. 7–27). Palgrave Pivot. https://doi.org/10.1057/978-1-137-52998-5_2.

Worth, J., & Van den Brande, J. (2020) Teacher autonomy: how does it relate to job satisfaction and retention?. National Foundation for Education Research. https://www.nfer.ac.uk/publications/teacher-autonomy-how-does-it-relate-to-job-satisfaction-and-retention/.

Trott, D. C. (1991, October). *Anthrogogy* [Paper presentation] American Association for Adult and Continuing Education, Montreal, Quebec. https://eric.ed.gov/?id=ED342887.

Tung, C., & Chang, S. (2009). Developing critical thinking through literature reading. *Feng Chia Journal of Humanities and Social Sciences, 19*, 287–317.

UNICEF. (2021, Sept. 29). *Curriculum reform to meet the individual needs of students (Uzbekistan)*. Unicef.org. https://www.unicef.org/documents/curriculum-reform-meet-individual-needs-students-uzbekistan.

Zak, P. J. (2015, Feb. 2). Why inspiring stories make us react: The neuroscience of narrative. *Cerebrum: The Dana Forum on Brain Science*, 2. https://www.ncbi.nlm.nih.gov/pmc/articles/PMC4445577/.

Zhang, Y. (2022). The research on critical thinking teaching strategies in college English classroom. *Creative Education, 13*(4), 1469–1485. 10.4236/ce.2022.134090.

Appendix 1: Excerpt from Learner Created Material (V3)

Prayer of Albert Goodson

Please be kind, be kind My Lord

As I plunge my heart, on your holy sword chopping organs, as I grind my bones words did break me, not sticks and stones Obedient to mother, to the world I was kind *Love is in Charity,* But you took what I find

A faithful girl, a wine bottle and a bean

showed such mercy, on her crushed spine and spleen

the likes of which, I've seen in no prose

Vacant eyes, ventilators, as she faded out; comatose

after that Blessed sunset, no day was dull

I clutched at what was left of her…

and dragged a living corpse to her funeral.

She looked serene in white, my stomach did a lurch

I looked for you My Lord, as the choirs sang in church

After laying her in ground, a priest asked for the cost

all my money was with You, so the wine bottle I lost

Made of tinted black glass, it's mouth closed with tapes

had a homemade smell, cause my lover plucked the grapes

On that same evening, with his friends he gulped it down

As I walked to my home, but I walked out of town

thoughts of loss in my head, and yet I was feeling fine

It is what it is. Nothing bad….but nothing kind.

Then I walked into the woods, which just lay out of our senses keen. lined with melting trees and mossy floors, on which I found a red bean Poisonous it was maybe, but Your fruit I couldn't deny a taste

my mouth filled with miasma, and my tongue rotted, …and went to waste

Nothing reached my head, for knowledge I wasn't feeding But your mercy was the same as her,

I was blur, blue, bleeding.

Where my body now lies, no one has ever seen Away from the eyes of… Jesus, Mary Magdalene. Your prayers might drown, my faith had such depth Now I am nothing, no one…I am all

by Tanishq Barol ©

Appendix 2: Sample of Students' Negotiation Responses Put Up on the Board (V6)

Group 1	• Independence • Convince your mother • Going in group of girls • Social examples to convince her father
Group 2	• Automobile fare • Convince her mom • A small business meeting • Her friend's marriage • Without telling her parents
Group 3	• Office work • Friends • Convincing parents • Without telling
Group 4	• Cancel the trip in respect of father • Wait till situation gets normal • Father is strict but loving • Look for the best time to talk • Ask for the trip again
Group 5	• No more holidays available for the entire year • Personal space • Face the truth and confront • Cheap/low-cost rip • Going as a mental break from stressful work • Want to respect you, not fear • More restrictions, more differences in our relationship eventually

Appendix 3: Sample of Peer Feedback (V7)

S. No	*Name of Student*	*Group No*	*Feedback*
1.	Mandar	1	• Clarity of thought • Lack of creativity • Focus too much on writing rather than active listening • Good communication skills
2.	Hardik	3	• Very late entry • First half focused on writing rather than listening

S. No	Name of Student	Group No	Feedback
			• Interrupted others candidates on one instance • Points were out of the box • To make up for lack of opportunity he summarised in the end-good.
3.	Arjun	4	• Good points • Good eye contact with others • Fresh perspective • Brownie points for concluding
4.	Vaibhav	5	• Last entry • Clarity in communication • Very few entry • Lack of creative points even on broad topic
5.	Saumyata	6	• Good opening • Proper structure and logic behind the points • Bringing out new points which was driving the GD forward. • Clarity in points and communication
6.	Steven	7	• Very late entry • Clear communication • Creative points • Need to bring some energy

Appendix 4: Mind map Used in Class (V8)

Nagamandala

Girish Karnad

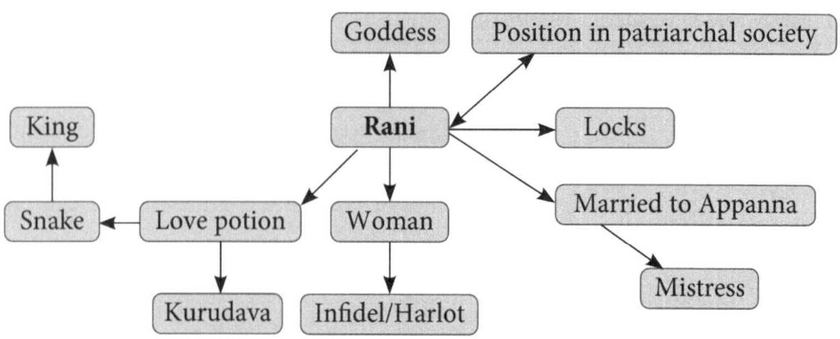

8

Looking Beyond the Compulsion of 'Need to be Told'

An Attempt at Anthrogogicity in the Undergraduate Literature Classroom

Diganta Ghosh

While there is no dearth of methodologies, materials, and research scholarship in the pedagogical space, the tertiary level has not received enough attention. Students at this level are perceived to be adults and therefore assumed to be capable enough to be educated without too much emphasis on teaching-learning methodologies. Universities do not bother to come up with anything beyond a sketchy syllabus, leave aside a detailed curriculum, nor are teachers required to be certified as trained. Beyond this, however, the teaching-learning paradigm in a tertiary classroom is heavily tilted towards pedagogy. Theoretically and practically, teachers, parents, and other stakeholders base their methodologies, assessments, expectations, and aspirations on pedagogical standards. In reality, therefore, the student is viewed as a child, irrespective of the level at which s/he is in. Take, for example, the teacher's need to establish order, control, and discipline in the classroom in order to get his/her ideas across to the students. No wonder, then, that the whole education system is referred to as 'pedagogy' in general educational discourse, in curricular and policy documents, and also in the psyche of all stakeholders. Consequently, the teaching curricula, classroom setting, orientation of teachers, prevalent teaching methodologies, and evaluation systems are all designed to treat the student as a child. For example, even in a subject like Education—which ought to be more aware of such a distinction—most of the educationists whose philosophy and perspectives are taught in undergraduate syllabi are developmental psychologists who focus on pedagogy.

The argument put forward in this chapter is that one of the characteristic features of pedagogical thought is the phenomenon of the 'need to be told'. Though it is predominantly presumed to be practiced in pedagogical space, it does extend beyond pedagogy and moves into the realm of andragogy. It is possible to look beyond the compulsion of the 'need to be told' when we adopt the principles and practices of anthrogogy (Trott, 1991; Deepa, 2022a, 2026; Durairajan & Deepa, 2026). Anthrogogy can loosely be defined as an educational philosophy based on inclusivity and humanism and is primarily focused on the education system beyond the secondary level. This chapter further examines the possibilities of anthrogogicity in an undergraduate English literature classroom.

The phrase 'need to be told' stands as a contrast to Malcolm Knowles' 'need to know' principle as postulated in his theory of andragogy. The foremost assumption in Malcolm Knowles' andragogical model of learning is that adult students are concerned about what benefit will accrue from learning something, and, hence, they 'need to know why they need to learn something before undertaking to learn it' (Knowles, 1990, p. 64). However, the adults' need to know ought to go beyond the beneficial nature of learning. In most teaching–learning situations there is a gap between what the teacher says and what the student understands. The more adult the student, the wider the gap. The students' schema provides for numerous interpretations of the teacher's instructions, which is why different students react differently to the same instruction. In order to bridge the gap, the student as well as the teacher feels another kind of need: the need to be told.

In the current education system both the student and the teacher believe that there is a need to be told. The keyword 'need' serves as two-way traffic. In the case of the student, 'need' is a noun, suggesting a range of associations—from an involuntary and impersonal 'requirement' to an active and voluntary 'desire' that s/he should be instructed. From the teacher's perspective, 'need' is a modal verb—suggesting his/her belief that the student 'needs to be told'. In other words, the student is thereby bound by his/her necessity of the teacher, whereas the teacher is bound by the conviction that the student is a *tabula rasa*, completely reliant on the teacher. The teacher performs the role of the active agent, while the student remains the passive recipient. It is easy to imagine that such a scenario would be familiar in a pedagogical environment where adult teachers deal with young students. Nonetheless, this phenomenon is so pervasive that it goes beyond primary or secondary levels and, more often than not, spills over to the tertiary level, including the domain of research. Many researchers, we are aware, share a comprehensive 'need to be told' type of relationship with their supervisor while it is also possible to provide a space for learner voices and agency in the context of research supervision and academic writing (Chandrasekharan & Sultana, 2026).

There is, of course, a well-established body of teaching–learning processes variously called adult education, adult literacy, adult continuing education, et cetera—coming under the umbrella term 'andragogy'—that envisions a mature, adult student, self-motivated and learning out of self-interest. While this system spreads its wings beyond the scope of the formal school to a university classroom-based education system, there is a complete dearth of studies that focus exclusively on the teaching methodologies of undergraduate students within a formal setup. 'Undergraduate' being a generic notion having multiple facets to it, approaching it with an open-ended methodology that takes into account the appropriate benefits of pedagogy as well as andragogy, becomes necessary. In this respect, anthrogogy emerges as a viable alternative. The focus of this chapter will be to highlight anthrogogical practices and possibilities in an undergraduate English literature classroom.

Ever since Knowles popularised andragogy as a branch of study beyond pedagogy, many educationists have tried, in their own ways, to find a way to formulate a new approach by uniting these two branches. Metagogy (Strohschen & Elazier, 2019) tries to provide a philosophical and theoretical framework to educators who shift from one methodology among 'a variety of "-gogies"—pedagogy, andragogy, critical pedagogy, etc.' to another when one methodology does not work. Peterson and Ray (2013) refer to metagogy as, 'While pedagogical and andragogical approaches are sometimes still discussed as though they are mutually exclusive, metagogy is inclusive of an andragogical approach but also includes conventional pedagogical approaches as they are appropriate to a task at hand depending on the context, student needs, or stated goal' (p. 82). In essence, according to metagogy, any and every methodology can be appropriated to suit teaching–learning needs. This makes it too open and too free.

Heutagogy has most of its principles sourced from andragogy, yet goes beyond its scope 'towards truly self-determined learning' (Hase & Kenyon 2000). It presumes the student to be extremely motivated and mature, and so can function with an enormous amount of learner autonomy (Blaschke, 2012). None of these methodologies, however, focus their attention on the group of learners that fall into that space where pedagogy ends and andragogy begins.

In parts of South Asia, and particularly in India, the field of English language learning and teaching is routed through the teaching of English literature, which is one of the relics of our colonial past. It is pertinent to note that even with whatever little popularity the andragogical approach received through research, the andragogical perspective has stayed clear of the discipline of teaching literature at the tertiary level. This is a serious research gap which this chapter proposes to fill. As such, it becomes imperative to look at the domain of literature teaching in andragogy. Within that scope, scholars have noted that literary texts have been used only for functional (Kazemek & Rigg, 1986) or transactional (Britton, 1982) purposes; that is, the use of literary texts as a means to an end, and not for the appreciation of literature. Kazemek and Rigg further note that the adult learners taking up these courses are those who have had low grades in the formal educational setup and are not exposed to 'high literature'; they need to be given carefully curated or simplified texts. They further recommend a three-step technique to teach poems: read aloud by the teacher without the text in front of the student; re-read with the text; and discussion by inviting comments and without telling the meaning. The last suggestion has been used by me quite a number of times and I shall enumerate one such example in a later part.

The situation within the boundaries of formal education is different. There is a prescribed syllabus for the students to negotiate; there is an examination system that expects them to achieve a certain level. The choice of texts for study and the mode of examination are static and pre-determined. In other words, the texts choose themselves and so does the examination system.

In this part I shall concentrate on the teaching of English literature to rural undergraduate students who have very little knowledge of the English language. These students have passed the secondary level of education with very little exposure to the English language in their everyday lives. Beyond their English textbook, they have had little access to English through books, magazines or newspapers at home or in libraries, in the type of entertainment they consume, or in the hoardings they see around them. In spite of these odds, they want to graduate in English literature because they see it as a step in the right direction to learn the language. With this limited knowledge of English, they are expected to negotiate not just the canons of English literature (Ghosh, 2010), but also its socio-economic historicities, philosophical, political and psychological underpinnings. To overcome these obstacles is undoubtedly very challenging for the students who have a bare minimum understanding of the language. We as teachers use different strategies to make these canonical texts approachable so that the students can gain some amount of literary capability (Ghosh, 2010), and not just take refuge in rote learning or help from bazaar notes. This is where the scope for anthrogogy comes in, based on the belief that there is huge anthrogogical potential in the English literature classroom. Normally, a New Critical approach is used in the classrooms, involving a close reading of the text. However, such an approach, while working wonders with students who know the English language, does not help students with very little knowledge of English.

Anthrogogy targets the education of adults, and the term 'adult' refers to those students who are foraying into formal education at the tertiary level. The term is remarkable in its all-inclusivity including within itself all genders, multilinguality, multiculturality, and also taking into account variable capabilities of the students. Among the many characteristics of anthrogogy (Deepa, 2022a, 2026) I shall highlight a few that are relevant to my discussion.

An adult's learning takes place through 'interpretative spaces' (Deepa, 2026). In terms of semiotics, an interpretative space refers to that gap between the sign or signifier and its signification which gives the reader the freedom to interpret words and texts autonomously. The adult learner, therefore, needs to have enough mental space to ruminate and come up with an independent interpretation. This implies that in a literature classroom there will be multiple interpretations of the same text and it is our duty, as teachers, to accept these interpretations in a non-judgmental manner and see how we can inculcate these interpretations in alignment with the authoritative one. Even if these interpretations are way off from expected responses, we have to think of the learners as intelligent human beings, as adults who have their own experiences and learning. So, we have to identify the underlying thought from where they have arrived at such an interpretation. Once we are able to do that, we will find that the acceptance of their interpretation will also enrich us as students of literature. In some scenarios we may have to deal with inferential questions which are opinionated and not necessarily accurate or knowledge-based. This will lead to knowledge co-creation. We also have to accept that the learners come with variable capabilities. Not everyone will learn at the same time, nor will everyone process data and knowledge in the same manner, and we must be alright with that.

We must also accept the concept of multilinguality. These students may be weak in the English language, but they do have sufficient proficiency in their L1 and they also have knowledge of literature in L1. We must be in a position to exploit that knowledge (Ghosh, 2010). In fact, this writer believes that the learner's knowledge of L1 is more important than being just a resource or an asset. It is actually, as we say in Sanskrit, a 'sampad', a lexical term that does not have an actual English equivalent. In narrow semantics, sampad means an asset, but it has wider connotations of 'success, profit, advantage' (Bodewitz, 2003, p. 233) and also as an 'acquirement' (p. 234) if we look at its etymology. In *Natyashastra*, it is described as a compounding of 'sama' (equal) and 'pada' (quartet/stanza) ("Sampad, sampat, saṃpat, saṃpad"). Likewise, the learner's knowledge of L1 is his/her 'success, profit, advantage', his/her 'acquirement'; and giving the linguistically-disadvantaged learner the freedom to use his/her L1 in the English literature classroom provides them with a sense of dignity, equality and equity.

When the teacher acknowledges the learner's sampad of his knowledge of L1 as well as of his/her knowledge of literature in L1, the teacher essentially acknowledges the learner as an individual who is aware of their shortcomings and also of their strengths. Further, when the teacher acknowledges the learner as a knowledgeable adult and provides him/her with adequate freedom and space to express him/herself, it is quite easy to get the learner excited. It is possible to see real-time progress being made by such learners who had given up, with the teachers also having given up on them.

Another interesting idea is that of the 'thought seed' (Deepa, 2022b). Adults are able to carry a thought and act on it at a later stage. A teacher can exploit this by deliberately planting a thought—like sowing a seed—in the learners' mind. By dropping a literary thought in the mind of the learner, there to gradually take root and sooner or later blossom into an urge for new learning, the teacher can open newfangled avenues that learners can explore at their own pace.

In the next part I enumerate some examples from my classroom, where I have made use of the principles and practices of anthrogogy at the tertiary level in the English literature classroom. When provided with adequate impetus, we can see that both teachers and learners use strategies of their own to learn in their own ways, which perhaps would not have happened if the teacher and the learner answered to the burden of the 'need to be told'.

The Use of Interpretative Space

While reading Dickens' *Oliver Twist*, we reached the chapter where Bill Sykes meets his end attempting to escape using a rope, but being accidentally killed by hanging on the same rope. One student asked if it can be seen as the role of fate. Though initially surprised by the reference to a literary concept like 'role of fate', I realised that this question came from the study of Shakespeare's play *Macbeth* in the previous year, where they had learned the concept of tragic fate. Instead of giving a clear answer, I asked the students if they can think of other such examples from the text where fate plays a part. One by one, they came up with other instances, such as Oliver meeting the Brownlows. In the course of this discussion, one student also used the term 'chance and coincidence'—again an unexpected use of a literary concept. I realised that this is a term they have picked up from the reading of another text in the previous semester, which is Thomas Hardy's novel *Far from the Madding Crowd*. This gave me the opportunity to discuss Dickens' narrative technique of using coincidences. Later I also suggested that they present a paper on how Victorian writers use coincidence as a narrative technique, but that has not yet borne fruit—existing perhaps as a 'thought seed' at the moment and will germinate once ready.

The Experience of Shared Learning

While teaching Samuel Beckett's play *Waiting for Godot*, when we got to the end of the play, it was quite anti-climactic for the class that Godot does not come. They were not used to a text that was open-ended and so could not quite comprehend the fact that the play ended in an open manner. Among many questions on the play's ending, one was 'What would happen if Godot actually came?'. The extrapolative nature of this simple question caught me off guard because being conditioned to accept the views of the author, as the teacher, I had never contemplated such a scenario myself. For me, that Godot will not come was a given and central to its absurdity. So, I found it very difficult to answer that question. I, however, managed the situation by throwing open the question to the class where the students, in their own understanding, responded that Godot may have come at some other time, at some other place, and therefore may have not met the tramps. I, on my part, have not yet found a satisfying response to the question 'What if Godot came?', but my quest to find an answer has contributed to my understanding of the play.

The Exploitation of Knowledge of Literature in L1

I have found that the students are more responsive when we move out of the syllabus and introduce shorter, simpler texts to discuss literary concepts. In a class where I was to read Edgar Allan Poe's short story 'The Purloined Letter', I introduced another simpler short story, Kate Chopin's 'The Story of an Hour', in order to talk about the characteristics of a short story. When I read the story and identified the twist in the tale, the students could relate to stories they had read in Bangla which had similar features, particularly Moti Nandy's short story 'Ekti Khuner Sambad' ('The News of a Murder'), which was in their Bangla literature syllabus.

The Use of Thought Seeds

At the end of the reading of Sylvia Plath's confessional poem 'Daddy', where the poet confesses about her complicated relationship with her father, I put forward a question to the class to think about: if the gender roles were reversed, that is, if the writer was male, could he have written a similar poem about his mother? Would such a poem have gained acceptability? This is a thought I have planted in their minds which I think will germinate in due time and, I think, will manifest itself in different people in different ways. For my part, I am yet to receive a response; but when I do, I plan to introduce them to the male confessional poets like Robert Lowell and Allen Ginsberg.

These are a few of my personal experiences where I have been successful in engaging the students in a productive discussion when I treated them as adults, gave them sufficient space to form their own interpretations, comfortably use their own knowledge of literature they have gained from the learning of literature in their L1, or gave them sufficient time for some of their thoughts to grow. In none of these instances did the learners feel a need to be told as they came up with their own literary interpretations, nor did I as the teacher sense the compulsion that the learners need to be told. In other words, the learners and the teacher were cohesively able to transcend the need to be told.

References

Blaschke, L. M. (2012). Heutagogy and lifelong learning: A review of heutagogical practice and self-determined learning. *International Review of Research in Open and Distance Learning*, *13*(1), 56–71. https://doi.org/10.19173/irrodl.v13i1.1076.

Bodewitz, H. W. (2003). The concept of "sampad" in the Arthaśāstra, the vedic prose texts and the Gītā. *Indo-Iranian Journal*, *46*(3), 231–259.

Chandrashekaran, D., & Sultana, S. (2026). Anthrogogicity and learner agency in academic writing. In S. Deepa & G. Durairajan (Eds.), *Anthrogogy in use: A handbook for language educators* (pp. 122–135). Orient BlackSwan.

Deepa, S. (2022a). Pedagogic scaffolding and anthrogogic learning contexts: Issues in metaphor mismatch. *ELTIF*, *XIII*(2), 3–7.

Deepa, S. (2022b). Thought seeds in anthrogogic learning contexts. *Journal of Indian Education*, *48*(2), 58–70.

Deepa, S. (2026). Principles of anthrogogic language education. In S. Deepa & G. Durairajan (Eds.), *Anthrogogy in use: A handbook for language educators* (pp. 3–26). Orient BlackSwan.

Durairajan, G., & Deepa, S. (2026). Prolegomena: Moving from pedagogy to anthrogogy. In S. Deepa & G. Durairajan (Eds.), *Anthrogogy in use: A handbook for language educators* (pp. xix–xxviii). Orient BlackSwan.

Ghosh, D. (2010). *Transfer of L1 literary capability to L2: A study at the tertiary level* [Unpublished MPhil dissertation]. EFLU, Hyderabad.

Hase, S., & Kenyon, C. (2000). From andragogy to heutagogy. *ultiBASE In-Site*, *5*(3), 1–10.

Kazemek, F. E., & Rigg, P. (1986). Four poets: Modern poetry in the adult literacy classroom. *Journal of Reading*, *30*(3), 218–225.

Knowles, M. S. (1990). *The adult learner: A neglected species*. Gulf Publishing Co.

Knowles, M. S., Holton III, E. F., & Swanson R. A. (2005) *The Adult Learner* (6th ed). Routledge.

Peterson, C. M., & Ray, C. M. (2013). Andragogy and metagogy: The evolution of neologisms. *Journal of Adult Education*, *42*(2), 82–85.

Sampad, sampat, saṃpat, saṃpad: 20 definitions. (2023, February 20). In *Wisdom Library*. https://www.wisdomlib.org/definition/sampad.

Strohschen, G., & Elazier, K. (2019). The metagogy theorem: A framework for educating adults. *International Forum of Teaching and Studies*, *15*(1), 3–15.

Trott, D. C. (1991, October). *Anthrogogy* [Paper presentation]. American Association for Adult and Continuing Education, Montreal, Quebec. https://eric.ed.gov/?id=ED342887.

9

Unveiling Anthrogogic Practices

Teaching Novels to English Literature Students

Narji Baruah

Reading a novel for pleasure is different from reading a novel to comprehend and analyse it from multiple critical lenses. A simple reading of a novel, penned in English, featuring an unfamiliar setting and plot, will only lead to a basic understanding of the narrative. This means that such a simple reading of a novel gives only a rough overview of a novel. It involves reading the novel with limited or no questions from the reader at all. Moreover, readers of this kind do not focus on discovering connections, references, or associations with various texts, experiences, society, or culture. On the other hand, careful and conscious reading of a novel leads the readers to understand and examine the novel from critical perspectives.

Literature is taught to adult learners with the expectation that they will engage with texts on a deeper intellectual level. Students who are adult learners of English literature are therefore expected to approach a novel not only to critically read, comprehend, and analyse it, but also to reflect on its thematic relevance, cultural significance, and narrative techniques. However, such an approach to reading a novel cannot be inculcated in students all of a sudden. It is a gradual process and needs to be taught by the teacher in class so that the student can eventually become a self-sufficient critical reader. Critical thinking and reading work in tandem. Critical thinkers are willing, persistent, flexible, open-minded, and confident in using certain cognitive skills when it is necessary and appropriate (Ennis, 1987; Facione, 1990; Halpern, 1998, 2003, cited in Lun, et al., 2010). They question not only what was said, but also what was implied and suggested. In addition, they are aware of their interpretations, revising and refining them constantly (Mahshad, 2017). If a student can analyse a text critically, it is indicative that such a student is a critical reader.

Most students of English literature face difficulties in comprehending and being able to identify and state, while reading, the climax or that

moment in the narrative where things reach a breaking point, where tension is at its peak, or when some significant discovery occurs for which they need to use their 'interpretative space'. This space can be defined as the mental space that readers use to delve deeply into a text in the context of literary analysis. It emphasises the need to delve deeper, taking into account other interpretations, points of view, and all the minute nuances that give the whole text depth and richness. To fully understand the author's message, cultural context, and writing processes, readers are encouraged to go further into the text rather than merely reading it in a cursory manner.

The principal reason behind students facing such difficulty in understanding moments of climax in these novels, amongst many others, is that the language and setting of the novels prescribed for students of English literature in India are not familiar to them. The plots are set in unfamiliar locations and the language in which the text is written is often their second or even third language, English; hence, interpreting the text becomes challenging for the students.

As an illustration, we will look at the oft-prescribed Jane Austen's *Pride and Prejudice* which, as the teacher–researcher, I taught to degree-level students of English literature in a college in Assam, India. The narrative of this novel unfolds from Hertfordshire in the southeast to Derbyshire in the East Midlands, England. The storyline takes place against almost indistinguishable backgrounds, showcasing comparable cultural norms and social hierarchies. The unfamiliarity of this setting was a challenge for students attempting to understand the novel. Students who were from a regional-medium background faced more difficulties in fully grasping those moments when tensions reached their peak.

It should be mentioned that it takes careful planning on the part of the teacher to enable comprehension of texts written in English and placed in foreign settings, especially in places like Assam where English is the second, or even third language. It is crucial to accept the basic idea of an anthrogogic way of looking at a text which gives importance to the incorporation of different cultural contexts while dealing with the same.

When literature is taught from a pedagogic perspective, lectures play a crucial role in exploring the themes, characters, and contextual complexities of a novel. During these sessions, the teachers may delve into historical and cultural contexts, providing valuable insights to assist students in understanding unfamiliar settings within the narrative.

But it is the teacher who has to take on the onus of providing all this information. In contrast, when literature is taught from an anthrogogic perspective (Deepa, 2026), classroom discussions and interactive sessions offer students a platform to articulate their interpretations, and exchange cultural perspectives which contribute to a cooperative and collaborative understanding of the novel.

Anthrogogy (Deepa, 2022, 2026) can be defined as a set of multifarious learning principles that operate on the foundations of unity in diversity of experiential differences, with multilinguality and pluriculturalism as the venous network that acts as the propulsive force from within. Hence, a comprehensive approach that incorporates the principles of anthrogogy strives to cultivate an inclusive and dynamic learning environment. By doing so, it empowers students to overcome the obstacles posed by novels set in foreign contexts and composed in a language that may not be their primary means of communication.

Teachers can solve the problem of disconnection, mentioned earlier, by implementing an anthrogogic perspective while planning their classes. This could entail offering additional materials to students in both the local language and English in a judicious manner, promoting group conversations that facilitate language interchange and integrating cultural context in the process of teaching and learning. As explained by Durairajan, Nainala, and Ghosh, 'the teacher deliberately uses the L1, to tap knowledge of the world, or knowledge of L1 and about the L1 to enable language capability in L2' (2011, p. 29) The teacher–researcher here, contemplates whether exposing students to the background of a text (here, novel) and encouraging connections with their cultural contexts would enable them to grasp the intended information of the author and analyse it through a critical lens.

In this chapter, the background of the students refers to those concepts and ideas which students are familiar with. When students dive into a novel set in a foreign land, their previous beliefs and ideas play a big role in how they understand the plot of the text. Drawing on schema theory, background knowledge or schemata are used to help readers strengthen memory or activate their existing knowledge structure to bridge the gap between what they have already understood and the whole details expressed in the passage for achieving the outcome of reading comprehension (Xue Jinyu, 2022, as cited in Ren, 2023). In such a case, the teacher can exploit the background knowledge of the students to enable them to make such connections. It highlights the

importance of considering what the students already know when they're processing stories set in different places or countries, and with a different set of cultural assumptions. As they read, students bring along mental frameworks filled with pre-existing notions about social norms, cultural practices, and geography. These mental guides help them make sense of the narrative in an unfamiliar setting. Whether it is knowledge about historical events, cultural standards, or the lay of the land, having these ideas in mind enhances the reading experience.

In an era, when almost all references to materials are accessible through Google, a teacher teaching a text based on a different sociocultural setting not familiar to the students, usually brings in pictures or videos to make the students understand and relate to what is being taught. For example, while coming across a description of 'Thrushcross Grange' (the large estate on the Yorkshire moors in *Wuthering Heights* by Emily Brontë) the students may not be familiar with the notion of what a grange is. In such a case, a video clip from the movie *Wuthering Heights*, or an image from Google can be shown to the students to get a clear idea of the word 'grange'. In this scenario, while it is accurate to acknowledge that such a viewing may help the students gain a general understanding of the meaning of the word, there exists a potential drawback as relying solely on providing direct references to students may foster a habit that limits their approach to interpreting texts; similar to how, from a pedagogic method of teaching literature, lecture notes are dictated. This approach may confine them to viewing a given text from a narrow perspective, hindering the development of a more comprehensive understanding. Furthermore, this method may inadvertently discourage students from establishing meaningful connections between the foreign literature they are exploring and their native literary traditions, which are inherently rich. Thus, the risk lies in unintentionally restricting students' interpretative skills and hindering their ability to appreciate the broader cultural and literary contexts at play. Along with providing a direct reference to the novel in which it is set, connecting the text with the students' background and native literature will result in developing critical thinking and reading skills among readers. In this connection, Naskar and Jha, (2017) point out that 'he [the reader] must be able to put himself in a position where he would read a text critically with the help of his cultural knowledge but not become prejudiced by it.' (p. 175). This indicates that the cultural knowledge of the readers should help them to look at the text from a wider perspective, and it should not negatively interrupt their thoughts and thereby the process of reading the text.

An anthrogogic approach to teaching a text is centred on recognising and leveraging students' diverse backgrounds, experiences, and perspectives to enrich their understanding (Ghosh, 2026). It recognises that students' interpretations of texts are shaped by a multitude of personal experiences and cultural factors. This helps students draw parallels and contrasts between books written by well-known authors in well-known settings, which leads to a deeper understanding of the characters, settings, and contexts of these different texts. The anthrogogic approach acknowledges that instruction ought to embrace and integrate students' diverse viewpoints rather than sever them from their cultural heritage. It also seeks to develop students' critical thinking skills by giving them the means to evaluate novels critically. It encourages engaging conversations in which students can express their ideas, viewpoints, and points of contention, fostering a vibrant and welcoming learning atmosphere that honours and respects the students' varied experiences. Essentially, teaching a text in an anthrogogic manner gives students the confidence to approach literature with a wider perspective and an open mind. The results benefit both teachers and learners to proceed gradually from the initial stage of the 'interpretative space' (Deepa, 2026) to its climax.

This chapter critically examines a few anthrogogic practices that were used to bridge the gap between the reader (student) and a text (novel) written in English by relating it with the backgrounds of the students. This study is the first-hand experience of the teacher–researcher teaching English literature at the tertiary level, with thirty-five, fourth semester students registered for a BA in English Literature, in a women's degree college in Assam, India.

The novel *Jane Eyre* has been taken as an example to support the argument raised by the researcher regarding the usefulness of using anthrogogic practices to teach critical reading skills. At first, these second-year literature students were asked to read the text at the beginning of the semester. This was expected to be done before the actual classroom teaching of the text as the total teaching hours cannot be used to only read one particular text. This setup was intentional, designed to catch the students' first, unguided responses to the material before any teaching influence. This way, the study aimed to watch and analyse how they initially grasped and interpreted the content, giving us valuable insights into their understanding and perspectives right at the start, without the immediate influence of formal teaching. However, they could not complete reading the whole text before actual classroom teaching due to various reasons such as reading other texts, completion of assignments, co-curricular activities, et cetera.

The students were asked to tell the teacher and other classmates what the novel was about and what it said. They were able to narrate the main plot and state that *Jane Eyre* is written by Charlotte Bronte; that the central character is Jane Eyre who is an orphan ill-treated by her aunt. They could conclude that she goes to Lowood Institution and later works as a governess. They were also able to understand that, in the end, she marries the owner of the house. The students were clear with the plot, but during this re-telling there were none or very limited critical observations.

This teacher–researcher started with an introduction to the author of the novel. The students were told that *Jane Eyre* was written by Charlotte Bronte under the masculine pseudonym Currer Bell. They were then asked to recollect the characteristics of Victorian society and the status of women during that period. There was a discussion with them on this issue and I pointed out that women during the Victorian era (1820–1914) had to face numerous challenges in every sphere of their lives. Victorian women were expected to take care of the home, family, and children. I also asked them to reflect on their own experiences of family life in India and whether such a status is true of India today. Women in the Victorian era were not allowed to become independent. More importantly, the writings of women writers were not taken seriously. At this point, the reason why Charlotte Bronte had to take a pseudonym became clear to the students. They were then asked to think a little more deeply about the status of women today, and whether women can write and publish their work with their real identity in the present era. The answers were affirmative. They named some famous female writers of the present era such as Arundhati Roy, Alice Walker, Margaret Atwood, Chimamanda Ngozi Adichie, et cetera. I added to the list and raised the students' awareness regarding female writers of the region like Nirupama Borgohain, Mamoni Raisom Goswami, Rita Chowdhury, et cetera, whose contribution to Assamese literature is worth mentioning.

The reading and analysis of the text went on simultaneously. Due to time constraints, students were asked to read the remaining portion of the text during their library hours and at home. The discussions took place in class. At the end of this reading and discussion, the movie

Jane Eyre was screened in the classroom so the students would be able to visualise the scenic views of England, Gateshead Hall, Lowood Institution, Thornfield Hall et cetera. As mentioned earlier, students often find it challenging to create a mental picture of the locale and actual setting of the novel when the text is in their second language (here, English) especially if it is set in a foreign place. While the screening of the movie provided a clear picture of the background, it did not help the students relate to the main character and understand her mental travails, for the dialogues in the movie are not only in English but also in the local dialect. To help them form a connection to Jane Eyre, I experimented with something very different. Instead of using a character from the English text to make comparisons, I got the students to draw parallels with a character from an Assamese folktale called 'Tejimola'. This folktale, penned by Lakshminath Bezbarua and forming part of his collection of short stories titled *Burhi Aair Xadhu* ('Old Granny's Tales'), served as a familiar reference point for the students. In that story, the main character—Tejimola—experienced the heartbreaking loss of her mother during her early years, echoing a similar circumstance to Jane Eyre. While Jane was orphaned, Tejimola's father remarried, leading to a challenging situation where she faced abuse from her stepmother. The parallel between Jane and Tejimola lies in their difficult childhoods, marked by a persistent atmosphere of fear. Both characters share a common thread of navigating through the hardships of their early lives, painting a poignant picture of the challenges they had to endure during their formative years.

In *Jane Eyre*, Jane is unaware of Mr Rochester's first wife Bertha Mason. Had she known about Bertha, there was a possibility that she might not have developed a liking for Mr Rochester. It was a dreadful truth that she was unable to accept and hence left Gateshead Hall. In a novel written by Sushmita Banerjee, *Kabuliwalar Bangali Bou* ('A Kabuliwala's Bengali Wife') when the main character (the writer herself) first went on to Kabul from Kolkata after getting married to Jaanbaaz (without her family's consent), to her surprise she found that her husband was married to Gulguti previously. In both instances, the female characters find themselves unaware of a significant and concealed aspect of their partners' lives, the fact that their partners were previously married. While the specific circumstances surrounding Jane and Sushmita differ, the common thread lies in the profound shock and difficulty each woman experiences upon learning this previously undisclosed information. The revelation of their partners' prior marriages introduces a complex emotional and psychological challenge for both Jane and Sushmita, highlighting the shared theme of undisclosed marital history and the subsequent emotional impact on the unsuspecting female characters.

The examples cited above were drawn from works in Assamese and Bengali literature. This choice was deliberate, considering that the students have familiarity with both Assamese and Bengali literary traditions, allowing them to readily connect with the contexts and situations referenced during class discussions. More importantly, they would be able to read and interpret those novels/short stories with ease, for Bengali/Assamese is the more enabled language for these students. By incorporating literature from these regions, the aim is to leverage the students' linguistic and cultural familiarity to enhance their engagement and comprehension of the material. The intent is to create a learning environment where students feel a strong connection to the content, facilitating a deeper and more meaningful exploration of the literary nuances present in Assamese and Bengali literature. This is evident in a study done by Durairajan, Nainala, and Ghosh, (2011) in which they stated that 'if the student's capability in the more enabled language is used as a vehicle for thinking, planning, organizing, analyzing, revising, etc. language/literary capability can be enabled more effectively' (p. 30).

Mustofal and Hill (2018) opine that life experience and the knowledge readers bring to a text play a significant role in their interpretation of the text. When the characters Tejimola and Sushmita in the context of the plot of *Jane Eyre* were cited as examples, students began to share similar situations that have happened in connection to these events. Student M said, 'Though the plot of Jane Eyre is set in a foreign land we've never been to, the hardships that Jane underwent as an orphan are prevalent even in today's era.'[1] Another student, Student N, contributed to the discussion saying, 'The themes of domination and subjugation depicted in the novel aren't confined to historical contexts; rather, they continue to influence the lives of women in today's society.' In this way, the students' comments added layers of real-world connection to the literary analysis, demonstrating how the universality of certain themes in Jane Eyre sparked reflections on their own lived experiences and societal observations.

---

[1] In order to maintain the confidentiality of the students their names have not been revealed. They are deliberately referred to as Student, M, P, et cetera.

Continuing the discussion on the anthrogogic approach to teaching literature, other students delved into their own experiences to enrich the exploration of Jane Eyre. Student P remarked, 'Tejimola's resilience is inspiring. It made me reflect on the strength we find within ourselves during challenging times. Jane's character feels like a companion in my own journey.' This insightful comment from Student P emphasises the personalised connection students establish with characters, underlining the novel's ability to transcend temporal and cultural boundaries. Student Q added a layer of complexity to the discussion by sharing, 'The expectations placed on women to conform to societal norms have lasting consequences, and it's not confined to a specific period or place.' Student Q's perspective highlights the intergenerational impact of societal expectations, showcasing how literature becomes a medium for students to articulate their reflections on broader societal issues. Student R offered a unique viewpoint by stating, 'Jane Eyre opened my eyes to the complexities of identity. Tejimola's journey in reconciling her past and present resonated with my own exploration of selfhood in the modern world.' This comment adds a layer of introspection, emphasising how literature serves as a catalyst for self-discovery and personal growth. None of these reflections and insights would have been possible, if this text had been taught from a pedagogic perspective, where only the teacher's insights and views would have been articulated. The novel and the experiences delineated in it would not have been 'owned' by the students. From an anthrogogic perspective, we need to understand that students 'do not need to be told' how to interpret the text (see Ghosh 2026 for a detailed discussion of this concept). Given the space and freedom to think, compare, contrast, analyse, and evaluate, they become critical readers who are able to go into their own interpretive space to make connections.

The additional comments by students, self-reflective and introspective, further illustrate the anthrogogic approach's effectiveness in fostering a rich and multifaceted engagement with literature. By incorporating their own narratives and observations, students not only enhance their understanding of the text but also contribute to a collective exploration of universal themes that transcend the confines of the novel itself.

Introducing *Jane Eyre* as a part of English literature, especially when connected to other familiar texts, opened up a rich space for multiple interpretations among the students; a kind of 'interpretative space' where diverse perspectives could flourish. The students' backgrounds, shaped by their unique experiences, played a crucial role in enabling them to approach the novel from various angles. By referencing texts penned by familiar authors set in known environments, students were encouraged to draw comparisons and contrasts between characters, settings, and contexts, enhancing their understanding.

It is worth noting that teaching directly from the text can sometimes lead to a disconnection from students' own cultural roots. Herein lies the significance of an anthrogogic approach to reading, which is a method that embraces and integrates students' cultural backgrounds rather than causing detachment. This approach, therefore, not only widens the intellectual horizons of the students but also provides them with the tools to critically engage with the novel. The students, armed with diverse inputs, are not just readers but active participants in discussions about the characters, plot, and setting of *Jane Eyre*. They bring forth their opinions and arguments, fostering a dynamic learning environment that respects and values the varied cultural and personal backgrounds of the students. By embracing this diversity, the anthrogogic approach gives rise to an environment where students feel empowered to explore literature from various angles, appreciate different viewpoints, and engage in meaningful discussions. It promotes a sense of inclusivity that allows each student to connect personally with the material, creating a more enriching and comprehensive learning experience. Ultimately, the anthrogogic way of teaching literature strives to cultivate not only a deeper understanding of the texts but also a more tolerant and appreciative mindset among students.

In the realm of pedagogic teaching, the focus often revolves around breaking down the literary nuances of classic works, and 'spoon-feeding' it to students. In contrast, it is essential to accept the dynamic responses from students when employing an anthrogogic approach. During my time teaching *Pride and Prejudice* by Jane Austen to college-level students, the anthrogogic method helped me to open up numerous perspectives. One student, drawing from their cultural background, remarked, 'Elizabeth's struggle against societal expectations resonates with the challenges we face in our communities. It's like Austen is speaking to us across time.' Another student, from a contrasting cultural background, added, 'The intricate dance of manners and etiquette in the novel is both fascinating and alien. It makes me question the expectations imposed on individuals in different societies.' These responses illustrate how the anthrogogic approach encourages students to merge their experiences and cultural contexts into the framework of the narrative. Such engagement not only deepens their understanding of the material but also nurtures a sense of connection and relevance, fostering a learning environment that transcends the boundaries of time and culture.

References

Austen, J. (1813). *Pride and prejudice*. T. Egerton.

Banerjee, S. (1997). *Kabuliwalar bangali bou*. Bhasa O Sahitya.

Bezbaruah, L. (1911). *Burhi aair xadhu*. Banalata Prakashan.

Bronte, C. (1992). *Jane Eyre*. Wordsworth Editions.

Deepa, S. (2022). Thought seeds in anthrogogic learning contexts. *Journal of Indian Education*, *48*, 58–70.

Deepa, S. (2026). Principles of anthrogogic language education. In S. Deepa & G. Durairajan (Eds.), *Anthrogogy in use: A handbook for language educators* (pp. 3–26). Orient BlackSwan.

Durairajan, G., Nainala, S., & Ghosh, D. (2011). Exploiting L1 knowledge in English teaching: Teacher education possibilities. In *Starting, stimulating and sustaining English language teacher education and development: A selection of papers presented at the International Conference in Hyderabad in January 2011* (pp. 27–31). British Council. https://www.britishcouncil.in/sites/default/files/tec11_conference_papers_0.pdf.

Ghosh, D. (2026). Looking beyond the compulsion of 'need to be told': An attempt at anthrogocity in the undergraduate literature classroom. In S. Deepa & G. Durairajan (Eds.), *Anthrogogy in use: A handbook for language educators* (pp. 165–173). Orient BlackSwan.

Lun, V., Fischer, R., & Ward, C. (2010). Exploring cultural differences in critical thinking: Is it about my thinking style or the language I speak?. *Learning and Individual Differences*, *20*, 604–616. https://doi.org/10.1016/j.lindif.2010.07.001.

Mustofal, A., & Hill, J. L. (2018). Understanding cultural context in responding to literature: Researching the teaching of literature in EFL classroom context. *English Language Teaching*, *11*(6), 108–114. https://doi.org/10.5539/elt.v11n6p108.

Nakar, G., & Jha, S. (2017). The role of cultural schemata in critical reading. *International Education & Research Journal*, *3*(5). https://ierj.in/journal/index.php/ierj/article/view/839.

Ren, Shiqin. (2023). The application of schema theory to the teaching of reading comprehension. *Journal of Education and Educational Research*, *2*, 86–88. https://doi.org/10.54097/jeer.v2i3.7578.

Tasnimi, Mahshad. (2017). Critical reading: An introduction. *Humanising Language* Teaching, *19*(6), 1–6, https://www.researchgate.net/publication/351428432_Critical_reading_An_introduction.

10

Thought Seeds as an Instrument for Assessing the Intercultural Competence of Adult ESL Learners

PANKAJ NARKE

Introduction

Education in the twenty-first century has undergone several changes in response to the demands of changing sociopolitical equations in different parts of the world. With increasing global trade and knowledge exchange, communication and collaboration skills have become immensely desired and are ranked higher in the modern education framework than mere language skills (Bernie, 2009). Empowering individuals to negotiate their thoughts in the integrated global system effectively has become a top priority of educational programmes. To facilitate this demand, a major prerequisite is optimum exposure to international cultures. One must possess adequate intercultural competence (IC) to function smoothly between two cultures.

While defining IC, it is difficult to zero in on a specific definition as it has been referred to using various terms like global competence, multicultural competence, and intercultural maturity (Fantini, 2009). Intercultural competence comes into play when two individuals from different cultural backgrounds engage in a reciprocal interaction based on their commonly agreed understanding and readiness to adopt, or at least accept, each other's perspectives. It is the preparation to interact appropriately and effectively with persons of a different culture (Sinecrope, et al., 2012). Some researchers explore the appropriateness of communication and define IC as an ethical orientation that highlights morally right ways of being, thinking, and acting (Jokikokko, 2005).

The need for developed IC became more intense with the advent of communication technology. The world is emerging as a common market for all, and an ideal place for graduates to look for professional opportunities. Most workplaces today recognise the significance of a multicultural environment, leading to wide outreach for their businesses.

Hence, working with individuals from various cultures is ubiquitous, requiring an openness of mind to learn new cultural practices and adjust one's own to meet a common understanding. The White Paper on Intercultural Dialogue by the Council of Europe (2008) clearly states that every individual should work to improve their IC as it is necessary for the development and maintenance of a sustainable democratic society.

Following the need for developed IC, one of the top priorities of educational institutions is to equip individuals with adequate cross-cultural communication skills. Consequently, educational policies and curricula worldwide have begun integrating cross-cultural content for teaching and assessment. One of the major reasons for this is that students at the tertiary level are at a constructive stage of their social development and start forming their world views based on their experiences. Students at the tertiary level are most likely to have serious discussions about their beliefs and values regarding cultural practices. Actions like negotiating identities, trying out different perspectives, accepting and rejecting views, et cetera, are frequent in higher education. Furthermore, students attempt to acquire and strengthen their employability or entrepreneurial skills at this stage. One of the objectives of higher education is to enable students to fit into the global set-up, which enhanced IC can facilitate.

In the context of international education, students are most likely to experience cultural shock, which refers to coming across cultural practices that are possibly different from one's own. In such situations, providing intercultural input becomes necessary for the teachers, yet remains challenging.

IC in the English as Second Language (ELS) Classroom

The intercultural approach to language teaching has been identified as very close to communicative language teaching (CLT) by several researchers (Derin, et al., 2009; Piątkowska, 2015). One of the reasons for this claim is that to develop IC, a learner has to engage in a meaning-focused task[1] that has relevance in real life. Further, learners must negotiate for meaning during communication, leading to an organic language acquisition process. Although all these aspects are factored

[1] A meaning-focused educational activity where students must employ both linguistic and non-linguistic resources to get a communicative end is known as a 'task' (Ellis, 2009).

into CLT, it does not necessarily focus on learners' socio-cognitive development with reference to the attitudes needed to be inculcated for communicating with people from a different culture. CLT does not focus on developing culture-specific knowledge among language learners to communicate cross-culturally. Therefore, the scope of the IC approach to language education is broader than that of CLT as it goes beyond communicative competence and ventures into developing attitudes, values, and perspectives. An interculturally competent speaker is not only linguistically accurate but also culturally appropriate. The objective of IC is to enable learners to handle complex situations, acknowledge multiple identities, and systematically avoid biases about other cultures during communication.

IC in language education has been highly influenced by Byram's prototype of intercultural communicative competence (ICC) (1997). This eclectic model integrates multiple disciplines such as applied linguistics, sociolinguistics, social identity theory, and cross-cultural communication. Byram underlined five important elements of intercultural communicative competence in his model, namely, knowledge, attitudes, skills of interpreting and relating, skills of discovery and interaction, and political education incorporating critical cultural awareness. According to this model, knowledge refers to the state of having a sense of the course of social interaction, cultural references, and their significance in meaning-making while communicating. Attitude encompasses the willingness to accept new knowledge and practices from a different culture and engage in interactions with openness. The skills of interpreting and relating denote the capacity to understand new contexts while communicating, and using cultural symbolism for the betterment of communication rather than leading to misunderstanding. Acquiring new cultural knowledge and integrating it into everyday communication effectively by understanding the sociocultural challenges indicates the possession of the skills of diversity and interaction. Finally, the ability to critically evaluate one's own and others' beliefs and practices indicates critical cultural awareness.

To implement the ideas of the IC model in a language classroom, Byram (2002) proposed three pedagogic methods. Firstly, a teacher can promote a comparative analysis of two cultures by presenting cultural facts from a foreign culture through teaching materials. Then, the teacher would guide students to find similarities and differences between their own and target-language cultures. Tasks like role-play, information gap, and simulation techniques can facilitate this. This technique aims to make students realise how the people from the target-language culture react and respond to specific situations. Secondly, the teaching and learning materials should be presented from intercultural and critical perspectives. Here, the teacher would present texts with a theme from a foreign culture and encourage learners to ask questions about unfamiliar concepts. Lastly, authentic materials from the target-language culture, including audio, visuals, and written texts, must be critically analysed. Encouraging learners to make judgments about the text enhances their text comprehension and enables them to understand the sentiments attached to a specific topic in the target language culture (Martínez-Flor, 2008).

Although these recommendations for integrating IC in ESL classrooms appear to be comprehensive, there is still great reluctance to practice IC by teachers (Alyan, 2011; Byram, et al., 2013; Garrido & Álvarez, 2006; Sercu, 2006), because they face several challenges while implementing the IC approach in their classrooms. Teachers require systematic orientation for using IC materials for teaching and assessment. In the case of adult learners, the teacher should be able to understand the scope of introducing IC elements and assess them accordingly. Adult learners bring more cognitive resources into the classroom, including perceptions, ideologies, emotions, and preferences. It is, therefore, important to provide learners sufficient space to utilise these aspects and form a balanced world-view. Teachers should be trained to alter their instructional methods and materials to suit learners' interests and cognitive levels.

However, there is no differentiation in the teaching method used for adults and children. The use of pedagogic tasks—common among young learners—in the teaching and assessing of adult learners restricts them from expressing their ideas openly. This happens because the pedagogic tasks have predefined output and structures (Breen, 1987). In such cases, adult learners have to stick to the task instructions without being able to express themselves freely and being able to develop their perspectives on the topics.

An example of a pedagogic task would be:

List the reasons the lawyer provided in 'The Bet', a short story by Anton Chekhov, for supporting life imprisonment as against the death penalty. Form groups of four students and discuss whether the lawyer's decision to accept the bet was right or wrong. Then, write your conclusions in 300 words.

This task is based on a short story, 'The Bet', taught to first-year Engineering students as a part of their syllabus. The task is pedagogic, as it has specific instructions for working procedures and a defined output size (300 written words). Although the task encourages group work to promote meaningful communication, it does not allow the learners to take the discussion outside textual contexts. The task has a specific learning objective: learners should understand the character's (lawyer) perspective and evaluate it based on the storyline. Although this task has the potential to assess learners' knowledge of the text, it does not encourage learners to apply the knowledge in their surroundings. In this task, there is no scope for the learners to criticise or compare their values about the topic. These features of a pedagogic task hinder an assessment of their cultural and cross-cultural knowledge.

To assess intercultural competence, the learners need space to express their perspectives without many restrictions. The absence of such appropriate assessment tasks results in inadequate integration of IC in the adult ESL classroom (Tran & Dang, 2014).

Assessment of IC

Very few models are available for assessing learners' intercultural competence to define a learner's communicative abilities. Hashem (1995) proposed a standard Cultural Test, which consists of multiple-choice questions that learners had to respond to. These questions were mainly based on cultural stereotypes and generalisations. Learners had to choose the appropriate options for given situations. Although this test was feasible to administer, it restricted the learners to fixed responses, which might not allow them to express their individual cultural experiences.

A similar challenge was faced by Fantini and Tirmizi (2006) and Allen and Herron (2003) in their intercultural diagnostic test, which used Likert scale-based questions. Learners are given predetermined responses and their only responsibility is to choose the probability of intensity that they may experience as a response to the given intercultural situation. Learners are not permitted to alter the provided factual information. They are rather forcefully pushed to connect with the given options and choose the one they think is most accurate. Hence, although learners choose one of the given options, that choice might not be the most authentic. Jackson (2005) suggested using reflective diaries where learners record their intercultural experiences to identify their level of IC. However, this method has been subject to criticism. First, the primary condition for using this tool is that the teacher has to believe every entry the learners have made. Sometimes, learners may not want to write about their uneasy intercultural experiences to save themselves from wrong impressions. However, these experiences are most significant in intercultural knowledge acquisition. Further, interpreting these diary entries is subject to external factors such as teachers' beliefs, motivation, and awareness. Teachers' beliefs and understanding of a specific culture may affect their judgments about learners' experiences. Sometimes, their unawareness of certain cultural practices would also hinder their interpretations. These factors may influence the interpretation (Gillespie & Cornish, 2009).

Learners should involve their personal experiences while judging cultural facts, interpreting cultural practices, and performing comparative analyses between two or more cultures. Therefore, the instrument for assessing IC should allow learners to express their ideas, but not in a predetermined framework like language tasks. Thus, not having an appropriate perspective for assessing learners' IC knowledge poses a problem for teachers in integrating IC into the language classroom.

Anthrogogic Perspectives for IC

Adults learn differently than children, as their concerns and perceptions of the world differ from those of young learners. Therefore, pedagogy is inappropriate for describing the adult teaching–learning process (Deepa, 2022, 2026). Knowles (1998) used the term 'andragogy' to illustrate the process of adult education and lists some fundamental features of adult learners and learning. Adults come with various life experiences to the classroom and have developed cognitive abilities for higher-order thinking skills. Therefore, problem-based instructions are more effective when they collaborate with peers to exchange ideas and opinions to develop solutions. Adults are autonomous learners who can decide their learning goals depending on their personal needs. They are intrinsically motivated to learn and practice their knowledge in real-life situations. One of the reasons for this is that adults learn when they feel they need the knowledge for a specific purpose.

While all these facts about adult education are right, Trott (1991) proposed the term 'anthrogogy', to make the concept of adult learning more gender-neutral and to concentrate on education as a lifelong process. The anthrogogic approach considers learning a collaborative process and the learner an interdependent entity. Learners' existing knowledge plays a vital role in acquiring and assimilating new knowledge. They critically evaluate new knowledge, associate it with their existing experiences, and store it in their long-term memory. For adults, learning is a holistic process, which means they evaluate knowledge, check its applicability in their lives, and select and eliminate portions of knowledge. Deepa, (2022, 2026) used the term 'anthrogogy' to refer to a philosophy of learning that finds its roots in plurality, multilinguality, and inclusiveness. In this view, an adult learner is a part of the ecosystem and one who takes responsibility for its sustainability.

In addition to the principles discussed so far, this chapter explores the cultural dimensions of the anthrogogic approach by highlighting the significance of IC as an essential factor for existing in a pluralistic society. Intercultural knowledge acts as a cement in maintaining a healthy relationship between people from different geographical, cultural and linguistic backgrounds. The spirit of IC lies in a person's ability to appreciate differences, display respect and empathy, and recognise multiple realities (Ruben, 1989). Similar to Byram's models of IC discussed earlier in this chapter, adults must understand the different practices in various societies and their cultural significance to create healthy social relations. They must protect themselves from stereotyping, discriminating, and developing biases against people based on their cultural practices. The anthrogogic approach can help educators integrate social and scholastic skills to ensure learners can use these skills to coexist with people from different identities.

Although various curricular frameworks worldwide have expressed the necessity of developing sustainable education to create a harmonious society, there are very few instructional guidelines for implementing it. Several researchers have offered theoretical frameworks (Byram, 1997; Risager, 2007; Jokikokko, 2005; Liddicot, 2004) to develop and assess IC. However, there is a requirement for efforts to define the kind of assessment tools that can be used for teaching and assessing IC at the university level. Moreover, in the Asian context, very little literature is available on assessing IC among adult learners, indicating the need for more research.

Thought Seeds as a Tool for Assessing IC

To achieve the anthrogogic objectives of IC, we need to have specifically designed tools for assessment that would empower learners to express their thoughts, feelings, interpretations, questions, et cetera, without being restricted. Such tools enable learners to apply the classroom knowledge in the practical world, open them up to challenge their perspectives about society, and give them opportunities to alter their world-view whenever required. In adult ESL classrooms, it is common practice to use tasks to elicit responses from the learners which later helps the teacher determine the success rate of learning. Tasks, as a tool, are particularly successful in language learning and acquisition as they ensure that the learners use the target language for an authentic communicative purpose while focusing on meaning and form. Some of these task types are information exchange, problem-solving, personal response, judging, evaluating, et cetera (Scarino & Brownell, 1994). Learners are required to complete the task which has specific objectives and learning goals. Upon completing the task, it can be assumed that the learner has learned the focused language skill. While this is proven to be effective in learning language skills, the extra-linguistic development of the learner is usually not the focus.

To understand adult learners' intercultural knowledge, their values and perspectives towards the world must be triggered. Consequently, they also need to be provided with an uncontrolled space of expression that could be beyond the framework of a task. Deepa (2022a, 2022b) proposes the concept of a thought seed which finds its inspiration from a Japanese agricultural practice: the creation of seed balls. Seed balls are created by covering seeds in a layer of mud and then randomly thrown in the field. With exposure to rain, the seeds in the seed ball start sprouting, thereby developing the field into a forest. A thought seed is an anthrogogic solution to the problem of shrinking the thinking space of teachers and learners in the adult classroom. It creates the space for expressing life experiences learned outside the classroom. The objective is to create an avenue for lateral, pluricultural, and multidisciplinary discourse. Unlike a task, the thought seed does not have an expected outcome; rather, it provides the scope for different responses based on learners' life experiences, reflections, and judgments. Instead of problem-solving and completing the tasks, learners use metacognitive skills to process their knowledge while responding to thought seeds. A series of questions can be seen as the seeds which sprout after being sown in the contexts of experiences and observations of the learners. Learners develop their ideas with the help of these questions. Learners' responses to thought seeds are not uniform but subjective. Learners must think critically to produce responses, support ideas with logic and facts, and interpret situations by empathising.

In this chapter the thought seed has been modified to suit the purpose of IC assessment. Originally, a thought seed has the following features:

- Relatable to real life and does not necessarily depend on the classroom context.
- Does not have one correct response, has scope for logical thinking and a variety of expressions.
- Does not have a specific boundary for expression (word limit).
- Students can decide whether they want to submit the assignment or not.
- Students can draw knowledge from any source they want to, without specific reference materials.
- Learners' responses are subjective.
- No specific criteria for evaluation. (Deepa, 2022b)

In this chapter, as the thought seed is used for assessing learners' intercultural knowledge based on the text provided in the classroom, certain features have been modified. First, a preamble to the thought seed was added, briefly capturing the text's theme. Through this preamble, the thought seed was made relevant to the classroom context and the reference materials. A series of questions were also posed to the students in order to trigger learners' thinking processes from their own cultural perspectives. Learners did not have to answer these questions separately but rather combine their thoughts in response to them and provide one reply in the written mode. The traditional examination environment was avoided, such as setting strict word limits, a rigid exam-hall sitting pattern, timed exams, invigilation, et cetera. Learners were encouraged to take the assignment home and respond to the thought seed over a week. They could submit it whenever they were ready.

This study was conducted to answer the following research questions (RQs):

1. How did the thought seeds assist in observing the intercultural knowledge of adult learners?
2. What are learners' perceptions about thought seeds as a prompt for expressing their feelings about another culture?

Description of the Study

The study was conducted at a private university in India with twenty ESL students studying in the first year of their BTech programme.

The learners were between 17 and 19 years old and were selected for the study using the random sampling technique. The three-week-long study involved reading texts and watching videos, followed by discussions.

The data was collected using two thought seeds (TS1 and TS2) that were designed based on a short story and a video. The literature text and video were selected based on the scope of their intercultural discussion. It is generally acknowledged that literature texts carry cultural baggage and are influenced by social context, just as language and non-verbal communication infuse a society's social and cultural norms. Literature combines information about social systems, conversational techniques, socialising, and thinking styles. Different conceptions of time and place are well illustrated (Andernovics, 2009). This makes literary pieces ideal for cross-cultural inputs.

For TS1, a short story by Earnest Hemingway titled 'Hills like White Elephants' was selected as it was also a part of the syllabus. The story has rich content for intercultural interpretation, particularly themes like relationships, abortion, and gender dynamics. For TS2, a video interview of a famous Indian actress, Aishwarya Rai, interviewed by David Letterman was used (available on YouTube). Similar to the story in TS1, the video in TS2 also has several instances of intercultural exchanges, negotiation of understanding, and discussion on cultural stereotypes.

Table 10.1: *Description of the Thought Seeds*

Thought Seed 1	Thought Seed 2
Preamble: In the story 'Hills like White Elephants', written by Ernest Hemingway, we read about a couple's dilemma regarding having a baby. Both the characters in the story behaved differently concerning their expectations for future life, their feelings for the baby, and their opinions about abortion. Do you think it is acceptable to have a difference of opinion	*Preamble*: In the video, you see that the interviewer and the celebrity talk about various cultural differences between two societies: American and Indian. They talk about how Western culture influences Indian culture by citing the examples of Bombay and Bollywood. They also talk about how many languages people can speak in the two countries. Interestingly, the term 'young' can be different in both contexts and may make people uneasy. Further, they talk about the family system and compare it. They also

Thought Seed 1	Thought Seed 2
between a man and a woman on an issue like abortion? Does patriarchy have a role in the decision-making process? In the case of disagreement on the issue of abortion, whose opinion should be given more value? Why? If we imagine the couple in the story as Indian, would they arrive at the same decision as the couple did? Finally, would you have liked this story to end differently? How? Write your impression of this story with the help of the given questions.	comment on the movies produced in the two countries. Source: https://www.youtube.com/watch?v=CEPjPhbGK Do you think that Western culture has an influence on the Indian entertainment industry? Indian cinema appears to be more musical than Western. Does this indicate something? What do you think about family systems in the Western and Indian cultures? Can children have the right to decide whether they want to live with their parents or independently? Is being multilingual a good quality, or should there be a common language for all? Compare the facts from both cultures based on your knowledge, analysis, and judgments. Write your response.

Each thought seed consisted of a preamble and a series of questions to prompt the learners to think of the content from multiple dimensions about the topic of discussion. The preamble aided the process of activating schema related to the text. Every question in the series aimed at making learners reflect on their cultural beliefs, think critically by comparing and contrasting cultural practices, form judgments, and understand stereotypes. The themes in the thought seeds were related to everyday discourse in the current global contexts, making it relatable. The respondents had the freedom to agree or disagree with the theme of the text with a range of possibilities. There was no specification regarding the use of language, length or style of response, or particular success criteria. After discussing with the students, it was decided that they would submit their responses in one week. Along with critical thinking, the thought seeds aimed to observe respondents' abilities to express complex cultural concepts, thoughts, and opinions in the English language.

Data Analysis and Results

The data gained from the thought seeds was qualitatively analysed to identify instances of cultural reflections and intercultural understanding by the learners. The categories of intercultural reflections in fifteen responses from each thought seed (selected randomly) were coded to understand the patterns in learners' expressions and how thought seeds created the space for their expressions. The following categories[2] were observed prominently while analysing the data.

Critical Judgment

Critical judgment involves an unbiased and logical perspective toward a culture that is new to an individual. This category suggests that the learners have developed the ability to think based on facts and observations, question the texts, and personalise the knowledge. Instances of inferring, reasoning, cause-effect analysis, and drawing conclusions based on facts were considered in this category. The following table shows the representative data presentation and analysis.

Table 10.2: *Critical Judgement Analysis*

Data Excerpts	Analysis
TS1, P3: 'The man might not be as serious in the relationship as the girl was. As the girl is involved emotionally and physically in the relationship. In today's world abortion is a risky operation and if it goes wrong, Jig (the girl) can lose her life. Therefore, her confusion about the operation is valid.'	In this data sample, the learner is making their judgment about the character's state of mind based on the context of the situation, as well as considering their own knowledge about the topic being discussed. This excerpt suggests that the learner has gone beyond the text to understand its meaning and can relate it to a real-life situation. This data sample also indicates that the learner has developed a sense of sympathy for the character.

[2] The data instances have been deliberately presented in tabular form along with the analysis to enable us to club the expressions from different respondents in the same category. These various instances across the data strengthen the presence of each category.

Data Excerpts	Analysis
TS1, P8: 'I believe that both characters are right in their place. Each and every individual has their own ways of facing a problem or have their own perspectives in viewing things. Not all individuals face their problems in the same manner. Here, the man might have decided to go for the abortion taking society into consideration.'	Like the previous data sample, in this example also the learner is drawing their judgment from their own understanding of the social arrangement without judging the character negatively or positively as presented in the original text. This statement indicates the learner's ability to have a balanced point of view and reason out things based on real-life observations.
TS2, P2: 'The influence of western culture can be seen in Indian cinema as Indians believe western is modern. The choice of music in Indian cinema is changing which could be a result of western pop culture. The old classic Indian musicals are rare and the young generation does not like them much. This could be the reason why there is a lot of western influence.'	In this example, the learner justifies the reasons for the influence of Western influence on Indian cinema with different examples such as the popularity of pop culture, social perspectives towards Western culture, and the absence of Indian classics in modern times. This shows the learner's ability to think critically.
TS2, P14: 'The family systems in India and western countries are different and this could be because of their different perceptions about relationships. Parents in India take care of the children even at the age of marriage and beyond. Children also stay with their parents till their last moments. As it is observed in many western cases, parents train their children to take care of themselves at an early age and make them independent. That's why in India we have more joint families and in the USA they have smaller families.'	A clear reflection of critical judgment can be seen through this example as the learner compares the situation in two different cultural contexts before forming an opinion. While understanding the difference between two cultures, the learner can figure out the practical reasons behind it.

The series of questions in both the thought seeds enabled the learners to reflect on their understanding of the text from multiple dimensions. They could give reasons for their judgments, and each participant interpreted the stories provided through the text and video differently.

Forming a critical judgment is a complex cognitive process that requires several rounds of filtration of information, which is evident in these examples. These examples prove that thought seeds enable learners to think back and forth, compare and contrast, and find real-life references for their beliefs about a different culture.

Comparative Cultural Reflections

Under this category, the responses indicate how the learners interpreted the events in another culture by comparing them with their own. Instances of comparison of social systems, beliefs, gender roles, and acceptable and non-acceptable cultural elements were considered under this category. Some of the examples are discussed here.

Table 10.3: *Comparative Cultural Analysis*

Data Excerpts	Analysis
TS1, P4: 'In the Indian culture, family's involvement in the decision-making process is very normal. However, the Western culture gives more freedom to the individuals. This could be the reason that the couple is taking such a complex decision (of abortion) on their own.'	A comparison of the decision-making process in two cultures and the significance of individual opinions in two cultures has been discussed. This is a constructive understanding of another culture.
TS1, P9: 'Abortion is a very serious topic in the Indian context and something that is considered taboo. People do not discuss it that openly because they are judged. In the Western culture people discuss it openly and are more independent in their decision making.'	This example discusses how the discussion of certain topics is taboo in a certain culture and perfectly normal in another. Such comparative understanding helps in developing knowledge about another culture.
TS1, P11: 'I think patriarchy is prevalent in all the societies in the world. In this story, the man is very persistent about getting the operation performed despite seeing that the girl is hesitant about it. This is not much different from Indian society. Here also men take most of the important decisions. '	In this example, the learner identified a similarity in the problems existing in different cultures. Such understanding prevents them from forming a bias about a culture.

Data Excerpts	Analysis
TS2, P7: 'Indian cinema is more musical because music is one of the important features for making business. In 90s, it was music that made the Bollywood movies superhit. However, that is not case with the western movies I think. They rely on a strong story and action. The music industry flourishes separately.'	In this example, the learner discusses the reasons for cinema becoming popular in two cultures. This is another example of being able to understand the differences and critically reflect on them.

This aspect of learners' responses indicates that learners assimilate the newly learned knowledge with their existing schema about some cultural practices. Learners carefully record their observations and develop their views based on these observations. Such practice prevents learners from developing biases about another culture. These comparative reflections also suggest that the learners can identify the similarities and differences between the two cultures. It is also important to know that these comparisons and differentiations do not necessarily lead to forming good or bad opinions about any culture, a much-expected characteristic of an interculturally aware individual. In instances where the learners get an opportunity to interact with a person from another culture, there is a rare possibility of them experiencing cultural shock. Comparative analysis of the cultural facts enables learners to conduct an autonomous discovery of world-views (Byram, 2002).

Discovery of New Cultural Knowledge

While reading the story and watching the video, the learners discovered some unknown facts about the other culture. Such identifications of new cultural facts were based on the differentiations from their own culture. The responses with the elements of such discovery were marked in this category.

Table 10.4: *Discovery of New Cultural Knowledge Analysis*

Data Excerpts	Analysis
TS1, P10: 'While having a tense discussion over the abortion the couple orders drink after drink. As the weather in Barcelona is very cold, drinking	This example suggests the learners' moment of discovering the logic behind consuming alcohol and its cultural

Data Excerpts	Analysis
alcohol might be helping them keep warm. Also, we often see in Hollywood movies that they often have tensed discussions while drinking.'	appropriateness. Such understanding prevents an individual from judging one culture based on an understanding of another.
TS2, P5: 'In America, children usually move out and live an independent life after eighteen. This could be the reason why they need to check with their parents if they are available for dinner. Smaller families could mean more independence.' TS2, P14: 'In America majority of the people are not multilingual because they can easily communicate only in English. That is the reason they speak only one or two languages (monolingual and bilingual).'	These examples indicate that the learners learn about the different equations between parents and children and the various reasons behind them. Similarly, they also seem to understand the reason the majority of the people are monolingual in a specific culture.

Discovering new facts about another culture is a learning experience that comes from having an open mind to accept the unknown. Cultural exploration of this kind fills the knowledge gaps about other cultures among learners. Independent discovery of cultural facts and practices blocks the possibility of misinterpretation and forming biases. Furstenberg (2010) identified the dynamic process of discovery, inquiry, and exploration as a collective, constructive approach to learning. While being oriented to a new culture, individuals must be able to figure out the uniqueness of that culture in order to be able to appreciate the differences.

Recognising Biases

Having discussed the text about a foreign culture, the learners recognised that certain things they thought about that culture were based on biases. This was a process of unlearning something they had heard of and relearning new information based on their inquiry. The responses where the learners believed they had wrong notions about the target culture fall under this category.

Table 10.5: *Recognising Bias Analysis*

Data Excerpts	Analysis
TS1, P11: 'We think that patriarchy is effective only in our part of the world but that doesn't seem to be the fact. The American man in the story is passively patronizing and expects the girl to go for the operation. He is the one ordering all the drinks and also translating the names of the drinks from Spanish to English. It's about the power structure.'	In this example, the learner understands the role of gender bias in two different cultures and is able to interpret the situation based on the same.
TS2, P4: It is not always true when we say Indians like to live in joint families. The modern Indian society is much different. My cousin got married last year and he moved to Bangalore with his wife. Both of them have a job in an IT company there. They prefer to live away from their parents because it is convenient for them.'	Here, the learner can counter the stereotype about a particular culture by citing real-life examples. This ability enables learners to have a bias-free understanding of the events in various cultures.

Distinguishing between biases and facts is highly significant while learning about another culture. This could be done by closely observing social practices and understanding the circumstances when events happen. Intercultural competence can only be developed when an individual has an objective orientation toward another culture. Biases act as blocks in the process of the acquisition of cross-cultural knowledge. They prevent individuals from appreciating differences and make them culturally rigid. In the process of active inquiry about another culture, learners get an opportunity to correct their perceptions.

Learner Perceptions About Thought Seeds

After administering the thought seeds, the learners were asked to talk about their experience responding to them. It was the first time the learners were given this kind of exercise. Thought seeds differ significantly from the regular pedagogic tasks used to teach and assess. Pedagogic tasks have specific areas of focus on a text or a video. Any information provided outside the scope of a pedagogic task is irrelevant or incorrect. On the contrary, the thought seed expresses a holistic understanding of the text. Here, learners can use their personal life experiences to interpret the texts.

Some expressions of the learners' experiences are presented here:

> *P3*: 'In the beginning, it was difficult to process all the questions in the thought seed. We normally get one question and answer it. But these questions were interlinked. It was a lot of thinking but responding to this was like storytelling.'

> *P7*: 'When we answer questions in the exam it is like summary writing. This was different. Here there were questions from all the dimensions. I had to think, make connections between the other culture and mine and then respond.'

> *P10*: 'I normally read a lot of literature, like stories and novels. I love the characters from these stories and novels. But I normally do not pay attention to their social contexts. This exercise made me think of these characters as they actually live in a society like ours. It was nice to think of them as common people.'

> *P12*: 'It was like I can say what I wanted to. While watching the video I was really upset to know that the journalist had very limited ideas about India and Indian cinema. I could totally express my unhappiness about it.'

These perceptions suggest that thought seeds expanded the boundaries of learners' thinking. From the assessment point of view, thought seeds could extract learners' opinions, beliefs, and judgments on various aspects of the text. This helps a teacher to understand whether the learners have observed the cultural differences they are willing to accept or reject, whether they draw parallels between their own culture and the other culture, et cetera. The excerpts from learners' responses indicate that thought seeds involve learners emotionally as well as critically while they respond. The learners were not anxious about answering the questions as is usual during examinations. Further, no answer was correct, so every response was valid and valued.

Discussion and Conclusion

The data analysis helped us answer the RQs, which were set at the beginning of the study. To answer the first RQ—'How did the thought seeds assist in observing the intercultural knowledge of adult learners?'—it can be said that the anthrogogic approach helped assess adult learners' IC in several ways. The questions in the thought seeds enabled the learners to think about cultural practices from multiple perspectives and establish a meaningful connection among these perspectives. These questions certainly accelerate critical thinking ability among learners. They felt curious to know more about the target culture, and knowledge acquisition happened through active inquiry. Learners engaged in complex cognitive activities such as comparison, contrast, evaluation, assimilation, and accommodation in this process. The questions in the thought seeds encouraged learners to search for references from their own lives while evaluating various cultural practices. This process was autonomous, as there were no specific guidelines for the learners to follow while articulating their thoughts. Learners did not have to seek validation for their responses. The validity of their responses was decided by themselves as they evolve with a new version of cross-cultural knowledge.

To address the second RQ—'What are learners' perceptions about thought seeds as a prompt for expressing their feelings about another culture?'—the data suggests that learners could clearly reflect on the differences between the pedagogic tasks and thought seeds. The assessment of cultural knowledge becomes a learning moment for the learners as they discover various aspects of the target culture. Recognition of biases and unlearning happens when the learners are encouraged to ask questions and think critically about cultural practices of their own and others. Adult learners can think independently and have a good storage of life experiences. Thought seeds require them to actively make use of their existing intercultural knowledge chunks while taking a stance about the target culture. Challenging their own beliefs is the first step in the process of developing a democratic worldview. Thought seeds enable a democratic thinking process among adult minds.

It is a common observation in the Indian context that intercultural knowledge does not receive enough attention, particularly in the tertiary-level curriculum. As a result, the traditional language and literature assessment models must have the components of intercultural knowledge assessment. This is paradoxical as literature texts are one of the best sources of intercultural inputs. Along with a literal and factual understanding of the text, learners can also develop perspectives for the target culture. Therefore, an instrument like a thought seed becomes important to assess learners' intercultural understanding.

References

Allen, H., & Herron, C. (2003). A mixed-methodology investigation of the linguistic and affective outcomes of summer study abroad. *Foreign Language Annals, 36*(3), 370–385.

Alyan, A. A. (2011). *Exploring teachers' beliefs regarding the concepts of culture and intercultural communicative competence in EFL Palestinian university context: A case study* [Doctoral dissertation, University of Massachusetts Amherst]. ProQuest Dissertations and Theses. https://doi.org/10.7275/5682560.

Andernovics, S. (2009). Developing and assessing intercultural communicative competence: A guide for language teachers and teacher educators, to get to know each other leads to better mutual understanding. *ELT Journal, 63*(4), 443–445. https://doi.org/10.1093/elt/ccp076.

Breen, M. (1987). Learner contributions to task design. In C. Candlin and D. Murphy (Eds.), *Language learning tasks* (pp. 23–46). Prentice Hall.

Byram, M. (1997). *Teaching and assessing intercultural communicative competence*. Multilingual Matters.

Byram, M. (2009). Intercultural competence in foreign languages: The intercultural speaker and the pedagogy of foreign language education. In D. K. Deardorff (Ed.), *The Sage handbook of intercultural competence* (pp. 321–332). Sage.

Byram, M., Gribkova, B., & Starkey, H. (2002). *Developing the intercultural dimension in language teaching: A practical introduction for teachers.* Language Policy Division, Directorate of School, Out-of-School and Higher Education, Council of Europe.

Clark, J., Scarino, A., & Brownell, J. (1994). *Improving the quality of learning: A Framework for TOC renewal in Hong Kong*. Hong Kong Bank Language Development Fund/Institute of Language in Education.

Council of Europe. (2008). *White paper on intercultural dialogue*. Council of Europe: Intercultural Dialogue. http://www.coe.int/dialogue

Deepa, S. (2022a). Pedagogic scaffolding and anthrogogic learning contexts: Issues in Metaphor mismatch. *Journal of English Language Teachers' Interaction Forum, 13*(2), 3–7.

Deepa, S. (2022b). Thought seeds in anthrogogic learning contexts. *Journal of Indian Education, 48*(2). 58–70.

Deepa, S. (2026). Principles of anthrogogic language education. In S. Deepa & G. Durairajan (Eds.), *Anthrogogy in use: A handbook for language educators* (pp. 3–26). Orient BlackSwan.

Derin, A. Ç. Z., Pinar, E., Özlem, K., & Gökçe, K. (2009). Turkish EFL teachers' opinions on intercultural approach in foreign language education. *Procedia-Social and Behavioral Sciences, 1*, 1611–1616.

Ellis, R. (2009). Task-based language teaching: Sorting out the misunderstandings. *International Journal of Applied Linguistics, 19*(3), 221–246.

Fantini, A. E., & Tirmizi, A. (2006). Exploring and assessing intercultural competence. *World Learning Publications.* Paper 1. http://digitalcollections.sit.edu/worldlearning_publications/1.

Fantini, A. E. (2009). Assessing intercultural competence. In D. K. Deardorff (Ed.), *The Sage handbook of intercultural competence* (pp. 456–476). Sage.

Furstenberg, G. (2010, August). A dynamic, web-based methodology for developing intercultural understanding. In *Proceedings of the 3rd international conference on Intercultural collaboration* (ICIC '10) (pp. 49–58). Association for Computing Machinery. https://doi.org/10.1145/1841853.1841861.

Garrido, C., & Alvarez, I. (2006). Language teacher education for intercultural understanding. *European Journal of Teacher Education, 29*(2), 163–179.

Gillespie, A., & Cornish, F. (2009). Intersubjectivity: Towards a dialogical analysis. *Journal for the Theory of Social Behaviour, 39*(1), 1–24.

Hashem, M. E. (1995, November 18–21). *Assessing Student Learning Outcomes in Teaching Intercultural Communication* [Paper presentation]. 81st Annual Meeting of the Speech Communication Association, San Antonio, Texas, United States. https://eric.ed.gov/?id=ED394158.

Jackson, J. (2005). Assessing intercultural learning though introspective accounts. *Frontiers, 10*(2), 165–186.

Jokikokko, J. (2005). Interculturally trained Finnish teachers' conceptions of diversity and intercultural competence. *Intercultural Education, 16*, 69–93.

Knowles, M. S., Holton, E. G., & Swanson, R. A. (1998). A theory of adult learning: Andragogy. In M. S. Knowles (Ed.), *The adult learner: The definitive classic in adult education and human resource development.* 47–84. Gulf Publishing Company.

Lázár, I., Huber-Kriegler, M., Lussier, D., Matei, G. S., & Peck, C. (2007). *Developing and assessing intercultural communicative competence: A guide for language teachers and teacher educators.* Council of Europe. https://book.coe.int/en/education-and-modern-languages/3907-developing-and-assessing-intercultural-communicative-competence-a-guide-for-language-teachers-and-teacher-educators.html

Liddicot A. J. (2004). Conceptualization of the cultural component of language teaching in Australian language in education policy. *Journal of Multilingual and Multicultural Development, 25,* 297–317.

Piątkowska, K. (2015). From cultural knowledge to intercultural communicative competence: changing perspectives on the role of culture in foreign language teaching. *Intercultural Education, 26*(5), 397–408.

Risager, K. (2007). *Language and Culture Pedagogy: From a National to a Transnational Paradigm.* Multilingual Matters.

Ruben, B. D. (1989). The study of cross-cultural competence: Traditions and contemporary issues. *International Journal of Intercultural Relations, 13,* 229–240.

Sercu, L. (2006). The foreign language and intercultural competence teacher: The acquisition of a new professional identity. *Intercultural Education, 17*(1), 55–72.

Sinicrope, C., Norris, J., & Watanabe, Y. (2007). Understanding and assessing intercultural competence: A summary of theory, research, and practice (Technical report for the foreign language program evaluation project). *Studies in Second Language Acquisition, 26*(1), 1–58.

Tran, T. Q., & Dang, H. V. (2014). Culture teaching in English language teaching: Teachers' beliefs and their classroom practices. *Global Journal of Foreign Language Teaching, 4*(2), 92–101.

Trilling, B. (2009). *21st century skills: Learning for life in our times.* Jossey-Bass.

Trott, D. C. (1991, October). *Anthrogogy* [Paper presentation]. American Association for Adult and Continuing Education, Montreal, Quebec. https://eric.ed.gov/?id=ED342887

Usó Juan, E., & Martínez Flor, A. (2008). Teaching intercultural communicative competence through the four skills. *Revista Alicantina de Estudios Ingleses 21,* 157–170.

11

Incorporating Thought Seeds as an Assessment Tool in Anthrogogic Contexts

Tabitha Chekuri

Introduction

Assessment is integral to language education, serving as the cornerstone that shapes and influences learning experiences, and eventually, both educational objectives and outcomes. This is true for all education in general and language proficiency development in particular. It guides instructional strategies, provides insights into students' linguistic competencies, and facilitates continuous improvement in language learning and teaching. Ultimately, effective assessment practices enhance both teaching approaches and students' language learning processes. Back in the 1950s, it was postulated that educational objectives, learning experiences, and evaluation procedures must be linked with each other and influence each other (Furst, 1958), which in a sense is the precursor to the washback argument (Alderson & Wall, 1993; Chang, 2000). Brown (2004) also highlights three primary purposes of assessment in language education: to measure learner progress, to diagnose individual strengths and weaknesses, and to inform instructional decision-making. Through systematic assessment procedures, teachers acquire valuable insights into students' language competencies across various areas such as listening, speaking, reading, and writing (Alderson, 2005).

In anthrogogic contexts in general, and in the context of this study in particular (which focuses on communication courses), where the aim is to focus on actual language use, assessment serves as a tool for evaluating learners' communicative abilities, including their capacity to understand and produce meaningful discourse within real-life contexts. Employing a range of assessment methods—from conventional tests to performance-based tasks and portfolios—enables teachers to identify students' learning styles, preferences, and individual learning trajectories, thereby fostering personalised and differentiated instruction (Brown & Abeywickrama, 2010). Alternative assessment practices provide a more thorough understanding of students' accomplishments and also provide genuine insights into their knowledge, capabilities, skills, attitudes, and competencies nurtured throughout the instructional journey (Letina, 2015). These approaches prioritise the practical application of skills, providing concrete proof of students' capacity to address real-world issues across different subject areas. Assessment of learning, which is summative, has now been supplemented with assessment *for* and *as* learning which is formative in nature (Black & William, 1998). The possibility of learning through assessment has also been mooted (Deepa & Durairajan, 2023).

Assessment practices in language teaching have evolved over the past fifty years to embrace a communicative approach, emphasising the importance of assessing learners' ability to effectively communicate in real-life situations (Hughes, 2003). This shift towards communicative language assessment reflects a broader pedagogical philosophy that prioritises language use and interaction over rote memorisation and grammar drills (Bachman, 1990; Bachman & Palmer, 1996). Ultimately, assessment stands as the essential element of language learning and teaching, encouraging innovative teaching methods, student engagement, and eventually in the development of communicative competence. But the development of such competence alone is not sufficient. As adults, these students need to use language for communication in everyday life, and the whole course needs to be of value to the students after the course is over. Drawing on a formative and, where possible, summative assessment argument, in the context of this study conducted in an autonomous university, it is important to not just consider washback—for which the sit-down exam is an example of negative washback—but also wash-forward into the professional and everyday lives of the adult learners (Deepa & Durairajan, 2023; Durairajan, 2026). This will enable all assessments in general and assignments in particular, to have genuine predictive validity (Messick, 1989).

Nature of Communication Courses

Undergraduate level communication courses are programmes aimed at equipping the adult learner with the most vital skill of being able to interact with other human beings in order to express thoughts, ideas, needs, emotions, et cetera. In these courses, students typically learn how to convey their thoughts effectively, adapt to various types of audiences and situations based on culture, context and need, and also how to respond effectively in order to reach a desired end.

While these communication courses can be categorised and placed in various baskets based on the need for communication and audience—like mass communication, technical communication, digital communication, public speaking et cetera—the crucial form of all of them which is used most regularly and becomes essential for the basic survival of human beings is interpersonal communication. The aim of this chapter is to delve into the nature of interpersonal communication, ways to effectively impart interpersonal communication skills to adult learners, and most effectively evaluate the learning progress in a way that ensures the learners' ability to implement the learnings in their day-to-day interactions rather than acquiring theoretical knowledge.

The nature of interpersonal communication can be complex. It requires the skill to interact one-on-one, in small groups, or with a larger group of audiences while keeping it engaging and ensuring the message is understood and bought into. It is the most dynamic form of communication requiring immediate adaptation to the audience, mood, and context with little to no preparation time. It is in real-time, ever evolving and requires both verbal and non-verbal communication styles.

As communication courses aim to equip students with the knowledge and skills required to excel in various contexts, it is crucial to assess these skills in a meaningful and effective manner. Learning in communication courses demands more than rote memorisation and repetition of facts. Instead, it necessitates critical thinking and effective application of knowledge which shows a learners' ability to apply its principles in actual use/contexts. While sit-down, end-semester exams have long been the standard, they fall short in adequately evaluating this multifaceted nature of communication. These exams typically focus on assessing a student's ability to recall and reproduce theoretical knowledge within a limited time-frame. However, effective communication involves a complex interplay of skills, including active listening, empathy, adaptability, and the ability to respond appropriately to various interpersonal dynamics. Sit-down exams do not capture these nuanced aspects of communication because they do not provide opportunities for students to demonstrate their practical application of these skills in real-world scenarios.

Assignments offer a better alternative, as they allow students to engage with the material more deeply and apply their knowledge in more practical contexts. For example, written assignments can require students to analyse communication case-studies or reflect on their own communication experiences. However, assignments also have their limitations. Some assignments may be overly prescriptive, dictating specific formats or restricting students' exploration of diverse perspectives. This can limit students' ability to think critically and creatively about communication challenges, which are essential skills in real-world contexts. Additionally, traditional assignments may not always promote the kind of self-reflection and personal growth necessary for developing strong communication skills. Students may focus more on completing the task according to requirements rather than using the assignment as an opportunity for meaningful introspection and improvement.

Incorporating thought seeds, therefore, into the assessment process presents a more effective approach. Thought seeds prompt students to engage in deep reflection on their learning experiences, encouraging them to think critically about how they apply communication concepts in real-life situations (Deepa, 2022). This method fosters self-awareness, accountability, and the ability to consider multiple possibilities and solutions. By integrating thought seeds into term papers and other reflective assignments, teachers can provide a more comprehensive and authentic learning experience that better captures the complexities of communication, and one that will prepare students for real-world communication challenges.

While college/university level communication courses are often seen as platforms to teach specific communication techniques, it is essential to recognise that they should go beyond imparting mere instructions. Instead, these courses should shift towards term papers and reflective assignments that enable adult learners to gain self-awareness and a deeper understanding of their own learning as communicators. Communication courses for adults should prioritise self-reflection and the development of meta-awareness over rote instruction. Understanding the rationale behind this shift is essential for creating effective educational experiences that truly enhance communication skills in adult learners. In other words, prioritising self-reflection and the development of meta-awareness in communication courses for adults provides numerous benefits over rote instruction. It enhances practical application, fosters critical thinking and emotional intelligence, supports diverse learning styles, encourages lifelong learning, and builds accountability. These factors collectively contribute to more effective and meaningful learning experiences that prepare adult learners for the complexities of real-world communication.

Adult Learners and Anthrogogy

The adult education system has undergone significant transformation since Malcolm Knowles (1970) introduced his theory of adult education. The definition of 'adult education' has expanded to encompass a wide spectrum of formal, informal, and non-formal learning experiences, including those individuals who return to education after a break following regular studies (Knowles et al., 1998; Merriam & Brockett, 1997). Typically, 'adult learners' are individuals aged 25 and above (Chao et al., 2007), with some overlap between the categories of non-traditional student and adult student. Adult students are those pursuing vocational certificates, degrees, or training aiming to enhance work-related skills, often balancing multiple life-roles and responsibilities (Ross-Gordon, 2011). However, this chapter uses the term 'anthrogogy', as introduced by Trott (1991), with a broader interpretation than what Trott visualised, focusing on gender inclusivity. Here, anthrogogy' is used as a more inclusive term than alternatives like andragogy, aiming to include diverse aspects of learner identity and experience. Anthrogogy emphasises treating adult learners as adults rather than adopting a pedagogical approach more suited for children. While adult learning theories have been discussed in the literature, there has been a lack of research focusing on adult learning in mainstream higher education contexts, rather than just within vocational or literacy contexts (Deepa, 2026). Moreover, in conventional adult learning settings, instructional methodologies often adhere to pedagogical principles designed for younger learners, which may not fully address the unique needs and learning styles of adult students. As a result, there is a growing recognition of the importance of incorporating anthrogogical approaches that emphasise self-directed learning and the relevance of education to adult learners' real-life experiences and goals.

Learning and evaluation processes have evolved very little over the years, particularly in this domain of communication courses and this is reflective in how we teach and evaluate our adult learners by continuing to apply the principles of pedagogy. It is important to understand that one size does not fit all. Adult learners are unique and come with prior learning experiences, beliefs and prejudices which cannot be eliminated from the learning process. Adult learners are also self-aware and motivated by goals which are most often aimed at filling specific gaps in their skill set. This makes them autonomous or self-directed learners.

Evaluation of their learning progress demands practical application and relevance to everyday life to truly assess its success. Keeping this in view, it is imperative that adult learning programmes are learner-centred, and that the evaluation processes are practical, anthrogogic, self-reflective, and collaborative rather than theoretical and pedagogic in nature (Durairajan, 2026).

Anthrogogy and Thought Seeds

Having established that adult learners only need reflection simulators and not task-based evaluation mechanisms, to spark off their learnings in such a way that it leads to real-time performance and self-reflection, thought seeds work best in this scenario. A thought seed is a 'catalyst (written, spoken, a picture, a meme, a video, an advertisement, et cetera.) usually followed by a series of statements and questions which will persuade the teacher/learner to build a thinking platform, process information divergently and go meta over the "apparentness" found in the trigger' (Deepa, 2022, p. 64). While task-based activities are given to the learner with a prescribed way of solving the problem and with an intention for the learner to arrive at a predetermined outcome which is purely teacher centric, thought seeds allow learners to use a more autonomous way of arriving at solutions that best suit a particular situation in their real lives. They further provide the learner the opportunity to engage with tasks that are relevant to them personally based on the audience, context and the situation. Typically task-based assessment has very explicitly detailed steps that need to be followed to arrive at the desired solution/outcome and works best with learners (like children) who might not have a very evolved ability to learn through reflection. However, for an adult who is a language user and more evolved in terms of critical thinking abilities, the pedagogic approach can not only limit but also hamper the learning process when the process itself is prescribed to them.

For example, a typical task-based essay question in interpersonal communication could be: Imagine you are a manager overseeing a team project where two team members have conflicting ideas about the direction of the project. Using the Thomas-Kilmann Conflict Model (TKI), analyse the conflict and propose a resolution strategy. Your essay should include a description of the conflict, an assessment of each team member's conflict-handling style using the TKI framework, and recommendations for resolving the conflict based on your analysis.

In this task-based assignment, the steps and expectations are explicitly detailed: students are required to apply the TKI framework to analyse the conflict, identify conflict-handling styles, and propose a resolution strategy based on their analysis. While this approach provides clarity and structure, it may limit adult learners from exploring alternative conflict resolution strategies or reflecting deeply on their own communication approaches beyond the prescribed framework. Adult learners, who bring diverse life experiences and professional insights to the table, may find such prescriptive tasks less engaging and less conducive to meaningful learning experiences that foster personal growth and real-world application of communication skills. Thus, while task-based assessment has its merits, it may not fully tap into the potential of adult learners who benefit from learning environments that allow for flexibility and encourage reflective thinking.

Thought seeds, on the other hand, provide the adult learner with what seems like just soil, but has seeds that can germinate at will and encourages them to apply learnings to various real-life situations set in different contexts and with a varied set of audiences, giving them an opportunity to really put to the test all the concepts learnt and assess the efficacy of their learnings effectively. It also provides them a chance to reflect on what went well and what did not, and encourages them to course correct as required.

For example, a question prompt incorporating thought seeds would be:

> Describe, in detail, a recent interpersonal conflict you have experienced. How did your basic conflict-handling style influence your actions? Was your conflict-handling style appropriate or inappropriate to this specific situation? To what degree do you believe your conflict-handling style is flexible? Justify using examples from your experiences.

While learning is generally goal-oriented for most adult learners and they are largely self-motivated/driven to learn, application of the learning and reflection of its efficacy does not happen naturally most times, and, unfortunately, seldom as a part of course requirements. As such, if we want to ensure effective learning and give our adult learners an understanding of how the course enables them to fill the skill gaps identified while signing up for a course, it is imperative that we provide a sincere opportunity for them to push themselves beyond their comfort zone and put their learnings to the test. The assessment administered should enable the learner to apply their learnings and reflect on the outcomes. A learning programme for an adult learner can never be effective unless the learning and the application of their learnings can go beyond the classroom. They gain little to nothing if they are only able to reproduce some theoretical concepts out of a book or a worksheet to 'pass' the course but unable to understand how to or have the opportunity to take these learnings beyond the exam.

This is even more important for courses on communication as the very nature of such courses is to enable proficiency in skills. The evaluation process is not to test if the candidate heard what was spoken in the classroom and if they are able to reproduce the same, but to assess if they will be able to utilise these learnings in a significant and meaningful way in their day-to-day interactions. A teacher/facilitator can assume the success of the programme when there is enough evidence to prove that the learning has percolated into the learner's real-life scenarios and that the learner has the ability to tackle the problem at hand differently than before being equipped with these new skills. In fact, the exams should be like the last class of the learning programme: the act of answering the paper should be both challenging, and exhilarating. It should push them to turn a corner not turned before in their learning and their language-using journey to utilise everything in a way that proves that the learning imparted will stay with them for a lifetime; that the learning has the ability to make an impact not only in their own lives but in the lives of those around them that gain from their newly acquired abilities. This is anthrogogic predictive validity that does not confine them to performing in a fish bowl, but teaches them how to swim in a lake and, when needed, even in the ocean (Durairajan, 2026).

Context for the Study

The context for this study is an elective course on 'Interpersonal Communication' offered to a group of fifteen final-year undergraduate students, in a private university in India. Some of the topics covered include 'Listening and reading nonverbal messages', 'Providing feedback', and 'Sending interpersonal messages', among others. With the aim to evaluate the effectiveness of the end-semester evaluation process, thought seeds were used as questions for a term paper submission. It was interesting to see how the learners were not just answering based on theoretical concepts learnt but went beyond the classroom and the course, delving into their personal experiences and evaluating their communication style before and after the course was taught. The learners were able to reflect on their own learning and understand the shift in their behaviours, as well as notice and appreciate the evolution of their communication style as they applied the learnings to their personal situations.

Incorporating Thought Seeds as a Tool for Assessment

The assessment format incorporated thought seeds to enable both the teacher and the students to gain deeper insights into the practical application of interpersonal communication concepts. To examine the validity of this hypothesis, a significant modification was made to the assessment structure to enable reflection based on thought seeds. The focal point of this change was the term paper, which evolved into a personal application assignment. The aim here was not only to evaluate students' comprehension of interpersonal communication topics but, more importantly, to encourage thoughtful reflection on how these learnings translated into their real-world experiences. In other words, the term paper prompt was written in such a manner that it was a personal application assignment which required the students to reflect on key learnings on various topics covered in the course on interpersonal communication, analyse their communication style, reactions and observations, and talk about the application of the concepts in real life, out of the classroom experiences.

For example, in a sit-down, end-semester exam a typical question would be 'What is emotional competence? List and explain three behavioural skills you need to apply emotional intelligence effectively.' Such a question only requires a regurgitation of information that is available in any textbook on factors of emotional competence. This then becomes an empty speech act (Spolsky, 1990). However, while using thought seeds to assess their learning on the topic of 'Applying Emotional Intelligence', the prompts given were:

a. Think of a situation which was difficult or challenging for you. How did you react/respond during that time? What do you think was the experience of people who were involved in the situation? Would you change any aspect of your behaviour/communication if given a chance to undo the experience for yourself and others involved? If yes, how/what would you do differently? If no, why?

b. "Self-management is the ability to understand your feelings and to use this understanding to effectively deal with emotional situations." Rate yourself according to the above statement on a scale of 1-10 and justify your score using at least two examples from your experiences.

Analysis of Student Responses to Thought Seeds

In this revised assessment format—in the form of a term paper that incorporated thought seeds—students engaged in self-reflection by responding to thought seeds. The thought seeds served as catalysts for introspection, prompting students to delve into their own communication style, responses, and observations. This enabled the students to go beyond the course and exam and think about how they used the learnings and applied them to real-life situations and not limit it to the classroom activities. The intention was to encourage a comprehensive analysis of their communication behaviour, both in and out of the classroom setting. By encouraging students to analyse their communication experiences outside the confines of the classroom, the assessment aimed to bridge the gap between theoretical knowledge and real-world application. The students were prompted to consider how the concepts learned in the course manifested in their daily lives. This involved a critical examination of their interactions, conflicts, and communication patterns in diverse settings such as the workplace, social events, and personal relationships. By doing this, the assessment helped students understand how interpersonal communication theories can be used in real-life situations outside of academic settings.

The personalised nature of the assignment allowed students to recognise their strengths and areas for improvement. Through the reflection on their communication styles and behaviours, they became aware of the gaps in their skills, areas that required further learning, and patterns of successful communication that led to positive outcomes. This awareness contributed to a holistic understanding of their communicative competence that was not just limited to the know-how of communication but extended to the application and use of the language in real-life situations.

Furthermore, the assessment encouraged students to not just discuss but also celebrate their successes in real-life situations. By emphasising the application of communication concepts in authentic scenarios, the assignment provided a platform for students to acknowledge instances where their learnings led to positive outcomes. This celebratory aspect not only boosted their confidence but also reinforced the value of the interpersonal communication course in equipping them with practical, transferable skills.

Responding to thought seeds through the term paper corresponds to an anthrogogic perspective that transcends traditional assessment methods, offering students a comprehensive and transformative learning experience. Each dimension of this approach contributes to the development of critical thinking skills, self-awareness, and the practical application of topics discussed in class. Let's delve into each aspect to explore how these elements were interwoven in the responses recorded in the term paper submissions, indicative of a rich and reflective learning experience for the students.

Reflection on Learning

Engaging with thought seeds prompted students to delve into their learning processes and beliefs about communication. This aspect of the term paper encouraged metacognition—the awareness and understanding of one's own thought processes. For example, a student reflected on how their upbringing or cultural background influenced their communication style, fostering a deeper understanding of the roots of their communication behaviours.

> *S1*: 'I realized that I was not self-aware of my emotions in this situation, my parents had to read my emotions but after I expressed and communicated better, I got better advice and help from them. If I were better at expressing it, I would not have it all bottled up in the first place. I also now realise that one of the main reasons to be so hesitant is my inability communicate better at home, which I think is both the problem and part of the solution.'[1]

Another student reflected on his experience as a leader in one of his projects, recognising the importance of effectively communicating, guiding discussions, and delegating tasks across different project phases while adapting his role using the concepts taught in class.

[1] The student responses have been reproduced as such. No attempt has been made to correct any language accuracy errors either in grammar or choice of words.

> *S7*: 'Aero 2021-2022, I think this is when I gave my best at being a leader. Teaching phase: I had to teach them how's and what's of fluid dynamics and everyone in my team are from ECE, EEE, and AI, so I had to explain all the concepts from the ground up. And I was patient with them to grasp the concepts. Now that I reflect back, I was selling those concepts and theories to them. Designing phase: Plane modelling is a world apart from applied fluid dynamics but all the theories almost apply and this is when I tried participating in the discussions and letting them come up and debate with their doubts and ideas. As much as I wanted them to come up with a design by themselves. I had to switch between selling and participating in a lot of aspects. Manufacturing phase: In this part of juniors took over, as I was able to successfully delegate major parts of manufacturing.'

Other instances of reflection on learning include detailed accounts of experiences when a student noticed a pattern in his/her communication style that requires improvement or changes, along with deliberation on what they would do differently when faced with a similar situation again. Excerpts providing evidence of this are given below:

> *S15*: 'I'll make sure that just one thought is provided at a time when I'm trying to convince someone, and that the other person can understand what I'm trying to convey. I should present the data I gathered to them gradually so that they can process it.'

> *S6*: 'I want to learn to give negative feedbacks such that it won't be taken in a wrong way, at the same time, it should not be taken lightly. In case of personal relationships, I can't do certain things easily, like greeting etc., Like yesterday, one of my friends wished me, and somehow, I couldn't reply back to her actively, it looked as if I wasn't interested. I kept thinking about it the whole day, but when a similar situation occurs again, I do the same thing. So, I want be able to provide proper feedbacks.'

> *S7*: 'When I confronted this junior about what happened, he didn't care as much and kept doing what he was doing. I had to stop him from touching power tools that day, which meant they had to delay manufacturing for that day. I wish I knew a better way to handle that situation. But the rationale was to not let any work be done rather someone gets hurt.'

> *S7*: 'If I can redo everything, I would jump less into interactions with strangers or, even if I have to go through those days, I think I will ask

for help and be more open and talk about it without hesitation instead of building walls around me.'

Ownership of and Accountability for Learning

Responding to thought seeds empowered students to take ownership of their learning journey. In the term paper, they were not passive recipients of knowledge; instead, they actively shaped their educational path.

For instance, a student reflecting on active listening identified specific strategies such as asking questions and paraphrasing in order to enhance this skill in future interactions, demonstrating a proactive approach to learning and improvement.

Another student acknowledges his responsibility in ensuring clear communication of feedback, recognising past misunderstandings as a consequence of his failure to confirm interpretation. He also writes about a solution/future course of action, demonstrating accountability for effective communication.

> *S11*: 'One of the major areas where I have to focus is to ensure that the recipient has a clear and full understanding of my feedback. By default, I don't have the habit of checking if my message had been interpreted in the way it was meant to. Due to this there were some misunderstandings too. Once my friend was talking with me about his future career choices and plans. The moment he started listing his career choices [(The student then went on to narrate an incident where honest feedback was misinterpreted as discouragement.] ... I will double check whenever I provide my feedback (especially negative feedback!!) and make sure that it is interpreted properly. I would ask the recipient to rephrase the feedback that I gave him and correct it if needed. I would also be more careful about the vocabulary that I chose and the way I construct my sentence.'

Through their responses to thought seeds, another student identifies his communication patterns in discussions, realising the importance of passive facilitation for effective persuasion. He acknowledges past beliefs/misconceptions and express a willingness to practice passive facilitation, indicating ownership of their communication style and a commitment to improvement.

> *S11:* 'I think I really need to practice more passive facilitation. I tend to get excited usually when trying to persuade. Hence, I end up speaking a lot and also reiterate facts a lot of times. Looking back now, I realize

> that there hadn't been a situation where I tried to put passive facilitation to practice. I always believed wrongly that speaking more increases the chances of persuading a person. I used to get blinded by my very own instinct.'

Another finding shows that a student acknowledges the importance of listening in communication and anticipates opposing arguments. She expresses a desire to work on her listening skills alongside other aspects of persuasion, showing accountability for improving their ability to understand and respond to different viewpoints.

> *S5*: 'I would equally also like to work on my listening skills simultaneously, so as to anticipate what the argument from the other side could be like.'

> *S9*: 'I want to improve on a few things when it comes to persuasion. The first one is to sound logical. I always try to tell what I believe in, but people get convinced by facts rather than what you think. I also want to improve on first deciding what to speak and to whom because you have to say different things to different people when trying to convince them to do a specific task.'

Multiple Possibilities/Answers

Thought seeds challenged students to move beyond binary thinking and consider multiple possibilities or answers. This aspect of the term paper mirrored the complexity of real-world communication. For instance, when reflecting on a miscommunication, a student considered various factors such as cultural differences, tone, and non-verbal cues, demonstrating a nuanced understanding of the multifaceted nature of interpersonal interactions. The student reflects on her experiences with different team members, acknowledging both successful and unsuccessful practices. She recognises the need for different approaches based on individual team members' competencies and communication styles, indicating an ability to consider various factors influencing team dynamics and leadership.

> *S14:* 'This was successful with Y, but it turned into a case of reverse delegation with P, where I ended up doing the majority of the work... We were moving closer to the deadline, and none of us could afford a conflict. I noticed that having just one teammate in this condition could affect how he views the team, so I took special caution to let him know that he did his best, which was true because his problem

> was competence. I tried to avoid the conflict and focused on the other teammates... Next time I'm asked to be in such a position I will have a full-fledged conversation and set realistic and efficient rules with my co-head together that will also prevent conflict.'

Another example includes a student's reflection on the lack of self-awareness regarding emotions and the impact on communication with her parents. The excerpt given below indicates an ability to consider alternative approaches to improve communication within personal relationships.

> *S1:* 'I realized that I was not self-aware of my emotions in this situation, my parents had to read my emotions but after I expressed and communicated better, I got better advice and help from them. If I were better at expressing it, I would not have it all bottled up in the first place.'

Findings also indicate that a student reflected on the challenges in balancing individual needs and team objectives. He proposes ways to improve leadership, demonstrating an ability to think of multiple solutions to address interpersonal and team-related issues.

> *S9:* 'There have been a few times when my leadership attempts were not successful. One of the aspects that I could not control was trying to satisfy everyone's needs and the expectations they had of themselves on the team. As a leader, you need to know how to understand and manage people's emotions and how that can work well for the team and improve the team. Being in a team sport, I haven't found the middle ground between putting the team in the best position and handling my teammates to have a positive attitude. The team's morale does depend on everyone's ego and emotions. I have failed to keep that under control and haven't been able to satisfy everyone's needs while leading the team to the highest level. A few relationships with some of them have started to deteriorate since I have had to make a tough decision not to let them play. I can be a better leader by talking to my teammates and trying to make them understand that a few decisions will be taken only to make the team better and make the most out of the team we have. I must be more assertive in my communication since my emotions get the better of me sometimes, since I value the relationships I have built more. But when it comes to the team, I need to think for the better so that we are more successful. I believe setting tasks and maintaining objectives can help everyone have a chance to prove themselves and reward the ones who have shown the best results.'

Self-Assessment of Performance/Competence

The term paper introduced a unique dimension of self-assessment, asking students to score their own performance and competence in interpersonal communication. This process required a critical evaluation of their strengths and weaknesses. For example, a student assessed their active listening skills on a scale and articulated areas for improvement, indicating a heightened sense of self-awareness. The assessment here was not only left to the teacher's score or grade but a student's genuine understanding of how they performed and what they could do to improve further.

The data proves that the ability to self-evaluate is a fundamental aspect of adult learning behaviour. Self-evaluation fosters a sense of autonomy and empowerment in learners, allowing them to take ownership of their learning process. By assessing their own performance/competence, students become more actively engaged in their learning journey, leading to greater motivation and commitment to learning. The reflective nature of the term paper also enabled students to carry out a realistic evaluation of their behaviour. They were challenged not only to identify their actions but also to delve into the underlying reasons for those behaviours.

> *S6*: 'But I lack some communications skills which hinder me from happily allocating work to a person as I might not be able to freely discuss and settle the work. And I still need experience in figuring out the talent each person has. Also, one of the most important external factors to delegate is the motivation of the person to do the work. In such instances, we should be capable of motivating others. I lack that special skill.'
>
> *S12*: 'I would rate myself 4 out of 10 for self-management of emotions. This is because as the definition says self-management involves the ability to understand your feelings. I am someone for whom processing emotions and expressing what I am feeling is difficult.'
>
> *S14*: 'With a primary focus on self-awareness and self-management when talking about emotional intelligence, I want to work on being able to accept my feelings first, then theirs and, act upon them using my other interpersonal skills.'

Application of Concepts to Real-Life Experiences

The thought seed-driven term paper facilitated the integration of classroom concepts into students' daily lives. This connection between theory and practice enriched their understanding of the practical relevance of interpersonal communication concepts. For example, a student studying conflict management described personal experiences to illustrate how they applied negotiation strategies in a real-life scenario. Another student who reflected on conflict resolution concepts wrote about how these theories played out in a disagreement with a friend.

> *S12*: 'Though in the exercise of finding your preferred style of conflict management, **I got a higher score for collaboration,** it is true only in professional settings. **Avoidance or accommodation is what I practice the most in real life** especially with people that I am close with. With outsiders, I feel I either use collaboration or compromising. For example, there have been many conflicts within my family and friends and I have never once openly spoken about how I feel or how those events are disturbing me. I always choose avoidance because it is easier than explaining them why I am feeling that way because I do not understand why I feel what I feel... **Knowing and learning theory is one thing and applying them in reality is another thing and I feel making the decision to not avoid is going to be a huge and challenging step.**'[2]

Another student describes how they applied persuasion techniques in a real-life scenario. By detailing specific strategies used and their outcomes, the student illustrates how the concepts discussed in class were practically applied in a real-world context.

> *S15*: 'I believe I made use of a few of my persuasion techniques during this incident. By gathering data on the company and speaking with those involved in the sector, I provided social proof, and by outlining the situation with COVID, I convinced my father that the medical industry is a better place to invest. My father gained the confidence to invest in this business by making an effort to investigate that industry. It establishes credibility. I reasoned that making an emotional plea would also be beneficial, so I enlisted my mother's assistance in convincing my father to launch this enterprise.'

Drawing on his experience in sports, a student demonstrates the application of interpersonal communication concepts in a practical setting, showing the integration of theoretical concepts to their own lived experiences.

---

[2] The sentences in bold are in the original.

> *S9*: There has to be a balance between being task-oriented and relationship-oriented. I've had to build relationships and communicate with my teammates and learn how they think and communicate off the court so that it helps us on the court.'

In essence, the altered assessment structure served as a bridge between the academic realm and the complexities of real-world communication. By prompting reflective thought and personal application, students were not confined to the boundaries of course content and exams. Instead, they were challenged to consider how their academic knowledge translated into meaningful actions and outcomes in their lives. This approach not only enriched the assessment experience but also aligned with the broader goal of education—to empower students with knowledge and skills that extend far beyond the classroom.

The Need for Incorporating Thought Seeds for Assessment

Traditional assessments such as sit-down exams and term papers often fail to capture the complexity of communication as a skill-based, context-specific discipline. Exams typically emphasise memorisation and theoretical knowledge, offering limited scope for students to demonstrate practical proficiency in real-life interpersonal scenarios. While term papers allow for more flexibility, they can still be disconnected from lived experience of students and can lead to a high probability of having issues of academic integrity.

Thought seeds, on the other hand, provide an alternative that encourages students to personalise their learning, applying communication theories to situations drawn from their own lives. This not only enables deeper engagement and critical thinking but also supports the development of self-awareness—an essential characteristic of effective communicators. For adult learners in particular, whose educational goals are often tied to immediate professional or personal learning needs, this approach offers a more meaningful and motivating form of assessment. By bridging theory and practice, thought seeds can be used to align assessment more closely with the realities and demands of everyday communication.

Application

While the transition from sit-down exams to using thought seeds offers numerous advantages, it also presents challenges. Some of these challenges include the need for clear guidelines and effective feedback mechanisms.

Here are the main distinctions between assessment practices from an anthrogogic and pedagogic perspective that can serve as a quick check list for teachers. A detailed discussion of the differences between pedagogic and anthrogogic assessment practices in general is in another chapter in this book (Durairajan, 2026).

1. Anthrogogy involves collecting and analysing data to enhance current and future performance/learning for the teacher and student, while pedagogy entails making judgments based on standardised criteria to assign final grades or scores.
2. Anthrogogy is diagnostic, aiming to identify areas for improvement, whereas pedagogy is evaluative, providing learners with an overall score.
3. Anthrogogy provides feedback to enhance learning, while pedagogy determines whether criteria have been met. Feedback in anthrogogy reflects on strengths and weaknesses, while pedagogic feedback depends on the level of achievement against predetermined criteria.
4. Anthrogogy focuses on continuous assessment, aiming to improve performance during the learning process and beyond the course, while pedagogy only aims at assessing the learning to indicate programme's completion.
5. Anthrogogy examines and focuses on the process, while pedagogy assesses the outcome.
6. In anthrogogy, the relationship between the teacher and the learner is student-centered, relying on jointly defined and agreed upon standards. In contrast, in pedagogy, every student is evaluated against predetermined standards mostly set by the teacher.

Conclusion

In summary, the transition from sit-down exams to term papers in communication courses is paramount for fostering comprehensive learning experiences that align with communication's skill-based nature. Communication courses should transcend the mere measurement of memorisation and regurgitation of information, aiming instead to cultivate critical thinking and application of communication theories and concepts to real-life interactions. If we continue to rely on sit-down exams, we risk testing the content of interpersonal communication rather than the actual skills. Therefore, by solely relying on sit-down exams, the assessment of communication ability is limited to students' knowledge of theoretical concepts without adequately evaluating their ability to apply these concepts in authentic everyday situations. This approach will definitely lead to a disconnect between academic performance and real-world communication competence, thereby limiting the overall effectiveness of communication courses.

In particular, responding to thought seeds through term papers represents an anthrogogical approach that fosters holistic learning. It weaves together reflective practices, critical thinking, and practical application, providing students with a nuanced understanding of interpersonal communication. By actively engaging in self-assessment and connecting theoretical concepts to real-life experiences, students not only enhance their academic knowledge but also develop the skills and awareness necessary for effective communication in diverse contexts. While challenges exist, careful planning and support can ensure a successful integration of thought seeds into assessment practices, elevating the quality of communication education and preparing students to excel as skilled and adaptable communicators in today's complex and interconnected world.

References

Alderson, J. C., & Wall, D. (1993). Does Washback Exist? *Applied Linguistics, 14*, 115–129. http://dx.doi.org/10.1093/applin/14.2.115.

Alderson, J. C. (2005). *Diagnosing foreign language proficiency: The interface between learning and assessment.* Continuum.

Bachman, L. F. (1990). *Fundamental considerations in language testing.* Oxford University Press.

Bachman, L.F., & Palmer, A.S. (1996) *Language testing in practice: Designing and developing useful language tests.* Oxford University Press.

Black, P., & Wiliam, D. (1998). *Inside the black box: Raising standards through classroom assessment.* School of Education. King's College London.

Brown, H. D. (2004). *Language assessment: Principles and classroom practices.* Longman.

Brown, H. D., & Abeywickrama, P. (2010). *Language assessment: Principles and classroom practices.* Pearson Education.

Deepa, S. (2022). Thought seeds in anthrogogic learning contexts. *Journal of Indian Education, 48*(2), 58–70.

Deepa. S. (2026). Principles of anthrogogic language education. In S. Deepa & G. Durairajan (Eds.), *Anthrogogy in use: A handbook for language educators* (pp. 3–26). Orient BlackSwan.

Deepa, S., & Durairajan, G. (2023). Learning through assessment in anthrogogic contexts: Wash-Forward. In A. L. Gokturk-Saglam, & E. Sevgi-Sole (Eds.), *Emerging practices for online language assessment, exams, evaluation, and feedback* (pp. 99–118). IGI Global. https://doi.org/10.4018/978-1-6684-6227-0.ch006

Durairajan, G. (2026). Principles of anthrogogic testing and assessment: The need for humane joyful practices. In S. Deepa & G. Durairajan (Eds.), *Anthrogogy in use: A handbook for language educators* (pp. 27–55). Orient BlackSwan.

Furst, E. J. (1958). *Constructing evaluation instruments.* Longman, Green and Co.

Hughes, A. (2003) *Testing for language teachers* (2nd edition). Cambridge University Press. https://doi.org/10.1017/CBO9780511732980.

Knowles, M., Holton III, E., & Swanson, R. (1998). *The adult learner: The definitive classic in adult education and human resource development.* Elsevier.

Letina, A. (2015). Application of traditional and alternative assessment in science and social studies teaching. *Croatian Journal Educational, 17*(1), 137–152.

Merriam, S.B., & Brockett, R.G. (1997). *The profession and practice of adult education: An introduction.* San Francisco.

Ross-Gordon, J. M. (2011). Research on adult learners: Supporting the needs of a student population that is no longer nontraditional. *Peer Review, 13*, 26–29.

Spolsky, B. (1990). Social aspects of individual assessment. In J. H. A. L. De Jong, & D. Stevenson (Eds), *Individualizing the assessment of language abilities* (pp. 3–15). Multilingual Matters, Ltd.

Trott, D. C. (1991, October). *Anthrogogy* [Paper presentation]. American Association for Adult and Continuing Education, Montreal, Quebec. https://eric.ed.gov/?id=ED342887.

12

Teaching Questioning in Anthrogogic Classrooms using the Samvaad Method

A. Amaratheja

Introduction

As human beings, all of us use questions in our day-to-day lives: we use them to get information, seek knowledge, clear doubts, et cetera. Children also ask a lot of questions to know more about the world they are living in. From ordinary scenarios to the most demanding circumstances, the art of questioning remains an enduring skill within us which we, as adults, teach our children. For instance, it starts with teaching a child to answer or pronounce their name for the question, 'What's your name?' and then the child goes on to ask, 'What is this?', and so on. Thus, human lives involve asking and answering questions that fulfil the process of communication and comprehension. In this modern era, questions and answers generally lead us to know more about the person's rationale, logic, structure, and development. Asking and answering questions in our own first language is a natural phenomenon prompted by observation, understanding, and reflection. Thus, questioning is an art that we learn to master as we grow up. Among the many challenges of the present education system, however, is that the art of questioning in real-life situations is rarely taught. In addition, when it comes to other languages that we learn, it is assumed that we need to be taught how to ask questions in that language. This is truer of English as a second language (ESL) where, because of the colonial hangover, it is assumed that such 'learners' need to be taught the forms of asking questions as well.

Current Teaching Regarding the Nature of Questioning

At the school level, in ESL classrooms we teach students the art and skill of questioning by focusing on the form first. This is done by teaching them the grammar of asking questions in English by inverting the subject and verb as it is done in the structural syllabus. In communicative language teaching, we give them role-play activities and teach functions of language where questions are used, like getting information, asking for directions, et cetera. When it comes to the classroom curriculum and syllabus at the undergraduate level, some Indian universities unfortunately still continue to re-teach the grammar elements, focusing on a structural perspective. As such, the focus is on the structure of forms rather than the pragmatic use of questions. For instance, the following excerpt has been taken from an undergraduate English textbook used in a South Indian university.

> To enquire is to ask for information from somebody. Enquiries can be direct/indirect. A few ways of making polite enquiries to seek information are:
>
> **Subject questions**
>
> These questions are about the subject of a sentence:
>
> - Who takes you to school?
> - Which is your favourite place?
> - What annoys you the most?
> - When is it convenient?
> - *Do not add the auxiliary verb 'do' ('do', 'does', 'did'): Who takes you . . . ? not Who does take you . . . ?* (Gowda, et al., 2021, p. 80)

From the above description, it is obvious that the textbook has tried to focus on the practice of form with no reference to any context. The forms are presented in isolation and do not have specific contexts that vary from each other. Such isolation of form and structure will not help the students/learners experience real-life contexts. Any grammatical item has three aspects: form, function, and meaning. All grammatical structures will be learnt only when they fulfil the above three aspects and are put into use. From the above extract, we can infer that questioning was taught in this particular text though the use of grammatical form rather than focusing on the function and meaning of the structure.

Another excerpt from the same textbook which focuses on the types of modal verbs to be used in questions, is reproduced below.

> *The common expressions for seeking permission and giving permission are:*
>
> 1. *Seeking permission:*
>   - May / Can / Could I ....?
>   - Do / Would you mind if I ....?

- Is it all right if I ....?
- If you don't mind, I would like to .... (p. 82)

From the above extract, we can see that although the focus is supposedly on the function of seeking and giving permission, the major focus is on the forms of language that have to be used to ask for permission. Thus, we can infer that the focus is on the structures rather than the actual context where these varied question forms have to be used. To make it worse, in the same textbook they also have a chapter on question forms where a short 'lecture' on question forms in English has been provided. The following excerpt has been taken from there.

> *QUESTION FORMS*
>
> In grammar, a question is a type of sentence expressed in a form that requires an answer. An interrogative or question word is used to ask a question, such as what, which, when, where, who, whom, whose, why, how etc. There are different types of questions (also known as interrogative sentences) that one can ask. Each elicits a slightly different response and is structured in a certain way. In this unit, we shall study the following types:
>
> - Yes-no questions
> - Wh-questions
> - Question tags (p. 90)

The above excerpt deals with the form and function of the question types in a way that focuses on the form: Yes/No, Wh-questions, and question tags. This extract, meant for adult students, focuses only on question forms and the structure and function of the lexical item. There is no information on the pragmatic perspective. The students will never learn to use these forms in real-life contexts by merely focusing on such form practice.

An attempt has been made to teach questioning from a functional perspective through contexts or situations. The following excerpt has been taken from the undergraduate English textbook for another university, which deals with functional English.

> Seeking/Granting/Refusing Permission:
>
> Below are a few expressions used in formal and informal situations to seek permission.
>
> a. Could I have your permission to...? (formal)

b. We'd like your permission to . . . , please, (formal)
c. Could we . . . , (please)?
d. Can I . . . please? (less formal than Could I...)
e. May I . . . , (please)? (formal) (Panikkar, et al., 2019, p. 121)

From the above extract, we can see that the instructions suggest that the expressions can be used in formal and informal situations, but the text still focuses on asking questions through modal auxiliaries that focus more or less on the practice of form and not the function. The same issue can be seen in another extract reproduced below.

Common questions to be asked when Asking for Directions.

a. Is it far? / Is it close?
b. How far is it? / How close is it?
c. Could you please give me directions?
d. Where is the nearest bank / supermarket / petrol bunk? (p. 125)

In order to focus on teaching questioning techniques or forms, they use modal auxiliary, wh-questions, or yes/no questions. The form practice of these lexical items is given more priority than the context and the meaning. Since there are many ways of asking questions in English, ESL or EFL learners will only get confused when the focus is on form alone. It would help if we taught learners through tasks and activities that rely on real-life experiences. From these texts, we understand that these extracts would fall under 'empty' information-gap activities rather than real-life experience activities.

It is not enough to merely present empty role-play activities to teach questioning techniques. The NEP 2020 has mandated that 'Indian "Knowledge of India" will include knowledge from ancient India and its contributions to modern India and its successes and challenges, as well as a clear sense of India's future aspirations with regard to education, health, environment, etc.' (p. 16). There may be many other ways in which this could be carried out. Still, in line with NEP 2020, the attempt made in this chapter is to reach out to Indian knowledge systems and adapt/use the Samvaad method of questioning to teach questioning techniques in the adult ESL classroom.

Samvaad as a Questioning Technique

Samvaad is the theoretical framework using the art of questioning. We are not teaching adult learners how to question in terms of the content that has to form the question itself, but how to use questioning as a technique to get genuine information. In this regard, the Samvaad system of questioning will help adult learners construct real-life knowledge. Questioning through dialogue is said to help students merge previous knowledge with new information or ideas. Dialogic teaching invites students' thoughts and opinions, allowing them to 'think, interpret, and generate new understandings' (Nystrand, 1997, p. 11). According to Bakhtin, 'any utterance, whether spoken or written, that people use in communication with each other is internally dialogic' (Bakhtin, 1986, p. 63). In a dialogic interaction, speakers listen to one another actively, share, and construct new meanings collaboratively through reciprocal understanding. Samvaad teaching involves teachers' questioning techniques, which usually need to be understood beyond the classroom contexts (textbooks and printed texts) and the learners' real-life experiences. Samvaad questioning encourages students to develop a 'logic-based' approach to the concept and produce their own evidence and reasoning. It is an approach that supports the teaching and learning process through interactive dialogues, question posing, and answering them, leading to new questions, understandings, and ideas. The Samvaad paradigm, although not adhering to a liberal neutral point, permits individuals to be distinct and supports the diversity of groups and customs as well as their equality (Prince, n.d.) According to him, Samvaad consists of three steps: first, getting to know oneself in a way that allows one to understand the traditions that support the inquiring self, their logicism, their authoritative texts, and their story; second, understanding the other in their tradition and rationality, similar to picking up a new language; and third, engaging in dialogue with the other in order to fulfil the goal of dialogically coexisting. Samvaad teaching adopts open and divergent questions that lead learners to think, share, and generate different ideas between students and teachers toward the collaborative construction of knowledge.

In anthrogogic classrooms, adult learners are expected to act, behave and take responsibility as language users, whereas in pedagogic classrooms, the teacher enables students to learn by providing a scaffold whenever needed (Deepa & Durairajan, 2022a). The term 'anthrogogy' implies that adult learners should take responsibility for their academic purposes and keep to their deadlines for task/ assessment completion in mainstream higher education programmes and classrooms, both offline and online (Deepa & Durairajan, 2023a; Deepa, 2026). Using Samvaad as a questioning technique can be encouraged in anthrogogic classrooms because the learners are individual adult language learners who can think, interpret, and generate understandings on their own. Alexander (2008) states that dialogic teaching has five indicators: 'collective, reciprocal, supportive, cumulative, and purposeful'. This very fundamental approach in anthrogogicity optimises these five indicators to enhance teaching and learning by using Samvaad questioning techniques in ESL classrooms.

The majority of research on dialogic teaching, however, has focused on students in elementary and secondary school settings, so it must be acknowledged that there has been less research on adult learners (Fisher, 2009, 2013; Mercer, 2000; Mercer, et al., 1999). We observed through an analysis of the two textbooks that the questioning techniques taught at the undergraduate level are pedagogic and form-focused. Therefore, in order to teach and enable questioning strategies in an adult language user classroom, the Samvaad method of questioning was chosen for this study. The research questions that were behind the experiments are as follows:

1. What are the ways in which Samvaad questioning can be used in an undergraduate classroom?
2. How effective will Samvaad questioning be when combined with the use of a real-life task to enable students to ask relevant questions?

Methodology

This study adopts a qualitative approach to analyse and assess Samvaad questioning techniques in anthrogogic learning contexts. The author of this chapter is the observer of the classroom. The study is an intervention by the researcher through observation.

Sample

Undergraduate students registered for an integrated master's programme in the Humanities stream were subjects of this study.

Research Tools

The tasks used in the classroom, the teacher's diary, the reflective essays submitted by students, focused group-interviews with the students, and the researcher's diary.

Procedure

The study involves classroom tasks with the teacher's interventions. Here, the teacher is the facilitator or mentor, and the researcher is in the classroom observing the interactions and transactions. Before starting the task, the teacher introduced them briefly to the Vikram–Betal stories,[1] Nachiketa's questions, Yaksha Prashnas,[2] and other similar texts. The purpose of referring to these stories where questions were asked and answered in Indian lore was to motivate students to ask questions and also make them understand that questions are a significant part of conversations, and not merely a part of empty role-play activities.

The narration of a few of these old stories helped the students look at questions with fresh eyes and ears and made them curious about revisiting their own questioning techniques. Through these stories, the teacher made the students aware of the art of questioning in real-life experiences. In class, the task of asking relevant questions was divided into five steps with equal partnership from the students and the teacher through Samvaad techniques.

Step-1: Dynamic Grouping

As the first step, the class was divided into groups using the dynamic-grouping technique. According to Deepa & Durairajan (2023), it has been observed that not forcing students to work in randomised or teacher-selected groups, which is usually a pedagogical practice, is important. Instead we need to give them the freedom and choice to work in groups,

---

[1] The stories of Vikram–Betal have their roots in ancient India, where the main characters are King Vikram and the vampiric ghost Betal. Originally written in Sanskrit, these tales were meant to teach the audience moral lessons. According to the frame story, King Vikram had to take Betal on a journey without uttering a sound. Betal would narrate a story and pose a question but would fly back to his original haunt if Vikram answered it. Vikram is unable to keep from answering the questions, usually ones on the morality of a certain situation, and Betal flies back to his haunt. This continues through twenty-five such stories.

[2] In the epic *Mahabharata*, as the Pandavas approached the end of their banishment, Yudhishthira engaged in a series of questions and answers with a yaksha (celestial being/spirit) in order to revive his four other brothers. This dialogue is called the *Dharma-Baka Upakhyan*, or the 'Legend of the Virtuous Crane'.

with peers, or as individuals at their own comfort levels to attain the optimum learning outcome. Based on this group dynamic perspective, the students were formed into different groups/pairs or allowed to work on their own, as per their choice.

Step-2: General Instructions for the Task

The teacher used an advertisement pamphlet from a super bazaar or mall that consists of different offers on different items (Images 1 and 2), with some having fifty per cent off, and other items marked as having thirty, forty or fifty rupees off. The teacher gave the pamphlet to all the adult learners. The task assigned to them was to take on the role of finance manager on behalf of the teacher, like a personal shopper or co-shopper. The students were expected to help the teacher purchase items worth Rs 2800. They had to read, decide on what to do, make their lists, and start asking questions within fifteen minutes.

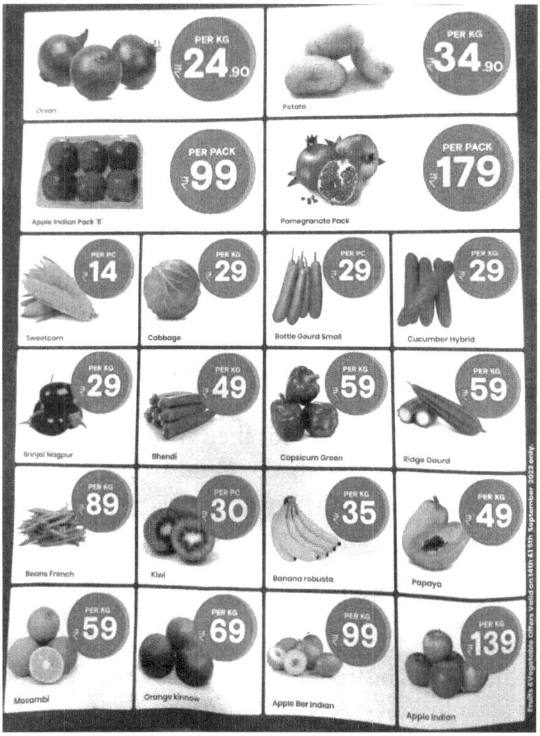

Image 1

Image 2

The teacher did not go with students to the mall/super bazaar, but the students were expected to buy items on behalf of the teacher. The teacher assigned points as scores for their initial budget list, and added an instruction that if students had chosen wrong or irrelevant items from the teacher's wish list, they may be given minus points after the Round 1 questions.

Step-3: Round 1 Questions That the Students Had to Ask the Teacher

After giving the general instructions for the task, the teacher did not give the students any physical currency, but an imaginary currency value of Rs 2800. Each group was told they had the option to ask the teacher three questions regarding the shopping trip. The teacher maintained that no group could buy something that the teacher would not use or something she didn't need. If the students did not adhere to this condition, the teacher would deduct points. Each group responded that they were okay with one or two questions, which would be enough. They asked the teacher a few questions through dialogues. The questions did not actually follow the pattern of questioning according to the grammatical rules of English. Initially, the teacher did not point this out but answered the 'questions'. The function of questioning had been fulfilled even if the interrogative form had not been used. Given below are a few such examples.

Q1. If any allergy or dietary restrictions?
Q2. For how many member(s)?
Q3. Food preferences (sweet, sour, spicy, et cetera.)
Q4. Preference of vegetables from the leaflet.
Q5. What would she choose from the second page of the leaflet?

Step-4: Simulated Shopping

As adult learners, the students came up with the idea that they would try out simulated shopping (online shopping through the internet, either apps or websites), where they could add items to the cart that shows the final price of all products. During this process, one or two groups realised that for one product, the app/website was showing only 20% off; there was no mention of the MRP.

They brought this issue to the teacher's notice. The teacher asked them what they were trying to convey. Further, the teacher asked them to put this issue in the form of a proper question. These were genuine, real-life adult problems. The teacher directed them to do a Google search, find the product's value, and find out the final price by calculating. The teacher posed the question of whether they knew how to do such a calculation.

This is the Samvaad system, where the teacher does not give direct answers to the students but poses a few more questions so that they find the answers all by themselves. They all got the information needed independently because they were adult learners.

This is an example of anthrogogic experience among adults; a student does not have this kind of experience in a pedagogic setup. In anthrogogic learning contexts, Samvaad questioning is essential because it is dialogic.

Questioning or switching up how to question in an anthrogogic setup in the discipline of English language teaching (ELT) can enable adult learners to arrive at their solutions by themselves.

Finally, the groups drew up a list of items that could be purchased on behalf of the teacher. In the end, the teacher's declaration of the results was announced to each group in discussion mode, but not lecture mode. The teacher called each group and discussed how relevant their questions were to the task and gave them their scores.

As we saw, the teacher also used the Samvaad mode. Thus, teacher–student interaction/participation was equal for the first round of questions. In the Samvaad system, there is an underlying philosophy of equality between the teacher and the student, irrespective of the position and designation of the teacher; there is only debating through discussions and questioning.

Step-5: Round 2 Questions

After the declaration of results, the teacher announced that those students who did not fulfil the teacher's shopping cart requirements were less than fifty per cent. Those who did not use their first-round questions would now be able to use three more questions. The teacher asked if they wanted to use a reset button for the questions. The groups responded to the teacher that they all needed to ask a few more questions. The teacher allotted them three more questions and, in addition to that, unutilised questions from the previous round.

Those students who had made the shopping list with their own reasons and assumptions and did not pose questions to the teacher, found that their reasons and assumptions did not match the teacher's wish list exactly after the Round 1 discussion and results. This time, these students got clarity regarding what to ask in the form of questions. For instance, one group had put a kitchen utensil (a frying pan) on the shopping list. Since the teacher had enough utensils in the kitchen, she wouldn't need it. Then, those students posed questions related to the teacher's dietary preferences. Finally, their shopping list was finetuned without the teacher answering them directly.

By the end of the class, the teacher gave them a brief conclusion about how this questioning would be done in their adult lives and the importance of the art of questioning in constructing knowledge in real-life experiences.

Data Interpretation

The questions asked by the groups of students during both rounds of the task were related to dietary restrictions, number of family members, food preferences, preferences for vegetables, and health issues. The language used to frame questions was simple and comprehensible. The lists were made based on reasons and assumptions related to daily experiences. When asked why they had included items like tea and vegetables in the list, they came up with 'tea is very common in Indian households', 'vegetables are good for health,' and so on. As a post-task activity, students submitted reflective essays on the task. The following themes emerged from the reflective essays on the task: teamwork/group collaboration, decision-making, creativity/critical thinking skills, financial management, and learning/personal growth.

Team-work/Group Collaboration

Students emphasised the novelties and the challenges of working in groups to finalise a shopping list. They mentioned the need to coordinate with teammates, consider different perspectives, and arrive at a consensus, which added complexity to the task.

As student D said, 'The time bound nature of the task was not really an issue, it was more difficult to actually co-operate with other people as we had to reach a consensus and take decisions as a team, making something as mundane as buying groceries quite a bit more complex.'[3] The student identified the importance of coordination with teammates.

Student G said, 'With the help of our group members, we completed the list considering healthy diet of the elders who are in good shape.' The students stressed the importance of group work in completing the task.

Decision-Making

Students highlighted the challenges of the decision-making process, especially regarding budget allotment and item selection. The time-bound nature of the task added pressure and complexity, requiring quick thinking and decision-making.

---

[3] The statements made by the students in their reflective essays have been reproduced as such, with no changes.

Student A said, 'Working under stress, making conclusions from the limited questions we had, framing the questions in a way we get max intel added on to the spirit. We could even discover our skill sets in making judgements at a given time frame and how we could justify them.' Student A identified the complexity of the task as making decisions and framing questions with skills.

Student H said, 'The task made me understand that our questions should never be of the manner that it gets dodged back at us. Propelling our questions with the right tools and aiming it at the right directions is something that'll aid us.' Student H identified the importance of asking the right questions to get the correct responses.

Empathy

Some students mentioned the challenge of shopping for someone else with little information, requiring them to make assumptions about other people's choices. They highlighted this as an attempt to put themselves in the shoes of the person they were shopping for.

Student E said, 'It was quite tricky to choose the list because it was not for ourselves. I had to put myself into my mother's shoes and rely on whatever experience I acquired while shopping with my mother. Now, I am slightly aware about what to enquire if I am asked to shop for someone else.' Student E pointed out that shopping for others was a challenging task and identified that one should have empathy to do such things.

Student F said, 'Shortly I had fun realising about daily shopping routine of another person, managing health & finance, etc.' Student F expressed the joy of shopping for another person and caring for them, and showed the empathetic nature of shopping.

Grammar as a Barrier to Creativity

Some students noted that conventional grammar rules sometimes restrict creative expression, suggesting that grammar can inhibit imaginative thinking.

Student K said, 'Whereas grammar mostly is done in conventional methods, puts a halt on our creative minds. Some of them are just rules that creates domains within which we should limit our work. No doubt it's unavoidable, but it overlays our imaginary skills.' Student K rightly pointed out that conventional grammar sometimes is a barrier to creativity.

Creativity and Critical Thinking

Some students compared the task to detective work, highlighting the need for creativity and adaptability in framing questions and reaching conclusions. Students mentioned the need for critical thinking skills to frame questions strategically and to get the required responses. Problem-solving skills were highlighted as students navigated constraints such as limited questions and time pressure to finish the task.

Student H said, 'Framing questions is indeed an art whose mastery needs both analytic and deductive skills, this may also slightly vary according to the situations. We need to make some assumptions, that designs our format. The key lies in the fact whether those judgements favor or go against our motives, which requires some observation skills as well.' Student H found that the framing questions in real-life situations needed analytic and deductive reasoning. From this we can see that for framing questions one also needed creativity and critical thinking.

Student K said, 'It spreads out more area for creativity, and freedom to capture it with our own hint of magic. each one of us took it in very many beautiful ways.' They identified the fact that the task involved a lot of creativity and reason.

Financial Management/Awareness

The task brought awareness of the reality of expenses, emphasising the importance of budgeting and financial intelligence. Students reflected on the challenge of staying within the budget and making the right choices to improve savings.

Student F said, 'I'm a kind of person who doesn't likes to spend too much money especially on the things I know I won't be using much so I think it's a good habit of mine to save money which also a part of our Indian culture i.e., culture of savings but it doesn't means to compromise the basic needs to have a healthy lifestyle.' Student F expressed that the task made them aware of how to save and manage money.

Learning and Personal Growth

Students reflected on what they learned from the task, such as increased awareness of financial management, empathy, and teamwork skills. They acknowledged the educational value of the task in preparing them for real-life situations and enhancing their perspectives.

Student B said, 'After careful planning and using the resources provided to us we managed to finalize everything and even made some savings. I think classes like these help us more in real life situations.' Student B figured out that the task was helpful in coping with real-life situations.

Student H said, 'In short, we could get a deep insight to the facets and the differences between simply asking questions versus a more structured and weighed discipline of asking them.' Student H observed through this task that simply asking questions would go in vain, whereas structured questions would fetch them good results.

These themes collectively highlight the task's complexity and the variety of learning opportunities it provided to students, including collaboration, judgment, empathy, critical thinking, and personal development. More importantly, the students learnt to ask relevant and appropriate questions in a meaningful authentic context.

Conclusion

The chapter discussed how Samvaad questioning techniques were introduced and explored in anthrogogic learning contexts. When students need more straightforward answers, they can arrive at answers by further questioning. This implies that the teacher can move far away from teaching the syntax of the interrogative, which usually does not happen in many language classrooms in India. The Samvaad system shows us that it could be used in English language classrooms where one respects knowledge. In contrast to conventional classrooms, this technique allows for the appreciation of cultural background and worldview, and helps clarify learners' thoughts, words, and actions.

As the observer-cum-researcher of this anthrogogic classroom, these are my reflections. This dynamic grouping helps students find the optimum learning environment to work in according to their comfort levels. It also encourages learner autonomy, to be independent and grow individually, to acquire knowledge in real-life experiences. The equal-partnership approach is generally said to be very effective because the anthrogogic classroom really works for it. The teacher–student relationship is not just a classroom connection; it helps construct and share knowledge. The conventional methods of teaching questioning would focus only on structural and functional syllabus implementation in the classroom, whereas this anthrogogic classroom brought an engaging task to the students to make it authentic and as real as possible, that is, linked to daily-routine budget shopping. The material used for the classroom task was a simple newspaper pamphlet and it was circulated through the class WhatsApp group. When classroom materials are simple but real and the tasks authentic, students will involve themselves with these tasks, put in a lot of effort and show enthusiasm. Teaching the art of questioning through this activity gave scope to enhance or construct real societal knowledge rather than teaching them question forms, question tags, and interrogatives in isolation. Samvaad (dialogic) teaching–learning has scope to enhance anthrogogic classrooms and make them more viable than the conventional lecture/teacher-centered classrooms.

References

Alexander, R. J. (2008). *Towards dialogic teaching: Rethinking classroom talk* (4th ed.). Dialogos.

Bakhtin, M. (1986). *Speech genres and other late essays.* (W. V. McGee, Trans., C. Emerson, & M. Holquist, Ed.). University of Texas Press.

Carey, T. A., & Mullan, R. J. (2004). What is Socratic questioning? *Psychotherapy: Theory, Research, Practice, Training, 41*(3), 217–226.

Deepa, S. (2022a). Pedagogic scaffolding and anthrogogic learning contexts: Issues in metaphor mismatch. *Journal of English Language Teachers' Interaction Forum. XIII*(2), 3–7.

Deepa, S. (2022b). Options in multiple choice questions: Oh really! Yours sincerely adult learners!. *Language and Language Teaching, 11*(2.22), 81–86.

Deepa, S. (2022c). Thought seeds in anthrogogic learning contexts. *Journal of Indian education, 48*(22), 58–70.

Deepa, S. (2022d). Pedagogic practices in higher education and Peter Pan syndrome: An appraisal. *Fortell, 45*, 164–173. https://www.fortell.org/wp-content/uploads/2022/10/July-2022-164-173.pdf.

Deepa, S. (2026). Principles of anthrogogic language education. In S. Deepa & G. Durairajan (Eds.), *Anthrogogy in use: A handbook for language educators* (pp. 3–26). Orient BlackSwan.

Doukmak, R. (2014). Are you sure you don't have any questions? Dialogic teaching as a way to promote students' questions. *English Language Teacher Education and Development, 16*, 27–33.

Gowda, T. N. T., Poornima, P. S., Firdose, A., Vedha Surendra, V., Basavaraju, B., Priyadarshini, S., Mallikarjunappa, G., Mamatha Subraya, M., & Rashmi, L. (2021). *Luminous-I: I semester B.A./B.S.W./B.A. (Music) generic English.* Bengaluru Central University Press.

Mercer, N. (2000). *Words and minds: How we use language to think together.* Routledge.

Mercer, N., Wegerif, R., & Dawes, L. (1999). Children's talk and the development of reasoning in the classroom. *British Educational Research Journal, 25*(1), 95–111.

Miyazaki, K. (2023). Questioning in Bakhtinian dialogic pedagogy and argumentation theory. *Dialogic Pedagogy: A Journal for Studies of Dialogic Education, 11*(3), A42–A64. https://doi.org/10.5195/dpj.2023.544.

Nystrand, M. (1997). *Opening dialogue: Understanding the dynamics of language and learning in the English classroom.* Teachers College Press.

Pannikkar, C., Veerappa, M., Rama Devi, N., Vasudha, A. R., Aziz, N., Obed, N., Balagam, S. K., Gowtham, A., & Badrinath, P. (2019). *Word and image 1: Communicative English handbook for I semester B.A. Communicative English.* Bengaluru Central University Press.

Paul, R., & Elder, L. (2006). *The thinker's guide to the art of socratic questioning. Foundations for critical thinking.* Foundation for Critical Thinking Press.

Prince, B. (n.d.). *The Religious Freedom in Hindu Traditions.* Retrieved 29 April, 2025 from https://www.academia.edu/36408009/Religious_Freedom_in_Hindu_Traditions.

Trott, D. C. (1991, October). *Anthrogogy* [Paper presentation] American Association for Adult and Continuing Education, Montreal, Quebec. https://eric.ed.gov/?id=ED342887.

Walsh, J. A., & Sattes, B. D. (2011). *Thinking through quality questioning: Deepening student engagement.* Crowin/Sage.

Yang, Z., & Brindley, S. (2023). Engaging students in dialogic interactions through questioning. *ELT Journal, 77*(2), 217–226.

Yildrim, S., & Uzun, S. (2021). An overview of dialogic teaching and its implications on learning. *International Journal of Education, Technology and Science, 1*(2), 135–153.

13

Modified Tasks for Writing

An Anthrogogic Revamping of Classroom Practices

SRUTI NARRA

Introduction

Humans may learn at times through passive reception but most often learn through inquiry, challenges, arguments, and experiences, primarily due to the active involvement that necessitates imbibing of knowledge\learning of the skills to a better degree. The next question is whether adults learn differently compared to children. The answer to this question might depend on what is being learnt and many other factors such as the field of expertise, skill set of adults, familiarity to the context, motivation, and the like. However, adults bring much more to the learning table than children, like their knowledge of concrete and abstract concepts and schemata, life experiences, metacognitive awareness, and pluricultural backgrounds, most of which have been identified as advantages in language learning (Ausubel, 1964). They are also guided by their learning preferences, learning goals, and intrinsic motivations. On the other hand, they might be limited by individual differences in terms of short-term memory, brain structure, and motivation levels. While children might have some of the above in common, like learning preferences or motivations, they are still exploring everything around them and adults are more settled in their ways and preferences.

In neuroscientific terms, a 'sensitive period' refers to the notion that the effects of environmental stimuli on the developing organism are stronger during certain periods of development. The term 'critical period' is used when a specific environmental stimulus is needed to cue normal development, whereas the term 'sensitive period' is used when the development is more easily influenced by a negative environmental event (Bodin, et al., 2011). The sensitive periods in children make them the most flexible\plastic. While adults can learn and form memories and new neurons throughout their life, they have less plasticity as they become more specialised towards adult functions. However, this plasticity is something adults could alter through experiences (whether abstract, emotional, conceptual) and physical activity and hence, it is not a limiting factor for adult learning though there are suggestions regarding the possible difference in expected learning rates among children and adults (Knowland, & Thomas, 2014). Also, the relevance and potential of the adult learners' experience and background cannot be overemphasised.

In addition, the change in attention among adults and children is also relevant here. While children are immersive, adults are selective; as such they shift from environmentally-driven behaviour to internally-driven behaviour (Craik & Bialystock, 2006). Hence, it is important to make a clear distinction between teaching children and adults. One of the ways of achieving this distinction might be by altering the learning environments accordingly to maximise learning outcomes. Unfortunately, mainstream education for adult learners in India and South Asia, though in theory aims to develop valuable and relevant professional capabilities through self-directed tasks and foster learner autonomy, in practice and even in theory still relies heavily on pedagogic theories. For instance, in the National Education Policy document, though the aim is to foster learner autonomy, the guiding principles are pedagogic in nature (NEP 2020). Therefore, there is a need to study adult learning in detail to examine the application of adult learning theories and related challenges in the Eastern context (Chan, 2010; Deepa, 2022a; Tezcan, 2021; Muduli, et al., 2018; Sharma, et al., 2020).

Scope of the Chapter

This chapter discusses a few aspects related to teaching writing in the light of anthrogogy and aims to put forward some of the practical applications of anthrogogic principles in classrooms with reference to the teaching of writing. A few writing tasks used to teach undergraduate learners in India are critiqued and some modifications suggested with respect to the instructions of these tasks to align them with anthrogogic principles. The objective here is to show how existing tasks can be made anthrogogic. These modifications were presented to the same set of undergraduate learners. The teacher conducted informal discussions with these students to find out their preferences related to the modifications suggested, and if they would be interested in tasks that would be modified based on such suggestions. A retrospective report based on the group discussion was put together by the teacher. This data along with the tasks used in the actual classroom and the suggested modifications are discussed in a later section.

Theoretical Background

Andragogy

Andragogy was defined as a set of core adult learning principles that can be applied to adult learning situations in the context of distance education, open learning and non-formal adult education programmes, and lifelong learning (Knowles, et al, 2015; see Loeng, 2018 to trace the historical development of andragogy in different countries). However, it has never been applied to mainstream education. More importantly, Knowles' theory of andragogy does not provide a systematic approach to apply these principles. Since there can be a lot of factors determining the success of the approach, it may be useful to think of ways of adapting it in line with the variables that need to be considered. The context, goals, and purposes for which these principles are applied can result in changes in the learning process or the emphasis of the learning process.

Purwati, et al., (2022) discuss six principles of andragogy and their application in English as foreign language (EFL) contexts in face-to-face and virtual classrooms. Purwati's study aimed to discuss these principles vis-à-vis material design, teaching activities, and assignments. Though the ideas for implementing these principles give a sense of direction to teachers, they are still very generic and most of the suggested activities—like project-based learning, tasks involving adults inside and outside the classroom—are already in use in Indian classrooms. Though active engagement is a step forward, learners engaging in set ways that the teachers expect and providing autonomy only in aspects like selecting the seating arrangements in the classroom, or using the polling feature in Zoom to assess student engagement, would still keep the teacher in the steering seat. The study also fails to address the issue holistically as it, for instance, seems to assume that children and adults have clearly defined differences and generalises adults motivation and self-directedness, ignoring the potential differences in learning capabilities, stages, and personalities which affect the degree of self-directedness and motivation among adults.

Choy and Delahaye (2003, 2005) divide learners into four stages. The first is children where high pedagogy\low andragogy is recommended; the second is young\adolescent learners where high pedagogy\high andragogy is relevant; while stages three and four are posited for adult learners where low pedagogy\high andragogy is suitable. Nevertheless, the application of this concept would depend on variables such as prior learning contexts and experiences, exposure, home environment, et cetera, as they might shape the expectations of the learners and would also have an impact on their learning style, ability, or skill. As such, the stages might not be as distinct and predictable as stated in the study.

Anthrogogy

In this chapter, the term 'anthrogogy' (Trott, 1991) is preferred as it is an inclusive term; a detailed delineation of the construct has been attempted by Deepa (2026). This shift in attitude from the prevalent pedagogic practices can bring about a change in the role of teachers and learners, the kind of syllabus and materials relevant for adult classrooms, group dynamics among peers and administrative practices (Deepa 2026), and testing and assessment practices (Durairajan, 2026).

Though adult learning theories have been discussed in the literature, there were very few studies focusing on adult learning holistically and not just in the vocational or adult literacy contexts. Also, mainstream adult learning contexts are still guided by pedagogic principles, if at all loosely modified for adult learners. Hence, there is a need to discuss the key principles, explore them, and study them in the context of adult learning to determine their feasibility in our language classrooms. There are many factors like the learners' stage of learning, varied capabilities and experiences, and backgrounds that can affect the relevance of these anthrogogical principles. Some learners who are new to the anthrogogic style of teaching might need guidance to adapt to the new learning environment and to become self-directed over time. The teacher in such contexts could progress from pedagogic to anthrogogic strategies. The goal for adult learning environments should always be this direction of improvement rather than subjecting the learners to pressure or expectations that are not well-founded (Knowles, et al., 2015). There are studies that have problematised the challenges of applying anthrogogic principles in some adult classrooms and some with very successful outcomes given the varied attitudes and readiness of learners (Deepa, 2022b). As such, it should be a learner-centred decision that is negotiated between the learner and the facilitator, and in such environments the teacher guides the learners to become gradually more self-directed. On the other hand, even adolescents and children could be prepared to become more self-directed learners and hence anthrogogical principles can encourage and guide pedagogic approaches to focus on this direction of improvement as their larger goal. To enable such a movement it is necessary to enable adults to reflect on their learning, collaborate, and also be able to metacognise.

Reflection and Metacognition

Abbas (2016) studied the effect of reflection-supported, process-based writing instruction for second year students at a college of education in order to assess their writing performance and attitude. In this study, the focus was on the reflection on students' writing (Deti, et al., 2023 is a replicative study in a different context). The paper reports that the method tested was effective in developing a stronger writing performance and encouraging a positive attitude related to writing. It would have been interesting to find out the effect of reflection at a deeper level, for instance, while reading texts or instructions or inputs\samples as part of the writing class. In this study reflection was encouraged through a writing reflection sheet where there were questions encouraging reflection throughout the process of writing. This being a good start, reflection during the teacher–student interactions with the content could clarify the concept of reflection and teach them how to reflect and what to reflect on. The writing reflection sheet asks the student to respond to questions like—'What was well in my performance and what was not so well?' To be able to reflect appropriately on such general and abstract questions, the student needs to be able to differentiate good and bad writing, self-assess one's writing, identify the bits that are well and those that are not so well, and then take necessary actions. Teacher feedback and orientation can help the students through the process. However, when starting to encourage reflection in a writing classroom, starting with simpler and clearer steps might be better. For example, helping students reflect on one concrete aspect of writing like use of cohesive devices, purpose of writing, target audience, et cetera, might lay the foundation better.

Mulugeta (2021) discusses an interesting study about students' strategy use in reading-to-writing tasks. The reading-to-writing tasks are defined in the study as follows: 'an activity that involves both comprehension and production and calls for complex interaction in the process of reading to create one's own text in writing' (p. 79). Graduating students were part of the study and the author observed that students whose writing was 'competent and average' used different strategies more frequently compared to students who produced 'less competent writing'. Moreover, students who produced 'competent writing' preferred metacognitive strategies whereas students whose writing was 'less competent' preferred social/ affective strategies. The author encourages the integrated approach to teaching reading and writing skills and the strategy training in academic contexts. Reflection while reading to write is the right focus and the use of metacognitive strategies in such tasks can help the students imbibe textual features and apply them while they construct texts.

The teaching–learning cycle Derewianka discusses (VicTESOL, n.d. p.1–9) has four stages:

- The first stage involves building content knowledge relevant to the field.
- The second and the third stages, supported reading and learning about the genre, could be realised through tasks like text deconstruction, use of annotated sample texts, group and peer discussions about the text to focus explicitly on the genre, discourse features, and meaning construction.
- The fourth stage, supported writing, is where the teacher and the student(s) jointly construct a text.
- The final stage is independent use of the genre.

The second and the third stages in this cycle are relevant in this discussion. Discourse and genre deconstruction to explicitly discuss textual features, structure, and meaning construction, making all these concepts explicit, and developing a metalanguage among learners is important. Sedita (2013) also stresses on explicit strategy instruction at each step of the writing process.

Collaborative Writing

Collaboration has been widely researched but in this section it will be discussed briefly in connection with teaching writing to adults. Lingard (2021), in an article that elaborates on strategies and activities for collaborative writing, lists seven core activities, namely, brainstorming, conceptualising, outlining, drafting, reviewing, revising, and editing. These activities could be performed collaboratively and, based on the writing genre and the task in focus, some activities might be more necessary than others. The author also emphasises the importance of establishing and critically thinking about one's collaborative writing practices, and states that being purposeful and explicit about a collaborative writing strategy can help the team achieve its goals and minimise challenges.

Stell (2018) discusses the use of collaborative writing in an EFL classroom context. This study explored the effects of collaborative writing on complexity, accuracy, and fluency. One of the findings of this study is that pairs in a collaborative task achieved better accuracy and fluency. The study also found that collaborative writing helped students to resolve meaning-related issues in their texts. The author states that the learners focused more on vocabulary and spelling during the collaborative writing activities than the structural aspects. This might explain the low effect of collaboration on text complexity in this study. Apparently, some groups worked collaboratively resolving issues in a co-constructed manner and equally contributed to the task, while some used the approach of task distribution where they would interact with each other. However, they did not write and discuss simultaneously and thus the sections were divided and treated as solitary acts in some cases. While both the interactions are useful, the author observes that 'when the pairs wrote and discussed simultaneously, their constant change of roles gave them the opportunity to engage further with the task, thus balancing the levels of equality and mutuality to create a collaborative relationship' (Stell 2018, p. 87). The study puts forward these pedagogical implications: 'paper-based collaborative writing can be effective for learners who are used to exam-oriented EFL classrooms. The interactive process involved in collaborative writing can encourage students to revise, recall and apply language forms and functions effectively' (p. 87).

Wigglesworth and Storch (2012) bring together the studies related to collaboration in writing and writing feedback especially focusing on small group and pair activities. Based on existing research this paper concludes that processing feedback in pairs gives learners opportunities for language learning and, when engaged in pair activities involving processing feedback and writing, learners can engage in cognitive processes that promote language learning. The study gathers that collaboration affords learners with opportunities to deliberate about their ideas, to give and receive feedback from peers, and can encourage learners' deliberation on particular features of language based on the context of the writing task. The study also observes that learners drew on their explicit knowledge of language, language rules they were familiar with, and their linguistic intuition while involved in collaborative writing.

It would be useful to study the effect of collaborative writing on the learners' ability to reflect and develop metacognitive skills especially in adult language classrooms, in Asian contexts.

Critique of Writing Tasks & Learners' Response to Suggested Modifications

The following inputs and tasks were adapted or created for a business\ professional communication course for students studying for BBA or BTech degrees at a private university in India. The classroom teacher is an Assistant Professor in this institute and has been teaching there for more than six years. The identity of the teacher has been kept anonymous for purposes of confidentiality. Eighteen students participated in this study. Most of these students had low intermediate to high intermediate level of proficiency in English, while there were a handful with low advanced level of proficiency (the range of proficiency in CEFR, Council of Europe, 2001, for most students would be B1–B2). The teacher, in an informal discussion, said that in their teaching context some of the challenges in the language classrooms were 'lack of learner motivation, learners' hesitation to participate in the classroom activities, and high student-teacher ratio in a classroom'.

This English teacher of the BBA and BTech degree programme was asked to share a random sample of the writing tasks that were used as part of the language courses. The author of this chapter received five tasks, amongst which one was a complete writing section from the prescribed text book with pre-writing tasks and other exercises/activities building up to a writing task. The purpose in requesting this random sample was to understand how writing is taught in these programmes. The teacher believed that the tasks selected and sent were a good representation of such teaching/enabling. The objectives of these tasks were to prepare the students for the writing needs in their field and to equip them with skills needed to write independently when they start working after graduation.

The selected materials were critiqued for their relevance to the learner group, the principles they adhere to and reflect in terms of both pedagogicity and anthrogogicity, and their relevance also in terms of the target language use domain of the learners. After the tasks were critiqued, some modifications were suggested to the teacher. The teacher took these suggestions and modifications to the learners and had a discussion with them to understand their preferences and opinions about the modifications. The learners' preferences and opinions about the modifications were collected using informal discussions and the English teacher put together a retrospective report based on the discussions with the students.

For analysis, four writing tasks (one writing section + three writing tasks) will be discussed. The task that the teacher had submitted is described first, after which the modifications suggested for each task are presented. Lastly, the learners' and teacher's responses are qualitatively discussed. These responses dealt with aspects such as the modifications and changes in the tasks\instructions\choices given. The learners' preferences—for instance, whether the learners would like to do a task with the modifications mentioned or if they prefer the original version of the task—were also collated. To gather this information, the teacher had to explain to the students the differences between the task they had done and the suggested modifications to the task. The learners were divided into 3 groups (Student Group 1, 2, and 3; in the chapter referred to as S.G. 1, 2, and 3), where they discussed and expressed their preferences and opinions. The teacher put together a retrospective report based on their responses in the discussion and expressed their opinions about the modifications as well as paraphrased learner responses.

Writing Section

The writing section used in the teacher's classroom is the fourth section in a textbook unit called 'Describing an Event'. The previous sections covered the function and theme of the unit, giving students practice through exercises focusing on the skills and elements in the following order—reading, grammar and vocabulary, listening and speaking. It is beyond the scope of this chapter to discuss the approach of the entire unit; hence the focus is only on the writing section which consists of a set of pre-writing exercises and tasks that lead to a final writing task.

This writing section begins with a brainstorming question (Exercise 1) and progresses to writing exercises that expect students to choose the right words from the given choices to complete three posters and a table with details of the events being discussed in the posters (Exercises 2 and 3). The poster\table-filling is followed by some vocabulary exercises where students need to find adjectives from the posters that match the words\ phrases given ('interesting', 'very good', 'big' are the words students need to find matches for) in Exercise 4, and completing sentences with the correct information (phrases like 'I've listened to', 'I've watched', et cetera., are given, and the students need to write complete sentences using these phrases) is Exercise 5). After the sentence completion, the learners need to describe an event they have seen. Here, the phrase 'I've just arrived at ...' is given and one can assume that the students need to complete the sentence. The instruction given for this task was: You have arrived at one of the other events. Describe what you have seen on your first day'. It is important to note that no further instructions regarding word count or the number of sentences to be written were given; this was marked as Exercise 6. This was followed by a 'Plan Ahead' section that began with a reading text which was about 200 words, and had four short paragraphs (Exercise 7), followed by four questions (Exercise 8). The questions focused on the tone of the text, intended audience, organisation of the text, finding examples of conversational language in the text, some adjectives in the text and informal punctuation. The reading text was followed by exercises that dealt with the present perfect tense (Exercise 9) and a note-making task where the learners write about a festival they attended with phrases learners could use under each paragraph, like 'have you ever ...?', 'I've just ... there are lots of ... fantastic ... fascinating ... and exciting ...' and the suggestion is to 'use four paragraphs' (Exercise 10). The section ended with a writing task where the learners were asked to write an article describing their first day at a local festival or one of the events in the poster. Learners were expected to write about 150–180 words, and they could refer to the texts in the section if needed. There were suggestions related to 'using the right register and attracting the reader at the beginning' (Exercise 11, "Festival Fever", 2007, p. 49).

Critique and Suggested Modifications

Given their awareness and practice in writing by this stage of the unit, though the level of proficiency is basic to intermediate, the learners could be asked to create a poster by giving them the key details of the events (in place of Exercises 2, 3, 4 and 5). This could be a pair or group task and poster making can be a useful skill for business communication making the task relevant in terms of target language use domain.

The 'Plan Ahead' section seems useful as it makes the learners think about the passage in terms of style, audience, organisation, and word choice. However, the instructions are direct and focused and do not provide any space for alternative responses. Questions 2 and 3 and 4 in Exercise 8 could be modified as:

> Q2. Can you find examples in the first and last paragraph of conversational language?
>
> Modification: *What do you think are the examples for conversational language in this article?*
>
> Q3. What adjectives does Isabelle use to interest the reader?
>
> Modification: *What words does the author use to grab the readers' attention?*
>
> Q4. What informal punctuation does Isabelle use?
>
> Modification: *Is there any punctuation in this article that is appropriate here but might be inappropriate for formal texts?*

It is a small article (~200 words), and the learners would be able to find the answers without clues. However, it would be more anthrogogic for the teacher to provide the clues only if required while the task is being completed rather than providing them at the beginning itself, which is tantamount to an underestimation of their capabilities.

Exercise 9 is very pedagogic and focuses on surface-level, system-oriented features which could have been focused on much later in the writing process. Post brainstorming, organising ideas and writing, if learners have used an inappropriate tense or structure, they could be made aware of their surface-level errors during the drafting or feedback session. This is easily possible for the example article\reading text is also available for them to extrapolate the appropriate tense and structures for the writing task.

Exercise 10 is focused on 'Completing the Notes', but this is really not something that needs to be used to make the learners use the right sentence structure. Here again, the correctness or appropriate use of structures could have been focused on at a later stage. As it stands, this exercise is part of the 'Plan Ahead' section. Asking the learners to write a set number of paragraphs—in this case four—and providing phrases to be used at the planning stage itself to enable such writing makes the exercise pedagogic. The learners are not even given a chance to think and come up with relevant ideas for their text. They need to fit their ideas into the given mould. More importantly, adult learners need to be encouraged to make notes in points or using graphic organisers. There is no need to emphasise the use of complete sentences and appropriate structures while making notes, organising ideas or planning the draft.

Exercise 11 could become a writing task better suited for adult learners by making simple modifications. The modified task is given below:

> Would you be interested in describing an event like the ones mentioned in the unit? If not, can you think of any other event or an eventful day you would like to describe? If not, can you put on your creative hat and make one up? Writing at least 150-180 words can help the readers follow your event, if you can be succinct yet complete in lesser words, you are encouraged to try. You can go through the articles presented in the unit if that can help you get started, but always start with an open mind while writing, try not to get too influenced by the other authors' style, try to find your style of writing. Do come to the facilitator for any clarifications.

Learners' and Teacher's Response

For Exercises 1–6, with reference to the suggestion about making a poster, the learners showed interest and said 'they would like an activity like that instead of the grammar exercises' (S.G. 1, 3). An interesting improvisation the learners suggested was making an infographic instead of a poster and thought it would be easier to do as they were familiar with the process of making infographics. Accepting such suggestions is a good anthrogogic principle, which implies that materials that need to be used in an adult classroom should be like a resource-book and be eminently tamperable with by the teacher in the classroom (Prabhu, 2019b).

The classroom teacher also felt the same and said that even for learners with lower to upper intermediate proficiency, tasks that engage them meaningfully can and will generate interest. The teacher also liked the idea of deleting a few grammatical exercises and discussing surface-level errors and issues during teacher feedback. The teacher agreed that this would individualise feedback for the learners as they would receive help and guidance where needed based on their language errors. The teacher also realised that it is an efficient use of time as currently all grammatical aspects are discussed equally for all the learners, and in such individualised sessions, both class time and student time is better utilised.

The teacher found that the instructions for Exercise 11 generated interest among all levels of learners and some of them stated that 'they could choose something based on their interest and the amount of time they can spare for the task' (S.G. 1). The teacher observed that they felt more in control when they exercised their choice rather than being dictated by the teacher completely. This again needs to be interpreted as evidence that teachers in adult classrooms need to have the freedom to modify exercises or tasks based on the context, level and interest of the learners.

Input Example

The input used in the teacher's class is titled 'Thesis Statements: The Bad and the Better'. This handout introduces thesis statements, their purpose, use, and relevance. In the handout are a few examples that are labelled 'Bad and Better'. The handout is followed by a graphic organiser titled 'Writing the Three-part Thesis Statement', which has questions and instructions to supposedly guide the writers. The questions read as follows:

- Pose a question or restate the question posed by the writing prompt (Section 1)
- Make a claim or state your opinion (without using the personal pronoun 'I') and
- Make sure to write your answer as a complete sentence, not a question or phrase' (Section 2)
- Write down three main points (pieces of evidence) that you will explore in your paper. These will become topic sentences in the body of your essay (Section 3)
- Now put it all together (Section 4)

The section questions are followed by examples like 'What are the primary causes of climate change?', 'Climate change is caused by human activities.', et cetera. ("Thesis Statements: The Bad and the Better", p. 012519).

The questions and instructions form four sections in the graphic organiser and there are boxes under the sections where the students can make notes: Sections 1, 2, and 4 have one box, and Section 3 has three boxes.

Such explicit instructions make this whole task pedagogic for there is no space for any individualised thinking or writing. It is as though these adult learners need to be held by the hand and taught how to put together a thesis statement.

Suggested Modifications

Given that the input is for adult learners, using absolute terms like 'bad' and 'better' to label thesis statements and presenting prior labelled statements makes the input pedagogic as the learner is not given a chance to think about the statement with an open mind as it is already labelled and presented. Instead, the use of descriptors like 'Simple–Elaborate', 'Indicative–Clearer', 'Can be controversial–safer', 'Correct–more appropriate' can make a lot of difference as the focus is shifted to the reader rather than being unnecessarily subjective, binary, dismissive and absolute. The learners should be asked to use the mentioned sets of labels to tag the sentences. This can make the input appropriate for adult classrooms and can turn a passive handout into an interesting task that encourages reflection and raises metalinguistic awareness. This could also be a collaborative activity that encourages metalinguistic discussions amongst learners.

Though the idea of using a graphic organiser to help learners organise their writing is a good start, the instructions make the task pedagogic. For example, the materials producer has decided how many specifics\ details need to be provided, how the essay is going to start, how the claim will be made, and even the number of evidence statements the writer would provide. This kind of heavy hand-holding or scaffolding dulls the learners' thinking as it is not being demanded or encouraged, does not provide any scope for a free flow of ideas, and discourages learner creativity. Adults do not need scaffolds, only road signs that they can use, as and when required, if they do not know or are a little unfamiliar with the route (Deepa 2022b, 2022c; Deepa & Durairajan, 2023).

In an adult classroom, where learners come with their own skill sets, their own investment, (Prabhu, 2019a) there are likely to be some who can think out of the box in contexts like these and stand out: others in class, may need encouragement from the teacher who should work as a facilitator. The main drawback of this task is the inflexibility of the instructions. Instead, using a flexible graphic organiser where the format could be altered can make the task more anthrogogic as the learner is given a resource and the choice to use it as and when needed. The existing instructions are like a guided writing task, where very little thinking and system oriented blank filling, accompanied by a few cognitive operations are all that is expected of the learner.

In the modified task the facilitator could use the following instructions:

- Look at this graphic organiser, does it seem useful?
- How would you like to use it?
- Can you use it to make notes before writing your essay?
- Try it in your next pre-writing stage if you like.
- Here is the softcopy of the same. Play with the format and adapt it to your requirements.

Another aspect to note here is the examples; whenever we provide examples, it is important to state that they are just indicative and meant to merely provide students with a starting point. It is important to indicate that there are many other ways of saying the same thing, especially when the learners need to shift from a pedagogic to an anthrogogic set of expectations. It is important not only for clarity and completeness, but also for reiteration whenever possible and not just whenever required. This is a paradigm shift and it cannot happen without such conscious and consistent changes in our teaching style.

Learners' and Teacher's Responses

Student Groups 1, 2, and 3 found the modifications useful and relevant. Most learners preferred the modifications suggested. Some of them stated that *by* 'filling in the details' (S.G. 1) in an organiser like this, they would be able to 'arrange and organise their ideas in order' (S.G. 3).

However, no learner suggested modifications to or attempted to modify the given format and the teacher stated that this was because of low motivation among the learners. This implies that the learners liked the flexibility that was suggested, where the format of the graphic organiser was open and they could modify it according to their needs. However, in spite of preferring a flexible model during the discussion, the learners did not change anything in the model when they had the chance in some of their tasks to modify the format. This could be attributed to the existing strict nature of the classroom where materials are not perceived as a resource which can be played around with. Anthrogogicity requires a mindset change, not just with teachers, but also with learners.

Set of Pre-writing Exercises for Argumentative Writing

A description of the pre-writing task used in the teacher's classroom is as follows. The handout describes argumentative and evaluative type of essays. There are short texts labelled A, B, and C ('the first draft is A, the second is B and the third draft is C', as mentioned in the handout). These three 'texts' are followed by yes\no questions like, 'Is it a convincing comparison of cars or buses?' and 'Would you refer to it as a persuasive piece of writing?'. After these texts with questions is a table summarising the themes of A, B, and C. There are steps to guide the students in how to analyse the texts like, 'Underline the key words in the themes of the three texts', 'How do the themes in Texts A, B show the way the writing is developed?' and 'Draw a circle around the words or phrases in the Themes of Text C which show how the writer's argument is structured'. Such explicit questions make this task pedagogic and structured ("Module 6: Writing an Argument", 2012, pp. 1–3).

Critique and Suggested Modifications

Though the idea of making the learners analyse text drafts is a good start, the approach is pedagogic. The fact that the learner is provided information regarding which version is which draft and what it has done is a lost potential for critical thinking and discussion.

Instead, the learners could be asked which of the texts, according to them, is the first, second, or third draft. If this exercise is likely to be perceived as difficult for the learners because of their proficiency level, it could be converted into a pair or a group exercise.

Another problem with the task is that the themes have been predetermined and given away to the learners. This is an underestimation of adult capabilities and another lost potential in the task to enable reflection and metacognition. Instead, the facilitator could ask the learners to arrive at the themes of the texts which, if required, could be carried out as a pair or group exercise while the facilitator guides the learners as required towards the appropriate themes.

Last of all, asking them to analyse the text, connecting the themes and the phrases in the text as a whole-class activity could be interesting and useful provided the texts are appropriately challenging for the group.

Learners' and Teacher's Responses

The teacher observed that in the given suggestions, the 'pair work idea yielded some good responses from the learners' (S.G. 1, 2). They also liked the possibility of guessing the themes of the text and felt that 'they could participate actively in such a task as they need to come up with a response and cannot just listen' (S.G. 2).

For the final analysis of the text and connecting the themes and the phrases in the text, the teacher preferred it to be a pair activity instead of a whole-class task as the number of students in the class was high and a whole-class activity would have elicited responses only from the most active students; many other relevant or different responses may not have been taken into account, only because of lack of time.

The teacher liked the idea of a pair/group activity better for the task as each pair/group gets enough time to complete the activity in peace and ask questions when needed, and the teacher can go from pair to pair to clarify their doubts.

Letter Writing Task

In the material used by the teacher in the classroom, a letter writing task which has two situations was used. It was a pair activity where the pairs choose one situation. The situation describes a context where a letter needs to be written and there are suggestions for note-making, and underlining the phrases and expressions in the letter as well as on a worksheet.

One situation read as follows:

> You are Head of Human Resources at a/an ... company. You have been in touch with an IT Training company about training some of your staff. You have now received information about the training but need to change some of the details. With a partner, think of what kind of changes you might need to make (for example the number of people taking the training course). Now underline the phrases and expressions in your own letter and on worksheet 2 which you could incorporate into the letter. Write the letter with your partner. (Morley, 2006)

This task is not as pedagogic as the others that have been discussed; however, there are some aspects which could be modified to make the task an anthrogogic one.

Suggested Modifications

This task at the outset looks fine. The topics seem appropriate to the target language use: there is a collaborative writing opportunity and some guidelines for planning writing are given.

However, there are only two situations to choose from, and if giving many choices is time-consuming, we could at least let the learner decide whether they would like to choose something else. The problem here, which is primarily caused by a pedagogic perspective, is that we are trying to fit all learners into a box—with only two alternatives provided—only for the sake of practicality.

The guidelines for pre-writing are also pedagogic in nature as they instruct the learner to do very specific things like underlining the phrases and expressions. Instead, the facilitator could state 'You might want to make notes at this stage if you are such a writer that benefits from note making before writing'. This kind of a statement could in turn make the learner think about their style as a writer or their preferences during pre-writing. We should, where possible, let the learner arrive at their preferred way of learning and organising their thoughts. This can eventually make them self-aware. Otherwise, they are just doing what they are asked to do without knowing the purpose of it or alternatives to achieve the same.

When a shift in paradigm is the objective, there is a need to reflect on our current practices with a critical eye because simple aspects become patterns in our teaching. In an already pedagogically-dominant context (in India and other such similar contexts), we need to take extra measures to change such styles before they become strong patterns in our teaching. Such changes can benefit learners at all proficiency levels as the indications and guidelines are still there but there is flexibility, choice, and opportunities to think and become metacognitively aware of their learning.

Learners' and Teacher's Responses

The teacher agreed with the suggestion that asking the learners to write complete sentences when not necessary—for instance, while making notes—can be demotivating for them. The teacher observed that giving them the option to make notes at the pre-writing stage was better, as most of the learners stated that 'it would be useful to make notes at that stage and said that they would try making short notes first when they have to write' (S.G. 1, 2). The teacher also agreed that asking the learners to make notes in the form of bullet points can encourage hesitant writers and provide them with a starting point.

Tone in Textbooks: Suggestive or Prescriptive?

Across the four tasks (accompanied by exercises within the task) that have been analysed in this chapter, one theme that runs through them is the nature of language used and the tone that is reflected in the materials, particularly in the teacher's handbook. The argument made thus far in the chapter is that even the instructions that are meant for adult learners needs to be more anthrogogic. If this is the case, it is paramount that teachers should not be given 'instructions' to be followed in the classroom, but suggestions on how the materials could be used, on a 'use if required' basis. When materials developers produce content for an adult language classroom, it needs to be seen as providing ideas to the teacher on how to use or, more importantly, modify the materials in the classroom.

When such ideas are delivered through textbooks or other forms of materials, the tone of this delivery communicates the expectations of the materials producer to the teacher and this can impact their role in any classroom. The argument that materials should be eminently tamperable-with by the teacher in the classroom (Prabhu, 2019b) was made with reference, not even to adults, but pedagogic school classrooms. As such, this ought to be the rule and not the exception in adult classrooms.

The appropriacy and applicability of tasks and activities for any language classroom depends on many factors, such as the size of the classroom, learners' proficiency level, their current learning needs, goals, difficulties, or challenges. As such, the tone needs to be suggestive, where there is scope for negotiation between the teacher and learners, and teachers are encouraged to make decisions based on their classroom context. A prescriptive tone or attitude is when the material developer takes all the decisions and prescribes them to all teachers who are likely to use the materials, leaving no room for any modifications or individual, local, context-based decision-making. It should always be possible for a teacher to move away from a textbook and take decisions that are appropriate for their classroom. Textbooks can then become a good medium that will enable teacher autonomy, inculcate a culture of negotiation between the teacher and learners, and inspire teachers to be facilitators.

As an illustration of such tone, a section from Unit 1 of a textbook titled *English* for *Engineers* (Ibbotson, & Day, 2008) was selected. Before examining the section selected, the introduction for Unit 1 from the teachers' version of the textbook will be described. This is to ensure fair coverage of content. For instance, the introduction to the unit might cover aspects like the approach or methodology appropriate for the unit, and might also discuss key ideas teachers could apply while delivering the unit.

The author starts with a suggestion to hold an introductory discussion in class. Here the teacher is instructed to use ('use' is the verb used) questions like, 'What field of engineering are you in\would you like to go into?' (a listing of the various branches of engineering are also provided), followed by a question like 'In what kinds of situations do you use English at work?'. For this activity, the author suggests ('could use' was the verb used) pair work or small-group work in large classrooms. After the orientation, the author instructs the teacher to introduce the book by showing the contents and explaining the emphases on listening, speaking, active use of language, and practice through activities like role plays and discussions. It is obvious that the teachers are instructed to merely 'carry out these procedures', for the phrases used in the teacher's handbook include 'hold a ... discussion ...', 'use the following questions ...', 'invite the students ...', 'explain the themes ...', 'emphasise that ...', et cetera. The only context where prescription could be seen as replaced by suggestion is in the use of the modal verb 'could' as in 'students could work in pairs ...' (Ibbotson, 2008, p. 1)

A description of a section from the same unit in the student's book (Ibbotson, & Day, 2008, p. 9) is presented below, followed by an analysis of the notes to the teacher for the same section (Ibbotson, 2008, p. 5).

This section from the book had activities like reading a note from a space elevator-research team in pairs, discussing the questions raised in the note, arriving at possible solutions, making notes, giving a small talk in small groups using the notes they had made, and finally writing two to three paragraphs summarising the talk.

The teacher's notes for this section carries suggested answers for the tasks, and the instructions read: 'Students analyse the notes in pairs and read them out in full', 'Students complete the task in pairs and compare their ideas to the suggested answer', 'Students complete the task in small groups', 'Students complete the task either in class or as a homework activity'. At the end of this set of prescriptive, constraining instructions is a note titled 'Emphasising the Technical Advantages' which includes a list of words that the teacher would find useful while teaching the section: 'conventional', 'eliminate', 'superior', et cetera. (Ibbotson, 2008, p. 5).

The tone in the unit above is imperative and prescriptive. There is hardly any difference between the sections in the textbook and the teacher's notes. Most importantly, the teachers are not provided any thinking space or opportunities to come up with ideas on how to conduct their class, the approach that they could use, or a choice in the aspects that they could choose to focus on. The introductory paragraph from the same unit also has a similar tone and even lists the questions the teacher could use to guide the discussion. This neither leaves any room for teacher creativity or adaptation based on student needs, nor is the teacher given the freedom to modify the content to make it relevant to their classroom.

The modifications suggested to the writing tasks in this chapter have been attempted with this suggestive and perspectival tone in mind. The teacher and the learners should be able to collaboratively take decisions in the classroom that can further their learning. Many factors like the proficiency level, purpose of participating in the task, personal writing goals, cultural familiarity\practices, learning context, and so on, can determine the suitability of such modifications.

The aim of this chapter was to provide a few suggestions to the teacher and the learners as plausible possibilities/alternatives. The modifications are therefore worded using modal verbs like 'can' and 'could' with no impositions and no use of imperative sentences.

On a personal note, if I were the teacher in that classroom and if I had found such suggestions\possibilities in my textbook\teachers' guide in addition to or in place of activities to be completed for each unit, they would instil an immediate responsibility within me to decide whether it is a good suggestion or not and, more importantly, they would make me pause and think of other possibilities. A change in the language of instructions and a suggestion of alternative possibilities could go a long way in developing a teacher's sense of plausibility (Prabhu, 1987).

Conclusion

The modifications suggested to the writing tasks have been intended to transform and revamp the pedagogic tasks into ones that are anthrogogic in their orientation. In order to do this, over and above the language of instructions and in a few cases, the focus of the tasks themselves, the focus was, wherever possible, to provide space for teacher learner negotiation and discussion, in order to enable learner reflection, collaboration and metacognition. One section took this to a higher level and critiqued the nature of suggestions provided in the teacher's handbook. Adults come to any classroom with their own skill sets and their own learning preferences. Materials meant for adult classrooms, and all teachers handbooks need to move away from pedagogic prescriptive methodologies and materials, and provide suggestions that can be picked up and used or modified by all teachers who can and will use their own sense of plausibility.

References

Abbas, S. (2016). The effect of reflection-supported process-based writing teaching on Iraqi EFL students' writing performance and attitude. *Arab World English Journal, 7*(4), 42–62. https://doi.org/10.24093/awej/vol7no4.4

Ausubel, D. P. (1964). Adults versus children in second–language learning: Psychological considerations. *The Modern Language Journal, 48*(7), 420–424. https://doi.org/10.1111/j.1540-4781.1964.tb04523.x.

Bodin, D., Yeates, K. O., & Cass, J. (2011). Sensitive periods. *Encyclopedia of Clinical Neuropsychology*, 2255–2256. https://doi.org/10.1007/978-0-387-79948-3_1593.

Chan, S. (2010). Applications of andragogy in multi-disciplined teaching and learning. *Journal of Adult Education, 39*(2), 25–35.

Choy, S., & Delahaye, B.L. (2003). Youth Learners: The Authentic neglected species learning for an unknown future. In H. Mathews, & R. McKay (Eds.), *Proceedings Annual International HERDSA Conference* (26), (pp. 100–107), Christchurch, NZ.

Choy, S., & Delahaye, B. L. (2005). Some principles for youth learning. In Blakeley, J (Ed.) *Emerging Futures—Recent, Responsible and Relevant Research AVETRA 2005*, (pp. 1–21). www.avetra.org.au/publications/Conf05Papers.

Council of Europe (2001). Common European framework of reference for languages: Learning, teaching, assessment. Council of Europe. https://rm.coe.int/16802fc1bf.

Craik, F. I. M., & Bialystok, E. (2006). Cognition through the lifespan: mechanisms of change. *Trends in Cognitive Sciences, 10*(3), 131–38. https://doi.org/10.1016/j.tics.2006.01.007.

Deepa, S. (2022a). Thought seeds in Anthrogogic Learning Contexts. *Journal of Indian Education*. *48*(2), 58–70.

Deepa, S. (2022b). Pedagogic Practices in Higher Education and Peter Pan syndrome: An Appraisal. *Fortell* (45), 164–73. https://www.fortell.org/wp-content/uploads/2022/10/July-2022-164-173.pdf.

Deepa, S. (2022c). Pedagogic scaffolding and anthrogogic learning contexts: Issues in metaphor mismatch. *ELTIF*, *XIII*(2), 3–7. https://www.academia.edu/81011272/Pedagogic_Scaffolding_and_Anthrogogic_Learning_Contexts_Issues_in_Metaphor_Mismatch.

Deepa, S. (2026). Principles of anthrogogic language education. In S. Deepa & G. Durairajan (Eds.), *Anthrogogy in use: A handbook for language educators* (pp. 3–26). Orient BlackSwan.

Deepa, S. & Durairajan, G. (2023). Scaffolds or road signs for anthrogogic language learners: A critical enquiry. In P. B. Nair, P. Ramalingam, & B. Nagalakshmi (Eds), *Teaching of English: Theorising from the classroom* (pp. 11–25). Tamil Puduvai.

Deti, T., Ferede, T., & Tiruneh, D. (2023). The effect of reflection supported learning of writing on students' writing attitude and writing achievement goal orientations. *Asian-Pacific Journal of Second and Foreign Language Education*, *8*(1), 29. https://doi.org/10.1186/s40862-023-00202-8.

Durairajan, G. (2026). Principles of anthrogogic testing and assessment: The need for humane joyful practices. In S. Deepa & G. Durairajan (Eds.), *Anthrogogy in use: A handbook for language educators* (pp. 27–55). Orient BlackSwan.

Festival Fever. (2007). Pearson.pl. Retrieved April 25, 2025, from https://www.pearson.pl/fileadmin/poland/english/products/files/sample_files/9781405884129.pdf.

Ibbotson, M. (2008). *Cambridge English for engineering: Teacher's notes.* Cambridge University Press. http://www.cambridge.org/elt/englishforengineering.

Ibbotson, M., & Day, J. (2008). *Cambridge English for engineering: Student's book.* Cambridge University Press.

Knowland, V. C., & Thomas, M. S. (2014). Educating the adult brain: How the neuroscience of learning can inform educational policy. *International Review of Education*, *60*(1), 99–122. https://doi.org/10.1007/s11159-014-9412-6.

Knowles, M. S., Holton, E., & Swanson, R. A. (2015). *The adult learner: The definitive classic in adult education and human resource development.* Routledge, Taylor & Francis Group.

Lingard, L. (2021). Collaborative writing: Strategies and activities for writing productively together. *Perspectives on Medical Education*, *10*(3), 163–166. https://doi.org/10.1007/s40037-021-00668-7.

Loeng, S. (2018). Various ways of understanding the concept of andragogy. *Cogent Education*, *5*(1), 1–15. https://doi.org/10.1080/2331186x.2018.1496643.

Module 6: Writing an argument. (2012). Learning Centre, University of Sydney. Retrieved on April 25, 2025, from https://www.sydney.edu.au/content/dam/students/documents/learning-resources/learning-centre/writing/writing-an-argument.pdf.

Morley, C. (2006).*Worksheet 3: A business letter.* Teaching English.org. Retrieved on April 25, 2025, from https://www.teachingenglish.org.uk/teaching-resources/teaching-adults/activities/upper-intermediate-b2/business-letter.

Muduli, A., Kaura, V., & Quazi, A. (2018). Pedagogy or andragogy? Views of Indian postgraduate business students. *IIMB Management Review, 30*(2), 168–178. https://doi.org/10.1016/j.iimb.2018.01.008.

Mulugeta, Fekadu. (2021). Addis Ababa University students' strategy use in a reading-to-writing task. *The Ethiopian Journal of Education, 41*(1), 75–111. https://ejol.aau.edu.et/index.php/EJE/article/view/2021.41.1.75.

Ministry of Human Resource Development (2020). *National education policy 2020.* https://www.education.gov.in/sites/upload_files/mhrd/files/NEP_Final_English_0.pdf.

Prabhu, N. S. (1987). *Second language pedagogy.* Oxford University Press.

Prabhu, N. S. (2019a). Materials as support: Materials as constraint. In G. Durairajan (Ed.), *Perceptions of language pedagogy* (pp. 82–93). Orient BlackSwan.

Prabhu, N. S. (2019b). Rethinking language pedagogy: An interview. In G. Durairajan (Ed.), *Perceptions of language pedagogy* (pp. 314–30). Orient BlackSwan.

Purwati, D., Mardhiah, A., Nurhasanah, E., & Ramli, R. (2022). The six characteristics of Andragogy and future research directions in EFL: A literature review. *Elsya : Journal of English Language Studies, 4*(1), 86–95. https://doi.org/10.31849/elsya.v4i1.7473.

Sedita, Joan. (2013). Learning to write and writing to learn. In Hougen, M. C. (Ed.), *Fundamentals of literacy instruction and assessment,* (pp. 6–12). Paul H. Brookes.

Sharma, N., Bansal, A., Jain, S., Sharma, L., Jain, C., & Madaan, M. (2020). Students' perception regarding pedagogy, Andragogy, and heutagogy as teaching–learning methods in undergraduate medical education. *Journal of Education and Health Promotion,* 9(1), 301. https://doi.org/10.4103/jehp.jehp_221_20.

Stell, Annita. (2018). Exploring the use of collaborative writing in an EFL classroom context. *University of Sydney Papers in TESOL, 13,* 63–97.

Tezcan, F. (2022). Andragogy or pedagogy: Views of young adults on the learning environment. *International Education Studies*, *15*(1), 136. https://doi.org/10.5539/ies.v15n1p136.

Thesis statements: The bad and the better. (2021, December 12). EBSCO. Retrieved April 25, 2025, from https://www.ebsco.com/sites/g/files/nabnos191/files/acquiadam-assets/Thesis-Statements-Handout.pdf.

Trott, D. C. (1991, October). *Anthrogogy* [Paper presentation] American Association for Adult and Continuing Education, Montreal, Quebec. https://eric.ed.gov/?id=ED342887.

VicTESOL. (n.d.). *A teaching and learning cycle* (pp. 1–10). Victorian Association for the Teaching of English to Speakers of Other Languages. Retrieved from https://victesol.vic.edu.au/wp-content/uploads/A-Teaching-and-Learning-Cycle.pdf.

Wigglesworth, G., & Storch, N. (2012). What role for collaboration in writing and writing feedback. *Journal of Second Language Writing*, *21*(4), 364–374. https://doi.org/10.1016/j.jslw.2012.09.005.

14

Observations and Experiences from an Anthrogogic Classroom

A Learner's Perspective

MEGHNA ANAND and NIDHI D. M.

Introduction

In contemporary higher education, the nature of learning in adult learners is acknowledged to be distinct from that of young learners (Deepa, 2026). However, many courses offered for adult learners continue to follow pedagogic instructional methodologies that can obstruct the holistic growth potential of these learners. While pedagogic approaches have been designed to cater to the needs of young learners, it is insufficient to accommodate the unique personal, cognitive, and experiential needs of adult learners. In an effort to provide independence and flexibility in the learning processes at higher educational institutions, courses were planned using an anthrogogic approach. Deepa uses the term 'anthrogogy' (2022a, 2026) to refer to all the teaching and testing principles that are associated with adult learners. An anthrogogic approach allows learners to take ownership of their learning, including deciding what and how they learn. The experiences and advantages of adopting this approach are discussed in the later sections of the chapter.

The educational world witnessed a significant metamorphosis during the time of the COVID-19 pandemic. At a time when most people were unhabituated to online learning practices, everybody had to depend on technology and learn ways to cope with the situation. While some saw this as taxing, others made optimum use of it to come up with creative ways to engage learners in the process of learning. At the postgraduate level, two online courses were designed for students innovatively by bringing in novelty not just in the mode of learning, but in the whole process of learning itself. We, as students of these two courses, would like to describe our experiences and observations, and reflect on our learning process.

Two content courses were offered to postgraduate students at a central university. The courses intended to help learners understand how language operates within the purview of the specific areas of education and media. They were offered to the same group of learners in two consecutive semesters. Since it was during the pandemic, classes were conducted online. An abrupt transition from offline to online mode was perceived as a serious impediment to the sphere of learning, but these courses took advantage of such a shift to optimise the learning experiences of the learners.

The Course Trajectory

The distinctiveness was ingrained in the instructional approach. To begin with, a WhatsApp group and a Google Classroom were created to build a virtual space to proceed with the course. A wide variety of materials like research articles, academic texts, Facebook posts, YouTube videos, viral memes, movies, letters, advertisements, jingles, reels, and many more such materials from an array of sources were brought to this learning space. These resources were presented to the class as prompts or thought seeds in the WhatsApp group. A thought seed is a 'catalyst (written, spoken, a picture, a meme, a video, an advertisement, et cetera.) usually followed by a series of statements and questions which will persuade the teacher/learner to build a thinking platform, process information divergently and go meta over the 'apparentness' found in the trigger' (Deepa, 2022b, p. 64). A continuous engagement in the learning space happened through discussions sparked by these thought seeds. For instance, the course instructor shared a video titled 'Is ugly produce the key to our food waste problem?' This video initiated a whole new discourse on how a label like 'ugly' can modify the way people look at things. Learners delved into what people discern as ugly. They debated on how things that look different are considered ugly and are not qualified to meet the standards of the supermarket. Learners came up with examples and anecdotes from other contexts to investigate how the words 'ugly', 'perfect', 'imperfect', 'beauty', 'flawed' operate in society to create dogmas in the minds of the masses. The language used on the one hand affects the individual thoughts and beliefs, and on the other hand it affects larger systems like the market and economy. They were able to indulge in constructive criticism and reconstruct their thoughts.

Image 1

Image 1 was also shared by the course instructor as a thought seed (Deepa, 2022b). It sparked a classroom discussion around the ambiguity of language and how language can be used for effective communication. People don't always say what they mean and don't always mean what they say. Language is never absolutely clear and for effective communication to take place, language needs to be properly interpreted. Learners delved into the various elements required for effective communication. They discussed that language for effective communication need not only be spoken or written language, but is often a manner of how it is combined with paralinguistic elements. The discussion further led to another important criterion for effective communication to take place, that is, to understand and be aware of the speaker/listener's social context. Art, music, dance, and theatrics are also some ways through which people try to communicate and express their feelings. The learners discussed that in this particular image, 'yes' and 'no' are ineffective to put meaning into the already given sentence. Yes and no have contradictory meanings, but when put into these particular sentences, neither of them give a different meaning of their own nor change the meaning of the already given sentence. Therefore, in this context they fail to effectively express meaning.

Learners were encouraged to post comments and engage in peer discussions on specific constructs using Google Classroom discussion boards. It consciously created a dialogical online platform where the learners also started identifying resources and materials that were pertinent to the course and started sharing them with the group. A gradual role reversal took place where the adult learners now took charge of their own learning and encouraged others to contribute to their mutual learning space.

In addition to this, the course instructor invited experts in the field to educate the group. A transgender person was invited to talk to and sensitise the learners towards the role language plays in portraying gender, and how language can be more inclusive so as to not discriminate against any section of society. This led to an awareness of language-related choices that depict gender identity and how the community has been dealing with the enigma around the terms associated with them being used to portray their reality by the media and people in general.

Another expert discussed cyber security, hacking and online safety through anecdotes and shared safety measures that people should be informed about. One more professor who is a language professional made an incognito appearance throughout the duration of the course as an audit student. She provided remarkable inputs through her responses to the prompts and feedback on the student responses, and initiated dialogue within the group. The learners perceived her as a student and her inputs and questions were well received and responded to without any hesitation. This removed all kinds of affective inhibitions to participate in the class. This was different compared to a guest expert participating through a lecture because it not only gave information but also facilitated learners to think and educate themselves through the deliberate negotiation of thought and observation in their learning space.

The students' perceptions, arguments, and discussions related to the prompts were continuously recorded in the form of journal entries which the students called a 'thought seed diary'.

We conducted a survey aimed at eliciting responses from students enrolled in these courses regarding their experiences and perceptions of the applied anthrogogic approach. When asked about the thought seed diary, one answered that 'My diary helped me analyse the way I engaged with whatever videos, lectures or texts that were shared in the class.

Initially, some things that were shared in class just seemed to look like any social media forward message but with guided discussions, I could interpret it critically and this I note as my progress.' Another student said, 'From a superficial level of understanding, I was able to go beyond and look deeper, and within the lines. My critical thinking expanded and this was easily seen through the progress in the thought seed diary.'

We learners were assessed on the thought seed diary entries we chose for assessment. We also had the liberty to select those tasks for assessment we felt that we had performed our best in. Before our performance was assessed by the course instructor, we had to do a self-assessment to decide the tasks in which we had given our best. In this process, we evaluated our own performance based on the rubric we collaboratively created. We also had the responsibility to assess the prompts that we had selected and justify the reason for choosing them. We all commented on our individual progress that we observed on reflecting on each of these thought seeds and the peer responses to them. The modes of formative assessments were thus diverse and well-planned to cater to students' progress. This progress was measured by nudging the students to show their ability to perceive things and act differently based on the experience of classroom discourse. The overall assessment therefore included self-assessment, peer-assessment and, more importantly, assessment of the course by the learner. In the survey, when asked about the method of self- and peer-assessment, one student answered that it provided them with the opportunity to analyse their own work, and the process of peer reviewing opened them to multiple perspectives other than their own about the same work.

A Shift from a Conventional Pedagogic to a Distinct Anthrogogic Approach

The divergent nature of these courses provided a unique learning experience for the learners that did not allow them to rely on traditional methods. Generally, courses that follow a traditional approach perceive learners as children and adhere strictly to a pre-determined syllabus with a limited number of texts listed by the course instructor. One-sided lectures are the primary mode of instruction, where learners assume passive roles while the teacher dominates the discourse. These sessions are predominantly didactic. Post-lecture discussions, though they do occur, offer minimal opportunities for learner engagement. Learning materials are disseminated in the form of texts or PowerPoint presentations utilised during lectures. Assessment methods centre solely on written examinations, demanding learners reproduce the delivered content.

Highlighting the nature of adult learners, Deepa (2022a, 2026) remarks that they are responsible for everything in their own lives, including taking charge of their own learning, and that the pacing of their learning often stems from prioritising and juggling other adulting responsibilities. Thinking, planning, and execution are major tasks that permeate each day for adults; organisation in adults often amounts to prioritisation even when it is learning. Using a conventional approach for adult learners leaves no room for thinking, planning, or execution. Ott (2011) suggests four main points to differentiate between young and adult learners: 'First, … the learner [is] self-directed and independent in the pursuit of information. Second, the real-life experience of the learner must be acknowledged and built upon. Third, the readiness to learn is driven from the learners' occupational and social roles. Finally, the learner is driven by the possibility for immediate application of the knowledge or skill' (32).

The two content courses taught with an anthrogogic perspective had taken into consideration all these aspects in carefully crafting the course. The course instructor understood individual learner needs and preferences instead of looking at them as a homogenous group of learners with common preferences. Consequently, she brought in diverse materials and tasks that created rich learning experiences. The course was self-directed but the teacher facilitated the learners in organising their experiences. These courses were highly dependent on experiential learning which were not only meant to provide experiences throughout the course but also brought the learners' previous experience as a resource to foster learning, and created a conducive environment by developing reciprocal relationships between the learners and between the teacher and the learners. By doing so, they were motivated to voluntarily take charge of their learning and become autonomous learners in a community of practice.

The course design aligned with recommendations provided by Muñoz, Welsh, and Chaseley (2018) for adult educators, encouraging educators to involve learners in planning their learning, draw on learners' rich experiences, ensure topics are relevant to the roles of specific learners in your classroom, include activities in your instructional plan to help you get to know each learner as an individual, and be aware of the biases and assumptions that are brought to learning.

These recommendations can be taken into consideration in every anthrogogic learning space. Throughout the courses we experienced, the learners could plan, organise, and assess their learning. They could integrate learning materials, experiences, and knowledge intricately. They found everything relevant to the real world and found ways to apply their knowledge to practically analyse language outside the course domain. The learners developed critical thinking and creativity. This reflects in a student's comment: 'The course made me realize how powerful language is when used either negatively or positively. It is especially important in these two fields as they could shape the listener or reader's point of view and perception, which would result in their reactions over any matter that's being discussed.'

An Emic View through the Learners' Lens

In a peer discussion on course feedback, one of the students expressed that she felt that on completion of the course, her vision had transformed while she came across advertisements, movies, social media messages, reels, and stand-up comedies. She was no more viewing them as a mere reader or listener. She was able to critically analyse the intention, language choices, and portrayal of characters. She also made an effort to view them from an ethical perspective. Another student opined that the approach of the course was so unconventional and novel that though the course demanded continuous engagement, it did not induce any anxiety and stress. Most of the classroom activities were centred around real-life contexts and materials that we come across in daily life. This made everything seem relevant and all the tasks were completed with admirable ease and delight.

We, as students, were allowed to work largely at our own pace and never felt the pressure of an impending deadline. By allowing us to choose our own learning goals, the course built in us the confidence and desire to take ownership of our learning, and a sense of control over our progress. The final deadlines felt more like an opportunity to showcase all of the knowledge we had gained instead of perceiving it as a doomsday. As a result, we hardly felt much pressure and enjoyed studying these courses. When asked about the methodology of this course in the survey, a student responded, 'The absence of pressure of examinations or deadlines made the process very easy. The innovative methods aroused interest and curiosity to participate in the class. This in turn made me feel comfortable to perform in my assessments. In fact, I didn't realise where teaching stopped and testing began. It was all intertwined.' As Knowles' theory of andragogy states, we did feel like we thrived in this environment that allowed for self-direction with a focus on problem solving and application of knowledge (Knowles, Holton III, & Swanson, 2014).

There was no pressure of being either right or wrong or not knowing enough as well. All perceptions were accepted in the classes. There were no specific right or wrong answers. We all arrived at a general consensus, sometimes nudged towards it by the professor, through classroom discussions. This parallels what Muñoz, Welsh & Chaseley (2018) had noted, that adults bring experience, wisdom, and insight to the learning community; the discerning facilitator fosters an exchange of knowledge. Everybody was encouraged to participate in these discussions and nobody was judged for their answers. Due to this, students felt motivated and encouraged to take part in discussions and put forth their viewpoint. In this kind of scenario, it is easily observable that learner autonomy exists in and beyond the classroom with minimum teacher intervention. Students are more likely to engage in higher-order thinking processes and gain a deeper understanding of the subject matter when given the freedom to explore and learn on their own. This approach is effective in promoting critical thinking, problem-solving, and collaboration skills (Jonassen, 1994).

Retrospective Insights and Transformative Journey

Initially, the abrupt transition to an online mode of instruction, combined with an unconventional teaching–learning approach was met with apprehension. The anthrogogic approach—which placed an emphasis on learner autonomy, self-directed learning, and a break from the instructor-centric paradigm—challenged our preconceived notions of education. Having grown accustomed to more structured and prescriptive learning experiences, the prospect of navigating a course in which the learning trajectory was mainly determined by the learners themselves seemed both new and unsettling. Our scepticism was further stoked by the emergence of a wide range of educational resources, from viral memes and social media content to scholarly texts and research articles. The unconventional inclusion of seemingly unrelated materials as prompts or 'thought seeds' made us question the course's relevance and coherence. The deliberate blurring of lines between educator and learner raised concerns regarding the efficacy of this unconventional approach in facilitating meaningful discussions and knowledge exchange.

However, as the classes progressed, doubts increasingly gave way to engagement. The diverse materials, which were initially met with scepticism, were catalysts for thought-provoking exchanges that extended beyond the confines of conventional academic discourse. In hindsight, the reservations we had throughout the earlier stages of the classes became an essential part of our transformative journey. It was a precursor to the profound shifts in our perspectives, prompting us to reevaluate our notions of effective pedagogy. One of the students in the survey commented on the methodology and stated,

> Conventional methods, I feel, include predefined templates to use for content delivery and assessments but the methodology used for teaching this course was unique and was not too challenging at the same time. Yet, it enabled me to sit and think of certain things which I would not spend my time pondering on, otherwise. Which, I now feel is essential.

The students went on to work in various different fields. Some who went on to work in offices said that the ability to critically analyse language choices, intentions, and character portrayals has become second nature for them. They no longer passively consume content, whether it is commercials, films, or social media messaging; they actively scrutinise it from ethical and linguistic perspectives. The real-life settings woven into classroom activities transmitted seamlessly into relevance in their daily lives. When asked about the influence of this course, a student answered, ‘the knowledge of how to use language was what I was acquainted with but this course drew my attention to what goes behind the conscious use of language and what follows after something is said or written.’

Some of the students went on to pursue further studies, like us, for example. As PhD research scholars, the ability to plan, organise, and assess our learning honed during the courses, seamlessly integrates with the demands of academic research. Critical thinking and metacognitive skills developed in an anthrogogic environment are essential instruments now in our research endeavours. Learner autonomy, observed in and beyond the classroom, aligns with their ability to explore, learn independently, and engage in higher-order thinking processes. One of the students from this class is now pursuing a PhD. Her significant takeaway from these courses was:

> Words said or written can be interpreted, translated or even relayed without any motive and still affect people in different ways. And that I should leverage that thought while using my language in daily life. Academically, it is even more important to fine-tune my language and thoughts, to convey it correctly so the intended message or idea is not lost to confused conceptions.

The anthrogogic approach promoting critical thinking, problem-solving, and collaboration skills, has now become an integral part of their academic identity.

The pivotal learning outcome was enabling the learners to think critically. This is clearly expressed by a student who felt, 'The major take away for me was the ability to critically recognise how language operates at multiple levels to affect the people interacting in the field. The class could together understand the negotiation of meaning, motives behind language use.' The anthrogogic courses were more than just transformative experiences during our postgraduate years; they were catalysts for continued growth, influencing both our professional and academic pursuits. With its emphasis on autonomy, critical thinking, and real-world applicability, the anthrogogic method continues to impact our journey in 2026 and beyond. The classes' unconventional nature, which originally sparked scepticism, eventually became the foundation of an innovative and enriching learning experience.

Recommendations for Course Instructors

The overwhelmingly favourable response received from the learners of these courses stand as a testament to the effectiveness of this approach. Adopting this approach can bring about a transformation in the higher educational milieu. Here are some takeaways for the course instructors who teach adult learners. The instructors need to acknowledge what the learners bring to the table. They come with rich and diverse life experiences that the teacher can use as a resource in the classroom helping them create a democratic and inclusive classroom. Learners should be provided with ample opportunities to participate and contribute in the classroom. One of the effective ways to achieve this would be to encourage them to bring in materials that they find relevant. They, however, must be guided to justify why they find it relevant. This will not only provide them with a sense of ownership and responsibility for their learning, but also promote critical thinking and creativity in adult learners. Teachers need to bring about a change in the assessment to make it more learner-centred, offering flexibility and accommodating various modalities. The assessment process of learners needs to be crafted through continuous assessment, peer-assessment and self-assessment at various stages of the course. Course instructors can adopt various strategies with an objective of making their learners independent and responsible for their own learning.

Conclusion

Adopting an anthrogogic approach to design and implement two master's-level courses has proven to be a profound and enriching experience for the learners. The educational landscape has undergone significant changes as a result of the shift from traditional pedagogical approaches in favour of learner autonomy, critical thinking, and creativity. These courses have empowered learners to take ownership of their education by utilising diverse and authentic materials, and collaborative learning. This has fostered a sense of confidence and increased engagement and motivation amongst the learners.

This approach has had an indelible impact on students' perceptions extending beyond the classroom, impacting several domains of their lives. The success of these courses highlights the urgent need for a paradigm shift in adult education, with an emphasis on learner-centred strategies that value student autonomy. The anthrogogic approach equips educators with valuable insightful ideas and strategies for designing inclusive, intriguing, and impactful learning experiences as they continue to navigate the evolving landscape of education.

References

Deepa, S. (2022a). Pedagogic practices in higher education and Peter Pan syndrome: An appraisal. *Fortell, 45,* 164–73. https://www.fortell.org/wp-content/uploads/2022/10/July-2022-164–173.pdf

Deepa, S. (2022b). Thought seeds in anthrogogic learning contexts. *Journal of Indian Education*, *48*(2), 58–70.

Deepa, S. (2026). Principles of anthrogogic language education. In S. Deepa & G. Durairajan (Eds.), *Anthrogogy in use: A handbook for language educators* (pp. 3–26). Orient BlackSwan.

Jonassen, D. H. (1994). *Thinking technology: Toward a constructivist design model.* Educational Technology Publications.

Knowles, M. S., Holton III, E. F., & Swanson, R. A. (2014). *The Adult learner: The definitive classic in adult education and human resource development.* Routledge.

Muñoz, M., Welsh, L. A., & Chaseley, T. L. (2018). Developmentally appropriate practice for adult learners. *YC Young Children, 73*(4), 70–76. Ott, K. D. (2011). Technology and adult learning: Understanding e-learning and the lifelong learner. *International Journal of Technology, Knowledge & Society, 7*(3), 31–36.

Part III

A Compendium of Anthrogogic Tasks

Theoretical postulations and research applications in the domain of anthrogogy may not suffice to tempt teachers in adult classrooms to try out our approach. In this section we present a collection of anthrogogic tasks, twenty-six in total, that focus on language empowerment, enable critical awareness of literature, and various aspects of teacher education. We hope that interested teachers and researchers will be inspired to work with, modify or adapt one or more of these tasks in their own classrooms. These tasks are consciously anthrogogic in their framing. This does not mean that some of them cannot be used in pedagogic contexts, but for that purpose, the tasks will require a large amount of guided scaffolding which will obviously be age- and cognitive-level appropriate. The unique selling point of these tasks is that the contributors have attempted to explain why the task is anthrogogic and also describe what would have been a pedagogic alternative. The language used by the task creators to describe objectives is not uniform and there are intra- as well as inter-author variations. These variations have been respected and valued to celebrate the spirit of anthrogogicity.

This compendium of tasks can be used in a variety of ways: either as a muse to create other tasks, or as a resource book to dip into in the domains of both teaching and research. They are rooted in real-life contexts and are intended for undergraduate students of language or literature, postgraduate students who are required to augment their higher order language skills, or participants who have registered for a teacher-education programme. The tasks expect both students and participants to engage deeply with them by applying their knowledge, analysing information, evaluating arguments and perspectives, and wherever needed creating their own responses.

Eleven tasks focus on language empowerment at the undergraduate level. Shree Deepa and Shravasti Chakravarty have presented tasks that integrate personal experiences with academic content and expect students to make a presentation, write an academic report, and go through an interview experience. The possibility of learning language through gaming is explored by Shadab Khan in his four tasks, while Pankaj Narke presents a task that enhances intercultural communicative ability. Sruti Narra has put together three academic writing tasks.

The enabling of critical awareness in literature at the undergraduate level is the focus of two tasks. The task by Sweta Mukherjee is about being able to read a novel critically, while the task by Shravasti Chakravarty is on poetry reading with a twist, where students are expected to make a creative presentation based on a poem.

At the postgraduate level there are three tasks that focus on language empowerment. Shravasti Chakravarty's task is on enabling critical thinking through the interpretation of a novel. Sayan Chaudhuri's task intriguingly focuses on the processes in the mind of the student needed to develop a critical awareness of language use, and not on the outcome. Sajida Sultana's task is on empowering students to fine-tune their academic writing skills.

The compendium ends with ten teacher-education tasks which can be used at either the pre- or in-service levels. Shree Deepa's first task is in the area of syllabus and materials development, and expects participants to critically examine language exercises. The next three tasks, also by her, are from a course on the use of language in media. In these tasks, participants are expected to critically assess an article by identifying arguments that have influenced them, respond to a thought seed, and follow that up by creating a thought seed. The first of Geetha Durairajan's six tasks expects the participant to categorise statements in linguistics based on the perspective reflected. The second and third tasks expect the participant to take on the role of an advisor in the area of bilingual education and provide feasible solutions to given scenarios. The last three tasks are from a course on classroom-based evaluation. In them, the participants are expected to use their knowledge of validity and reliability to evaluate and provide constructive criticism on a short piece of writing, and provide alternative assessment solutions to scenarios.

We hope that this section will enable and empower teachers and researchers to teach and assess anthrogogically so that their students/participants are able to actively engage with and empower themselves through this learning process. The tasks are drawn from the lived/taught experiences of the contributors and therefore stand as a testament to the value of an anthrogogic approach in fostering meaningful and lasting educational experiences.

Contents

15. Undergraduate Level Tasks

16. Postgraduate Level Tasks

15
Undergraduate Level Tasks

A. Language Empowerment

Task 1: English Language Proficiency Course

Shree Deepa

Background

Proficiency courses at the UG level are usually pedagogic in nature because they treat the students as deficient learners and perceive 'language' as a system of rules, whether grammatical, lexical, or discoursal. Tasks are, therefore, mostly system oriented.

Teaching students how to make presentations by getting them to make one is a routine task at the undergraduate level. Very often topics are just handed over to a group of students to 'work' on and then asked to make presentations. In the twenty-first century, students often download ready-made PowerPoint slides and read the text while calling it a 'presentation'. This makes it highly pedagogic as the only skill being used is minimal searching through engines like Google and using generative AI, while ending up 'loud reading' chunks of text on slides which are decorated in the garb of 'presentation skills'.

On the flipside, students at the anthrogogic level must be challenged and their agency increased to their full potential when asked to engage with the task of presentation. The anthrogogicity of such a task lies in the fact that the 'presentation' is a product of a full-fledged enquiry process. Hence, the teacher should rearrange the task in such a way that a 'copy-paste' method can be avoided.

Objectives

1. By the end of the task the students will be able to put together/ create a presentation and talk about their findings to their peers in the classroom.
2. The students will be able to write up an academic report on the project, its findings and implications.

Anthrogogic Task

There are many hostels in the university/college that serve you food. Go and visit them and research food wastage, food quantity management and waste disposal mechanisms in these hostels or messes. Please use whatever resources may be needed (interviews, observations, discussions, et cetera) to gather information. Populate your presentation with actual photographs, interviews, and videos as applicable.

Further identify and describe the problems therein and then provide tangible solutions for the problems; if possible, provide photographic or video proof/examples of these solutions in the presentation itself.

Finally, follow it up by writing a detailed academic report on the whole project. You are free to use online resources to select a suitable academic report format. It is not necessary to use PowerPoint and you are free explore alternative forms of presentations such as skits, musical presentations, short films, et cetera.

A pedagogic alternative to this task would be 'What is food wastage? Make a presentation on it'.

Timeline: 2 weeks

Task 2: Presentations

Shravasti Chakravarty

Background

Learners of English as a Foreign Language usually focus on improving their speaking skills to help them be more effective in their IELTS exam. Therefore, they could at best speak at length for three to four minutes after which they were often at a loss for words. This task provided learners the space to broaden their horizons in a non-testing sphere in which they could expand their opportunity to speak. It was akin to the internal resetting of the English-speaking clock to incorporate more time and information. They could make it conversational, thereby adding to the task's difficulty level according to their comfort level.

Objective

The learner should be able to develop and deliver an interactive session on a topic that integrates elements of IELTS preparation, demonstrating clear organisation, effective communication, and engaging delivery.

Anthrogogic Task

Make a presentation on a topic of your choice and speak for around seven minutes. You are free to make it interactive. Ensure your presentation topic feeds into your IELTS preparation.

The pedagogic task would be 'Pick a chit from those provided and make an impromptu speech for about 3–4 minutes'. This task would be more like a test with very little interaction. Also, the opportunity to respond to queries and therefore, engaging in a real conversation would be lost.

Timeline: 1 hour

Task 3: Developing Interview Skills — Shravasti Chakravarty

Background

Before the task, learners were introduced to the concept of asking questions in different ways. For this task, the only instruction provided to the learners was that they needed to collect a particular piece of information—what foreign tourists enjoyed the most in their country. Every other parameter—such as the place, time, manner and modality of gathering the data—was left to the discretion of the learners. This gave them an unprecedented amount of autonomy while making them accountable for the information gathered. They were, however, requested not to work individually to ensure ease of data collection. Thus, one student could wield the camera while another could ask the questions.

Objectives

1. The learner will conduct informal conversations with foreigners in their country, preferably in English, focusing on their travelling experiences.
2. The student will record these interviews, analyse the data, and present the findings in a chosen format, demonstrating effective communication and analytical skills.

Anthrogogic Task

Talk to foreigners in your country and have an informal conversation with them, preferably in English. Ask them about their travelling experiences. Record your interviews, analyse the data and present your findings in any format you prefer.

The pedagogic alternative could be to provide more structured instruction regarding data collection. In place of the unstructured interview, a structured interview could be used for uniformity of the data collected. Instead of the day-long excursion that gives freedom of movement and therefore autonomy, learners could also be instructed to stand outside the university and approach passersby in the vicinity.

Timeline: At least 7 hours outside the class

Ctrl+Alt+Play: Unlocking Language Through Gaming

SHADAB KHAN

Background

The following activities (Tasks 4–7) integrate language learning with critical thinking and real-world discussions, using gaming as a thematic context to develop LSRW skills, persuasive communication, and collaborative problem-solving. They are anthrogogic because they

1. encourage self-directed critical analysis of societal norms and personal assumptions, aligning with adult learners' ability to reflect on real-world social dynamics.
2. focus on real-world relevance (career choices, financial stability) and peer collaboration, catering to learners' need for practical, applicable knowledge.
3. emphasise experiential learning and teamwork, mirroring professional environments where the learners solve problems collaboratively.
4. foster authentic conversation practice by engaging learners in real-life persuasive dialogue, encouraging emotional connection through personalisation, and promoting interactive learning that moves beyond scripted responses to spontaneous negotiation.

Objectives

By the end of these activities, learners will be able to:

1. Develop LSRW skills through discussion, debate, and creative tasks.
2. Use persuasive and descriptive language effectively in spoken and written communication.

3. Analyse and challenge stereotypes in gaming and career choices using critical thinking.
4. Expand topic-specific vocabulary related to gaming, careers, and argumentation.
5. Collaborate and present ideas clearly in academic and professional contexts.

Task 4: Gaming Preferences and Stereotypes

Matching & Reflection: Students analyse stereotypes by matching demographics to game genres (for example, elderly man → Puzzle/Strategy; young woman → Fantasy Role-playing Game [RPG]) and reflecting on biases.

1. Think about the following individuals and the kind of video games they might enjoy playing:

Person 1

Person 2

Person 3

Person 4

2. Now, look at the list of game genres below. Match each individual to one of the genres and explain your reasoning.

Puzzle/Strategy Game)

Fantasy RPG

Sports Simulation Game

Action-Adventure Game

Game Genre	Who Would Play It?	Why?
Sports Simulation Game		
Action-Adventure Game		
Puzzle/Strategy Game		
Fantasy Role-Playing Game (RPG)		

3. After completing the table, answer the following:
   a. Did you match the elderly man with an action-adventure game? Why or why not? What influenced your choice?
   b. Do you think gender or age plays a role in determining gaming preferences today? Support your answer with examples.

Note: Consider how personal interests, social norms, and technological advancements shape gaming habits across different demographics.

The pedagogic alternative would be a lecture on game genres with no discussion of stereotypes or personal reflection.

Timeline: 30–45 minutes

Task 5: Exploring Careers in Gaming

Group Research, Debate, Case Study: Collaborative exploration of gaming careers, debates on legitimacy, and scenario-based decision-making.

Part 1: Brainstorming Careers in Gaming

What comes to mind when you think of careers in gaming? Write down your ideas and then categorise them into different career paths. Some possible categories include:

- **Content Creation** (Streaming, YouTube, Twitch, gaming influencers)
- **Professional Gaming** (E-sports athletes)
- **Game Development** (Designers, programmers, narrative writers)
- **Support Roles** (Marketing, event management, coaching, QA testers)

After listing your ideas, discuss how the gaming industry is expanding globally and in India.

Part 2: Research & Group Presentation

Divide yourselves into four groups. Each group will research and present on one of the following career paths:

1. Game Streamer/Influencer
2. E-sports Professional
3. Game Developer/Designer
4. Gaming Industry Entrepreneur (Startup founders, app developers, et cetera.)

For your assigned career, identify and present:

- The key responsibilities and skills required
- Potential earnings and career growth opportunities (globally & in India)
- Pros and cons compared to traditional jobs

Each group will share their findings with the class.

Part 3: Case Study Analysis

Read the following scenario and discuss in pairs:

Ravi, a final-year engineering student, has to choose between a stable IT job offer and pursuing his passion for e-sports. His family prefers the IT job due to job security and societal respect.

1. What factors should Ravi consider before making his decision?
2. What are the risks and rewards of both career paths?
3. How do personal values, financial stability, and societal expectations influence such career choices?

Summarise your discussion and share your thoughts with the class.

Part 4: Structured Debate

Motion: *Gaming should be recognised as a legitimate career in India.*

Form two teams:

1. *Affirmative Team*: Argues in favour of the motion
2. *Opposition Team*: Argues against the motion

The rest of the class will act as a judging panel, listening critically and voting for the most convincing argument.

Consider the following points while debating:

- Employment stability vs. income volatility
- Cultural perceptions of success
- Mental health considerations in high-pressure careers
- Economic contributions of the gaming industry

Part 5: Reflection & Wrap-Up

Write a short response to the following question: *Would you consider a career in gaming? Why or why not?* Reflect on your personal interests, career aspirations, and societal influences while forming your answer.

The pedagogical alternative would be to have a textbook chapter on gaming jobs with fill-in-the-blank exercises.

Timeline: 2–3 hours

Task 6: Game Design

Creative Group Project: Teams design a game concept and pitch it to 'investors'.

In groups, choose 3–4 pictures representing a character, a setting, and an obstacle in a game. Use these images as inspiration to develop your own game concept.

Discuss and define the following elements:

- Who is the main character, and what is their goal?
- Where does the game take place?
- What challenges will players face?
- How do visuals enhance these challenges?

Now, draft your game concept using the following template:

1. Title
2. Setting
3. Goal
4. Visual Features
5. Obstacles
6. Rewards

Each group will present their game idea using slides or posters. The rest of the class will act as investors, asking questions and giving feedback. Finally, the class will vote on the most engaging and feasible game concept.

The pedagogical alternative would be a worksheet listing game elements to label (for example, 'Match the obstacle to its definition').

Timeline: 1–2 hours

Task 7: Adult Real-Life Role-play

Dialogue Writing: Persuasive conversation about outdoor play versus screen time.

Image 1

Image 2

- Try to imagine that this is your daughter or son.
- Write a dialogue between yourself and the girl/boy, convincing them that they should be playing in the garden.

The pedagogic alternative would be a lecture on the benefits of outdoor play followed by a quiz.

Timeline: 20–30 minutes

Note: All images used in this activity are sourced from Freepik.com. These images are used under Freepik's free license.

Task 8: Intercultural Communication

PANKAJ NARKE

Background

This task is used in Intercultural Communication classrooms at the tertiary level. The target learners have a fair proficiency in English language skills and have the ability to use it for academic and non-academic purposes.

The given task is anthrogogic in nature as it has a broad scope and does not restrict learners' expressions in terms of the output modality or the length of expressions. The task does not limit the learners to the text itself but encourages them to take the discussion outside the text and relate it to their life experiences. Learners' world knowledge has meaningful space in this task, and the situation presented is realistic.

Objectives

1. Building emotional mindfulness in intercultural communicative situations. Analysing Anna's mental state and its possible impact on her communication would enable learners to consider the prior factors that change communication and to adapt their style to accommodate such changes to sustain meaningful and cooperative communication. This would also make learners understand the role of cultural differences in communication.
2. Identifying the effect of cultural generalisation and its impact on communication. Learners critically reflect on cultural assumptions and how they can create impressions among people. They will also understand needing to be sensitive towards such issues and will avoid judgments, but try to bridge the gaps.
3. Reflecting and critically thinking learners will reflect on their life experiences and think critically about their communication

strategies in such situations. By applying the situation to their life, they broaden their perspectives on such cultural issues.

Anthrogogic Task

The reading text for this task is a case study titled 'Home Country', published in *Case Studies for Intercultural and Conflict Communication*, edited by McKay-Semmler. The main character in this case, Anna, is a media student from Moscow who goes to attend an international conference at her university. As the infrastructure at the conference venue is not disabled-friendly, she finds it challenging to settle down and is in discomfort due to the arrangement. She meets McKenzie, an American student, who is empathetic towards Anna and ensures she feels comfortable by giving her company. She then invites Anna to visit her campus, which is accessible for disabled students and considers their needs. The narrative underlines the challenges encountered by those with impairments and the value of empathy and intercultural communication.

After you read the text, try and answer these questions in as detailed a manner as possible:

1. The text has words that represent feelings of a mixed nature, such as 'nervous', 'excited', 'proud', 'hope', 'embarrassed', 'sympathetic', 'confused', 'quiet', 'grin', and 'struggle'. How do these words capture Anna's state of mind, and why does she go through these mixed feelings? Are these feelings likely to have any effect on the way she communicates? Is McKenzie's gesture of sitting with Anna, unlike her other classmates, significant in bridging the cross-cultural gap? Think about these points and write/record/discuss your impression of the entire situation.
2. Why do you think public infrastructure ignores the needs of differently-abled people in different parts of the world? Can this be related to cultural generalisation? Can such differences lead to communication gaps among people of different physical abilities? Share your expression in any mode of your choice (verbal, visual, or auditory) with reference to the text and your observations about society with regard to this issue.

To make this task pedagogic, many teachers may ask some reading comprehension questions at the information recall level. For example:

1. *Why was Anna excited to meet students from other countries?*

2. *Write a short note on Anna's discomfort in the classroom and the issues she raised.*
3. *Why does McKenzie choose to sit with Anna? How does this reflect her empathetic nature? Explain in 300 words.*

Timeline: 1 hour

Reference

McKay-Semmler, K. L. (Ed.). (2021). *Case Studies for Intercultural and Conflict Communication*. Cambridge Scholars Publishing.

Introduction to Academic Writing

SRUTI NARRA

Background

This course was developed for HAMK, Finland in 2024 by the author and is either a compulsory course or one of the elective courses in Bachelors' programs like Smart and Sustainable Design, Bachelor of Business Administration, and Engineering in Sustainable Urban Design in the institute.

The course is divided into 10 sections: Paragraph Writing; Argumentation; Expository Texts; Audience vs Purpose; Text Organisation; Style; Abstracts; Research Proposal; Report Writing; and Citation & Plagiarism.

The course is designed for independent study for Bachelors' students. It consists of activities and tasks students can do to become familiar with the basic concepts in academic writing. It is a self-paced course designed to be completed in 8 weeks and is worth 2 credits\ECTS (European Credit Transfer and Accumulation System). In each section, students read academic texts and complete tasks to ensure they comprehended the material, and grasped the topic accurately. HTML 5 Package (H5P) activities were used in each section for giving students opportunities to use the academic writing features they studied in the section. At the end of the section, students need to reflect on their learning and give concrete examples of what they have learned in the section.

The three tasks described below (Tasks 9–11) are anthrogogic as they are closely related to the real use of language (in the context of the current course-academic use) and do not focus on surface level features, but rather on awareness raising of the concepts important in the context of academic writing. Students are not penalized for being wrong while learning, they get ample opportunities to make mistakes, learn at their pace, and spend the time and resources needed to master the concept before progressing to the next. The focus is also on the application of the concepts learnt and not on the theoretical aspects of the course. The exam is also an open-book exam and the student' awareness of the concept and the ability to apply the concepts learnt is tested.

The first section of the course deals with paragraph writing, where claims, evidence, and analysis are discussed. Students practice these features by doing tasks on characteristics of claims, elements of a paragraph, features and types of claims. The second section is on argumentation, where students study simple arguments and their structure, features of arguments, and ways to develop and strengthen their arguments.

Here are two example H5P tasks used in the section 'Argumentation'.

Task 9: H5P activity on Moodle Learning Platform (A)

Objective

To raise learners' awareness about the use of counter arguments in argumentation and give them an opportunity to apply the concept

Anthrogogic Task

Select the possible counter arguments for the claim in the question.

Claim: To promote digital literacy among children, schools need to give children access to technological devices in every classroom.

Counter Arguments (options):

1. Research has been showing the negative impact of devices such as TVs, phones, and tablets. The behaviour and learning of children get affected by long exposures to such devices and giving a green flag to the same in the schools could make the situation worse.
2. This can ease the process of getting familiar with new technological devices in the future.
3. Our grandparents' generation could not adapt to the change in technological developments and needed constant support in the process. To avoid such a repetition, the current generation needs to get enough exposure to technological advancements.
4. Reading ability in children is declining lately and exposure to devices like phones, tablets, et cetera, at the expense of books and tactile material is seen as a major reason for the decline.

Timeline: self-paced task designed to be completed within 5 minutes

Task 10: H5P Activity on Moodle Learning Platform (B)

Objective

To raise learners' awareness about the use of evidence\supporting statements in argumentation and to give them an opportunity to apply the concept.

Anthrogogic Task

Choose suitable evidence\supporting statements that support the claim in the question. There can be more than one answer.

Claim: I have a healthy lifestyle.

Statements (options):

1. I hate exercising, I like to watch movies all day.
2. I also try to eat balanced meals. I have learnt over time that planning my meals ahead helps me cut down on the junk I might eat otherwise. I give myself a cheat day or two in a month if I have achieved my goals. I don't indulge like crazy though, this can undo all the work done and I am aware of it.
3. I am not conscious of the food that I eat, it is too much work to plan my meals, I just eat whatever is available. Some days my meal could be a bag of chips.
4. I exercise regularly. There are some lazy days, but I try to stay motivated. Sometimes, changing the type of the exercise helps.

Timeline: self-paced task designed to be completed within 5 minutes

Task 11: Testing Task

Background

The course ends with a final exam that assesses the students' awareness about the concepts and their ability to apply them in indirect writing tasks. Given below is an example task from the final exam.

Objective

To test the learners' ability to comprehend the gist of the abstract and choose the appropriate title for it.

Anthrogogic Task

Read the abstract of an article given below and choose the right title for it.

Abstract: Djousse, et al. 2024

Background

Data on the relation of potato consumption with risk of type 2 diabetes (T2D) are limited and inconsistent. It is unclear whether the plant-based diet index (PDI), which is a novel and comprehensive tool to assess overall dietary pattern, modifies the association of potato intake with T2D.

Objectives

We examined the association of total, combined baked, boiled, and mashed potatoes and fried potatoes with risk of T2D and tested the interaction between PDI score and potato consumption on T2D risk.

Methods

We conducted a de novo, harmonized, individual-level data from 7 United States cohorts ($N = 105{,}531$). Cox regression was used to estimate hazard ratios (HRs) separately in each cohort adjusting for anthropometric, demographic, and lifestyle factors and cohort-specific results were pooled using an inverse-variance weighted method.

Results

Mean age ranged from 25 to 72 y, 65% women, and mean consumption of total potatoes ranged from 1.9 to 4.3 times per week. In the primary analysis, total potato intake was not associated with T2D risk: multivariable adjusted HR of 1.01 (95% confidence interval [CI]: 0.95, 1.08) for consumption of 1–2 servings/wk; 1.01 (95% CI: 0.93, 1.10) for >2–3 servings/wk; 1.05 (95% CI: 0.99, 1.12) for >3 to <5 servings/wk; and 1.07 (95% CI: 0.99, 1.16) for 5+ servings/wk compared with no potato intake. In secondary analyses, consumption of combined baked, boiled, and mashed potatoes was not associated with T2D risk, whereas fried potato consumption was positively associated with T2D risk: HR were 1 (ref), 1.07 (95% CI: 1.02, 1.12), and 1.12 (95% CI: 1.03, 1.22) for intake frequency of 0/wk, >0 to 1/wk, and >1/wk, respectively (P-trend = 0.04).

There was no significant interaction between PDI score and potato consumption on T2D risk.

Conclusions

Although consumption of total potato is not associated with T2D risk, a modest elevated risk of T2D is observed with fried potato consumption.

Title Options:

1. Potatoes Compared with Rice in Meals with either Animal or Plant Protein Reduce Postprandial Glycemia and Increase Satiety in Type 2 Diabetic Adults: A Randomized Crossover Study
2. Potato Consumption and Risk of Type 2 Diabetes Mellitus: A Harmonized Analysis of 7 Prospective Cohorts

Some pedagogical versions of these tasks could be according to a regurgitation model and be similar to the following:

1. *What is a claim? Explain with an example.*
2. *Define counter argument.*
3. *What is a supporting detail and how can it make a claim stronger?*
4. *What is the purpose of an abstract in academic articles?*

Timeline: 2 hours for the test; 10 minutes for the task

Reference

Djousse L, Zhou X, Lim J, Kim E, Sesso HD, Lee IM, Buring JE, McClelland RL, Gaziano JM, Steffen LM, Manson JE. Potato Consumption and Risk of Type 2 Diabetes Mellitus: A Harmonized Analysis of 7 Prospective Cohorts. J Nutr. 2024 Oct;154(10):3079-3087. DOI: 10.1016/j.tjnut.2024.07.020. PMID: 39289134.

B. Literature Teaching

Task 1: Teaching Literature—'Introduction to the English Novel'

Sweta Mukherjee

Background

A course on the English novel was taught as an Open Elective for second-year undergraduate students enrolled in the Liberal Education programme. The students were majoring in Computer Science and Engineering.

Objectives

The task will help students:

1. gain a basic understanding of the novel
2. understand different characters in the novel
3. respond to questions based on the novel
4. discuss the dominant themes of the novel

Anthrogogic Task

The students are asked to divide themselves into groups of five. The groups are based on their own choice. Next, they are provided with a choice of tasks that they would like to do in their groups. The tasks range from students suggesting an alternative ending to the novel; creating memes out of the characters that would represent the themes of the novel; making posters out of the dominant themes that have been identified; making the novel into a hypothetical film and deciding the actors who could play the lead characters justifying their choices; and also critically examining the relevance of the novel in the current syllabus.

Outcomes

I think the task gave the students the freedom to read the novel in a way that did not seem like an imposition on them. As they were free to form their own groups and choose a task that excited them the most, the learners had complete agency in learning the way they wanted to. The nature of the tasks was also not prescriptive, but rather exploratory. As they progressed with their chosen task, they voluntarily read parts of the novel. The tasks themselves acted as thought seeds and prompted learners to make choices that they were most comfortable with. The task ensured learner agency and learner autonomy.

A pedagogic alternative would be more teacher-directed. The agency to take decisions would also be with the teacher. The topics would be assigned to the students, and they would be completely guided by the teacher.

Timeline: 1 hour

Task 2: Poetry Reading With a Twist

SHRAVASTI CHAKRAVARTY

Background

This task is anthrogogic since learners were allowed to undertake this form of knowledge transfer in a manner conducive to their wishes. They had already studied the poem as part of their syllabus multiple times. Therefore, the opportunity to directly extrapolate their understanding to their lived experiences vis-à-vis the themes of the poem was akin to giving them autonomy in the choice of materials. Thus, it was anthrogogic. Learners wrote and sang songs, drew pictures on the board, and wrote alternate poems to express their understanding of the poem in the syllabus.

Objectives

1. The student will critically examine and interpret 'Elegy Written in a Country Churchyard' by Thomas Gray by analysing its themes, language, and imagery to clarify its key messages and aesthetic qualities. The analysis should demonstrate deep engagement with the text and the application of higher-order thinking skills from Bloom's revised taxonomy.
2. The student will synthesise an understanding of the poem by connecting its themes with personal experiences, thereby demonstrating intellectual engagement and emotional response.
3. The student will evaluate the contemporary relevance of the poem by assessing how its themes resonate with modern life and individual values.
4. The student will create an original presentation using a medium of their choice, such as PowerPoint or another format, to effectively communicate insights and personal connections, supported by relevant textual evidence and reflective commentary.

Anthrogogic Task

You have the poem 'Elegy Written in a Country Churchyard' by Thomas Gray in the syllabus. You have to present your understanding of the poem in any way possible. Your presentation can follow the usual system of using a PowerPoint presentation or any other means that you find convenient. Try to find connections between the theme of the poem and your own life.

The pedagogic model would entail the previous rounds of information transfer related to the poem. The teacher would share most of the information, and the learners would play a passive role by understanding the various components of the poem. Learners would at most explain what they thought the poet meant and summarize the content in their own words.

Timeline: 1 hour

16
Postgraduate Level Tasks

A. Language Empowerment

Task 1: Developing Critical Thinking in Literary Texts

Shravasti Chakravarty

Background

The mind map of the novel drawn/presented on the board had a few keywords that would seem random at first glance. It was left to the learners to connect the dots, add more information, and visual cues to complete the picture. Learners were also encouraged to take into consideration the whole syllabus to create these links. This meant they picked a character from one text and placed them in the context of a different text to rethink the progression of the story creatively.

Objectives

1. Analyse the mind map of the novel presented on the board to elaborate on its themes, characters, and social messages.
2. Connect the insights gained from the mind map to other literature they have encountered, demonstrating a comparative understanding of literary themes and perspectives.

Anthrogogic Task

Study the mind map of the novel presented on the board and elaborate on your understanding of the themes, characters, and social messages of the given text. Can you connect what you find here to any other literature you have encountered?

The pedagogical alternative would be to have the teacher introduce the themes and then have a discussion based on them. The information transfer will also be from the teacher to the learner in that teaching-learning scenario. The teaching methodology would primarily be a lecture method as is the norm in regular Masters-level courses.

Timeline: 1 hour

Task 2: Education, Literacy, and Justice

SAYAN CHAUDHURI

Background

This is a ten month course that I teach, as part of the Critical Writing programme at the Young India Fellowship, introducing critical debates in education and literacy in India. This task lends itself to the anthrogogic frame for two reasons. One, it actively interrogates both the 'distance' and the 'authority' of the teacher. The teacher does not stand aside as a subject of critique while everything else is—instead, the teacher and more specifically, teaching processes, are at par with every other element in the classroom to be critiqued. Second, the task builds a metacognitive and agentive understanding of the classroom for students—they are invited to be 'participant-observers' and study the classroom with the aim to potentially transform it, breaking against the normative frame of being students, as mere recipients of knowledge.

Objectives

The objectives of the task are aligned with a central objective of the course:

1. to cultivate in students a reflective understanding of how educational experience is mediated by social, pedagogic, and institutional factors
2. to cultivate observational and interpretive capacities in students, to be able to rigorously assess how educational experience is shaped
3. to collapse the divide between 'theory' and 'practice'. Rather than reading the text as distant from their local and immediate realities, the idea is to make students connect the ideas in the text to teaching and learning processes in the classroom.
4. finally, to help students develop a descriptive vocabulary for how they can read different elements in the classroom, including the teacher.

Anthrogogic Task

In this session, we will set up an experiment in class. Different groups will study different aspects of the classroom (teacher's speech and body language, student speech and behaviour, the social dynamics of the classroom) and will also conduct short interviews to develop a critical understanding of the classroom. We will conclude by deliberating on the various methodological aspects of doing such an exercise. Broadly, we'll mull over what it means to be participant-observers and ethnographer-practitioners in a classroom.

Group 1 and 2: Observe the social and pedagogic dynamics of the classroom.

This can include various social and pedagogic practices used and modelled in the classroom, body language of teacher and students, modes of interaction between different actors (teacher and student, student and student), use of technology/objects/textual material. Think of as many details as you can.

Group 3 and 4: Observe the linguistic dynamics of the classroom.

This can include the linguistic presentation of the teacher's content (rhetorical and storytelling techniques/choices, tone, use of examples, et cetera); how students talk, interject, question, respond; and anything else that you can think of.

Group 5: Interview the teacher.

Frame two questions that you think will help contribute to a critical reading of this specific class. These could be questions about the teacher's choices, attitudes, motivations, beliefs, and so on.

Group 6: interview Group 7

Frame two questions that you think will help contribute to a critical reading of this specific class. These could be questions about the student's quality of classroom experience, attitudes, motivations, learning styles, and so on.

Group 7: to be interviewed by Group 6

Reading: 'Being a Teacher in Contexts of Change' by Arathi Sriprakash (this reading will be directly relevant to the exercise in class; do read it closely).

A pedagogic alternative often used could be observational exercises carried out in the university setting, where students have to observe student dynamics and learning processes in different educational spaces. However, there is a crucial difference when they also critique their own classroom processes, studying themselves and the teacher.

Timeline: 2 hours

Task 3: Academic Writing—Drafting a Paragraph

Sajida Sultana

Background

The task becomes significant as the learners are adult, tertiary-level learners who need to read various journal articles and books, and write assignments with their own perspective. Some learners join a university after a couple of years gap to prepare for competitive exams. With constant preparation for various competitive exams, they seem to be more comfortable writing in bullet points and consider long-form writing a mechanical task that can be fulfilled with the use of generative Artificial Intelligence software. As the tertiary system of education is semester-wise, the necessity to learn a language skill becomes more important as the students want the skills learnt to be reflected in their upcoming assignments/dissertation submissions.

Objectives

1. To build an agency-enabling environment.
2. To develop learners to present peer perspectives.
3. To make learners share ideas on improving writing without hesitation.
4. To support learners to reflect on their writing style to build their agency.
5. To reduce learner-dependency on AI tools.

Anthrogogic Task

Requirement for the language teacher: A writing sample: dissertation chapter/assignment of a student.

First, the language teacher discusses ways of drafting a paragraph for writing an academic essay using the American Psychological Association (APA) 7th Edition Publication Manual or any other similar writing manuals followed by the university, if any. The teacher then shares a writing sample of one of the students with the class for them to understand what a peer-writing style is. The class reads the sample text in pairs/groups. The class reviews the structure of the text including the nature of paragraphs, and suggests ways they feel the paragraphs could be improved both in terms of content as well as language. The review is done using the 'Track Change' feature on MS Word. Each pair/group then presents their perspectives. As the pair/group presents, the language teacher also becomes part of their discussion and highlights if the students miss the use of logical transitions, forget to use first-person style to present their perspective, or miss any in-text citations, for example, as mentioned in APA 7.

In a pedagogic context, the all-knowing teacher gives individual feedback to each student about their work, and this mostly revolves around aspects of spelling and grammar. Students and peers are not considered capable of noticing important aspects of learner agency and slant (or perspective) and they are not considered capable of giving informed and non-parochial/non-partisan opinions about others' work. The element of trust in peers and fellow-learners is a deeply anthrogogic concept and this lies at the root of anthrogogicity in our understanding.

Timeline: This timeline is based on an average class size of thirty students with diverse language proficiencies:

- Teacher's discussion on drafting a paragraph – One hour
- Students' sample reading and peer discussion time – One hour
- Students' perspectives presentation with simultaneous teacher feedback – Two hours

B. Teacher Education

Task 1: Materials and Skills of Language Teaching

Shree Deepa

Background

Very often teaching and learning tasks in an ELT course, such as the one on materials and skills development, often focus on disseminating content to teacher trainees. Tasks are occasionally discussed as an application of the new knowledge learnt, but rarely are tasks seen as applicatory turfs. This makes them highly pedagogic. The verticals between the teacher and the student are like glass ceilings, even in a 'facilitation' type of course where teachers spout content and expect the students to regurgitate or even emit it on command with no processing of the content in assessment contexts.

Objectives

1. Critically evaluate the suitability of the provided exercise items for undergraduate students, identifying any inaccuracies.

1. Analyse the primary and secondary skills targeted in the tasks, utilising the Carroll table for detailed examination.
2. Assess the teaching methods employed in these items, determining whether it reflects an eclectic approach or aligns with Kumaravadivelu's post-method condition.
3. Identify applicable verbs from Anderson and Krathwohl's modified Bloom's taxonomy for each item, explaining their relevance and application.

Anthrogogic Task

Given below is one set of exercise items that was used in an undergraduate (UG) classroom in an autonomous university in India. Read it carefully and do the following in about 250 to 400 words. DO NOT solve the items.

Item Set

Pick the option that you think is the most appropriate answer for each scenario. Give clear reasons/rationales for your choice.

1. *You have been planning a surprise birthday party for your best friend for weeks. However, on the day of the party, your friend discovers your plans and confronts you about it. What response from you would help salvage the surprise and why?*
   a. I can't believe you found out! Well, I guess the surprise is ruined now.
   b. Oh no, you weren't supposed to know! Let's try to make the best of it anyway.
   c. I can't believe you ruined the surprise! You should have just pretended not to know.
   d. Well, since you know now, I guess there's no point in hiding anything.
2. *You're a new employee at a company, and you accidentally spill coffee on your colleague's important documents. What response from your colleague would make you feel less anxious and why?*
   a. You ruined my documents! This is unacceptable!
   b. It's alright, accidents happen. Let's see if we can salvage any of it.
   c. How could you be so careless? You need to be more careful!
   d. This is a disaster! I can't believe you did this!

1. Comment critically on the appropriacy of the task at the UG level. Do focus on inaccuracies if any.
2. What is the major skill and sub skill focus in this task? Critically explain this in detail using the Carroll table.
3. Add a critical comment on what 'method' is probably being used to teach this item. Do you think it uses an eclectic method or does it allude to the post-method condition as elucidated by Kumaravadivelu.
4. Refer to the modified Bloom's taxonomy (Anderson and Krathwohl's verbs) and add a note on which verbs are applicable for this set of items, and how and why they can be applied.

A pedagogic alternative to this task would read: 'Write short notes on the skills and sub-skills, link between task appropriateness and level, and between teaching methods and evaluation procedures'.

Timeline: 1 hour

Task 2: Language and Media (A)

Shree Deepa

Objectives

1. Critically assess the article by identifying at least five novel areas that have significantly influenced their understanding of its content.
2. Provide an evaluative commentary on these areas by inserting thoughtful critiques in square brackets (using a distinct color), demonstrating both analytical rigour and affective engagement.
3. Synthesise their observations and critiques into a comprehensive reflection that articulates how this exercise has reshaped their perspective on media discourse and the role of language in constructing meaning.

Anthrogogic Task

Read the article carefully and identify [highlight] at least 5 new areas that impacted you as you read the article. Add your critiques in square brackets in a different colour. This must be done as taught to you through the course.

The link to this article is given here for your reference. https://www.routledgehandbooks.com/doi/10.4324/9781315673134.ch3

A pedagogic alternative to this task would be 'Write a summary of the article that deals with the use of language in media'.

Timeline: 1 hour

Task 3: Language and Media (B) — Shree Deepa

Objective

After doing this task, students will be able to pull together their readings and discussions on a particular topic, place themselves at the centre, compare alternative treatments, and write about their perspective on it.

Thought Seed

How are biological phenomena treated in the media? Why does the advertisement of a sanitary napkin show blue liquid on it instead of red blood? Other biological phenomena, like hunger, are advertised in a glorious manner, say for example a McDonald's ad. Why is that? Think critically about why certain physiological phenomena are 'good' while certain other phenomena need to be hidden. Record your responses in your diary and submit them tomorrow. You also need to watch the first Indian movie on this theme, *Pad Man*, and add inputs from the movie as well.

A pedagogic alternative to such a task would be to ask students to read articles on how media treats certain phenomena and either summarise or make a presentation. Their evaluation of the domain is not likely to be tapped.

Timeline: 1 hour

Task 4: Language and Media (C) — Shree Deepa

Objectives

1. Select an item from any media, ensuring proper citation and details.
2. Create a unique thought seed inspired by the chosen item, avoiding replication of existing examples.
3. Analyse the language used in the item to identify any hidden agendas being promoted.

4. Justify their selection and articulate their personal reaction to the item.
5. Reflect on how this exercise has altered their perception of media and the role of language within it.

These objectives align with Bloom's taxonomy, progressing from the cognitive process of selecting (Remembering) to creating, analysing, justifying (Evaluating), and reflecting (Evaluating) on the media content. The freedom of choice that this task offers and the deployment of higher-order thinking skills together with the engagement of the affective domain challenges anthrogogic students and helps in knowledge co-creation. 'Thought seeds' are used as an alternative to tasks. Tasks limit the scope of responses while thought seeds expand the turf of expression and offer a chance to activate the schemata of the adult students and value them.

Anthrogogic Task

Pick up any one item from any media format (give all citations and other details) and convert that into a thought seed (do not replicate the ones that are already given to you, but choose a similar one) and analyse it for language and any hidden agenda that gets pushed. Rationalise your choice and your response to it, how this has changed the way you look at media, and how language operates there.

A pedagogic alternative to this task would be to expect students to critically analyse an advertisement based on theoretical inputs provided by the course instructor.

Timeline: 1 hour

Task 5: Linguistics for Language Teaching

GEETHA DURAIRAJAN

Background

The students were enabled to critically read extracts from Chomsky (*Aspects of the Theory of Syntax*) and Halliday (*Language as Social Semiotic*) and also taught to perceive the differences through a series of lecture-cum-discussion classes. The task below was given as a take-home assignment. Fifteen such statements were given. Five are reproduced here as a sample.

Objective

1. Students should be able to demonstrate that they can distinguish between arguments that are oriented towards formal (Chomskian) or functional (Hallidayan) linguistics by categorising them accordingly.
2. They should be able to give justifications about their categorising regarding the nature of language, language learning and use.

Anthrogogic Task

Given below are 5 statements. State whether each one belongs to the Hallidayan [H] or to the Chomskian [C] paradigm in linguistics; you are welcome to use the terms formal/functional if you prefer. Justify your classification in not more than 2 lines. Point form justifications are fine.

a. Language is a communicative tool that is reshaped by its users according to their needs.
b. Language is a cultural tool-kit.
c. Unless nutrition, in the form of exposure is denied, language growth in a child cannot be prevented.
d. An individual's actual language use may be error ridden, but this is never a reflection of his/her language incapability.
e. Speakers modify their language to suit the context and ability of their interlocutors.

A pedagogic model question on this topic would have been: 'Write a 500 word essay on the differences in perspective between the Chomskian and Hallidayan paradigm in linguistics'. Since the differences had been taught and discussed in class, this perforce must be given as a closed-book examination, and students would have had to memorise and reproduce the differences.

Timeline: Take-home assignment (maximum of 24 hours)

Task 6: Bilingualism and Bilingual Education (A)

GEETHA DURAIRAJAN

Objective

1. Students should be able to show their understanding and analysis of various bilingual education programmes.

2. They should be able to apply that knowledge to this context and create appropriate bilingual education programmes for this context.
3. They are pushed into applying what they learn and go beyond what they have studied to apply the concepts the way they would in real life.

Anthrogogic Task

Background: Danaca is a country where two major languages, Chrenf and Shinglin are spoken by 60 per cent of the population. These two languages are used widely for communication, and entered the country with invaders who conquered the land some 700 years ago. 25 per cent of the remaining population speak 3 local languages between them: Rumpa, Klioki and Kotnisip. The remaining 15 per cent are immigrants from neighbouring countries and speak 5 languages between them—Dishkurd, Meflish, Niffish, Lumati, and Ugulati.

Perspective: Imagine that you are a language education researcher who has gone to this country to learn about their differing language use.

Tasks

1. What are the different possibilities that exist as far as language education is concerned in that country? Consider the various permutations and combinations of languages and mediums of instruction. List these in point form.
2. From the listing provided by you in 1 above, look for patterns and separate them into an education policy that captures alternative stances that the government can take with reference to varied language use. For each stance, articulate the kind of language programme that is implied and the resultant nature of multi/bi/monolingualism that will result.
3. For each one of the language programmes stated by you, a 2 to 3 line explanation/clarification that explicates your articulation (and prevents me from reading less or more into it and creating or having to cope with ambiguities) is necessary. However, please remember that what is required is only 3 lines, not a paragraph, let alone a long essay. You are also welcome to provide your justification in point form, if you are happier with that.

Timeline: A take-home, 48-hour assignment.

Task 7: Bilingualism and Bilingual Education (B)

GEETHA DURAIRAJAN

Objective

1. Students should be able to show their understanding and analysis of various bilingual education programmes.
2. They should be able to apply that knowledge to this context and create appropriate bilingual education programmes for this context.

Anthrogogic Task

Background: Rashme Krishnakumar is the principal of a school run by Akshara, a non-governmental organisation in Keluchery on the Kerala–Karnataka border. Malayalam and Kannada are the two major languages spoken for purposes of wider communication. One-fourth of the population comprises migrant labour from neighbouring Tamil Nadu and they speak Tamil. A small but significant number of Tulu speakers also live in that town. These are second-generation inhabitants of Keluchery. Their parents moved to that city in search of work. At present, the Akshara-sponsored school is a State Board, English-medium one, but Akshara would like to be able to provide an 'alternative but effective yet adaptable to the mainstream' system of language education that will 'aid and abet' language maintenance and enrichment.

Perspective: Imagine that you have been invited as the language education expert to this school and are expected to advise the management on possible language policies and systems that are implementable. Since the organisation would like to stay with the State Board stream of education, assume that you will be providing advice on language education for primary and middle-school classes only. Also assume that all-possible facilities—namely infrastructure, trained language teachers, et cetera.—will be made available. As such, neither academic (in terms of board examination constraints) nor administrative constraints need prevent you from visualising (or dreaming up) alternative systems of language education.

Task: Write down the programme you would recommend, with justifications. Submit this as an essay of approximately 1000 words with appropriate justifications and references.

A pedagogic model question on this topic for both Tasks 6 and 7 would have been a closed-book question: 'Write an essay of 1000 words on the various bilingual education programmes. Try to provide one example of each kind of programme'.

Timeline: A take-home, 48-hour assignment.

Task 8: Classroom-Based Evaluation (A)

GEETHA DURAIRAJAN

Objectives

1. Students of testing should be able to recall their knowledge of the types of validity and reliability.
2. They should be able to distinguish between issues in the two constructs.
3. They should be able to apply that knowledge to real-time descriptions of tests and categorise the descriptions with justifications.

Anthrogogic Task

Given below are four descriptions of tests that have been perceived as problematic by the students who took them. Read the descriptions carefully and decide whether the problem is one of validity or reliability, or both. Then write down what can be done to make each test as valid and reliable as possible. You need not answer in complete sentences; even point form will do.

1. 20 students of a first-year, college-level English class, are asked to read aloud one of 5 texts that are chosen at random. The evaluator is primarily concerned with the accent that these English texts are read out in. On the basis of this evaluation, 3 students are selected from among this group to take part in an inter-collegiate debating competition.
2. This is a country which is largely dependent on agriculture, but there is also quite a lot of urbanisation; the divide between the rural and the urban is quite vast. In this country, there is a public English-language examination at the end of 7 years of English teaching. The paper is a test of language capability and has sections in grammar, vocabulary, reading, and writing. The reading section has two texts: one that talks about organic farming, and another

that deals with different kinds of industrial and noise pollution. The writing section asks students to describe in detail a circus that they have seen, or to describe a national level sports event. Many students, both from rural and urban areas, do badly on this test and feel that this is not a reflection of their true capability.

3. A village school conducts all its examinations, including final examinations, under a banyan tree, which is where all classes are also held. Some parents feel that there has been some discrepancy, and protest to the Public Education ministry because they felt that their children could have gotten better marks in the final examination.
4. A university in Australia feels that it is necessary to evaluate the English-speaking proficiency of foreign students who come to study there. To do this, the university asks all their teachers to follow these students for one week and observe their interactions with shopkeepers, bank officials, bus conductors, post office clerks, et cetera. Based on these observations judgements are made about who should get admission into the university and who should not. The students know that they are being observed.

A pedagogic version of this task would be a question that says 'Write a 500 word essay on the types of validity and reliability; give one example for each'.

Timeline: Part of an open-book, sit-down, end-semester examination: this section should not take more than 30 minutes to answer.

Task 9: Classroom-Based Evaluation (B) — Geetha Durairajan

Objectives

Students of testing should be able to exhibit their knowledge of issues in the testing of language, particularly scoring validity and the value of constructive criticism.

Anthrogogic Task

Background: One task prompt for the student of language and five short-answer responses from students, marked P1–P5.

Task:

1. Read the task and the five short-answer responses written by the students. Write down your scoring criteria for the task. (3 marks)
2. Evaluate the answer scripts using your criteria.
3. Write at least one comment per response to enable the student to improve or maintain his/her performance. You can write your feedback on the paper itself.

> Fill in the blanks in the passage given below by writing two or three short sentences. The passage has been taken from a letter. Read the information given to help you decide what needs to be written. Write your answers in the space provided.
>
> P. I have been a regular subscriber of PUSHTAK for the past two years. My subscription number for 2006 is P. 4779587.
>
> ....
>
> ....
>
> ....
>
> Please therefore ensure that the magazine is sent promptly, and send me the 2 back issues that I have asked for.

The 5 responses:

P1. *I have not been getting the magazine for the last two months. I am hereby writing my address for it might be of some help to you. I received the earlier magazines at the end of the month. So,*

P2. *I didn't get the last two copies of this magazine.*

P3. *For some unforeseen reason, I have not been able to get last three issues of the magazine, including this month.*

P4. *Usually your magazine reaches me very promptly, by the 5th of every month. But for the past two months it has reached me only after the 15th. Also, I shifted my residence in 2005 and probably because of that, I have not received the November and December issues of 2005.*

P5. *I have shifted my residence three months back and as such have not received the 2 back issues and this month's edition. My new address is:*

A pedagogic version of this task could have been 'Write an essay of about 400 words on the value of constructive criticism'.

Timeline: Part of an open-book, sit-down, end-semester examination: this section should not take more than 30 minutes to answer.

Task 10: Classroom-Based Evaluation (C)

GEETHA DURAIRAJAN

Objective

Students should be able to apply their knowledge of assessment practices and provide—with justifications—plausible alternative assessment practices that fulfil the requirements of validity, reliability and practicality.

Anthrogogic Task

Given below are descriptions of two students and their problems. Read them carefully and suggest (with justifications) the kinds of alternative assessments that would help them. Two alternatives per student will do. You are welcome to write your alternatives in point form. Assume that you have the authority to make decisions about the kinds of formative and summative evaluations that are possible.

A. Amrita is a first generation learner who is studying her content subjects through English for the first time in her Master's programme. She is never able to complete her test or examination papers, because her language of thinking is not English. She needs to read the questions, think of the answers in her own language, and then compose the answers in English.
B. Mukundan is a student of linguistics registered for a Master's programme. He usually reads all prescribed texts or articles and actively participates in class discussions. But when it comes to memory-based examinations he gets tense, forgets all that he has read, and sometimes even hands in blank sheets of paper.

A pedagogic version of this task could have been 'Write a 700 word essay on the different types of alternative assessments that you can recall. Write about the advantages and disadvantages of each'.

Timeline: Part of an open-book, sit-down, end-semester examination: this section should not take more than 30 minutes to answer.

Part IV

Ruminations on Anthrogogy

In most courses—whether at the undergraduate or postgraduate level—and even in teacher education, students/participants reflect and take stock of their own learning when they study for and answer examination questions. If they are ever able to own up to changes in themselves, look back and marvel at how far they have grown, it is likely to be a part of retrospection that takes place many years later (when and if this happens). Feedback for the teacher/educator is also usually only in the form of answers written in examinations along with any other incidental stock-taking. Such reflections may be sufficient in pedagogic contexts but in its highest form, education demands respect for the maturity, autonomy, and rich experiences that adult students bring to the learning environment. The reflective essay, far from being a mere academic exercise, can function as a space both for students and educators to engage in an ongoing dialogue—illuminating growth, challenges, and aspirations. This practice will encourage all participants to inhabit their own learning with intentionality, fostering shared meaning and a deepening relationship with knowledge, criticality, and self-evaluation.

In this section of the book, we present six reflective essays written by students who were either language empowered or introduced to a few nuances in teacher education anthrogogically. For us, these essays represent the proof of the pudding, or rather the anthrogogic *halwa* that the students were able to eat and relish. The theorisations, applications and tasks of the earlier sections find their culmination in these reflective student accounts which were written as part of their course work itself. The first four essays, written by Aniruth Sreenivasan, Pranav S., Samarth Majumdar, and Madhavaram S. as students of language registered for a compulsory English course at the undergraduate level, capture the wonder and joy of being taught English through a range of activities and projects, and how stimulating it was to be allowed to use technology in the classroom and experience an open-book/open-source examination.

The last two essays refer to content-based courses at the postgraduate level. Syed Musharafuddin discusses how case studies and thought seeds were used to teach syllabus development. Jeyalekshmi A. V.'s essay is an ode to the principles and practice of anthrogogy itself, where—to use her own words—her learning about anthrogogy extended far beyond the textbook.

We sincerely hope that teachers and researchers will be able to dip into these six essays and use them as thought specks, if not seeds, which will inspire them to take a few steps into the domain of anthrogogic teaching and testing.

17

A Course as a Course

R. Aniruth Sreenivasan

Stepping into the University of Hyderabad was a dream come true, although the nightmare of Basic Sciences—especially Physics—was the path I opted to spend the next five years of my life on. The freshman year started two months late for us compared to the other colleges and universities. Astonishingly, the first semester's coursework was not all sciences. We had two language courses of which one was EN111 English-I (Language). Yes! You're right; those were exactly my thoughts on this subject—'another half-year of sitting in an old lady's classes, going through long comprehensions, listening to boring grammar classes, and presenting on a topic which we have never heard before.' Clearly, I was mistaken, not about the instructor, but the coursework. Indeed, it was an old lady, but it was not like any of the regular English classes in high school or the other science courses.

Primitively, any teaching–learning process is one-way; the teacher speaks and the students listen. Although a good number of people desire to have students speak in their lectures, it is rare to see that happen because students are treated like children, and in the worst case, like 'primary standard kids'. Surprisingly, EN111 was different. We were allowed to think and, more importantly, discuss whatever we had in our minds without fear of judgment or needing very good vocabulary skills. For once, we were treated like adults and not like the locked minds of school children, trained to clear the board exams. Our confidence levels were boosted through such mind-blowing discussions and energetic arguments in debates with the professor and fellow classmates. The traditional locks did not tie us and we were free to learn at our convenience.

To begin with, have you ever had an AI and tech-enabled language class? Yes, it was one of the underlying necessities for our sessions. All the assignments—which were generally hand-written—were now to be done fully online, saving time for us students and the instructor. Moreover, we had the freedom to edit our assignments using AI grammar tools. Some people view this as an obstacle in grading the grammatical skills of the student. However, our teacher saw it as an opportunity for us to self-learn grammar in the most practical way possible, enabling us to be efficient in future jobs of writing articles and publishing papers. Besides, we had freedom in setting our submission deadlines, which acknowledged our lives outside the classroom. Through this, we experienced the work–life balance of an adult's life.

For the first time, there was no rush to complete the prescribed course's syllabus. Instead, it was a time for improving our grammar and vocabulary skills, and diving into new fields to learn something new. For example, I would like to quote my acquaintance with Parkinson's Law, which fortunately happened because of my professor. Our first group assignment, as I recall, was to submit an academic report of a survey we conducted and a skit that explains Parkinson's Law. During these assignments, I started to observe Parkinson's Law in our lives. We were given two weeks for the film presentation. We started discussing the plot and locations for filming on the very day of the assignment but we could complete the editing only the night before the presentation day. As the members were busy with their schedules, we met rarely and little importance was given to the project. Moreover, during the meetings we procrastinated, which prolonged the shooting. Instead of treating us like children and yelling, our professor extended the deadline by a week, as the whole class asked for an extension.

The skit presentation was a disaster. We were the first to present and we scored the least in class. There were many suggestions and comments from our professor as to the unavailability of subtitles, the plot's predictability, and the voices' vagueness. She gracefully allotted us another week to submit the improved version. As we recognised her adult-like treatment of us, we took the suggestions seriously, began adding the subtitles using Grammarly, and handled the voice issues.

On the final day, we re-presented it to our professor and got a hike in our marks. In addition to the marks, we got to experience the law in our lives; a task that was inadequately completed in three weeks was done within a week. If we had given more importance and effort to the assignment, we could have completed it on the first attempt. Likewise, I observed that I study for the exams only the day before when the pressure is high, even if I have free time the previous day. So, humans generally work according to their deadlines. I have been conscious since then, striving to be efficient and setting a pattern of completing my daily activities. This is an excellent memory as she cautioned us about Parkinson's Law by not pressuring us but letting us explore it independently, like an adult in their life.

Another activity I would like to draw attention to is Phantom Shopping[1]. As children, we have all seen our parents discussing and dealing with weekly and monthly budgets, including groceries, home appliances and accessories, electronics repair, and taxes. Several of us helped them calculate the savings and received working charges as pocket money. Our parents knew the requirements of each one in the house and worked accordingly to satisfy everyone in the family. However, what if you were asked to make a budget for a stranger whose interests you are unaware of by asking them three questions? Yes, this was our task; we were asked to present the budget worth Rs 2600—no more, no less—in groups for our professor from a pamphlet in a newspaper.

After exhausting two of our allotted questions, we appreciated the importance of questions and how we can shape anything with simple 'wh' questions, whether in this task or real life. I comprehended that our lives may be doomed if the right questions are not asked at the right time. The art of asking questions is a big philosophy which I would not like to discuss here. It also taught me the art of acceptance (which people lack nowadays) and working forward to use future opportunities instead of meddling with the past. After realising that the first set of questions was wasted and knowing that a new set of questions could be asked, we discussed it properly and used them. So we phrased the questions wisely and carefully, which resulted in knowing all the items required. Thirdly, we were able to think selflessly. We had to put ourselves in a stranger's shoes to understand the likes and dislikes of someone about whom we had no idea. A few groups had concerns for the professor's health, family members and grandchildren when making the shopping list. My creativity in presenting a bill showcasing the discount and amount saved, instead of a budget, was well appreciated. Aesthetics always result in a hike in grading, don't you think?

This particular activity was helpful to me in more than one way. I headed the Accounts team for two significant events in our university—the Pongal event of the Tamil community and the Freshers' party for 500

---

[1] Editor's Note: For a detailed discussion of this project see, A. Amaratheja's chapter in this volume (Ch. 12) where the nature of questioning used by the students while doing this project has been analysed.

newly-joined juniors. Also, as a coordinator of the Junior Science Club, I am able to better handle the accounts and bills apart from organising the events. All the activities of this course in my first semester have been continuously useful to me in various ways, especially now, when I am able to efficiently manage my academics along with the stressful job of organising events in the Science Club and making preparations in the free hours between classes.

The course was not all about group activities and encouraging teamwork. I remember one peculiar assignment, the Potentiality question. We were assigned twenty real-life scenarios and asked to choose and justify a choice of approach. The professor emphasised that the response may fall into one of three categories—constructive, neutral, and destructive. It was also made clear that the type of response to a single question may vary even for the same situation at different points in time and place. As a part of the assignment, we were required to create thirty such questions. While answering the questions, I found myself delving into my thoughts to consider how I would react or respond to the situation provided and how the response of another individual would affect me mentally. This exercise provided me with an opportunity to reflect on my actions and understand myself based on my response to those questions.

After bitter incidents, I have always regretted but never analysed my actions as what happened cannot be reversed, but this activity allowed me to think about how my actions in the future should not affect anyone. Indeed, one cannot satisfy everyone around them. However, I believe that a person is valued by the social life he has with his friends and society and I would like to create a positive environment around me, which is important in every adult's life.

Apart from allocating time to myself, it allowed me to ponder about one's life and its impact on others. Nobody has ever defined life, but every individual has several perspectives on life. I believe that the experience of situations such as those posed in the Potentiality questions contributes to and shapes one's opinion of how his/her life should be lived. I enjoyed this activity as it provided me with an opportunity to reflect on my thoughts amidst the hustle and bustle of life. Moreover, everyone needs to understand how they communicate their emotions to others, which can aid in their personal potential growth and development. In my opinion, the primary objective of this task was to examine ourselves and to make the required changes for a more effective life.

Any course that would be credited has to conclude with a semester examination that decides the fate of the students enrolled in the subject. Who likes examinations and tests? Literally, no one. Nevertheless, we have taken so many exams in our lives and are yet to take many more in the future. Exams are considered tedious because we need to starve and stare at given sheets of questions for hours together, while being stared at by the invigilators. It is a known fact that students are stressed on the day of the exam. Can you imagine having a pleasant experience of a semester exam (unless the question paper is leaked before the exam)?

It is said that the first impression is the best, but I say that the first experience is the best. By conducting an open-book examination, which means the usage of phones was allowed in the examination hall, our teacher broke the traditional lock of rules and regulations to provide us a sweet experience of what testing actual knowledge looks like in the world that awaits our adult life. Additionally, we were given refreshments during the exam for the first time. Generally, students are lethargic in English examinations but we were extra confident because our professor did not follow the traditional method of teaching the English language throughout the semester. We were not taught grammar concepts or asked to fill in random sentences with tenses, voice or speeches, which don't even make any sense. Instead, we were tasked with four assignments—Parkinson's Law, Phantom Shopping, story writing, and Potentiality questions. That was the syllabus for our exam. This was truly a test of our learnings.

As we all had just passed out of school, this exam showcased how a proper university exam should be. This approach towards education seemed broader compared to the usual memorising and vomiting method of the courses I studied in the second and third semesters, which will not do much good. All these years, it did not matter if we had a clear understanding of the concept; we studied, memorised and replicated it in the exam, and even secured A1 grades. However, this one was different; the marks did not matter to us. The only thing that mattered was to productively apply the learning outcomes and impact of the activities and assignments we did that semester. The examination focused on the creativity and learning from each assignment rather than grammar and regular, unchallenging questions. In the entire first-year English semester-exam question papers, only our question paper did not contain unrelated comprehension passages written by someone, incomplete sentences and paragraphs, and essay writing on random topics. It was pretty interesting and challenging for me as only creativity and innovation were tested.

The examination was time-consuming, but we were also given extra time. Moreover, we were given refreshments like tea, biscuits, and chocolates while writing the exam. Education is not only about gaining subjective knowledge, but also understanding what we learn through that knowledge and using it creatively in our routine life with emotionally aware and ethical conduct. This open-source exam was a good example of what a university education could be like. The experience was entirely new and nice.

I would also like to extend my gratitude to our course instructor, Dr Shree Deepa, for the fruitful experience of the exam as well as all the classroom discussions and the mature way she treated us. I am sure that more than the exam and the grades, she was concerned about our mental health. She always addressed us as 'young and aspiring physicists' and never as 'students' or 'children'; this is an example of the freedom we experienced as adults in her classroom. She made us look at language differently, by associating language with personality and development rather than merely a subject. I plan to carry the many lessons I learnt from this course with me throughout my life. In the end, the course EN111 was not merely an academic course worth three credits, but it has shaped the course of my life in many integral ways.

18

Unconventional Wisdom

A Journey of Self-Discovery in the Classroom

Pranav S.

I am a fourth-year Integrated Economics student at the University of Hyderabad. I was born in Kerala, and completed my school education in a CBSE school. The reason I chose this university as my destination for higher education is not only due to its cogent academic curriculum, but also because it provides immense experience for each student through various extra-curricular activities. Even though my major was Economics, I had an integrated course structure for the first three years which allowed me to pursue multiple courses simultaneously. From the first semester onwards, one such course that I always took was English, mainly to improve my communication and vocabulary. All the subjects I learned as part of the integrated course structure had the same pattern of three internal assessments, out of which the best two would be considered for a total of forty marks. The final evaluation was a sixty-mark external exam. Surprisingly, it was only in our third semester that a faculty member informed us that these assessments could be approached in an entirely different manner—an out-of-the-box approach which was indeed an eye-opener for me. This was successfully implemented by Shree Deepa ma'am, who taught us English in the third and fourth semesters.

It is not that her approach was entirely new to us; there were elements we were familiar with. Instead, what she did was help each student with the beautiful rediscovery of enjoying the learning process, rather than being a participant in the rat race to accumulate high grades. From her first class, we all felt something fresh had been brought to the table in our academics. The course structure unveiled to us was not limited to eight credits across two semesters, but it also had essential life lessons for each of us. A detailed explanation of how the course was unveiled is given below.

Semester 3

In the first class, Shree Deepa ma'am cogently outlined her teaching objectives and also explained her expectations from us. From the first whistle, we experienced being free inside the classroom where we could interact with fellow students and teachers, unlike the regular template where the teacher explains and the student listens. Shree Deepa ma'am never pressured us to do anything academically, but that in no way hampered our academic progress. We integrated various concepts of learning through constant interactions. My biggest takeaway from this semester was how she always created groups to do activities; it promoted strong interpersonal interactions where we could pitch our ideas to do the activities. On a personal note, hailing from Kerala, I forged a bond with four Telugu friends who were my classmates even before this English course. Still, we became so close to each other because we did several activities together throughout the semester.

The most critical project that I remember doing this semester was the presentation on the topic of Parkinson's Law. It was the first time that we had heard this term, which was very similar to the phrase *carpe diem*. That too was a phrase that went unnoticed in my vocabulary for a long time until I watched *Dead Poets Society* a few years back. In the movie, John Keating—played by Robin Williams—emphasised the importance of living in the moment through the idea of *carpe diem* (seize the day). Like that experience, there have been multiple moments in my life where the significance of time has surfaced as an undeniable truth—from the adage, 'time and tide wait for none', learned during my school days, to my recent encounter with the intriguing concept of Parkinson's Law.

Reflecting on the experience of that presentation on Parkinson's Law, I realise how impactful it was in shaping my understanding of time management and procrastination. The idea that 'work expands to fill the time available for completion' resonated with me. As a group, we procrastinated significantly throughout the process, yet the novelty of the topic and a sense of competition pushed us to put in genuine effort toward the end. We were a five-member group, and our first step was dividing the responsibilities—a plan laid out well in advance—yet we found ourselves scrambling in the last few days.

We used a shared Google document to collate our thoughts and ideas. Everyone contributed interesting concepts like Hofstadter's Law, the 80:20 principle, and references to the time management practices of Scandinavian countries found their way into our presentation. As Economics students, we wanted to anchor our presentation on the economic dimensions of Parkinson's Law. I was tasked with creating the content for the slides and the real brainstorming for me happened in the final two days. To make the presentation more engaging, I included references to *Interstellar*, Kafka, and other cultural elements, all of which were appreciated by the group.

What I appreciated most about this presentation experience was our freedom—from forming our groups to deciding the presentation's format. This creative liberty allowed us to think outside the box and personalise our approach to the assignment. Additionally, the open-ended nature of the assignment—which included data collection through interviews and the opportunity to create an academic report—made it more comprehensive. Unlike other subject presentations constrained by rigid structures, this experience allowed us to explore and express our thoughts more freely. Compared to other subject presentations, where strict guidelines and evaluation metrics dominate, this experience stood out for its relatability. The topic of time management and procrastination is something we all grapple with, often without realising. It was refreshing to break from rigid norms, witness creative presentations like interviews, musical performances and videos, and engage in a more genuine exploration of the subject.

As someone fascinated by movies, I loved weaving cinematic references into our narrative, and it felt rewarding when our efforts were acknowledged. Beyond the academic learning of report writing and understanding Parkinson's Law, this experience profoundly impacted my perception of time and the importance of making conscious efforts to change our habits. As the quote goes, 'They always say time changes things, but you have to change them yourself'. This experience made me realise that truth more profoundly.

Semester 4

After an exciting and one-of-a-kind semester experience with Shree Deepa ma'am, we were lucky enough to get her back for another semester. It was also an emotional journey for me since I have always loved the freedom I had during her English classes. English classes guided by Shree Deepa ma'am always compelled us to think uniquely, as she encouraged us to interlink our interests with academic ideas.

In continuation with the previous semester, ma'am gave us enough freedom to form our groups and approach different presentations. This semester, we were supposed to prepare a presentation on Ikigai. Ikigai is a concept that encourages people to find their purpose in life. Shree Deepa ma'am made us write reports for the presentations, which helped us upskill our academic writing skills.

Following the initial presentation, we were even allowed to choose the topic for a semester-long project, and our group chose 'Diploma Disease'. Diploma disease was an interesting idea that explained the reality of the job market. It explained the problem of qualification inflation, where degrees accumulate very quickly but, at the same time, the quality of education dips. For the semester-long project, we did intensive research on the topic and had questionnaires prepared as part of the research. It was the first time in my academic career that I had engaged in any research activity, but it gave me an experience that would help me in the future. The presentations also taught us about the potentiality of communication and different communication scenarios. Being able to communicate effectively with a good vocabulary has always been a quality that I strived for. In the previous English courses, we were taken through formality in speech, et cetera. But this potentiality assignment that highlighted the importance of speech behaviour that decided our attitude was discussed by ma'am for the first time. This was very new for me and will stay with me even when I get into professional settings. Further it will help me become a better person because I cannot speak anymore without introspection.

The approach to exams was also unique. The pattern of the question paper was thoroughly discussed before the exam, and the significant feature that made the English exam special was that everything in the question paper was based on classroom activity and projects. This was not seen in the question papers of any other subject. All the other exams I have attempted always had a template of reflecting on the topics from class notes or particular study materials, but this English examination was not limited to it. We were not asked to find out specific answers. Instead, we were asked to rationalise our stand, thus giving us the essential sense of freedom that no other subject did. The traditional question paper focuses on grammar, reading and writing, and is structured like a textbook where you are asked to find out if the sentence is a simple or compound sentence, or asked about past participles, et cetera. The question paper that we had included all these aspects, but it did not rely on any prescribed text. Instead, it was based on our classroom interactions and projects, which made it more connected to us. Our question paper contained editing, rational thinking through riddle-solving, essay writing, and dialogue writing. Thus, our question paper was not lacking in any way. What made it different was the freedom and relatability it had to our classroom interactions. Through the question paper presented in our exam, I got a different perspective on learning.

Another striking feature was how the exam hall was treated for the duration of the English examination. We were not detached from the world of the Internet, we were not forced to sit anywhere, and were given chocolates and biscuits which eased our stress and made us feel relaxed in order to be able to think and be creative. I liked this pattern of question papers of English exams where your perspective and creativity are given more weight than any study materials. If we can implement the examination structure of our English class in all our other subjects, we can make sure of at least easing the pressure in exam halls where students are well-supported by the faculty and facilities, which would reduce stress.

Through two semesters and eight credits, what Shree Deepa ma'am gave me, and the entire class, was a lifelong memory that was rare to experience in a competitive academic space. Building cohesion between people in the class and maintaining a friendly atmosphere throughout the class helped ease communication. It is a fast-paced world; she taught us that we could also take a pause to think differently, and teachers could make us think differently. This important life lesson was understood through this period. Through the assignments on procrastination and over-qualification, the classroom also made us introspect and present our better selves in front of the world. Writing reflective essays after each activity helped us garner knowledge and perform an in-depth analysis about each topic as well as reflect on the importance of these issues in real life. Thus, the method of learning English and the examination method was an enthralling experience for me.

Academically and non-academically, my experience with Shree Deepa ma'am was an eye-opener for me to chase my dreams and thoughts rather than just chasing academic degrees and grades. Being an Economics student, we always learn about the importance of long-term and short-term investments. Reflecting along economic lines, I feel that the English courses taught by Shree Deepa ma'am helped me to perceive academic struggle as more than just a mere accumulation of grades. The intensive discussions on procrastination and diploma disease helped me to tackle these problems in my personal life. I have always tried to incorporate my interests in every academic presentation I have made; the initial confidence for this came from these English classes I had. Besides that, I have already completed three research papers related to Economics, but the first kind of research work that I ever did in my academic life was in Shree Deepa ma'am's class, which gave me invaluable lessons for my academic journey.

19

Breaking Classroom Boundaries

SAMARTH MAJUMDAR

The EN111 course was one of the first courses I took as part of my undergraduate studies. Naturally, I didn't know what to expect. When academics began, I found that most of my core courses weren't too different from school, with familiar methods of teaching and learning. For instance, my first chemistry and math courses were almost precisely like school with the same teaching methods and lectures on how we must study harder to make our parents proud because they worked hard to send us here—the usual stuff students hear in school to motivate them.

However, this changed the moment I attended my first EN111 class. The experience was unlike anything I had encountered before. From the very start, it felt refreshingly different. Our professor immediately made the environment an easy-going one—no rigid rules—and we were encouraged to talk to friends and teammates to discuss ideas, use our laptops and phones freely, and even move around the room to form groups. This was a complete departure from the traditional classroom setting I was used to, where individual work and quiet attentiveness were the norms. In the very first session we were given our first assignment—a group project—and were instructed by our professor to form teams and start working on the assigned tasks. The spontaneity and freedom in the classroom was initially surprising but quickly became liberating. It set the tone for the entire course, emphasising collaboration, flexibility, and creativity over rigid structures.

The first assignment itself was unconventional in many ways. It required us to develop and apply various skills that I realised would be useful far beyond the classroom. We weren't simply memorising concepts or following textbook instructions—instead, we had to create surveys, write reports, conduct basic research, and collaborate effectively in a team environment. The practical nature of these tasks made the learning experience feel far more relevant and applicable to real life. For my group specifically, the first part of the course involved creating a survey, analysing the data we gathered, and compiling it into a structured report. Additionally, we conducted interviews as part of a video project. Taking the interviews was quite an experience in itself. It made me think quite hard about what needed to be done to make it an interesting and insightful conversation, not just for the interviewee but also for the audience watching it. Furthermore, I learned things that would otherwise be completely irrelevant to an English course, like video-editing and scripting.

After this was done, we started working on the report. Using the data gathered from the survey, we had to find trends, make correlations, and develop data to find meaningful connections. Doing the research was one thing but writing a research report for the first time was another, which was a fun experience. This hands-on experience allowed me to improve in areas I hadn't previously explored in depth, such as framing unbiased survey questions, interpreting data, and structuring findings into a coherent report.

A major highlight of this activity was learning about Parkinson's Law, which states that 'work expands to fill the time available for its completion'. Exploring this concept through practical application made it particularly impactful. It made me reconsider many of my ingrained habits regarding productivity and time management. For instance, I realised how often I unintentionally stretched tasks over long periods simply because I had more time, rather than focusing on efficiency. This newfound awareness motivated me to be more intentional with my deadlines and project timelines, making me more conscious of the way I work in the future.

The next part of the course shifted focus to creative storytelling, where we were tasked with collaboratively writing a fictional story using a set of given keywords. At first, the activity seemed simple but it quickly proved to be far more complex and challenging. With multiple people contributing ideas, the creative process became chaotic as everyone had their own vision for the plot and characters. There were moments of disagreement where conflicting ideas caused friction, and finding common ground became difficult. However, this challenge turned out to be one of the most valuable aspects of the activity. It taught me the importance of negotiation and compromise in a creative team setting. Despite the differing viewpoints, we were able to make multiple compromises, ensuring that everyone's input was reflected in the final story. This process of balancing creativity with cooperation was both rewarding and enlightening. By the end of the activity, we produced a relatively coherent and engaging story that reflected the diverse perspectives of the group.

Moreover, this experience improved my adaptability and problem-solving skills. I learned how to handle conflicting opinions with patience, while still contributing my own ideas. It was a practical lesson in teamwork that went beyond the classroom, preparing me for future storms that would come in academic and professional settings.

Following the creative storytelling exercise, we were introduced to what I consider the most significant takeaway from the course—reflective essays. Unlike standard essays which typically focus on analysis or argumentation, reflective essays required us to look inward. After each activity we were tasked with reflecting on our experiences, detailing the skills we learned, the challenges we faced, and what could have been done better. Initially, I found the process somewhat unusual as I was not used to analysing my own learning experiences in such detail. However, over time, I began to appreciate the value of this practice. Writing reflective essays encouraged me to become more self-aware and introspective. It made me consciously evaluate my strengths and areas for improvement, helping me identify patterns in my learning process.

This also carried over to times when I didn't need to write essays, as I became more open to the habit of reflecting on situations—not only to understand what I could have done better, but also how I treated people during an interaction and how I could have been nicer or kinder to them.

For example, after the survey project, I realised that while I enjoyed the creative aspects of making the video, I needed to be more methodical when analysing data. Similarly, during the storytelling activity, I became more aware of my tendency to be assertive with my ideas and learned the importance of stepping back and listening to others.

Another particularly memorable activity centered around the concept of potentiality, which encouraged us to explore the ways we react to different situations. This activity focused on the unpredictability of human behavior and made me reflect deeply on my own responses to various circumstances. We were given scenarios ranging from minor inconveniences to emotionally charged situations and asked to choose from multiple different reactions, which were marked constructive, neutral, or destructive, and then give a reason as to why we made that particular choice. More interestingly, we were also required to write our own questions for potentiality. This involved imagining a specific situation and then considering the multiple ways someone could respond to it. The process of constructing these questions was unexpectedly thought-provoking, as it made me examine my own behavior and also how others might interpret and respond differently to the same event. For example, when creating my own potentiality question, I imagined a situation where a person receives unexpected criticism from a colleague. I then explored various possible reactions, such as responding defensively, remaining calm, or seeking clarification. This activity definitely made me more open-minded, as it highlighted the diversity of human responses and the factors that shape them. It also made me more mindful of my own language and actions, particularly in challenging or emotional situations.

What made this class truly unique was its stress-free environment. Unlike my other courses, EN111 offered flexible deadlines, allowing us to submit assignments at a pace that suited us. This flexibility not only reduced unnecessary pressure but also fostered a sense of trust and responsibility. On some occasions, we didn't have formal classes at all. Instead, we were given free periods to work on our assignments. This autonomy allowed us to manage our time effectively and collaborate more productively.

The most striking difference, however, was that we were treated as adults. The professor believed we were responsible enough to manage our own learning, which was a stark contrast to the rule-heavy, micro-managed environment of school. This trust and independence made the learning process far more enjoyable and meaningful.

In the year and a half since I have taken this course, I have taken one more English course which was mostly about equipping us with skills that would be helpful in a research career, such as presenting, writing research articles, learning about the things involved in doing research, and so on. I didn't learn much from this course, not because the teacher was not good at their job but because these were skills I had picked up before and developed through self-learning and doing, which made the learning much more effective. Being a Physics student, I have since been a part of research projects in my field. I have used many of the skills I learned through EN111 during these, such as basic research and writing, among others. I have also been part of multiple clubs during this time, and much of my time in these clubs included organising events for other students. Obviously, a critical part of organising events is teamwork. I believe

I have become a much better team player because of the group projects I had to do during this course, especially in dealing with headstrong individuals and contributing constructively to the team effort.

There are many other lessons I continue to carry with me from this course. Beyond the practical skills of research, collaboration, and communication, EN111 taught me to think critically about many things I once took for granted. It made me question the rigid educational practices I had experienced for years and consider how my current courses could be made more effective and meaningful.

Most importantly, the course reshaped the way I perceive learning itself. It showed me that education is not merely about absorbing information, it's about developing skills, fostering creativity, and reflecting on personal growth. EN111 was far more than just an English course—it was a transformative experience that reshaped my perspective on learning and personal development.

20

Lessons That Linger

My Journey Through an Unconventional Classroom

MADAVARAM S.

There are some teachers who leave an impact so strong that their lessons stay with you long after the classroom experience ends. Dr Shree Deepa was one such professor for me. Learning under her was unlike any academic experience I had encountered before. It was engaging, unpredictable, and, most importantly, it felt meaningful in a way that traditional coursework often fails to achieve. Her classes didn't feel like just another set of lectures to sit through, take notes on, and forget after the semester ended. They felt alive. They felt like something that was shaping us, not just as students but as individuals who would eventually step into the real world.

When I first enrolled in EN201, I had a fairly standard expectation of what an English course would be like—grammar, comprehension exercises, structured essay writing, and maybe some discussions on literary texts. What I walked into, however, was something entirely different. Right from the first class, it was clear that this wasn't going to be the kind of course where we mindlessly memorised rules and formats. Dr Deepa had a way of making sure that what we learned in the classroom actually mattered beyond the walls of academia. She taught in a way that made us question, analyse and, most importantly, understand the nuances of language and communication in ways I hadn't encountered before.

One of the most fascinating classes I remember was when she introduced us to Parkinson's Law. At first, the name didn't ring a bell, and I had no idea what to expect. But as she started explaining it—that 'work expands to fill the time available for its completion'—something clicked. It was one of those moments where a simple concept changes the way you look at everything. It explained why assignments that could be completed in two hours somehow stretched into two days, why meetings always seemed to last exactly as long as the time scheduled for them, and why deadlines were the single greatest motivator for productivity. It was such a simple yet powerful insight into human behavior, and what made it even more impactful was how she connected it to our own academic experiences.

That class was not just about understanding Parkinson's Law—it was about seeing it in action. She asked us how many times we had delayed working on assignments simply because the deadline was far away. We all laughed because we knew it was true. Then she challenged us: what if we set our own deadlines, much earlier than the actual one? Would we be able to complete our work in a shorter time simply because we believed we had to? It wasn't just a theoretical discussion; she wanted us to test it out. And that led to one of the most memorable assignments I have ever worked on.

For this assignment, instead of just writing an essay on Parkinson's Law, we had the freedom to present our understanding of it in any creative format we liked. Some students made infographics, some created interactive presentations, but I chose to make a short film. This was something I had never attempted before for an academic project. A PowerPoint presentation would have been the safer, more predictable choice, but Dr Deepa always encouraged us to go beyond the ordinary. And so, I found myself diving into scriptwriting, storyboarding and video editing, all in an attempt to creatively capture how Parkinson's Law operates in real life.

The experience of creating that short film was an education in itself. It was more than just an assignment—it was a lesson in time management, storytelling, and communication. And, in a fitting ironical twist, I realised that Parkinson's Law applied even to this very project. I had initially given myself a week to complete it, but despite all my planning, I found myself racing against time in the final hours before submission. It was as if the assignment had become a self-fulfilling demonstration of the very principle we were studying.

What stood out to me the most about that experience was how much freedom we had. In many classes, assignments follow a strict format: a set word limit, rigid structure, a defined way of answering questions. But in Dr Deepa's class, there was no single 'correct' way to do things. It was about how well you could express an idea, how creatively you could engage with it, and how much you could make it your own. There was something incredibly liberating about that.

This openness extended beyond just assignments—it was the way she structured her entire teaching approach. Discussions weren't limited to a single perspective; they were built on the exchange of ideas, the curiosity of students, on debates that naturally arose when people with different viewpoints engaged with the same topic. Since our class was interdisciplinary, with both English and Language Science students, the diversity of perspectives made these discussions even richer. One question could lead to five different interpretations, and that was not just allowed, it was encouraged.

Even our exams were unconventional. I still vividly remember the day we were allowed to use our phones during an exam. It felt so strange at first. We had spent years being conditioned to associate exams with stress, strict invigilation, and the constant fear of being caught for something as minor as glancing around the room. And yet here we were, being told that we could use our devices. Not to cheat, but to think. The moment the exam began, I realised what she had done. It wasn't about memorising information; it was about understanding it, analysing it, and using whatever resources we had at our disposal to communicate our thoughts effectively.

There was a sense of trust in her teaching that I hadn't encountered before. She believed that students, when given the right environment, would want to learn for the sake of learning rather than just for grades. And she was right. The way we approached that exam was different from any other I had written. Instead of worrying about whether I could recall a specific fact, I found myself focusing on how to structure my answers, how to articulate my thoughts, and how to engage with the questions in a meaningful way.

This trust was present in every aspect of her class. She trusted us to meet deadlines without enforcing rigid penalties. She trusted us to engage with the material even when there were no immediate consequences for not doing so. And, perhaps most importantly, she trusted that learning was something that happened best when students were given autonomy, rather than being micro-managed at every step.

One of the biggest lessons I took away from her class wasn't just about English or Language Science—it was about the way education itself should work. So often, students go through their academic journeys treating learning as a chore, as something to be endured rather than enjoyed. But her class showed me that learning, when done right, is something that excites you, that sparks your curiosity; something that makes you see the world a little differently.

Even now, long after those semesters have ended, I find myself applying the things I learned in her class to everyday life. I catch myself thinking about Parkinson's Law every time I procrastinate on a task. I recognise the power of communication when I see how subtle changes in language can influence people's perceptions. I find myself questioning traditional methods of assessment and whether they truly measure learning or just obedience. These aren't just classroom lessons; they are perspectives that continue to shape the way I navigate the world.

Looking back, I realize how rare it is to find a professor like Dr Deepa—someone who challenges the conventional norms of education, who fosters an environment of trust and creativity, and who truly believes that learning is about more than just passing exams. I consider myself incredibly lucky to have been her student. Her classes were more than just courses I completed. They were experiences that shaped the way I think, the way I learn, and the way I engage with knowledge. And for that, I will always be grateful.

21

More Than a Degree

A Journey of Reflection, Growth, and Purpose

Syed Musharafuddin

From the moment I first set my sights on the University of Hyderabad, I knew that it was where I wanted to be. It was not just about academic excellence—it was about the prestige, the intellectual atmosphere, and the opportunity to grow in a space that had nurtured some of the finest minds in English studies. My dream was finally realised when I cleared the entrance examinations for both English Literature and English Language Studies. But amidst all the excitement, there was one crucial realisation: my passion leaned more toward language than literature.

A linguistics paper in my final year of undergraduate studies had first sparked this interest. The intricate structures, the evolving nature of language, and its profound impact on communication fascinated me. I saw language as more than just a means of expression; it was a dynamic force shaping society. With this newfound clarity, I eagerly looked forward to my journey in English Language Studies at the University of Hyderabad. Little did I know that the journey would not unfold as expected.

A Shift to Online Learning: The Pandemic's Unseen Challenges

2021 arrived with an unforeseen challenge—the COVID-19 pandemic. Just when I thought I would immerse myself in the rich academic environment of my dream university, the world shut down, and education transitioned to an online mode. For many, adapting to online learning was difficult, but for someone like me—with a visual impairment—the challenge was even greater.

Online platforms, despite their advantages, often fail to provide an inclusive learning experience. Accessibility remains an afterthought and navigating unfamiliar digital spaces requires an additional layer of effort. Reading dense PDFs, following slide presentations, and engaging with course materials in a way that matched my learning style was an ongoing struggle.

Beyond the technical difficulties, the emotional toll was equally challenging. University life thrives on in-person discussions, debates, and collaboration, but online learning lacked that energy. I missed the dynamic classroom interactions that fuel motivation. The distance and isolation of online education made it difficult to stay consistently engaged. However, despite these hurdles, I remained steadfast in my goal—I wanted to complete my master's degree and enter the teaching field.

A Gamechanger: Syllabus Design and Materials Development (SDMD)

Just when my motivation wavered, a particular subject changed the course of my academic journey—Syllabus Design and Materials Development (SDMD). More than the subject itself, it was the instructor who made all the difference. Dr Shree Deepa, an Associate Professor, had an approach that redefined my perspective on learning.

From the very first class, she made us feel at ease. She was not just a professor; she was an approachable mentor, engaging with us like a peer rather than an authority figure. The classes, held via Google Meet in the morning, often began with casual conversations before transitioning into course content. What set her apart was not just the way she taught, but why she taught the way she did.

Dr Deepa used case studies to illustrate the importance of syllabus design, making abstract theories feel relevant and practical. She encouraged us to question the way materials are developed and challenged us to think from the perspective of both teachers and students. However, the real gamechanger was an assignment that went beyond conventional academic expectations—thought seeds.[1]

When Dr Deepa first introduced the concept of thought seeds, I was flummoxed. It was unlike any assignment I had encountered before. While other courses focused on structured academic writing, thought

---

[1] Editor's Note: For a detailed discussion of how thought seeds were used in an undergraduate classroom to enable and empower students on aspects of interpersonal/intercultural competence, see Pankaj Narke's (Chapter 10) and Tabitha Chekuri's (Chapter 11) work in this volume.

seeds was about maintaining a reflective journal—simply penning down our thoughts on the topics discussed in class.

She explained that we could choose any medium to record our reflections: we could type on our laptops or phones or we could even use pen and paper. Typing? This simple option gave me immense freedom. As a visually impaired student, writing by hand is often a challenge and digital tools provide far greater accessibility. For the first time, an assignment felt truly inclusive, allowing me to express myself without limitations.

Most instructors have revolutionary ideas, but often fail in implementing them effectively. Dr Deepa was different. She did not just introduce thought seeds as a one-time activity, she actively followed up, ensuring that we were truly engaging with our reflections. The core objective of the assignment was not to spoon-feed knowledge, but to make us think critically and learn independently.

Initially, I struggled. Writing in such an open-ended format felt unfamiliar. There was no rigid structure, no right or wrong answer—just my thoughts taking shape in words. But as I embraced the process, I realised how transformative it was.

Rethinking Examinations: A Trust-Based Approach

Another unconventional, yet eye-opening aspect of Dr Deepa's course was the examination system. Unlike traditional exams where students are closely monitored, our final exam was open-book. We could refer to textbooks, recorded lectures, and notes—a concept that initially felt both liberating and unsettling.

Having been conditioned to give strictly invigilated exams, my first thought was: What if someone cheats? Would this not compromise the integrity of the exam? However, I soon realised that cheating was not even a possibility, because the nature of the questions demanded original thought. They were not about memorising information; they required us to analyse, reflect, and synthesise concepts in a meaningful way.

What stood out the most was the trust Dr Deepa placed in us. She believed in her students' integrity and capability, which in turn motivated us to uphold that trust. This approach resonated deeply with me as I have always been someone who values uniqueness and originality. The SDMD course, in every aspect, was the perfect stage for me to thrive.

A Visually Impaired Perspective on Learning and Inclusivity

For a visually impaired student, written expression is both a tool of empowerment and a challenge. It serves as a means to articulate ideas, engage in intellectual discourse, and assert one's voice in academic spaces. However, the process of translating thoughts into structured writing is often accompanied by unique hurdles—navigating text-heavy materials, accessing complex resources, and ensuring that one's work remains both coherent and impactful despite technical limitations. The effort required is not just cognitive but also logistical; assistive technologies, screen readers, and alternative formats must be seamlessly integrated into the learning process.

Yet, in Dr Deepa's classroom, these challenges did not define my learning experience. The thought seeds assignment and the open-book examination liberated me from the rigid constraints of traditional academic assessments. Unlike conventional assignments that impose strict formatting, structured responses, and inflexible submission requirements, thought seeds allowed me to express myself authentically in a format that worked best for me. Whether typing on a screen or using text-to-speech tools, I could engage deeply with the course material without being hindered by accessibility barriers. This seemingly simple shift had a profound impact on my academic confidence.

For the first time, my learning was not dictated by how well I could conform to a prescribed academic structure, but by how effectively I could think, analyse, and reflect. The open-ended nature of thought seeds encouraged me to explore concepts in ways that felt natural and meaningful, rather than feeling pressured to fit within conventional academic expectations. I was no longer focused on merely meeting requirements—I was engaging with ideas in a way that was organic, personal, and intellectually stimulating.

The open-book exam further reinforced this sense of empowerment. Traditionally, visually impaired students face additional difficulties in exam settings: from time constraints to navigating physical or digital texts quickly. These challenges often make assessments feel like tests of endurance rather than genuine evaluations of understanding. However, by removing unnecessary barriers and focusing on critical thinking, Dr Deepa's exam format transformed the experience into one of true academic exploration. With access to my notes and resources, I was able to synthesise ideas, draw meaningful connections, and apply my knowledge in a way that felt both inclusive and intellectually fulfilling.

This approach not only improved my academic performance but also reshaped my self-perception as an educator. It validated my perspectives, proving that my insights—shaped by my unique experiences as a visually impaired student—were valuable and worthy of being heard. It reinforced the fact that education is not just about mastering content, but about engaging with knowledge in ways that empower students to think independently.

The Transformative Impact of Dr Shree Deepa's Teaching Methods

Dr Deepa's teaching methods were not just innovative; they were transformative. She redefined the way I approached learning, shifting my focus from a passive reception of information to active engagement with knowledge. Her approach was deeply student-centric, making every class an interactive and thought-provoking experience rather than a mere transfer of information.

One of the most profound aspects of her teaching was the way she broke the traditional professor–student barrier. She treated us as intellectual equals, valuing our thoughts and perspectives. Her classes on syllabus design and materials development were structured around case studies, real-world applications and discussions that encouraged us to analyse and critique conventional methods of teaching. Unlike many professors who emphasise a rigid adherence to curriculum, she focused on making us understand why a concept was important and how it could be applied in practical teaching scenarios.

Perhaps the most profound impact of Dr Deepa's methods was the way she instilled a sense of responsibility in her students. The trust-based examination system was not just about allowing open-book references; it was a lesson in academic integrity, autonomy, and ethical learning. By removing the pressure of surveillance, she shifted our focus from performance to understanding, from competition to personal growth. This approach fundamentally changed the way I perceive assessment—not as a measure of rote memorisation, but as an opportunity to engage with knowledge meaningfully.

Even beyond the classroom, her influence lingers in my everyday teaching practices. As an Assistant Professor, I strive to replicate her student-centric approach, ensuring that my teaching is not just informative, but transformative. I now see my students not as passive recipients of knowledge, but as thinkers, creators, and individuals with unique learning needs. The creative freedom and critical engagement she fostered in me are now values I hope to pass on to my own students.

Dr Deepa did not just teach a subject, she redefined my relationship with learning. Through her, I learned that education is not about merely completing a syllabus but about igniting curiosity, encouraging independent thought, and making knowledge accessible to all. Her teaching was a testament to the fact that a great educator inspires, challenges, and leaves a lasting imprint on the minds of their students.

A Vision for the Future

Studying at the University of Hyderabad was my lifelong dream and, despite the challenges brought by the pandemic, my experience has been profoundly transformative. My journey was not one of academic perfection; I was not a topper, nor did I earn a distinction in my master's degree. However, I have come to understand that true learning is not measured by grades alone.

What I gained from my education was something far more valuable—the ability to think critically, view learning from multiple perspectives, and implement innovative teaching methods. The knowledge I cultivated during my Master's programme continues to shape the way I engage with the world, encouraging me to challenge conventions, adapt to different learning needs, and embrace creativity in education.

Dr Deepa's guidance played a pivotal role in this transformation. She did not just teach a subject; she modelled the kind of educator I aspire to be—one who makes learning engaging, accessible, and meaningful. Her unconventional assignments trained me to think beyond textbooks, reflect deeply, and personalise learning. Through her, I learned that effective teaching is not about authority or rigid instruction, but about creating an environment where students can explore, question, and grow. Today, as an Assistant Professor, I strive to mirror Dr Deepa's approach. I incorporate interactive discussions, encourage self-reflection through journals, and ensure that my classroom is a space where every student—regardless of ability—feels heard. Just as she trusted us with open-book exams, I trust my students to engage critically rather than merely memorise. Her teaching lives on through my own methods. I encourage my students to think independently, just as Dr Deepa encouraged me. More importantly, I remain conscious of the diverse needs of my students, ensuring that learning is inclusive and accommodating, particularly for those who may face challenges similar to mine.

Looking back, my journey at the University of Hyderabad was not just about earning a degree, but about discovering my true purpose as an educator. As I continue my journey in academia, I hold onto the invaluable insights, experiences, and inspiration that shaped me. My time at the university, especially in the SDMD course, has given me the confidence and clarity to create a more engaging, student-centred learning environment—one where education is not just about what we learn, but how we apply it to empower ourselves and others. In the end, the true measure of education lies not in the distinction of a degree, but in the distinction of thought and action it inspires. And in that sense, I consider my journey a success.

22

Anthrogogy

Learning Beyond the Textbook

JEYALEKSHMI A. V.

When it was time to select elective courses in our third semester, I noticed that our department was offering a course titled 'Anthrogogy'. I must admit, I initially made a rather far-fetched guess as to the word's etymology. I wondered if it was some course on the evolution of teaching methods across various societies. In my prior educational experiences, from primary education to my bachelor's degree, learning was often perceived as a meticulously controlled, linear progression with set milestones and grades. However, new insights into anthrogogy and the philosophies underlying it have urged me to re-evaluate those assumptions, opening my mind to more holistic and dynamic perspectives on education.

As the course progressed, the guiding principles of anthrogogy began to resonate strongly. The various elements of an anthrogogic learning environment—from the dynamic between instructor and learner to the development of learner autonomy—appeared quite striking to me. It's through active contribution that learning becomes truly stimulating, I realised.

This focus on autonomy has made me a more motivated and engaged learner, and I've since incorporated this approach into my daily life. The techniques employed in our classroom seemed rather refreshing, or even radical, compared to conventional classrooms. They nurtured the importance of empowering individuals to own their learning, academically and beyond. The course has shown me that learning flourishes in environments where autonomy, self-direction, and experience are valued.

One of the distinct aspects of the course has been the discussion on the philosophy that upholds anthrogogy. The introduction to Ikigai—a Japanese philosophy concerned with discovering one's purpose and meaning in life, has encouraged me to explore my passions, talents, and skills in the context of our coursework—guiding me to focus on areas that support my personal and career goals. Integration of the Pomodoro method also instilled a sense of discipline in me. It allowed me to set realistic goals for each study session, making me more accountable for my progress. We also demonstrated how learning transcends the four walls of a classroom by conducting our discussions and activities under a campus tree, thereby redefining the traditional classroom experience.

Assignments: Finding Depth Beyond the Deadline

For those who view assignments as a necessary academic burden, this course provided a refreshing challenge. The pedagogy versus anthrogogy assignment offered a valuable comparison of educational approaches. Creating scenarios helped me critically examine my own schooling, highlighting anthrogogy's emphasis on learner autonomy—a concept sorely lacking in my past. This assignment revealed the limitations of pedagogy, especially with adult learners. To disregard the accumulated experiences of adult learners within the learning environment is akin to commissioning a master sculptor and then insisting they work exclusively with clay pressed into a prefabricated mould. You are squandering a rich source of unique perspectives and ultimately yielding a result that is generic and underwhelming.

The language potentiality assignment was equally engaging. It challenged me to explore the power of language and its ability to influence thought and understanding. It also fostered a new appreciation for language beyond communication, highlighting how word choice impacts lives. This course further encouraged me to reflect on how language can shape the outcomes of certain situations, and instilled an awareness of using inclusive and culturally sensitive language in our everyday communication.

The peer-review approach in this course was a revelation. Seeing how my classmates tackled assignments broadened my understanding of learning itself. Their diverse perspectives on the same scenarios challenged my own thinking, and their feedback was invaluable. Moreover, it shifted the approach of the assessment from evaluation to mutual enrichment.

Finding the 'Why'

Reflecting on my experience with collaborative marking on formative assessments, I've found it to be a very effective approach that has helped my learning process in various ways. My usual exam feedback experience was a masterclass in brevity, often consisting of a single number and its unspoken implication, 'Good luck figuring that out'.

However, the opportunity to negotiate and discuss our grades with the professor has transformed the grading process from the usual one-sided evaluation into a constructive dialogue between the teacher and students. This new method of scoring has fostered a sense of responsibility within me. The idea that my grades were determined through negotiation made me take the assignments more seriously.

Receiving direct feedback, along with the chance to discuss it with the instructor, was indeed a refreshing experience. Collaborative evaluation opened my eyes to perspectives I hadn't considered, and I realised my teacher paved the way to think differently—presenting ideas I hadn't thought of, but seemed obvious and rational once explained. This process also played a key role in preparing me for the summative exams. By using the feedback to guide my study approach, I was able to focus on areas that needed improvement, ultimately enhancing my performance when it counted.

Exams Can Be Fun? Who Knew!

This course has surely redefined my notion of examinations. Our typical exams are a high-pressure test of memory, where students race against time to recall memorised information, often leading to stress and cognitive overload. On the contrary, the anthrogogy final exam emphasised applying learned concepts rather than memorising facts, resulting in a calm and reflective atmosphere. I found myself thinking, 'Are we sure this is really an exam?'

However, what truly struck me was the unique format of the examination, which deserves special mention. The open-book nature of the exam initially seemed straightforward. The permission to use coloured pens and headphones put further emphasis on a relaxed and comfortable atmosphere. Nonetheless, the emphasis on labelling answers and copying questions beforehand hinted at a deeper purpose. This, coupled with the critical section requiring analysis of social consequences, made it clear that simply copying information wouldn't suffice. We had to utilise our critical thinking abilities and apply theoretical knowledge to real-world scenarios. The instructor further supported our writing experience by offering refreshments, embodying anthrogogy's foundational principle of valuing the learner and cultivating an environment that refines their cognitive performance. As I move forward, I'll carry the knowledge I gained and hope for assessments that serve as tools for growth, not just evaluation.

Anthrogogy: Beyond Theory

Students find no greater reward than to see classroom learning put into practise outside. For me, the most impactful outcome of this course has been the direct application of the course principles in my professional life. In a recent discussion about the key elements of developing e-learning materials for adults, anthrogogy was my immediate guide. I shared my understanding of anthrogogy—drawing from our collaborative classroom experiences—to emphasise the importance of understanding the professional context, the learner's language background and characteristics, as well as the specific needs of adult learners.

Rarely does classroom theory translate so directly to practical application, and this experience underscored the value of engaged learning. This course—alongside the instructor Dr Shree Deepa's Language Assessment course—has proven to be exceptionally beneficial for my professional development. Specifically, the insights gained regarding language choices, language testing, and Bloom's Taxonomy have become indispensable tools in my work. The course was truly one of a kind. I am sincerely thankful to Dr Shree Deepa for offering a course that valued both intellect and individuality, providing me with invaluable skills and insights that will continue to influence my personal and professional growth.

Editors and Contributors

Geetha Durairajan retired as Professor from the English and Foreign Languages University (EFLU), Hyderabad, India. She is the editor of *Perceptions of Language Pedagogy* (2019) by Dr N. S. Prabhu. Her recent research, publications, and projects focus on anthrogogy and language potentiality, while her earlier work explored multilingual education and language evaluation. Over an academic career that spans thirty-three years, she has taught and supervised several generations of ELT professionals, many of whom now teach at universities in India and abroad. She continues to contribute to the academic discourse through invited lectures and plenaries. She can be contacted at geetha@efluniversity.ac.in.

Shree Deepa is an Associate Professor at the Centre for English Language Studies, University of Hyderabad (UoH), India. With over thirty years of teaching experience, she has published more than fifty research articles and numerous book chapters with leading national and international publishers. She has edited volumes, delivered over a hundred invited talks, and contributed as an advisor, reviewer, and content writer for NCERT courses. Her research interests include anthrogogy, inclusive education, language potentiality, and teacher education. She has completed projects with the British Council and an IRM project initiative under Institute of English, UoH. For further communication, write to her at shreedeepa@uohyd.ac.in.

Contributors

A. Amaratheja is a doctoral research scholar in English Language Education working with Dr Shree Deepa at the Centre for English Language Studies, University of Hyderabad (UoH), India. His research interests include English Language Teaching (ELT), anthrogogy, multilinguality, higher education, culture, psychology, and Marginalised Studies. He has published several research articles and book chapters in reputed academic journals and edited volumes. His doctoral research examines the use of questioning techniques in higher-education ELE classrooms, with a focus on how both teacher- and student-questioning contribute to interaction, critical thinking, and meaningful learning. He can be reached at 22hgph02@ uohyd.ac.in.

Deepesh Chandrasekharan is Principal (in-charge) of Kumaraguru College of Liberal Arts and Science, Coimbatore, with over twenty years of experience in education and leadership. He holds a PhD in English Language Education from the English and Foreign Languages University, Hyderabad, India, and masters' degrees in linguistics (JNU) and English (University of Madras). A Cambridge CELTA-certified educator and former Executive Director of an Erasmus+ project, he is also an alumnus of the US State Department's International Visitor Leadership Program. His research explores the intersection of language, power, and education, focusing on multilingualism, critical pedagogy, and equity in learning contexts. He can be contacted at deepesh.chandrasekharan@gmail. com.

Diganta Ghosh has done his MPhil from the English and Foreign Languages University, Hyderabad, India, and his PhD from Savitribai Phule Pune University. He teaches English literature at Moyna College, West Bengal. He is actively involved in research in the domains of literature and language. He can be contacted at digantaghosh@gmail. com.

Meghna Anand is a PhD research scholar in the Department of English Language Education at the English and Foreign Languages University, Hyderabad, India. Her research explores the integration of authentic materials and ICT/AI tools to enhance legal language vocabulary. Her academic interests include materials development, educational technology and English for Specific Purposes. Meghna has presented at several national and international conferences, contributing to the evolving landscape of language education and the integration of technology in specialised vocabulary instruction. Her e-mail id is meghna.anand6@gmail.com.

Monishita Hajra Pande is an Assistant Professor in the Department of Training and Development, English and Foreign Languages University (EFLU), Hyderabad, India. Before joining EFLU, she worked in Ambedkar University (Delhi), Ashoka University, and Indira Gandhi National Open University. She has experimented with a low-cost peer learning model, led a group of writing instructors, and has deeply engaged with questions around language policies, equity, and social justice in higher education. Her research interests include the development of reading and writing skills, bi-/multilingualism, and language teacher education. She has worked on various teacher training, materials development, and proficiency enhancement projects. She can be contacted at monishita@efluniversity.ac.in.

Narji Baruah is an Assistant Professor in the Department of English at Women's College, Tinsukia, Assam, India. She is currently pursuing her PhD in the Department of English at Tezpur University. She is passionate about teaching English at the undergraduate level and takes a special interest in understanding and enhancing classroom interaction. Her work also focuses on developing inclusive teaching practices for blind and visually impaired learners. She strongly believes that education should be accessible to everyone, regardless of their abilities or background. She is deeply committed to creating meaningful learning experiences that inspire students to think critically and express themselves confidently. She can be contacted at narjibaruah18@gmail.com.

Nidhi D. M. is a doctoral scholar at the School of English Language Education, English and Foreign Languages University, Hyderabad, India. Her research interests encompass multilingual education, translanguaging, the history of English in India, and writing pedagogy. She has presented her work at several national and international conferences. She received the Gold Medal for academic excellence for her Masters' degree in English Language Studies from the University of Hyderabad. Her doctoral work investigates the effect of pedagogical translanguaging in developing writing skills among ESL learners. She can be contacted at nidhimohan18@gmail.com.

Pankaj Narke is an Assistant Professor in the Department of Humanities and Social Sciences at Mahindra University, Hyderabad, India. He holds a PhD in English Language Education from the English and Foreign Languages University, Hyderabad. His areas of specialisation include second language acquisition, intercultural communication, and multiliteracies. Besides teaching courses at the undergraduate and PhD levels, he has published in national and international journals and books on these areas. He can be contacted at pankaj.narke@mahindrauniversity.edu.in.

Sajida Sultana is Assistant Professor, Centre for English Language and Development at Tata Institute of Social Sciences (TISS), Hyderabad, India. She has an MA in English (TESL) and MPhil in English Language Education (ELE) from the former Central Institute of English and Foreign Languages (now EFLU), Hyderabad. She holds a PhD in ELE from EFLU. Her research interests include translanguaging, academic language skills in higher education, anthrogogicity, minority education, English language teaching to marginalised students, mentoring, language feedback, language pedagogy, sociology of education, and English language needs of the corporate sector. She can be contacted at sajida.sultana@tiss.ac.in.

Sayan Chaudhuri teaches courses on education, literacy, and language pedagogy at Ashoka University, Shiv Nadar University and the Lodha Genius Programme, and conducts critical literacy workshops with teacher and student communities across various educational settings. He completed his PhD in English Studies from Jawaharlal Nehru University (JNU), Delhi, where he studied the framing of English studies in Indian higher education. He has also worked as a subject advisor for the English curriculum at the Delhi Board of School Education (DBSE), and is a founding member of Aaina (@aaina_edu), an initiative to make critical educational perspectives more accessible to a larger public. He can be contacted at sayan.chaudhuri@ashoka.edu.in.

Shadab Khan is a research scholar at the Centre for English Language Studies, University of Hyderabad. His work engages with English Language Education, focusing on how technology can be meaningfully integrated into classroom practices. He collaborates with pre-service English as Second Language (ESL) teachers and teacher-educators to explore ways of embedding digital literacy in English language instruction through the use of various ICT tools. His research interests include technology-enhanced language learning, material design, and assessment in ESL classrooms. He can be contacted at kkshadab09@gmail.com.

Shravasti Chakravarty is an Assistant Professor in the General Management area at XLRI Delhi-NCR. She teaches on their flagship MBA programme and other online programmes. With a PhD (English Language Education) from the English and Foreign Languages University, Hyderabad and BA from Presidency College, Calcutta University, her teaching and research interests include enhancing communication skills, developing critical thinking, and learner-centred pedagogy. She has presented papers in Japan, Indonesia, Uzbekistan, Spain, France, Poland, Bangladesh, and New Zealand. She has taught at the university level in India and Uzbekistan. She is an ardent Toastmaster. She can be contacted at shravasti@xlri.ac.in.

Sruti Narra is a Senior Lecturer, International Business, Häme University of Applied Sciences (HAMK), Finland, teaching language courses for research purposes—like Academic Writing—to masters and bachelors students. She is also involved in Design Based Education (DBE) based business labs where students work collaboratively on real company challenges to offer research-backed prototypes and solutions. She has a doctoral degree in English Language Education from the English and Foreign Languages University, India where she specialised in teaching academic writing. Some of her areas of interest are teaching writing, argumentation, multimodal writing, generative AI and writing, and education in multilingual contexts. She can be contacted at srutinarra@gmail.com.

Sweta Mukherjee holds a PhD in English Language Education from the English and Foreign Languages University, India and has over eleven years of experience in higher education. She is an Associate Professor in the Department of English, School of Humanities and Social Sciences, GITAM (Deemed to be University). A Fulbright Scholar (2012–2013) at the University of West Georgia, she also earned a Higher Education Teaching Certificate from the Derek Bok Center, Harvard University. She holds copyrights on *Guidelines for Curriculum Design and Transaction* and *Grading Rubrics on E-Forms*. Her interests include emotional intelligence, faculty development, social-emotional learning, and AI in education. She can be contacted at smukherj4@gitam.edu

Tabitha Chekuri is an Associate Professor in the Department of Humanities and Social Sciences, Mahindra University, Hyderabad. Her research interests include teacher cognition, teacher training and professional development, and classroom-based research with a focus on language education. She is particularly interested in exploring how teachers' beliefs, identities and emotions shape their pedagogical practices and professional growth. Her work draws on reflective methodologies to understand teachers' experiences and inform teacher training in diverse educational contexts. She can be contacted at tabithachekuri@gmail.com.

Authors of Reflective Essays

R. Aniruth Sreenivasan, schooled in Kalpakkam, Tamil Nadu, is in his third year of an Integrated MSc in Physics at the University of Hyderabad. As a 2024 NIUS (HBCSE, TIFR, Mumbai) Physics scholar, he is a curious and driven learner with a deep interest in physics, materials science, and science communication. Passionate about problem-solving, organising events, and outreach activities, he served as one of the 2024–25 Coordinators of the Junior Science Club at the Centre for Integrated Studies, and is an active member of the Zenith Astronomy Club at the School of Physics, University of Hyderabad.

Jeyalekshmi A. V. works as a Hyderabad-based Instructional Designer at a multinational consulting firm. She holds a Language Studies postgraduate degree from the University of Hyderabad. Studying both linguistics and language-teaching have sharpened her writing and creative storytelling, fuelling her passion for effective adult learning solutions.

Madavaram S. is a final-year integrated masters student in Economics at the University of Hyderabad. His primary interests lie in competition policy, antitrust economics, and development economics. He has gained practical experience through internships at the Centre for Development Studies, Thiruvananthapuram, and the Indian Institute of Space Science and Technology. A keen researcher, Madavaram has presented and published papers in his fields of interest, demonstrating a strong foundation in economic analysis.

Pranav S. is a final-year student in the Integrated Masters Programme in Economics at the University of Hyderabad, and a Future Research Talent Scholar at the Australian National University. He has undertaken research internships analysing international economic crises, the marine economy, and women's labour participation. Currently, his research centres on health and development economics, examining early-life shocks and life-course health outcomes in low-and middle-income settings. Pranav aims to contribute actionable insights to global development and policy through interdisciplinary research.

Samarth Majumdar is an undergraduate student at the University of Hyderabad, pursuing a degree in physics. He is an aspiring astrophysicist with a keen interest in advancing his research career. Apart from his academic pursuits, he loves playing the guitar, cooking, and swimming.

Syed Musharafuddin is an Assistant Professor of English at the Rajiv Gandhi University of Knowledge Technologies (RGUKT), Ongole, Andhra Pradesh. His areas of interest encompass English Language Teaching, communication skills, and applied linguistics. Passionate about enriching language education in technical domains, he emphasises experiential learning, learner engagement, and communicative competence. This chapter marks his debut scholarly publication, reflecting his commitment to research, reflective practice, and academic excellence.